SO-AZT-377

LONGSTREET HIGHROAD GUIDE
—— TO THE ——

VERMONT MOUNTAINS

BY NANCY BAZILCHUK AND RICK STRIMBECK

LONGSTREET
ATLANTA, GEORGIA

Published by
LONGSTREET PRESS, INC.
a subsidiary of Cox Newspapers,
a subsidiary of Cox Enterprises, Inc.
2140 Newmarket Parkway
Suite 122
Marietta, Georgia 30067

Text, maps, and illustrations Copyright © 1999 by Longstreet Press, Inc.

All rights reserved. No part of this book may be reproduced in any form or by any means
without the prior written permission of the Publisher, excepting brief quotations used in
connection with reviews, written specifically for inclusion in a magazine or newspaper.

Great efforts have been made to make the information in this book as accurate as possible.
However, over time trails are rerouted and signs and landmarks can change. If you find a change
has occurred to a trail in the book, please let us know so we may correct future editions.
A word of caution: Outdoor recreation by its nature is potentially hazardous. All participants in
such activities must assume all responsibility for their own actions and safety. The scope of this
book does not cover all potential hazards and risks involved in outdoor recreation activities.

Printed by RR Donnelley & Sons, Harrisonburg, VA

1st printing 1999

Library of Congress Catalog Number 98-89178

ISBN: 1-56352-504-6

Book editing, design, and cartography
by Lenz Design & Communications, Inc., Decatur, Georgia

Cover illustration by Harry Fenn, *Picturesque America*, 1872

Cover design by Richard J. Lenz, Decatur, Georgia

Illustrations by Danny Woodard, Loganville, Georgia

Photographs by Rick Strimbeck

No Vermonters in Heaven

I dreamed that I went to the city of Gold,
To Heaven resplendent and fair.
And after I entered that beautiful fold
By one in authority there I was told
That not a Vermonter was there.

"Impossible, sir, for from my own town
Many sought this delectable place,
And each must be there with harp or a crown,
And a conqueror's palm and a clean linen gown,
Received through a merited grace."

The Angel replied: "All Vermonters come here
When they first depart from the earth,
But after a day, or a month, or a year
They restless and homesick and lonesome appear,
And sigh for the land of their birth.

"They tell of ravines, wild, secluded and deep
And of flower-decked landscapes serene;
Of towering mountains, imposing and steep,
A-down which the torrents exultingly leap,
Through forests perennially green.

"They tell of the many and beautiful hills,
Their forests majestic appear,
They tell of its rivers, its lakes, streams and rills,
Where nature, the purest of waters distills,
And they soon get dissatisfied here.

We give them the best the Kingdom provides;
They have everything here that they want,
But not a Vermonter in Heaven abides;
A very brief period here he resides,
Then hikes his way back to Vermont."

—Ernest F. Johnstone, 1915

Contents

V

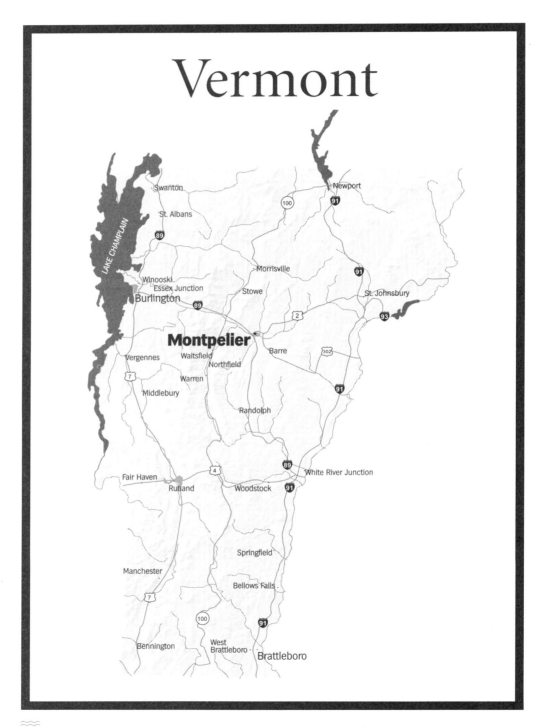

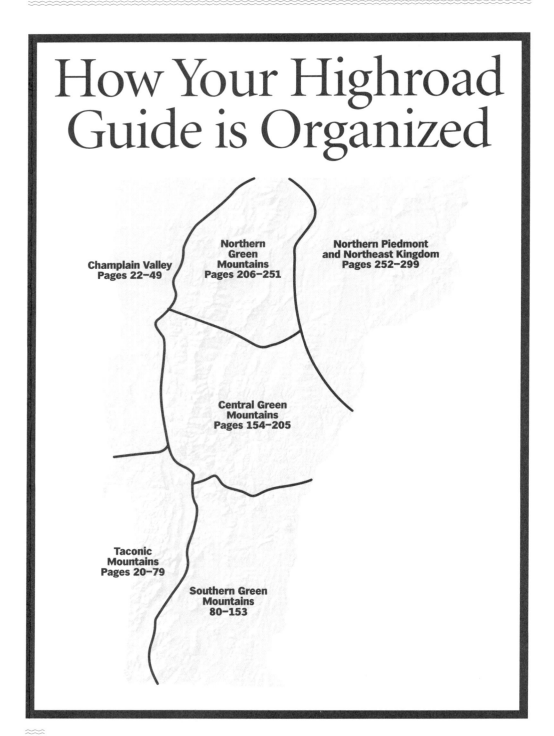

How Your Highroad Guide is Organized

Northern Green Mountains
Pages 206–251

Northern Piedmont and Northeast Kingdom
Pages 252–299

Champlain Valley
Pages 22–49

Central Green Mountains
Pages 154–205

Taconic Mountains
Pages 20–79

Southern Green Mountains
80–153

How to Use Your Longstreet Highroad Guide

The *Longstreet Highroad Guide to the Vermont Mountains* offers detailed information about the best places in Vermont to pursue your favorite outdoor activities, including hiking, camping, fishing, canoeing and kayaking, horseback riding, cross-country, downhill, and backcountry skiing, and snowshoeing. For most areas there are also detailed notes on the natural and human history, which can add dimension and depth to any outdoor pursuit.

The main part of the book is divided into five chapters loosely based on Vermont's physiographic regions. These are sandwiched between two additional chapters. The first tells the big-picture story of Vermont's rich natural and social history, from the tremendous geologic forces that shaped the rocks to the details of stone walls, barbed wire, and old apple trees on abandoned mountainside farms. The final chapter covers the long distance hiking and ski trails and waterways that defy the boundaries of the physiographic regions.

The maps in the book are keyed by figure number and referenced in the text. They should help both casual and seasoned mountain travelers get oriented. The legend below explains symbols used on the maps. While some Vermont trails have remained almost unchanged for decades, others may be rerouted or closed. Many mountain trails are closed for a month or so to prevent trail erosion during the spring "mud season," and some others may be closed to protect threatened or endangered species such as the peregrine falcon. When in doubt, call the recommended club or agency for up-to-date information. For extended hiking and skiing trips and especially whitewater adventures, you will likely want more detailed maps. Sources are listed on the maps, in the text, and in the appendices.

A word of caution: The mountains can be dangerous. Weather can change suddenly, rocks can be slippery, rivers can rise, and snow conditions can rapidly become difficult or impossible for skiing. Use common sense when in the mountains so all your memories will be happy ones.

Legend		
Amphitheater	Wheelchair Accessible	Misc. Special Areas
Parking	First Aid Station	Town or City
Telephone	Picnic Shelter	
Information	Horse Trail	Physiographic Region/ Misc. Boundary
Picnicking	Horse Stable	Appalachian Trail
Dumping Station	Shower	Regular Trail
Swimming	Biking	State Boundary
Fishing	Comfort/Rest Station	70 Interstate
Interpretive Trail	Cross-Country Ski Trail	522 U.S. Route
Camping	Snowmobile Trail	643 State Highway
Bathroom	Park Boundary	SR2010 State Route
		T470 Township Road

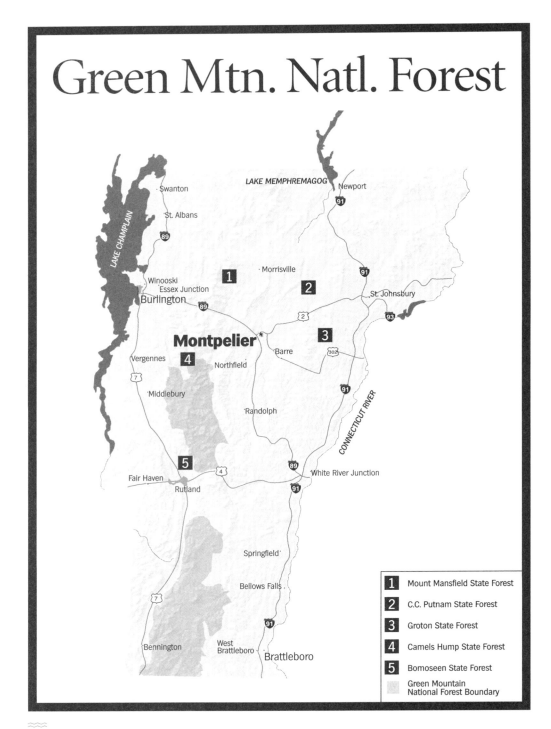

Green Mtn. Natl. Forest

LAKE MEMPHREMAGOG

Newport
91

· Swanton

LAKE CHAMPLAIN

· St. Albans
89

· Morrisville

1

2

St. Johnsbury

91

Winooski
Essex Junction
Burlington
89

2

93

Montpelier *

3

· Barre

302

Vergennes

4

Northfield

7

· Middlebury

91

· Randolph

CONNECTICUT RIVER

5

Fair Haven

4

Rutland

89

White River Junction

91

Springfield ·

Bellows Falls ·

7

91

Bennington

West
Brattleboro ·

Brattleboro

1	Mount Mansfield State Forest
2	C.C. Putnam State Forest
3	Groton State Forest
4	Camels Hump State Forest
5	Bomoseen State Forest
	Green Mountain National Forest Boundary

Preface

Vermont is named for its mountains. Early French explorers called them *les monts verts*, the Green Mountains. Sometime in prerevolutionary times the words got turned around and stuck. Vermont became the name for a region claimed by two rival colonies, New Hampshire and New York, but whose settlers claimed allegiance to neither. Ethan Allen chose the name The Green Mountain Boys for his vigilante band of settlers that chased New York surveyors back across the lake. They eventually became heroes for taking Fort Ticonderoga at the onset of the Revolutionary War, and later established Vermont first as an independent republic, then as the fourteenth state.

The Green Mountains are Vermont's defining characteristic, and lend their name to everything from the state license plate to Vermont's National Guard unit (still the Green Mountain Boys after all these years) to countless modern businesses. But there are other mountains here: the ancient Taconic Mountains in the southwestern corner of the state, the granite summits of the piedmont, and the hills of the Champlain Valley, which hardly seem deserving of the mountain surname—until you take in the views from their summits.

In this wrinkled land water follows its own laws and finds its way to every low point, cascading out of the mountains to form broad river valleys, ponds, lakes, and bogs, reshaping the land to create new habitats that dramatically contribute to the diversity of the Vermont landscape. This book is a unique guide to that landscape. Too often, the story of Vermont's rich natural history is told in the specialized language of science, and the state's human history is told without deep reference to the natural. We have tried to weave those histories together and tell them in lay terms, by explaining each place through the geological, ecological, and human processes that shaped it.

We began writing confident that we knew these stories and could tell them well, but we have finished somewhat humbled. In telling what we do know, we have gained a greater sense of how much we don't. In traveling to the far corners of the state to see firsthand many of the places described here, we've seen the state's beauty and diversity and how much Vermonters themselves cherish their links to the land. And everywhere we have gone we have learned new details that add strength and integrity to our own understanding of the complex fabric of the Green Mountain state.

We have tried to pass those details on to you. Consider this book a starting point for your own exploration of Vermont. Whether you choose to explore Vermont on foot, on skis, by bicycle or canoe, or a leisurely drive by car, we encourage you to keep your eyes open to the details we may have missed. For it is a wonderful, sometimes overwhelming property of nature that there will always be more to learn.

—Nancy Bazilchuk and Rick Strimbeck

Acknowledgments

Vermont's rolling green hills and craggy mountain peaks have always drawn those who love the outdoors and who make it their business to understand the whys and wherefores of mountain lore. We were fortunate as we worked on this book to draw on considerable expertise as we renewed old friendships and started new ones.

We're particularly grateful for the insights and wisdom of Charlie Cogbill, Brett Engstrom, Liz Thompson, and Jerry Jenkins, all of whom have spent hours in the field studying Vermont's flora and fauna. Their years of fieldwork and considerable body of scientific publications were invaluable in our work, and enlighten any naturalist who wishes to see the forests beyond the trees.

Some of Vermont's most dedicated public servants work at Vermont's Natural Resources Agency. Many staffers there were indispensable, but we owe a particular thanks to Ginger Anderson with the Forests, Parks, and Recreation Department, who read our manuscript end-to-end and offered many helpful suggestions, as well as help with ever-changing phone numbers and addresses. Charles Johnson, state naturalist, was kind enough to recommend us as writers and scientists capable of this task. Ed Leary, director of state lands, helped unravel land ownership puzzles and offered valuable insight on changing land use in state parks and forests. District Forester Jay Maciejowski helped us understand Tinker Brook, Coolidge State Forest, and the Plymsbury Wildlife Management Area.

Staffers with the Fish and Wildlife Department's Nongame and Natural Heritage Program were equally unstinting in their willingness to help. Particular thanks go to Program Director Steve Parren, as well as staffers Bob Popp, Everett Marshall, Eric Sorensen, and Linda Henzel. Wildlife biologist Cedric Alexander helped with information on wildlife management areas, particularly Victory Wildlife Management Area.

At the University of Vermont, we thank geologists Barry Doolan and Paul Bierman, Natural Areas Manager Rick Paradis, and Tom Hudspeth of the Environmental Studies Program.

The Vermont Chapter of The Nature Conservancy is steward of some of Vermont's rarer and more interesting habitats. Director Robert Klein and staffer Maryke Gillis were supportive and provided crucial information on Nature Conservancy sites.

Staffers with the Green Mountain Club have either walked every hiking trail in Vermont, or know someone who has. We are thankful for help with trail information from Lars Botzojorns, Glen Anderson, and Sylvia Plumb. Board member Bob Northrop offered unstinting moral support.

At the Green Mountain National Forest, ecologist Diane Burbank and information specialist Kathleen Diehl helped with information and advice.

Those who know and love a place are that place's best ambassadors. We thank Gerrit Kouwenhoven, director of Hildene in Manchester; John Wiggin with the Woodstock Ski Touring Center; and Ned Swanberg with the Vermont Institute of Natural Science's Taconic Field School for help understanding their corners of Vermont.

Every naturalist has his or her mentor. Ours is Hub Vogelmann, whose early work took him to all the fascinating places we've visited, and whose vision created the graduate program that gave us both the tools to study the landscape.

Finally, love and thanks goes to our families and friends, particularly our two children, Molly and Zoe, who waited patiently for mom and dad to finish writing the book. Rod and Kristen West, Steve and Cheryl Penney, Gaye Symington and Chuck Lacy, and Walter Poleman and Pat Straughan helped with friendship and childcare. A special thanks goes to Chelsea Martin, our tireless babysitter. Now, to the mountains!

—Nancy Bazilchuk and Rick Strimbeck

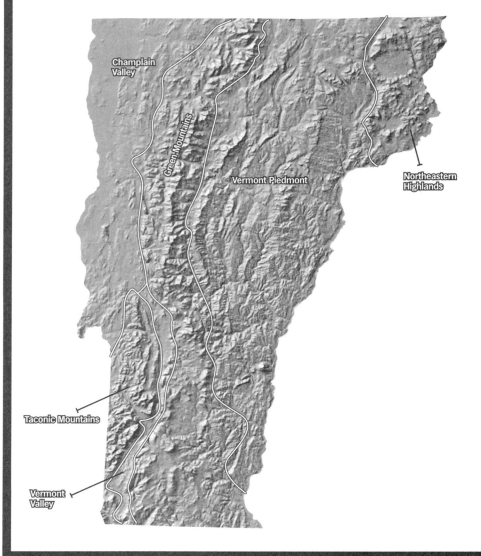

Vermont Physiographic Regions

The Natural History of the Vermont Mountains

The north/south-trending ridges of the Green Mountains roll across Vermont like great ocean swells frozen in time, cloaked in the verdant forests that give them their name. That analogy bears a grain of truth, for most of Vermont's rocks were formed from sediments that collected under a tropical sea, brimming with the first evolutionary burst of multicellular life, at the edge of a lifeless continent. These rocks were then thrust up on to the edge of the continent like a breaking wave, in two mountain-building events that spanned the time that the first plants and animals emerged from the sea to live on land, between about 450 and 350 million years ago.

Most—but not all—of Vermont's rocks can be traced to events that began more than 550 million years ago, when sediments were accumulating on a tropical continental shelf and slope—square miles of intertidal sands, subtidal limy mud, and deep water deposits of clay. Onshore stood the remains of an ancient mountain range, the

[*Above:* The Adams Apple and Lake Tear of the Clouds]

Geologic Time Scale

Era	System & Period	Series & Epoch	Some Distinctive Features	Years Before Present
CENOZOIC	**Quaternary**	Recent	Modern man.	11,000
		Pleistocene	Early man; northern glaciation.	1/2 to 2 million
	Tertiary	Pliocene	Large carnivores.	13 ± 1 million
		Miocene	First abundant grazing mammals.	25 ± 1 million
		Oligocene	Large running mammals.	36 ± 2 million
		Eocene	Many modern types of mammals.	58 ± 2 million
		Paleocene	First placental mammals.	63 ± 2 million
MESOZOIC	**Cretaceous**		First flowering plants; climax of dinosaurs and ammonites, followed by Cretaceous-Tertiary extinction.	135 ± 5 million
	Jurassic		First birds, first mammals; dinosaurs and ammonites abundant.	181 ± 5 million
	Triassic		First dinosaurs. Abundant cycads and conifers.	230 ± 10 million
PALEOZOIC	**Permian**		Extinction of most kinds of marine animals, including trilobites. Southern glaciation.	280 ± 10 million
	Carboniferous	Pennsylvanian	Great coal forests, conifers. First reptiles.	310 ± 10 million
		Mississippian	Sharks and amphibians abundant. Large and numerous scale trees and seed ferns.	345 ± 10 million
	Devonian		First amphibians; ammonites; Fishes abundant.	405 ± 10 million
	Silurian		First terrestrial plants and animals.	425 ± 10 million
	Ordovician		First fishes; invertebrates dominant.	500 ± 10 million
	Cambrian		First abundant record of marine life; trilobites dominant.	600 ± 50 million
	Precambrian		Fossils extremely rare, consisting of primitive aquatic plants. Evidence of glaciation. Oldest dated algae, over 2,600 million years; oldest dated meteorites 4,500 million years.	

rejuvenated, billion-year-old, deep roots of which now form the Adirondacks.

Erosion of these old mountains was the source of the sediment accumulating on the continental slope and shelf. There was no life onshore, and now-extinct life forms such as trilobites, crinoids, and ammonites crawled over and burrowed in the sands and muds of the submerged shelf. Their fossil remains can be found today in some of the rocks of the Champlain Valley.

About 450 million years ago, this slow accumulation of sediments was interrupted by the first of two major mountain-building events, called orogenies. These major geologic upheavals involve folding, faulting, and physical and chemical changes in rocks, and are driven by plate tectonics, the movement of large sections of the Earth's crust (plates) as they pull apart, collide, or grind past one another. Mountain ranges are formed where two plates converge, and the kind of mountains formed depend primarily on the kind of plates and their movement.

Geologists recognize two kinds of crust. Oceanic crust is thin and dense and contains high amounts of iron and magnesium, giving the minerals and rocks it forms generally dark colors. Continental crust is thicker and more buoyant, and the rocks are rich in silica, a compound of silicon and oxygen that is the most abundant substance in the outer crust of the earth, and makes lighter colored minerals and rocks. Like the first skin on a pool of candle wax, the plates that make up the outer crust of the earth float on the mantle, a layer of molten rock that extends more than halfway to the solid core.

Where two plate edges converge or collide and both are made of oceanic crust, one edge rides over the other, and the crust in the lower plate melts as it descends into the mantle. Over the 200-million-year life cycle of oceanic crust, it becomes coated with layers of muddy sediment that originates from erosion of the continents and settles to the ocean bottom. The underlying, dense oceanic crust is destroyed and recycled in the mantle, but the lower density continental sediment melts and bubbles back to the surface to form a curved chain of volcanic islands like the Aleutian Islands in Alaska.

As the last of the sediments that would become Vermont rock accumulated, just such a chain of islands was forming in the proto-Atlantic ocean that separated Vermont from its nearest continental neighbor, the future Africa. At the same time, the ocean between Vermont and the islands was slowly being eaten up. The islands gradually approached and finally crashed into North America, beginning about 345 million years ago. This island-continent collision caused Vermont's first mountain-building event, the Taconic orogeny. The heart of the Taconic mountains remains in southwestern Vermont and adjacent New York and Massachusetts.

The Taconic orogeny was followed by a 50-million-year period of relative quiet, during which the newly formed Taconic Mountains were ground down by erosion. The sediments from the mountains formed sheets of new sedimentary rock, some of which are still found in New York State, mainly south and west of the Adirondacks.

But during this period, the ocean continued to close, with future Africa and North America approaching one another like behemoth ocean liners on a collision course. The continental crust of Africa was riding over the oceanic crust attached to North America. In this second type of plate convergence, involving continental and oceanic crust, volcanoes and folded mountains form on the edge of the continent, similar to today's Andes Mountains on the western edge of South America.

Eventually all of the oceanic crust separating the two continents was destroyed, and the inevitable collision resulted in the much bigger Acadian orogeny, which lasted from 375 to 335 million years ago, and was actually part of a one-two punch that formed the entire Appalachian chain, including Vermont's Green Mountains, as well as associated mountains in Great Britain and Scandinavia. (These European peaks were later separated from the Appalachians when the Eurasian, North American, and African plates tore apart 200 million years ago.) This last crash is the third type of plate convergence, where continental crust meets continental crust, and both plate edges are too buoyant to be carried downwards into the mantle, so they collide in a kind of geologic train wreck.

In the Taconic and Acadian orogenies, the sediments on the continental edge were compressed and piled up by the force of the collision—imagine taking a sheet of clay 1 inch thick and 10 inches wide and squeezing it until it is 10 inches thick and 1 inch wide. The rocks folded and cracked along fault lines, and the squeezing generated intense pressure and high temperatures which "cooked" the rock, causing the minerals in the rock to partially melt and change into new minerals, a process known as metamorphosis.

The style of faulting, folding, and metamorphosis depended on how close to the plate edge and how deeply buried the rocks were. In western Vermont, in the Champlain Valley, the rocks were set back from the edge and close to the surface so that they were brittle and tore along long, jagged lines, forming horizontal slices that were then stacked up, a process known as thrust faulting. Although they have been altered slightly, these rocks are physically and chemically similar to the sediments that went into them, often with clearly recognizable sedimentary layers and fossil remains.

Farther east and in the heart of the Green Mountains, the more deeply buried and more plastic rocks responded to the temperature and pressure by folding, forming a series of wrinkles as in layers of cloth. In the Taconic Mountains, the rocks were so severely folded that a whole fold fell over to the west, then the whole mass slid farther west along a thrust fault, forming an overturned fold or nappe.

Metamorphism was also much more intense in the Green and Taconic mountains, so that they are now made mainly of "well-cooked," erosion-resistant rocks such as schists, like the shiny green chlorite schist that greets hikers on Camels Hump. The original sediments and layers in these rocks are no longer recognizable; scientists infer their origin as continental shelf and slope sedimentary rocks from their composition and geologic context.

Although they are also made of schist and similar rocks, parts of eastern Vermont close to the Connecticut River, along with a continuous band in western New Hampshire, belong to an entirely different geologic province. These are the compressed and altered remains of the volcanic islands that collided with the continent during the Taconic orogeny, now welded into the mix of rocks that make up the present day eastern edge of North America.

After the continental collision that created the Appalachian Mountains, North America and Africa were welded together as sections of the supercontinent of Pangaea, and remained so for over 100 million years, a time that saw the emergence of dinosaurs and extensive land-based ecosystems. About 200 million years ago, it all began to fall apart, beginning with the opening of an ocean basin between northern and southern supercontinents, then splitting each of these with the opening of the Atlantic Ocean, which continues to widen by a few inches a year today.

The events described thus far created most but not quite all of the rocks found in Vermont. One of the state's most famous rocks is the granite that is quarried in Barre and used in buildings and cemeteries all over the country. Granite and similar kinds of plutonic rock are formed when pools or bodies of molten rock (plutons), often at the roots of volcanoes, cool slowly deep underground. The Barre granite and similar rocks in the western White Mountains of New Hampshire were formed at about the same time as the Acadian orogeny (350 million years ago) when there was extensive melting due to the high temperature and pressure caused by continental collision.

Vermont has been geologically quiet for about 125 million years, but the bedrock formed over the past 550 million years continues to shape both the coarse and fine details of Vermont's natural history. The lay of Vermont's land—the mountain spine and the river veins—is largely controlled by the bedrock type and structure. The original mountains created during the mountain-building events so long ago are gone, ground away by hundreds of millions of years of erosion. But where rock-forming and mountain-building processes have put hard rocks close to today's surface, whether they form the summits of the Green Mountains or the low hills in the Champlain Valley, these rocks have resisted erosion, and stand higher than the softer rocks around them.

The general north/south grain of the Green Mountains and of the hills and valleys of western Vermont, which shows up clearly on regional topographic maps and in satellite photographs, follows the grain of the bedrock, which runs perpendicular to the compressive forces of the great continental train wreck. Regional and local climate is very much affected by this topography, as are Vermont's plant, animal, and human communities.

A second way that Vermont's rocks affect local natural history is through their chemistry. Most rock types can be loosely classed as acid or limy, but the acidity is not so much in the rocks themselves as in the soils that develop on them. Limestone and similar rocks contain minerals, chiefly calcite (calcium carbonate), that dissolve in water and counter the acidifying effect of the organic matter that plants contribute to soils, keeping the soil nearly neutral on the pH scale. The higher pH of limestone soils results in greater nutrient availability, so that growing conditions in soils developed over limy rocks can be considerably richer than in soils formed over acid rocks. Many of Vermont's rare plants, as well as our richest forest communities, are found in the limy lowland soils.

Because they are soft and dissolve slowly in water, limy rocks are also easily eroded. They are found mainly in the Champlain Valley and its southern extension, the Valley of Vermont, which separates the Taconic Mountains from the Green Mountains, lowland areas where erosion has scooped away the soft rock from between the harder rocks of the mountains. Some rock types in the Green Mountains contain intermediate amounts of limy minerals, enough to have some benefit for local soils and plant communities.

New England's geologic history encompasses most of the different kinds of geologic events that can happen in the Earth's crust, all of which are still occurring on different parts of the Earth today. They are all part of enormous cycles of continental movement and mountain building, which can take 500 million to 1 billion years to complete and operate over continent- and ocean-sized areas. Today the Atlantic Ocean is still opening, but we can anticipate a time in the far distant future when the sediments now accumulating east of Bangor and Boston will be shattered, wrinkled, and shot through with volcanoes to become New England's next mountains.

Hard Water

If the geologic changes of the last 300 million years could be made into a two-hour feature film, the mighty alpine mountain range created by the Acadian orogeny would melt away like a parking lot snow bank on an April day. All it takes is gravity and running water, slowly turning hard rock to gravel, sand, and clay and transporting the sediments, first to some distant ocean on the fringes of Pangaea and later to the widening Atlantic Ocean.

Water and gravity are still at work in Vermont today, but the finishing touches over most of Vermont's landscape were added by water in solid form, over only the last 2 million years or so. In the two-hour movie, the last ice age would be little more than a flicker of white in the last few seconds, but the continental ice sheets of the Pleistocene epoch have had an impact on Vermont's natural history far out of proportion to their brief duration.

On a global scale and over geologic time, the temperature and climate of the Earth as a whole has fluctuated dramatically—this last is not, by a long shot, the first ice age—responding at least in part to the continual rearrangement of the continents resulting from plate tectonics, the wobble of the Earth as it moves around the sun, and other factors. Beginning about two million years ago, the imbalances that lead to ice ages were well at work, and ice began to accumulate and spread over northern North America in the first of several successive waves of glaciation. The most recent wave of glaciation began about 100,000 years ago.

With its center in the middle of the Quebec-Labrador peninsula, the Laurentide Ice Sheet buried all of Vermont under 1 to 2 miles of ice by 18,000 years ago. At its farthest advance, it spread like a great white ruffled apron across central Pennsylvania and Ohio, then bending northwestwards through Indiana, Illinois, and on to Wisconsin. The islands off of southern New England—Long Island, Block Island, Nantucket, and Martha's Vineyard—are parts of the ice sheet's terminal moraine, which marks its point of farthest advance. Because so much water was locked up in the ice sheet, sea level was more than 350 feet lower than today, and the North American shoreline was much farther east.

Like running water, glacial erosion responds to the different rock types and to the overall lay of the land created by mountain building. As it flowed in a generally northwest to southeast direction, the ice sheet piled up against the Green Mountains like a surging tide, and began to overflow first through low points on the mountain ridges, carving deep, U-shaped notches like Hazen's and Smuggler's Notches in Vermont, and numerous others in the Adirondack and White mountains. The glaciers also carved high mountain cirques, or bowl-shaped depressions high on the mountains' sides. The most famous of these eastern cirques is Tuckerman Ravine in New Hampshire, but less dramatic examples may be found on the sides of Mount Mansfield.

Eventually the ice flowed right over the summits of the mountains, rounding off the summits and plucking at their flanks to create steep ledges and cliffs, like those on Camels Hump and Mount Mansfield. Glaciers erode rock by scouring and plucking. The scouring action is like sanding wood with sandpaper, with rocks embedded in the ice acting as the grit and the ice acting as paper. This scouring action is most evident in glacial striae, parallel grooves in the surface of eroded rocks that run in the direction that the ice flowed over the rock. The rocky summit ridge of Mount Mansfield is, in places, grooved like corduroy from this scraping, as are many other rock outcrops throughout the state.

In plucking, water finds its way into cracks in the rock and widens them as it freezes, so that blocks of rock are pulled loose and mix in the base of the glacier like raisins in bread dough—providing grit for abrasion. Thus, sediment is mixed into the glacier ice and carried along with it. This sediment can range from boulders the size of houses down to microscopic particles of silt, which has a floury texture when dry.

Glacier ice can carve rock, but it cannot destroy matter, so what is eroded in one place is deposited in another. When ice melts, all the sediment it carries is dropped as a chunky mixture of dirt, pebbles, rocks, and boulders called till. Most of Vermont's upland areas are covered by a blanket of till ranging in thickness from a few to tens

*A skier on Mount Mansfield,
Vermont's highest peak.*

of feet, so it is till, rather than bare rock, that is the starting point for soil formation in these areas. Rock fragments in till are sharp-edged or angular because they haven't been tumbled and smoothed by running water.

Melting ice also feeds streams and rivers that may flow over the surface of the ice, in tunnels under the ice, alongside ice lobes, or out of the glacier's snout. These streams pick up till sediments, carry them a distance, and deposit them in new landforms. Streams tumble the sediment, knocking off the corners so that the particles are rounded like the gravel and cobbles in a stream bed.

The energy of a stream allows it to sort sediment in layers of different particle sizes, because as the water speeds up or slows down, it tends to pick up or drop particles in different size ranges. The farther running water carries sediment, the more rounding and sorting there is. The kames, eskers, and deltas formed by these processes are the most important source of sand and gravel in the state, and some of the best places to see these sediments in profile are in quarries, ranging from big commercial operations like the one visible from VT 116 in Hinesburg, to small farm "borrow pits", sometimes found along local roads and trails.

Glacial geologists can read a landscape by looking at the kinds of deposits they find. Are the deposits a jumble of all different kinds of rocks with sharp edges? Then it's till. Are they alternating layers of sand and rounded cobbles? Then the deposits were carried by water, and may be dumped as a delta into a glacial lake, like deposits found near Lake Mansfield outside of Stowe.

Glaciers do more than move dirt: They create lakes. Lake basins, especially smaller ones, are ephemeral in geologic time, because they are rapidly filled in by sediment carried in by streams and rivers. Lake Champlain, the Great Lakes, and various other large, deep lakes in the northern tier of the United States and Canada were all scoured by ice sheets where they encountered already low-lying, soft rock. Smaller lakes are created where glacial deposits act as dams on small streams or as flooded glacial kettles, where a mass of ice left by a retreating glacier is buried in outwash and leaves a pond-sized or smaller depression after it melts away. Spectacle Pond in Brighton State Park is one of the best-known examples of this kind of pond formation.

The retreating Laurentide Ice Sheet also created even shorter-lived lakes, some lasting only a few hundred to a thousand years, not long enough to be seen as even a flicker in the two-hour film but plenty long enough to have a lasting impact on local natural history. As the ice began to retreat through the Green Mountains, a lobe of ice in the Champlain Valley dammed the westward drainage of the Winooski, Lamoille, and Missisquoi rivers, forming large lakes at elevations over 1,000 feet above present sea level in the upper reaches of these river valleys. These lakes drained as the ice retreated, but the gravel beaches and stream deltas that formed along their shorelines remain.

The Connecticut River was dammed by a glacial moraine in central Connecticut, forming 200-mile-long Lake Hitchcock, which extended nearly to the three-way border between Vermont, New Hampshire, and Quebec. There were also several smaller high-level, ice-dammed lakes on smaller streams in the Green Mountains and piedmont regions.

But the biggest lake by far formed in the Champlain Valley beginning about 13,000 years ago, when the glacier plugged the northward flow of water out of the valley and meltwater fed a water body geologists call Lake Vermont, which covered much of Chittenden and Addison counties with water. Later, as the ice retreated north across the St. Lawrence Seaway, the Champlain Valley was flooded by salt water, and for a few thousand years whales, seals, and numerous other saltwater and seashore species called Vermont home.

As with the high level lakes, the old shorelines of Lake Vermont and the Champlain Sea are marked by extensive beach and delta deposits. Some of these are the substrate for unique plant communities, like the pine barrens in the area around Burlington, which developed on a sandy delta deposited by the Winooski River as it flowed into the Champlain Sea.

With the final ebb of the brackish waters of the Champlain Sea, the overall lay of the land in Vermont came close to its modern form. But gravity never rests. The steep cliff faces created by glacial erosion are still under attack by frost and gravity, and Vermont's streams and rivers are once again tirelessly excavating till and outwash, recycling the materials as modern floodplains and deltas. And life, ranging from diminutive peat mosses to 200-foot white pines, from beaver to deer to humans, continues to shape the landscape.

Abenaki, Sheep, and Potash

As the glaciers retreated from Vermont roughly 13,000 years ago, they left a barren landscape that looked more like northern Canada than Vermont. Tiny tundra plants colonized the rubble left by the glacier, followed by hardy willows and alders. Woolly mammoths, mastodons, and saber-toothed tigers roamed this rugged landscape.

No one knows for sure when people moved in, but it wouldn't be too much of a stretch to imagine nomadic tribes venturing to the tundra in pursuit of arctic mammals, like the giant elk and caribou that lived on the glacier's southern fringes. Archeologists call these original Vermonters Paleoindians.

By about 9,000 years ago, archeologists have some evidence of scattered settlements, suggesting low population densities of no more than 10 people per 100 square kilometers. Camps have been found on high cliffs that would have overlooked glacial Lake Vermont and the Champlain Sea. Blackened stones from campfires and knives and other utensils chipped out of chert are all that we know of these early inhabitants.

As Vermont's climate warmed after the glaciers left, an army of trees slowly marched back into the Green Mountain State. First came spruce and balsam fir, the most cold-tolerant plants, which didn't have so far to travel. Because they're adapted to cold, these species inhabit the coldest, highest reaches of a mountain today; by the same token, when glaciers covered Vermont, these were the trees able to survive in closest proximity to the ice.

Less cold-tolerant trees, and those with heavy seeds, like oak, took longer to move north. By 12,000 to 11,500 years ago, however, scientists think that oak, birch, and maple trees found their way in small numbers to Vermont. By about 8,000 years ago, with maple, beech, and birch firmly established in the Green Mountains, bands of Abenaki people had taken up permanent residence throughout Vermont.

Water was their highway, so these settlers tended to concentrate along Lake Champlain and the Connecticut River Valley. Historians call this early period of Native American habitation the Archaic Period. These early Vermont residents lived lightly on the land, hunting deer, turkey, and bear and fishing the fresh cold streams and clear lakes for trout, landlocked salmon, and sturgeon. They made dugout canoes from trees, made or traded for beautiful cooking bowls crafted from soapstone, and had elaborate burial rituals, including cremating bodies and burying their remains with copper adzes and other tools.

Vermont's recent geologic past had a very real effect on at least some of these tribes: They buried their dead in the mounds of gravel left as glacial kames, as did other Native Americans in the Great Lakes region. A gravel pit in Isle La Motte is the only known glacial kame burial site in New England and is about 3,000 years old.

From about 3,000 years ago until the time of the first European settlers, or about 300 years ago, Vermont's native population made a major shift in technology. They used pottery instead of vessels made of stone for cooking and began using the bow and arrow. Birchbark canoes replaced the heavier dugout canoes, and elaborate burial rituals were widespread. Historians call this culture the Woodland Period.

During this time, and up until about 1,500 years ago, Vermont's climate was a few degrees warmer than it is today. Scientists call this warm period the Hypsithermal, and have found evidence for it throughout North America and Europe. In Vermont, at least some of that evidence is alive today. Some southern tree species made their way into the Green Mountains but weren't able to survive in the subsequently cooler climate. In Vermont's very warmest areas, typically in wetlands along Lake Champlain or the lower reaches of the Connecticut River, stands of black gum (*Nyssa sylvatica*) remain today as silent testimony to their peripatetic heritage.

While archeologists generally consider Woodland people to be farmers as well as subsistence hunters, Vermont's thin soils didn't do much to encourage native Abenaki agricultural efforts. "It would seem that Vermont's people were in no hurry to become farmers," wrote William Haviland and Marjorie Power in their book chronicling Vermont's first inhabitants, "The Original Vermonters."

Instead, archeological sites discovered on the lower reaches of the Winooski River suggest that residents continued to rely heavily on hunting, fishing, and gathering wild edibles, although at least one site from about 500 years ago shows that by then, native people were growing corn.

Native Americans who called Vermont home left fascinating artifacts the mountain explorer might be lucky enough to stumble upon. Green Mountain National Forest archeologist David Lacy has found places along the Long Trail where Native Americans traveled, camped and made stone tools out of quartzite outcrops. Probably the biggest find was one area at about 2,000 feet along the southern section of the Long Trail where the Abenaki mined a particularly rich quartzite outcrop for more than a kilometer along the side of a small ridge.

Some camps and other sites are scattered along the mountain ridge between Killington and Pico peaks; a reroute of the Appalachian Trail in this area was shaped by Lacy's finds, aided by the Abenaki, who worked with him to identify sacred sites. Still, the Abenaki and their forerunners didn't make large scale changes to Vermont's landscape. That would come in the last 300 years of European settlement.

In 1609, when the French explorer Samuel de Champlain first sailed south with 24 canoes from the Richelieu River into Lake Champlain, he would have seen Lake Champlain's shores populated with towering Eastern white pines, some 6 feet in diameter or more. At the mouths of many rivers, including the Winooski, the native people had planted vast fields of corn to take advantage of the fertile floodplain soils, evidence by that time that the Abenaki had perfected the art of growing corn in Vermont's short, harsh growing season.

Champlain noted seeing a grove of chestnut trees (*Castanea dentata*) on the Vermont shore, a report that had botanical historians scrambling to find evidence of his observation two centuries later. Chestnuts, while once a common component of the southern New England forest, are heavy-seeded trees and were just finally making their way northward into southwestern Vermont when the entire population of the Northeast was wiped out by chestnut blight in the 1920s.

Historians located chestnut stumps in the nineteenth century that validated Champlain's claim. The tree trunks were also evidence that the species had managed to migrate to northern Vermont during the warm Hypsithermal period 4,000 years ago. The stumps, high on a hill in what is now Burlington, meant one important thing: Champlain also traveled up the Winooski River in his early exploration of the lake.

Champlain probably wasn't too focused on the scenery, however. He was traveling with an escort of sixty Algonquin Indians, and at Ticonderoga New York, on Lake Champlain's southern end, they were challenged by Iroquois. Champlain won the battle that ensued, which ensured that the Iroquois would be forever enemies of the French. That hatred set the stage for decades of fighting in at least four different wars; the last best known as the French and Indian War, or Seven Years' War, in 1755-63.

Of course there was more to it than that, because both nations were fighting to control a valuable resource found in this new country—beaver (*Castor canadensis*), whose pelts were made into men's hats that were all the fashion in Europe. And the two nations were determined to control the future of Lake Champlain, because it was an important transportation corridor in those days, when the Green Mountains were a significant barricade to trade with the ports to the Southeast.

With the French aligned with the Algonquins and the British aligned with the Iroquois, Vermont became a kind of no-man's-land in these years of fighting. Raiding parties from French-held Quebec traveled south to attack British settlements in western Massachusetts and eastern New York. Britain's final decisive victory over the French in 1763 was a significant milestone for Vermont, because it meant settlers could brave Vermont's harsh climate without the additional burden of worries about raiding soldiers.

The aftermath of the war would extend far beyond lucky Vermont settlers, however. The fortifications that were built as a result of the seven decades of warring—in particular, Fort Carillon, later renamed Fort Ticonderoga by the British—would play into the outcome of the American Revolution.

In 1763, historians estimate about 300 European settlers lived in the Green Mountain State. By 1791, when Vermont was officially accepted into the United States, about 85,000 settlers lived here. Their settlement choices mirrored those of the Native Americans who preceded them: Because waterways were the preferred travel routes, areas along the Champlain Valley and the Connecticut River were first to be colonized.

Even before the end of the American Revolution, Vermont began to draw a flood of land-hungry settlers. It wasn't Vermont's climate that lured them northward, in fact, that was enough to keep most people away. It was money. Land was cheap, and in 1777, when Vermont declared itself an independent republic, settlers came to escape taxes.

At first the farms were subsistence farms, with families growing all they needed to survive. Hay, potatoes, and oats were early cash crops because they were more frost resistant than wheat. But the introduction of the merino sheep from Spain in 1809 and 1810 by William Jarvis, American consul in Lisbon and a Weathersfield, Vermont, farmer, had a profound impact on hill farming.

Sheep farming expanded the area of pastureland that farmers opened for their flocks, increasing the amount of cleared land to almost 90 percent. The cleared land was much more easily eroded. Some geologists estimate that the widespread clearing boosted erosion rates by a factor of 10, with heavy rains sending huge washes of gravel and soil down onto the bottomlands, in some cases burying cleared farmland in the valleys.

Merino sheep, with their long, soft fleece, were coveted for wool production, and Vermont's climate and relatively cheap land made it a natural home for sheep production. Wool was an ideal cash crop, since pound for pound, it was more valuable than many food crops. Its value made it worthwhile to transport,

Stone Walls and Barbed Wire

Sometimes the landscape holds subtle clues to its former inhabitants. None are so permanent as a stone wall or as evocative as the tatters of a barbed wire fence. Stumbling upon this hint of open fields and pastures in the middle of an 80-year-old forest opens a door on a tantalizing mystery: Who lived here, and when?

While it's difficult to date stone walls, it's possible to tell from their construction where the wall might have been constructed and for what purpose.

It wasn't until fields were plowed that stone walls began to sprout on cleared Vermont land. Farmers built single thickness stone walls with large stones for pastures. Double thickness walls were only built for extremely stony or cultivated fields. A double thickness wall is just what it sounds like: two walls built with a gap in between where smaller stones were tossed.

Barbed wire arrived in Vermont in the mid- to late 19th century. It didn't necessarily take the place of stone walls—farmers still needed places to pile all those rocks—but sometimes was used on top of stone walls. The pattern of barbs can help with the wire's approximate date of use. For example, "Crandal's zigzag," a pattern of teeth that juts from either side of the central strand, came into use in 1879. "Allis' buckthorn" was another pattern where the central strand was flattened in an oblong shape, with points all along the oblong; that came into use around 1881.

and farmers didn't have to worry about it spoiling. Historians estimate that there were as many as a million sheep in Vermont by 1836.

It's almost impossible to hike up to the ridge of the Green Mountains without seeing some evidence of Vermont's historic hill farms. Hillside farming, as it was known, made sense in Vermont because the valleys, while fertile, were areas where cold air collected. And narrow valleys tended to get darker earlier, a critical factor when combined with Vermont's short growing season. Some historians estimate that virtually every mountain slope below about 1,800 feet in elevation was cleared at one time or another.

Some farms have become present-day homes, but many more have been returned to the forest. Attentive hikers and outdoors people can pick up traces of these old settlements by looking for old cellarholes, stone walls, family cemeteries, and wells. Vegetation can also give clues to the land's past uses. If when hiking along, you find a big Eastern white pine (*Pinus strobus*) in the middle of the woods with thick branches on the lowest part of its bole, you can bet that it grew up in the middle of a field that is now grown over, because trees growing in the abundant light of open fields can grow outward as well us upward.

By about 1820, farmers were well enough established on the land that they had time to pay attention to their front yards: They planted paired sugar maples (*Acer saccharum*) at either end of the yard, sometimes called marriage trees as they were intended to grow with the married couple's relationship. The thrifty Vermonters who settled these hills found another use for these plantings: Since one tree was planted for the husband and one for the wife, these trees could be cut upon the death of the person it represented to be made into that person's coffin.

Other plantings that are a sure sign of early settlement include clumps of lilacs (*Syringa vulgaris*) or a small apple (*Malus pumila*) orchard. Later, more exotic trees were planted, including black locusts (*Robinia pseudoacacia*) and Lombardy poplars (*Populus nigra* var. *italica*).

Sometimes the remnant vegetation isn't the result of deliberate planting. Clumps of thistles (*Cirsium* spp.) and burdocks (*Arctium minus*) growing on large bumps on the ground are a sure sign of an old manure dump. Finding these clues in the middle of the forest is like finding ghosts of Vermont's past and is a fascinating reminder of the state's rich agricultural legacy.

Land above 2,000 feet may have been spared from the plow, but not from the ax. Even before the Revolution, there was money to be made from the forests. Burlington and Shelburne, with their strategic location on Lake Champlain, were centers of commerce where the trade was in lumber and other forest products like potash (wood ash extracts used in making soap and glass) and charcoal.

By the end of the nineteenth century, this frenzy of moneymaking had made some of the profoundest changes on the Vermont landscape since the passage of the glacier. Vermont, once so heavily forested that early settlers reckoned squirrels could travel the state from one end to the other without ever having to touch the ground, lost more than 75 percent of its forest cover. Making charcoal was a kind of cottage industry, and in some places in what is now the Green Mountain National Forest, observant hikers can see the pimplelike mounded remains of primitive charcoal kilns.

Changes in trade practices, improvements in transportation and the westward migration ended the profitability of sheep farming in Vermont just before the Civil War. It was replaced by dairy farming, which was able to exploit nearby markets for a profit. That heritage as a dairy state continues today. But the last century has seen an inexorable, piecemeal invasion of trees, reclaiming lost ground, so that now the state is 80 percent forested, and can once again live up to its nickname, the Green Mountain State.

A Mantle of Green

In his classic 1969 work on Vermont's flora, Frank Conklin Seymour calculates the state's flora has five times more variety per acre than New England's as a whole. Vermont's 1,400 native species of trees, shrubs, and other plants comprise about 60 percent of the total number of species found in the six New England states combined.

EASTERN WHITE PINE
(Pinus strobus)

Think of Vermont as a kind of crossroads, a place where plants from north, south, east, and west mix together to form different plant communities. Ecologists recognize in Vermont more than 70 community types, or unique plant assemblages. In the southern part of the state, and along the shores of Lake Champlain where the huge thermal mass of the lake helps moderate Vermont's chilly winters, look for red and white oaks (*Quercus rubra* and *Q. alba*) and shagbark hickory (*Carya ovata*), southern species you ordinarily wouldn't expect to find this far north. In the cold northeastern highlands, Canadian immigrants abound: white spruce (*Picea glauca*), tamarack (*Larix laricina*) and Labrador tea (*Ledum groenlandicum*) are but three of about a dozen northern migrants. And while Vermont's flora includes most of the species found to the east in New Hampshire and Maine, it also includes some midwestern species, such as Northern prickly-ash (*Xanthoxylum americanum*) that are at the eastern edge of their range.

Add to those crossroads conditions the overlay of the past land use itself. Virtually all of Vermont's 4.5 million acres of forest have been completely cut at least once in the past two centuries of European settlement. Whether the land was plowed or logged or used for pasture, the trees that reestablish themselves give subtle clues to the past. Eastern white pines (*Pinus strobus*) and grey birch (*Betula populifolia*) are two classic colonists in old, abandoned fields, for example.

The corrugated landscape adds a final dimension of complexity. For every 1,000 feet of elevation gain, the average temperature drops 3.6 degrees Fahrenheit, a temperature change that has a profound effect on the vegetation. Traveling to the barren summit of Mount Mansfield is like visiting the arctic. The miniature landscape of tiny arctic plants such as crowberry (*Empetrum nigrum*) and mountain cranberry (*Vaccinium vitis-idaea*) and dwarfed balsam fir (*Abies balsamea*) or black spruce (*Picea mariana*) are remnants of Vermont's glacial past. And then you can drop down 3,500 feet and find beautiful bogs peppered with tiny translucent orchids and weird insect-eating plants, like the northern pitcher plant (*Sarracenia purpurea*). It's a landscape that's fascinating to explore, and the purpose of the rest of the book

A round-leaved sundew has reddish leaves in a ring at ground level.

is to allow you to do that.

But before you venture into the Vermont woods, it's helpful to be familiar with the state's two most common vegetation types.

MAPLE-BEECH-BIRCH FOREST

On the flanks of the Green Mountains below about 2,400 feet, expect to find the Vermont state tree, the sugar maple (*Acer saccharum*) blending with yellow birch (*Betula alleghaniensis*) and American beech (*Fagus grandifolia*). This is the northern hardwood forest that dominates the Vermont landscape and turns flaming colors of red, orange, and gold in the fall. Walking through a rich northern hardwood forest can feel exactly like traveling through a long green tunnel. This trio of trees is often joined in lesser numbers by white ash (*Fraxinus americana*), hemlock (*Tsuga canadensis*), and black cherry (*Prunus serotina*). American basswood (*Tilia americana*) is the most common of several tree species that show up on more nutrient-rich sites, while red oak (*Quercus rubra*) joins in on warmer sites at lower elevations.

The understory plants have evolved to take advantage of the low light, often by growing enormous leaves to act like big solar collectors. Hobblebush (*Viburnum alnifolium*) and moose maple (*Acer pensylvanicum*), common understory shrubs, both have been known to grow leaves the size of dinner plates. The low light levels also explain why spring flowers are so plentiful and beautiful: Spring is the only time during the growing season when there's enough sunlight for the plants to grow, because the hardwoods aren't fully leafed out. Some of these understory plants, like squirrel corn (*Dicentra canadensis*) and bloodroot (*Sanguinaria canadensis*), have taken their low-light adaptation to the extreme: Once they've flowered and had leaves for a short while, the leaves shrivel up and disappear, leaving the plant to save its energy in a bulb or corm for the following spring.

The bounty of the northern hardwood forest attracts a variety of birds, mammals, reptiles, and amphibians, and at least some of these creatures leave record of their passage. Strange, round, dime-sized marks that scar some beech trees are a sign that black bear (*Ursus americanus*) have been feeding on the trees' nuts.

Vermont's hard winters mean that most of the state's roughly 150 bird species migrate south to spend the winter. But come springtime, the woods are alive with the calls of mating songbirds. What's most interesting about this immigration is how different returning species of birds manage to share the same habitat by feeding in distinct parts of the canopy, shrub, and ground layers. Ecologists use the word niche to describe this partitioning of habitat.

Some birds, like wood thrushes (*Hylocichla mustelina*) and veerys (*Catharus fuscescens*) forage on the ground and fill the early morning air with their ethereal songs. Black-throated blue warblers (*Dendroica caerulescens*) and red-eyed vireos (*Vireo olivaceus*) feed in the lower or mid-level tree branches. The black-and-white warbler (*Mniotilta varia*) creeps up and down tree trunks, gleaning insects from the bark.

The northern hardwood forest's thick layer of decaying leaves, plentiful streams, and tiny vernal pools provide rich habitat for six species of salamanders and seven toads and frogs. Like birds, these creatures share the forest by limiting their foraging to a specific kind of habitat. Gray treefrogs (*Hyla versicolor*) spend most of their time in rotted logs, under loose bark, and on the moss or lichen that covers the bark of older trees. In contrast, spring peepers (*Hyla crucifer*), while breeding in vernal pools, spend most of their summer on the ground or burrowed in the soil. In winter these frogs avoid freezing by wintering in the mud at the bottom of ponds, but wood frogs (*Rana sylvatica*) hibernate by burrowing into the upper soil layers, freeze solid as ice forms in the soil, and thaw out early enough to be the first frog species to begin breeding activity in the spring.

Probably the most well-known inhabitants of Vermont's northern hardwood forest are white-tailed deer, which now number about 250,000. They weren't always so abundant. Early settlers hunted them to near extinction, and those that weren't killed for meat found their habitat gobbled up by Vermont's early deforestation. So serious was their decline that the first laws to protect them were enacted in 1741, even before Vermont was a state. By 1779, the independent territory of Vermont had a closed season on deer, prohibiting hunting from January to June. But it was too little, too late.

By 1800, they were virtually extinct, and it became illegal to hunt deer in Vermont. In 1878, 17 deer were imported to Vermont in an attempt to reestablish their numbers. As today's numbers show, the effort was a success. Today's patchwork of mature forest and successional communities provides both winter cover and abundant summer browse, and deer may well be more abundant in Vermont than they were 300 years ago.

SPRUCE-FIR FOREST

Spruce-fir forest grows on the mountain slopes and ridges above about 2,500 feet and continues up to treeline, which in Vermont can dip as low as 4,000 feet. Confined as it is to the hills, it covers only about a quarter as much of Vermont as northern hardwood forest, but these are the forests that hikers will come to know best.

A hiker traveling from valley bottom to mountaintop would travel first through the northern hardwood forests up until about 2,000 feet. Then, in a transition to the spruce-fir forest, paper birch (*Betula papyrifera*) and red spruce (*Picea rubens*) begin to intermingle with the maples, beeches, and yellow birches.

Wood Sorrel

Wood sorrel (*Oxalis acetosella*) is a perennial herb that is abundant in acid forest soils, especially mid-elevation transition forests. Its leaves are anatomically and physiologically adapted to take advantage of the low, diffused light of the forest floor—so much so that direct light can potentially damage the leaves by overloading the photosynthetic system. Within a few minutes of exposure to direct sunlight, the three heart-shaped leaflets fold neatly down against the main leaf stalk, a process that involves an upward crease along the midrib of the leaflet as well as downward bending of the short stalk at its base. This minimizes light interception and allows the leaves to survive brief exposure to direct sunlight as occurs in sun flecks that reach the forest floor. The young leaves make a nice addition to a salad, in moderation; the tart flavor comes from oxalic acid, which could cause an upset stomach if leaves are eaten by the handful. As with many wild edibles, be certain of your plant identification before you eat the plant, or you run the risk of confusing it with other species that could cause poisoning.

Continuing the climb, balsam fir (*Abies balsamea*) and mountain ash (*Sorbus americana*) begin to appear, first in the cold drainages, but then more and more as the dominant trees in the canopy, until the hardwoods have dropped out. Spruce-fir forests have their beauty, but their typically high elevation locations, with associated cool temperatures and acidic soils don't make for such a hospitable place for understory plants. Look for club moss (*Lycopodium* sp.) or small flowering plants like bunchberry (*Cornus canadensis*), starflower (*Trientalis borealis*), wood sorrel (*Oxalis acetosella*) and goldthread (*Coptis trifolia*), so named because its roots are golden yellow.

Black-capped chickadees (*Parus atricapillus*) winter in these forests, but it is the summer breeding birds that capture most visitors' imagination. More than a dozen species of warblers either nest here or make stops here on their way north. Blackburnian warblers (*Dendroica fusca*), blackpoll warblers (*Dendroica striata*), and northern parula warblers (*Parula americana*) forage in the forest canopy's uppermost reaches. Ruby-crowned kinglets (*Regulus calendula*) use their fine tiny bills to pick insects and insect eggs off twigs and needles. Dark-eyed juncos (*Junco hyemalis*) flit about on the ground, searching for seeds and insects. But the biggest treat may be from the calls of the Swainson's thrush (*Catharus ustulatus*) or the gray-cheeked thrush (*Catharus minimus*), both high elevation inhabitants and each with their own distinctive flutelike songs.

As in the hardwood forest, warblers have found separate feeding and nesting niches in spruce-fir forest. For example, the parula warbler builds one of the forest's most distinctive nests out of the long green threads of old-man's beard (*Usnea* spp.), a lichen that grows on conifer branches. The Nashville warbler (*Vermivora ruficapilla*) invariably builds its nest on the ground, in well-hidden depressions in the sphagnum moss that often grows in the understory. And the magnolia warbler (*Dendroica*

Paper birch was one of the species heavily damaged by the 1998 ice storm.

magnolia) builds a more traditional looking nest right in the branches of a spruce or fir, using fine twigs and weed stalks. The use of different materials in nest construction limits competition for nesting supplies and increases the amount of time the birds have to forage and raise their young.

Although colder temperatures and fewer pools and ponds on the mountain slopes limit the numbers of reptiles and amphibians at higher elevations, it's still possible to find breeding populations of wood frogs (*Rana sylvatica*), spring peepers (*Hyla crucifer*), American toads (*Bufo americanus*), and a number of different salamanders. In one study of the distribution of amphibian populations along a transect up Vermont's highest peak, Mount Mansfield, researchers found 13 species at 1,200 feet, and seven species at Lake of the Clouds, a high-elevation pond at 3,930 feet. Because amphibians have moist, sensitive skin, some researchers think that acid rain and other airborne pollutants, like ozone, may also limit amphibian numbers and diversity at higher elevations, where pollutant doses are higher because the mountains intercept air masses coming from the midwestern states.

Acid rain has also been implicated in the widespread dieback of red spruce throughout the northern Appalachians and Adirondacks. The next chapter in Vermont's natural history will likely involve, once again, human impacts on the land and its inhabitants, working not only tree by tree or acre by acre as in the past, but through the regional and global effects of air pollution and climate change. Still, in view of the last 500 million years of upheaval and invasion, Vermonters and their guests can step into the twenty-first century with some confidence that the mountains of Vermont will remain green.

The Lay of the Land

Geographers generally describe five distinct physiographic regions in Vermont, each recognized by a suite of geologic, climatic, and ecological characteristics. Mountain building; erosion; and the invasions of ice, trees, animals, and people have all worked together to create these regions and their distinctive character.

THE CHAMPLAIN VALLEY AND VALLEY OF VERMONT

The Champlain Valley encompasses the low-lying area around Lake Champlain, and sends a finger south between the Taconic and Green mountains to form the Valley of Vermont. The bedrock is a complex mix of slightly altered Paleozoic sedimentary rocks that were only slightly "cooked" or metamorphosed during mountain building, including shale, quartzite, limestone, and dolostone. These rocks are sliced by a series of thrust faults, resulting in the formation of klippen like Snake Mountain and Mount Philo. In the Champlain Valley, low-lying areas are blanketed by lake bottom clays, bordered along the uplands by delta and other shoreline deposits. Otter Creek, Vermont's longest river, has built an extensive floodplain in the Valley of Vermont, with glacial deposits and carbonate rocks along its upland edges. The carbonate rocks, varied surficial deposits, and lowand topography, combined with the relatively warm and dry valley climate, support a rich array of plant communities, ranging from lowland swamps and bogs to oak-hickory and other rich hardwood forests in the uplands.

THE TACONIC MOUNTAINS

The Taconic Mountains in the southwestern corner of the state are a single, large, overturned klippe composed of folded slates, quartzites, and phyllites, with locally limy layers, and a moderate degree of metamorphism. The klippe forms a steep-sided mountain range with summits up to 3,800 feet at Mount Equinox, which supports a variety of hardwood and coniferous forest types, including rich hardwoods at the lowest elevations and spruce-fir forest at the highest.

THE GREEN MOUNTAINS

The Green Mountains form a series of long ridges that run north/south through the center of the state, with summits near or over 4,000 feet in elevation, from Jay Peak in the north to Killington Peak in the south. In the north, the Green Mountains are formed of strongly folded and moderately metamorphosed Paleozoic rocks of marine sedimentary origin. The southern end of the range is a high, hilly plateau formed of ancient Precambrian metamorphic and plutonic rocks. The high elevation makes for Vermont's coldest, wettest climates, with well over 100 inches of annual average snowfall on the mountain tops. At lower elevations, northern hardwood forests grade upward into spruce-fir forests. At the highest elevations, small areas of alpine tundra grow over exposed bedrock ridges and ledges. Steep ledges and cliffs carved by glacier ice and lowland lakes and wetlands add to the diversity of this region.

THE VERMONT PIEDMONT

The Piedmont forms a narrow band of low hills along the Connecticut River from Brattleboro to White River, then flares northward toward the Northeast Kingdom of Vermont. In the north, medium- to high-grade marine schists are interrupted by a large masses of granite around Barre. Deep soils made from glacially deposited till support northern hardwood forests in the southern part of the province and lower elevations of the north, while northern hilltops favor spruce-fir forest.

THE NORTHEASTERN HIGHLANDS

Except that it is on the wrong side of the Connecticut River, the extreme northeastern corner of Vermont may well have a lot more in common with the White Mountains of New Hampshire than the rest of the Green Mountain State. Geographers call this part of Vermont the Northeastern Highlands, but Vermonters call it the Northeast Kingdom. It is pocked by bodies of granite that rise to over 3,000 feet, forming an upland that rises above the Piedmont to support extensive boreal forests similar to those found farther north in Canada. The relatively low Victory and Nulhegan basins harbor extensive wetlands, including an isolated black spruce bog.

A substantial portion of the Northeast Kingdom's wooded landscape has a new owner, the Conservation Fund and the Vermont Land Trust. In December 1998 the two groups announced the $26.5 million purchase of 130,000 acres of Champion International Company's Vermont land—part of a 300,000-acre, $76.2 million deal that includes New York and New Hampshire. In Vermont, the groups will sell 90,000 acres, with conservation easements, to timber companies. The remaining 40,000 acres, mainly in the Nulhegan Basin, will be deeded to the state of Vermont and the U.S. Fish and Wildlife Service, with ownership depending upon funding.

Champlain Valley

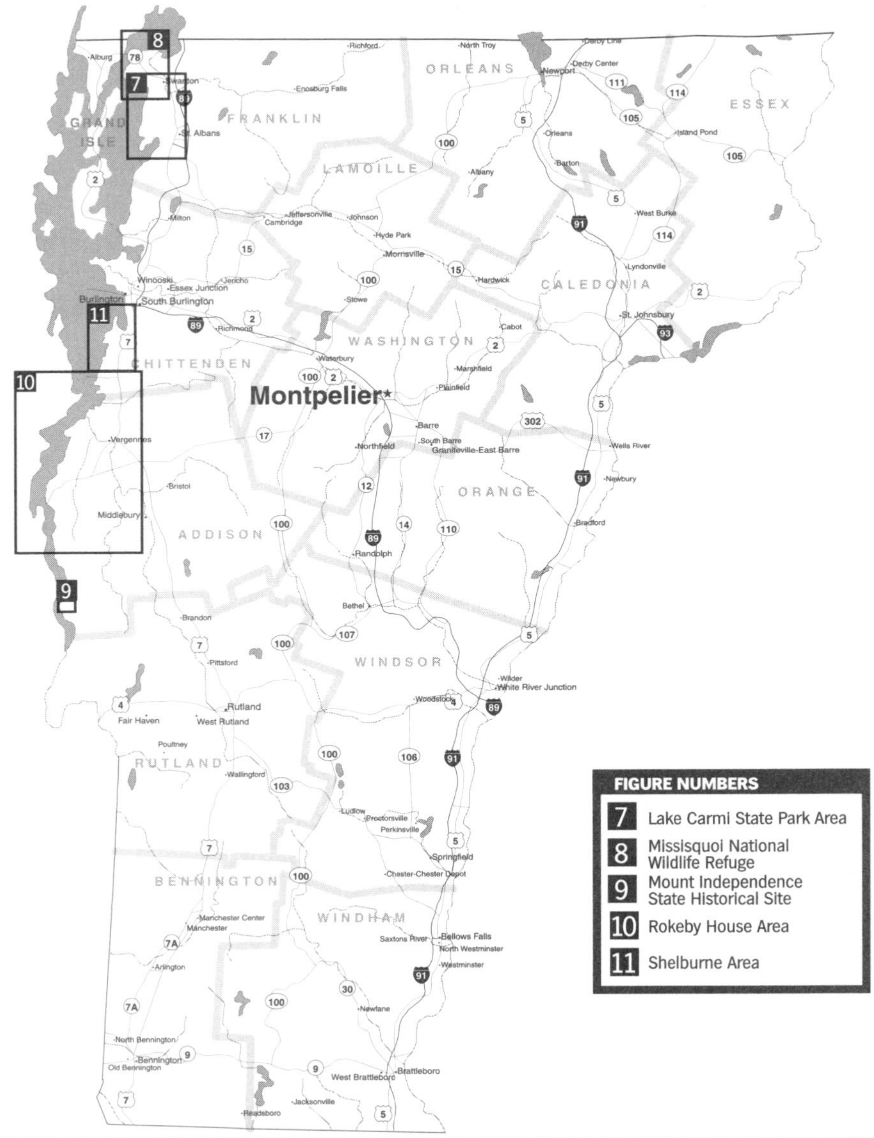

ORLEANS

FRANKLIN

GRAND ISLE

LAMOILLE

ESSEX

CHITTENDEN

CALEDONIA

WASHINGTON

Montpelier*

ADDISON

ORANGE

WINDSOR

RUTLAND

BENNINGTON

WINDHAM

FIGURE NUMBERS

7	Lake Carmi State Park Area
8	Missisquoi National Wildlife Refuge
9	Mount Independence State Historical Site
10	Rokeby House Area
11	Shelburne Area

Champlain Valley

Nestled comfortably in the broad lowland between the Adirondack and Green mountains, the Champlain Valley is one of Vermont's richest landscapes, with a variety of rock types, landforms, and plants and animals found nowhere else in Vermont. Scattered hills like Snake Mountain and Mount Philo offer sweeping views of the surrounding mountains and the rich farmlands and wetlands of the valley floor.

But not so very long ago, those hills were islands, and in place of today's verdant views, you would have looked out over a vast, surreal expanse of ice to the north, while wind-driven fleets of icebergs gathered in the bays and littered the shores of glacial Lake Vermont. A millennium later, you might have seen the spouts of whales feeding in the Champlain Sea, a cold inland arm of the North Atlantic Ocean.

Modern-day Lake Champlain drains northward, via the Richelieu River, through

[*Above:* Lake Champlain and the Adirondacks from Mount Philo]

The Vermont Whale

In 1849, workers on the new railway line between Rutland and Burlington were digging in deep, hard-packed deposits of blue clay when their picks struck bone. After some of the bone had been fragmented and carried off as fill (while the workers discussed at length just how a horse could have come to rest under 8 feet of sand and clay), a foreman noticed that the bones were most un-horselike, and had the workers continue the excavation a little more carefully. The collected bones and fragments where shipped to Zadock Thompson, a naturalist in Burlington, who eventually identified them as the remains of a 14-foot beluga whale (*Delphinapterus leucas*) that had found its penultimate resting place on the floor of the Champlain Sea. The skeleton now resides at the University of Vermont's Perkins Geology Museum in Burlington.

the lowlands of southern Quebec to the Saint Lawrence Seaway. But during glacial retreat, between 13,000 to 12,000 years ago, this northward drainage was blocked by the retreating Laurentide ice sheet, so the meltwater pouring off the glacier had to find its way to the Atlantic by some other route. Following the path of least resistance, it chose the Hudson River Valley, flowing into the Hudson River near Coveville, New York. This earliest stage of Lake Vermont began to develop when most of the Champlain Valley was still under ice and the Lake level was as much as 700 feet above the present level. A fjordlike finger of lake extended nearly 50 miles up the Winooski River Valley, as far as Montpelier. One side arm of the fjord joined with another from the Lamoille Valley to make an island of Mount Mansfield and the surrounding hills.

As the ice retreated north, Lake Vermont dropped in stages lasting a few hundred years each. At each stage, streams flowing from the Adirondack and Green mountains, well-fed with sediment-laden water from the melting glacier, rapidly built deltas along the lake shore. Wave action built gravel beaches along parts of the shoreline.

These old shoreline features now stand high and dry, under forest, field, and town, and can be recognized as terraces or more extensive flats with distinctive sorting and layering patterns in the sediments. Sometimes, they can be recognized by what people have built on them. For example, in the Champlain Valley, a disproportionate number of cemeteries have been put where sandy deltas formed in Lake Vermont and the Champlain Sea. In one survey by two University of Vermont students, 31 of 42 older cemeteries, or 74 percent, were found in these glacial deposits. Why not? It was easy digging, and flat.

By about 11,000 years ago, the ice had retreated north of the Saint Lawrence Seaway. The land was still depressed by the weight of ice to the north, and the Earth's crust was still rebounding from the recent removal of ice in our region. This allowed the cold salt water of the North Atlantic to invade the Champlain and Saint Lawrence valleys to form an inland sea now known as the Champlain Sea. The water level of the Champlain Sea dropped in stages as the land rebounded, eventually coming to a level somewhat lower than today's lake. As the land rebounded further, the region around the Richelieu River was lifted above sea level. It cut the Champlain Basin off from the sea to form freshwater Lake Champlain about 10,000 years ago.

SPINY SOFT-SHELL TURTLE
(Trionyx spiniferus)
The soft shell of this turtle is actually leathery skin covering a bony shell underneath.

As with Lake Vermont, the shorelines of the Champlain Sea are marked by raised deltas and beaches and are not quite level compared to today's shore. Due to continued rebound, Lake Champlain rose slowly over the last 10,000 years, putting some of the most recent marine shoreline deposits back underwater. The extensive sand plains around Colchester, now mostly under housing and industrial developments, are an example of an old marine delta surface.

In both Lake Vermont and the Champlain Sea, microscopic clay sediments washed out of the glacial till and were carried out away from the river mouths to settle slowly to the bottom, to form the clay belt agricultural soils in the broader reaches of the Champlain Valley. In the Lake Vermont bottom sediments, there is a curious juxtaposition: large fragments of rock, up to boulder size, embedded in the clay. These are dropstones, which melted out of icebergs that rafted them far out into the lake. Bones of seals and whales have been excavated from fields and forests of the Champlain Valley, buried in clay sediments deposited on the sea floor. The shells of North Atlantic clams and mussels, common in the lower reaches of the Champlain Valley, and remnant populations of marine shoreline plants like beach heather (*Hudsonia tomentosa*) and beach pea (*Lathyrus japonicus*) are further evidence of Vermont's brief tenure as the west coast of New England.

Addison/Weybridge

The flat, fertile fields that make Addison County ideal farmland owe their existence to the flooding of the area 12,000 years ago by glacial Lake Vermont and, later, the Champlain Sea. Lake-bottom clays are a boon to soil fertility, making possible the acres of cornfields that attract geese to Dead Creek Wildlife Management area, for example. But these same clays make farmers' lives miserable in the spring, because they so easily turn to mud, and make back road travel positively treacherous in

Vermont's fifth, prespring season—mud season.

In spite of the mud, farmers have flourished here since the first settlers came to Vermont in the early 1700s. Vermont's merino sheep industry thrived here in its heyday in the 1830s and 1840s. Dairying later took over as the number one agricultural pursuit, a position it retains today.

Standing atop Snake Mountain and other high points in the Champlain Valley, visitors will appreciate the care with which Vermont farmers tend their fields. From a high vantage point, the patchwork of emerald green fields below makes a breathtaking frame for the deep blue of Lake Champlain and the rugged peaks of the Adirondacks to the west.

DEAD CREEK WILDLIFE MANAGEMENT AREA

[Fig. 10(4)] Seen from the sky, Lake Champlain and its larger tributaries stretch between the Green Mountains and the Adirondacks like thin blue ribbons. Oriented almost perfectly north/south, Lake Champlain points like an arrow for northern migratory birds and ducks that will travel a thousand miles or more in the fall to reach their wintering grounds on the Chesapeake Bay and points south.

In fact, Lake Champlain is a major stopover for birds following the Atlantic Flyway, the migratory route followed by thousands of birds as they move between their wintering grounds in the south and their nesting grounds in the vastness of northern Canada. In the early spring and fall, the fertile wetlands and farmers' fields that ring the lake are alive with dozens of species not normally resident in Vermont, from the beautiful snow goose (*Chen caerulescens*) to ducks such as American wigeons (*Anas americana*), northern shovelers (*Anas clypeata*), gadwalls (*Anas strepera*), and ruddy ducks (*Oxyura jamaicensis*).

A number of wildlife management areas offer refuge to these migrants, including the Dead Creek area. At 2,858 acres, it is the largest wildlife management area Vermont owns along Lake Champlain, and probably the most heavily used because of its numerous boat accesses and the spectacular flights of snow geese in the spring and fall.

Dead Creek wasn't always goose heaven. Until the state began intensive management efforts at Dead Creek beginning in 1954, geese didn't even stop here during migration. Canada geese (*Branta canadensis*), which nest here now in great numbers, did not do so at all until 1960, after the state planted food crops, including clover, millet, and buckwheat, and built a series of dams to limit water level fluctuation in Dead Creek's numerous sluggish tributaries.

Biologists also introduced a flock of 44 Canada geese to the area in the late 1950s to encourage them to nest. Canada geese typically return to the same area to nest each year, so the state's efforts eventually bore fruit. A second benefit was to attract thousands of migrant snow and Canada geese to the area. Viewing is especially spectacular in late October, when the mowed cornfields to the south of VT 17 may harbor as many as 14,000 snow geese. From a distance the huge feeding flocks make the tawny yellow fields look as if they are covered by giant cotton balls.

The American bittern blends in with the reeds of its swamp habitat.

While geese may be the area's most spectacular migrants, Dead Creek is equally attractive for migrating ducks. In fact, along with the federally owned Missis-quoi National Wildlife Refuge, Dead Creek is possibly the best place in the state to see a wide variety of migratory ducks, including bufflehead (*Bucephala albeola*), redhead (*Aythya americana*), and ring-necked ducks (*Aythya collaris*). Blue-winged teal (*Anas discors*), wood ducks (*Aix sponsa*), American bitterns (*Botaurus lentiginosus*), mallards (*Anas platyrhynchos*), common merganser (*Mergus merganser*), and hooded merganser (*Lophodytes cucullatus*), all nest here. Green-winged teal (*Anas crecca*) are occasional and rare breeders at Dead Creek. There have been occasional reports that the state-endangered osprey (*Pandion haliaetus*) have nested here as well.

While much of the area around Dead Creek is cultivated farmland, when you see trees, look carefully. White oak (*Quercus alba*) and shagbark hickory (*Carya ovata*) are two of several southern tree species that reach their northern limits in the "ba-nana belt" of warmer climate that is associated with the lowlands around Lake Champlain. Refuge managers have worked with neighboring landowners to protect a 20-acre oak-hickory grove near Brilyea Dams, on the dirt road off of VT 17 just after the bridge crossing over Dead Creek.

Along the waterways, look also for black willow (*Salix nigra*) and a few Eastern cottonwood (*Populus deltoides*), whose fluffy white seeds are carried all over in the spring.

Fishing is mainly limited to warm-water species in the spring. Most common are bullhead (*Ictalurus nebulosus*) and carp (*Cyprinus carpio*). In the spring high water, lucky anglers might find largemouth bass (*Micropterus salmoides*), smallmouth bass (*Micropterus dolomieui*), yellow perch (*Perca flavescens*) and northern pike (*Esox lucius*).

The sluggish waters of Dead Creek, which gave the water body its name, are especially pleasant paddling with young children. The distances to paddle aren't too far—the farthest paddle at one stretch is about 3 miles—and the area is generally sheltered, although a stiff south wind can kick up wavelets. Children will delight in watching green frogs (*Rana clamitans*) and pickerel frogs (*Rana palustris*) bound into the water at their approach, and on sunny spring and early summer days quiet paddlers will find painted turtles (*Chrysemys picta*) basking on logs.

Directions: From the center of Vergennes, take VT 22A south to Addison Four Corners, or the junction of VT 22A and VT 17. Go right, or west, on VT 17; the wildlife

INDIAN CUCUMBERROOT
(Medeola virginiana)
This is identified by two whorls of leaves; greenish yellow flowers droop from the top whorl.

management area headquarters is 0.9 mile from this junction, and is on the north, or right side of the road. On the left are a series of pull-outs for cars where birders in the fall may watch snow geese, which feed in the cornfields to the south as they migrate. About 1 mile from the headquarters is the main canoe and boat access to Dead Creek. Parking and boat access are on the right side of the road; other boat accesses can be found north of the main refuge headquarters on West Road, off of VT 22A, and farther west from the refuge headquarters along VT 17 on the dirt road that turns left just after crossing the bridge over Dead Creek. Follow the dirt road about 0.5 mile until it forks, and take the left fork to the two put-ins. The first is just after the fork, and to reach the second continue until the road dead-ends. The fifth put-in can be found south of Addison Four Corners by about 1.5 miles; look for Nortontown Road on the right. Turn right onto Nortontown Road and follow it to the obvious put-in, about 1.5 miles on the left.

Activities: Birdwatching, duck hunting, canoeing, fishing, photography.

Facilities: Five canoe accesses (no boat trailer accesses) along the 6 miles of river owned by the state of Vermont.

Dates: Open year-round, but spring and fall are best. Since some areas are open to hunting in the fall, stop at the wildlife management area's headquarters on VT 17 to make sure you'll be out of the hunting areas if you just want to canoe or that you're in the appropriate area if you want to hunt. Staff will provide hunting season dates and a map of areas where hunting is permitted or prohibited.

Fees: None.

For more information: Vermont Fish and Wildlife Department, Essex Junction Regional Office, 111 West Street, Essex Junction, VT 05452. Phone (802) 878-1564.

SNAKE MOUNTAIN

[Fig. 10] Snake Mountain first began to take shape in the rumblings of the Taconic orogeny over 400 million years ago, when thrust faulting stacked more than 100 miles of sedimentary rock, formed on an ancient continental shelf, into the 10- to 20-mile-wide band of rocks that underlie the Champlain Valley. At Snake Mountain, the Champlain thrust fault, the lowest in a series extending eastward into the Green Mountain foothills, placed a slice of 550 million-year-old, rust-red quartzite on top of a gray shale that is about 100 million years younger.

More thrust faults to the east buried the entire region under thousands of feet more rock, all carried away by hundreds of millions of years of erosion, including all the rock of the upper thrust fault plate around Snake Mountain. The result is a klippe, a remnant of the upper plate of a thrust fault, isolated by erosion. The quartzite forms an erosion-resistant cap over the softer shale, but erosion scoops away at the edge of the shale, undercutting the quartzite to form the steep west face.

The combination of rock types and erosion makes for both acidic quartzite outcrops and limy cliffs, the latter a favorite of Vermont botanists because many of the state's rarer species tend to be found in calcium-rich areas.

The quartzite outcrops are colonized by red oak (*Quercus rubra*) and Eastern red cedar (*Juniperus virginiana*) with an understory that ranges from a shrub thicket dominated by shortleaf arrow-wood (*Viburnum rafinesquianum*) and choke cherry (*Prunus virginiana*) to a more open community of poverty grass (*Danthonia spicata*), sunflower (*Helianthus divaricatus*) and the occasional wood lily (*Lilium philadelphicum*).

Thrust Faults

Thrust faults occur as a result of convergent plate tectonic movement, as occurred during the Taconic and Acadian mountain-building events, in rocks that are not too deeply buried and are therefore brittle. The compressive force causes the rock to sheer in thin (by geologic standards), more or less horizontal sheets, which then slide one over the next. By this process, a section of crust that is a hundred or more miles wide may be compressed into a narrower, and correspondingly deeper, band of stacked-up slices of rock, with many of the original layers still intact but somewhat shuffled along the thrust fault lines. One outcome of this process is that older rocks end up lying on top of younger rocks, contrary to the rule for intact sedimentary rocks, which states that sediments accumulate upwards over time.

Below the quartzite outcrops are the limy cliffs. No trails pass this way, so would-be botanists have to bushwhack. Scattered here and there on the cliffs are columbine (*Aquilegia canadensis*), harebell (*Campanula rotundifolia*), bulblet bladder-fern (*Cystopteris bulbifera*) and smooth cliff-brake (*Pellaea glabella*), which is uncommon in Vermont.

You can follow the thrust fault's wavy trace by eye when you stand on the summit of Snake Mountain: to the north are the summits of Buck and Shelhouse mountains, Mount Philo, and Pease Mountain.

All the hills that formed from the Champlain thrust fault stood as small islands in the vast waters of Lake Vermont and the Champlain Sea, although only Mount Philo has had its lake deposits mapped. Still, hikers should watch for sands and wave-rounded beach cobbles as they traverse the lower sections of mountain's east slopes.

Snake Mountain is part of a larger, 1,215-acre wildlife management area owned by the state. Because of its sweeping view of Lake Champlain and the Adirondacks to the west, Snake Mountain is a fine hike, but the footing is best in summer or fall.

Winter hikers and skiers will have to contend with snowmobiles as there is a snow-mobile trail to the summit, and spring hikers will face muddy going, especially on the long northward traverse to the summit. Nonetheless, late spring can be one of the best times to enjoy the wildflowers that are especially abundant at low elevations.

Directions: From Addison Four Corners at the junction of VT 22A and VT 17, head south on VT 22A about 3 miles to Willmarth Road on the left. Turn onto Willmarth Road and go about 0.4 mile to the junction of Mountain Road. The trailhead is at a gated woods road straight ahead. Parking is along the shoulder of Mountain Road.

Activities: Hiking, photography, cross-country skiing, and snowshoeing.

Facilities: None.

Dates: Open year-round, but caution is urged in the early spring, and winter travelers may encounter snowmobiles.

Fees: None.

For more information: Vermont Fish and Wildlife Department, 10 South, 103 South Main Street, Waterbury, VT, 05671. Phone (802) 241-3700.

SNAKE MOUNTAIN TRAIL

[Fig. 10(5)] From the gated road, this blue-blazed trail climbs gently away from the lake through overgrown pasture gradually reverting to hardwood forest. After about 0.5 mile, the trail meets an old carriage road. Turn left uphill and begin a long traverse up the side of the mountain. In the mid- to late spring, look for trout lily (*Erythronium americanum*), so named because its pale leaves are mottled with brown much like a brook trout's skin, and squirrel corn (*Dicentra canadensis*), with its delicate, many fingered leaves and distinctive small white and yellow flowers. Deep water bars along this section of the trail testify to the volume of water during spring snowmelt. After another 0.5 mile, the trail begins a series of switchbacks to climb to the ridgeline. Once atop the wooded ridge, you'll enter what ecologists call a dry oak-hickory-hop horn-beam forest. Red (*Querus rubra*) and white oak (*Q. alba*), and shagbark hickory (*Carya ovata*) are the dominant tree species, with hop hornbeam (*Ostrya virginiana*), witch hazel (*Hamamelis virginiana*) and shadbush (*Amelanchier* sp.) the usual small trees and shrubs. At the southern end of the ridgeline at about 700 feet above sea level is a chestnut oak (*Q. prinus*) forest, an uncommon tree in Vermont. Many of these trees are more common to the south and are testimony to the moderating influence of the lake. Continue along the main footpath and ignore the numerous smaller roads that continue to intersect the trail. The trail reaches the summit clearing 1.8 miles from the road.

A cement slab, where you'll find yourself sitting to enjoy the view, is a reminder that Snake Mountain used to have an inn on its summit. The Grand View House opened in 1874, but closed in 1925 and was destroyed, first by the high winds during the 1927 flood and then by the 1938 hurricane. The foundation for the inn is overgrown now, and the cement slab actually dates from an attempt to build a house on the summit before the state purchased it in 1988.

Return to your car by the same route. For those willing to venture off the beaten track, a high-elevation bog can be found on a side trail off the main hiking trail about 0.5 mile from the summit. On your descent, take your first left off the main trail and follow this unblazed footpath east. After about 0.25 mile, the trail crosses a small stream, the outlet to a small pond, and then heads north, climbing into a thicket of hemlocks (*Tsuga canadensis*) that border the pond. The trail tops a crest and drops east into a hardwood forest. As the trail traverses a small bedrock outcrop, look to your right for a thinning of the trees and then a small trail on the right that goes into the bog. This small bog is ringed with tamaracks (*Larix laricina*) and black spruce (*Picea mariana*). Northern pitcher plants (*Sarracenia purpurea*), wren's egg cranberry (*Vaccinium oxycoccos*), leatherleaf (*Chamaedaphne calyculata*), and bog rosemary (*Andromeda glaucophylla*) abound.

Map turtles have a low ridge, or keel, along the midline of their carapace.

Trail: A 1.8-mile hike (one-way).

Elevation: 300 feet to 1,287 feet.

Degree of difficulty: Easy to moderate, with a few steep sections.

Surface and blaze: Well-worn, wide footpath with stony sections. Blue blazes.

WEYBRIDGE CAVE

[Fig. 10(5)] This 1,000-foot-long cave, the second largest in Vermont and one of the largest of its kind in New England, was virtually unknown until the early 1960s, when debris settled into a sinkhole, revealing a small entrance. The bedrock geology in this area is complex. The brook that formed the cave penetrated a small limestone ridge that is actually an overturned syncline, or a U-shaped fold of rock that was flipped over during the intense mountain building associated with the Taconic orogeny more than 400 million years ago.

Cavers report stalactites, stalagmites, soda straws, and anthodites, or cave flowers, although in the three decades since its discovery, vandals have harmed or destroyed many of the cave's more spectacular features. The small brook that cut the cave continues to course through it, making for wet passage, and almost immediately upon entering the cave, the spelunker is confronted with a series of vertical drops, one more than 40 feet, that require technical caving gear and ropes. The state Forests, Parks, and Recreation Department owns 97 acres around the cave in order to protect it for hibernating bats and the land is deliberately left undeveloped; 1 acre around the cave is

Spring Wildflowers

Wild ginger, spring beauty, bloodroot, hepatica, and three species of trillium are all early blooming spring wildflowers that share another, more subtle characteristic: ant dispersal. Their seeds have nutritious food bodies, called elaiosomes, that attract several species of ants, which collect the seeds and carry them into their underground nests, hiding them from other animals that might eat them. The ants eat the food bodies and may gnaw at the seed coat, then discard the seeds in abandoned parts of the nest, along with droppings and other waste materials that make good fertilizer. The seeds remain viable and will eventually sprout.

considered a natural area. Biologists are particularly concerned about the Indiana bat (*Myotis sodalis*), an endangered species in Vermont that may use the cave as a hibernaculum. The limestone bedrock supports a rich forest with a variety of wildflowers, especially evident in the spring.

Access to the cave requires parking on a narrow town road and crossing private land.

Directions: From the junction of US 7 and VT 17 at New Haven Junction, turn west on VT 17. Go about 4.5 miles to VT 23; take a left onto VT 23 toward Weybridge Hill. After 3.5 miles, take a left onto Hamilton Road. Take the first left off Hamilton Road, this is Cave Road. Go to the end of Cave Road, and look for a small Fish and Wildlife marker 40/41 on the roadside near a red ranch house. Walk north through the fields, and look for a sinkhole marking the cave entrance.

Activities: Caving, for advanced cavers with vertical caving skills only.

Facilities: None.

Dates: Should be avoided in the fall, winter, and spring because of the possibility that the cave is a refuge for overwintering bats.

Fees: None.

For more information: Vermont Department of Forests, Parks, and Recreation, 317 Sanitorium Road, West Wing, Pittsford, VT 05763-9358. Phone (802) 483-2314.

Mount Philo State Park

[Fig. 10(1)] If mountains were ranked by the views from their summits, then 968-foot Mount Philo would surely stand higher than many a wooded Green Mountain summit. The view from the top of the west-facing cliffs sweeps the patchwork fields and low hills of the Champlain Lowlands, over the broad waters of Lake Champlain to the summits of the Adirondack High Peaks. But the view from the summit is only part of the allure, for this small mountain was once a smaller island, and its slopes and ledges support a surprising variety of plant communities, both natural and otherwise, threaded by a loop road and a system of short trails.

Like Snake Mountain to the south, Mount Philo is a klippe, with steep west-facing cliffs of rust-red quartzite. The stabilized talus slope below the summit cliffs supports a diverse forest that includes black birch (*Betula lenta*) and shagbark hickory (*Carya ovata*) along with numerous more common species. A few big talus boulders adorn the uphill leg of the road just above where it splits to form a one-way loop, and they are in turn graced by clumps of columbine (*Aquilegia canadensis*), with showy, dangling red and yellow flowers appearing in late spring. A springtime botanical tour of Mount Philo's slopes may reveal other delights, such as bloodroot (*Sanguinaria canadensis*), mitrewort (*Mitella diphylla*), and large-flowered trillium (*Trillium grandiflorum*).

At the end of the last cycle of glaciation 13,000 years ago, the melting ice blanketed the area with till and left a kame terrace on the southeastern side of the mountain. During its retreat, Lake Vermont left gravel beaches on the flanks of the mountain and lake bottom clays around its base.

During the 1800s, the heyday of sheep farming in Vermont, Mount Philo was cleared for pasture right to the summit, with perhaps only the steepest part of the cliffs and talus spared from the ax and the flame. These pastures were abandoned in a piecemeal fashion so that a wide variety of successional species persist over much of the mountain, as patches of varying age and rates of regrowth work their way toward mature forest. The most recently abandoned pastures have dense stands of small trees and the occasional wide-spreading pasture tree. In the 1930s, Civilian Conservation Corps crews built the road and the summit buildings and planted several areas in European larch (*Larix decidua*), Norway spruce (*Picea abies*), and Scots pine (*Pinus sylvestris*).

As the road approaches the summit parking area, it passes by a small, parklike stand of red oak (*Quercus rubra*) and hop hornbeam (*Ostrya virginiana*) with a ground cover of woodland sedge (*Carex blanda*). This is a hint of the oak-hickory forest type that was once abundant on warm, dry, south-and west-facing slopes in the Champlain Valley.

More than 35 species of woody plants colonize Mount Philo, as do a wide range of wildflowers, ferns, and grass and related species. This diversity can be traced to the range of soil substrates, from bare limy rock to deep deposits of clay, sand, gravel and till; to the variety of microclimates that result from the overall shape of the mountain, from the warm and dry south-facing slopes to the relatively cool and moist north-facing slopes; and to human land-use patterns including pasture clearing and abandonment, the CCC plantations, and current forest management practices.

A more recent event has added another chapter to Mount Philo's already rich natural history. A severe ice storm in January 1998 (*see* page 173) damaged most of the trees on Mount Philo. The park remained closed over most of the following summer for a massive salvage and cleanup operation and the state has indicated that campground may remain closed or reduced in size.

Directions: Take VT 7 about 2.5 miles south from the traffic light at Church Hill Road in Charlotte or about 1 mile north from the North Ferrisburg crossroads, and

LABRADOR TEA
(Ledum groenlandicum)
Growing up to three feet
tall, this is an evergreen
with white blooms.

turn east on State Park Road, which goes .5 mile straight to the park entrance where the loop road begins.

Activities: Hiking, cycling, cross-country skiing, and sledding.

Facilities: Campground; picnic area with rain shelter and restrooms.

Dates: Road and campground, mid-May through mid-Oct.; otherwise year-round.

Fees: In season, there are fees for day use, parking at the summit, and camping in tents or lean-tos; no fees in the off-season.

Closest town: North Ferrisburg, 2 miles.

For more information: Mount Philo State Park, RD 1, Box 1049, North Ferrisburg, VT 05473. Phone (802) 425-2390 (summer). Vermont Department of Forests, Parks, and Recreation, 317 Sanitorium Road, West Wing, Pittsford, VT 05763-9358. Phone (802) 483-2001 (winter).

CLIFF TRAIL

[Fig. 10(1)] There are some easy, short paths linking together the various view-points on the summit of Mount Philo. This short but somewhat rough and steep trail links these with the park loop road, and it traverses right along the base of the cliffs. It can be reached by climbing up a steep spur trail that begins on the park road just below the gravel pit, by another steep link ascending from the downhill leg of the loop road, or by descending a trail from the summit area.

Near where the trail rounds the northern end of the cliffs, walking fern (*Asplenium rhizophyllum*) has found a home on top of several boulders of quartzite that have fallen off the cliff. A bit farther south, the trail is bordered by extensive beds of pale touch-me-not (*Impatiens pallida*) growing in loose scree, which, like talus, is a pile of rocks at the base of a cliff, but in this case the fragments are fist-sized or smaller and are often quite unstable. Farther along, under an overhang below the highest part of the cliffs, there is a porcupine den, recognized by an impressive pile of curved droppings and an occasional quill.

Trail: 0.3 mile from summit to park road and 1.2 miles to return via the road; to walk the road and trail from the park entrance is about 2.8 miles round-trip.

Elevation: About 400 feet at the park entrance, 700 feet where the trail joins the park road, and 968 feet at the summit.

Degree of difficulty: Moderate.

Surface and blaze: The trail is rocky in places, and the steep sections can be slippery when wet.

Shelburne Pond

[Fig. 11] "Pea soup" may be the first words that come to mind for many summer visitors to Shelburne Pond. Throughout most of the summer and early fall, the surface waters of the pond support a dense growth of algae that streams and swirls off the blade of a canoe paddle. Although the pond does not invite swimming, it is a remarkable example of an eutrophic, or nutrient-rich, pond, with a productive warm-water fishery, and it is bordered by rich wetland, limestone ledge, and upland field and forest communities.

The shoreline is undeveloped, and the pond is usually quiet, even on weekends. More than 500 acres of wetlands and low hills along the western shore of the pond, together with a section along the northeastern bay, form the University of Vermont's H. Laurence Achilles Natural Area, and a Vermont Fish and Wildlife Department boat ramp provides access for canoes and small boats. A short trail from the boat ramp runs through the upland forests along the southwestern shore.

On a geological time scale, lakes and ponds are ephemeral because they are gradually filled in by sediment and wetland vegetation, a natural process of succession. In the 10,000 years since glacial scouring and deposition dotted Vermont with lakes and ponds, many of the smallest have already been filled in. Although Shelburne Pond is medium sized (450 acres), the basin has an average depth of only 12 feet, and it is already about halfway through the filling-in process. Human activity, primarily farming, has accelerated this process by adding nutrients and sediment runoff to the lake, resulting in dense algal blooms in the summer.

Shelburne Pond is classified by the State of Vermont as ultraeutrophic. A 1981 study reported spring phosphorous concentrations, an indicator of nutrient status, 5 to 20 times those found in 25 other lakes sampled. Prolific algal growth at the bottom of the food chain supports dense fish populations at the top, including perch, smallmouth bass, and northern pike.

The pH of the lake water is usually around 8.5 in summer, chiefly because the bedrock in the lake watershed is limestone and dolomite, which outcrops on the steeper sections of the eastern shoreline. These exposed ledges are crowned by overhanging Eastern white-cedar (*Thuja occidentalis*) and support rare limestone ferns such as mountain spleenwort (*Asplenium montanum*) and purple-stemmed cliffbrake (*Pellaea atropurpurea*), along with a variety of more common shrubs and wildflowers.

If, at times, the water of the pond itself lacks charm, the wetlands along the north, west, and south shores make up for it. These are predominately cattail (*Typha latifolia*) marshes, but hidden by the western shore is a poor fen (a moderately acid peat bog) with the telltale crowns of tamarack (*Larix laricina*) trees poking up a short distance back from the water's edge. Since the pH of a poor fen is usually not more than 4.5, this means it has about 10,000 times the acid concentration of the nearby lake water!

Great blue herons (*Ardea herodias*), green herons (*Butorides striatus*), and

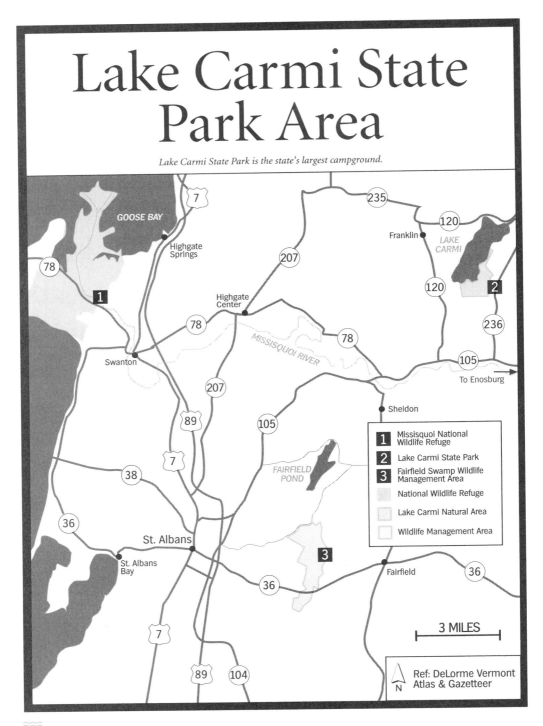

Lake Carmi State Park Area

Lake Carmi State Park is the state's largest campground.

GOOSE BAY

7

235

120

Franklin

LAKE CARMI

78

Highgate Springs

207

120

1

Highgate Center

2

120

78

236

MISSISQUOI RIVER

78

105

Swanton

To Enosburg

207

Sheldon

89

105

1 Missisquoi National Wildlife Refuge

2 Lake Carmi State Park

3 Fairfield Swamp Wildlife Management Area

7

FAIRFIELD POND

National Wildlife Refuge

Lake Carmi Natural Area

38

Wildlife Management Area

36

St. Albans

St. Albans Bay

3

Fairfield

36

36

3 MILES

7

Ref: DeLorme Vermont Atlas & Gazetteer
N

89

104

black-crowned night herons (*Nycticorax nycticorax*) are common along the shoreline, while many other wetland birds tend to stay out of sight in the cattails. The inlets at the northern end of the pond invite exploration by canoe and are good place to see beaver (*Castor canadensis*) and muskrat (*Ondatra zibethicus*), or at least their lodges and scent mounds.

Directions: From Burlington, take VT 116 south toward Hinesburg about 7 miles. Turn right on Pond Road, which becomes a dirt road, and look for a sign for the state fishing access at 1.5 miles on the right. If you come up VT 116 from Hinesburg, Pond Road is about 0.7 mile past the turnoff for VT 2A.

Activities: Canoeing, birdwatching, fishing, walking along the shore.

Facilities: None.

Dates: Open year-round.

Fees: None.

Closest town: Hinesburg, 5 miles.

For more information: University of Vermont Environmental Program, 153 S. Prospect Street, Burlington,VT 05405. Phone (802) 656-4055.

Lake Carmi State Park

[Fig. 7(2)] This popular campground—the state's largest—is next to Vermont's fourth-largest natural lake, which has a good warm-water fishery and a thriving walleye (*Stizostedion vitreum*) population.

But the real reason to visit the state park is the peat bog at the south end of the lake. Best of all, a trail traverses the northern end of the bog, making it easy to see this textbook example of a black spruce bog.

The 140-acre bog, the state's third largest, is dominated by spindly black spruce (*Picea mariana*) draped with old man's beard (*Usnea* spp.). Tamaracks mingle with the spruce, and the squishy sphagnum moss ground cover is dotted with Labrador tea (*Ledum groenlandicum*) and mountain holly (*Nemopanthus mucronata*). In the sunnier, more open areas of the bog and near the trail, look for three different species of cottongrass (*Eriophorum vaginatum*, *E. virginicum*, and *E. polystachion*). Leather-leaf (*Chamaedaphne calyculata*), sheep and bog laurel (*Kalmia angustifolia* and *K. polifolia*), northern pitcher plants (*Sarracenia purpurea*), and round-leaved sundew (*Drosera rotundifolia*) are scattered throughout.

Directions: From Interstate 89, take Exit 21 and head east on VT 78 about 12 miles. Two miles after passing through North Sheldon, look for VT 236 and turn left on it. The campground is 3 miles north on VT 236. The campground access road, VT 236, is also 3 miles west of Enosburg Falls.

Activities: Fishing, boating, swimming, hiking trails.

Facilities: 140 tenting or trailer sites, 35 lean-tos, 2 cabins, restrooms, 2 swimming

Missisquoi National Wildlife Refuge

The Missisquoi National Wildlife Refuge encompasses 6,000 acres.

N

Ref: Delorme Vermont Atlas & Gazetteer

1 Private Campground
2 Refuge Headquarters
3 Nature Trail
4 Canoe Put In
5 Shad Island
········· Canoe Route
‒ ‒ ‒ Railroad

MISSISQUOI BAY

GANDER BAY

GOOSE BAY

LAKE CHAMPLAIN

Missisquoi Bay Bridge

5

1

Campbell Road

78

4 P

Mac's Bend Rd.

DEAD CREEK

1 MILE

West Swanton

P

CHARCOAL CREEK

P

Shore Road

Tabor Road

MAQUAM CREEK

3 **2**

BLACK CREEK

MISSISQUOI RIVER

Central Vermont Railroad

MAQUAM BAY

Swanton **78**

1

beaches, a day-use area with picnic tables, a concession area, restrooms and rental boats, short nature trails.

Dates: Day use, open year-round; camping and services, open mid-May—Sept.

Fees: There is a charge for day-use admission and for camping and cabins.

Closest town: Enosburg Falls, 6 miles.

For more information: Lake Carmi State Park, RD 1 Box 1710, Enosburg Falls, VT 05450. Phone (802) 933-8383 (summer). Vermont Department of Forests, Parks, and Recreation, 111 West Street, Essex Junction, VT 05452-4695. Phone (802) 879-6565 (winter).

Missisquoi National Wildlife Refuge

[Fig. 8, Fig. 7(1)] In the northeasternmost bay of Lake Champlain, which crosses the international border into Quebec, the Missisquoi River has built an extensive and complex delta that supports a wide variety of wetland communities, including one of the largest bogs in Vermont, extensive swamp forests, and hundreds of acres of wild rice—a paradise for boaters as well as waterfowl and other wildlife. The 6,000-acre Missisquoi National Wildlife Refuge offers canoe and small boat access to delta waterways and has a 1.5-mile nature trail along small waterways in the southern portion of the delta.

A few thousand years ago, the Missisquoi River emptied south into Maquam Bay, and built up the plug of sediment that fills the gap between the uplands of Swanton to the east and Hog Island to the west. Finding its way blocked by its own pile of sediment, it eventually turned north and began to build the modern delta that now extends well into the shallow waters of Missisquoi Bay.

As in other deltas, the river splits into distributary channels before reaching the lake, but this delta has an unusual form: The levees along the distributaries form long narrow strips of relatively high ground extending well out into the bay. On a map it looks like the leg and toes of a bird (in this case, an upside down one), earning it the moniker "birdfoot delta." This kind of delta forms where there is little temperature difference between the river water and the water body that it empties into. If the river water is warmer or colder (and thus a different density) than the water body it's flowing into, it tends to fan out and form a broad delta front. But when the lake water and river water are nearly the same temperature and density, the water and sediments squirt out in a narrow jet and form the birdfoot shape.

Missisquoi Bay is so shallow (about 13 feet at most) that it warms right to the bottom in the summer, unlike most other sections of the lake. Rather than fanning out over the surface or sinking to the bottom, the river water with its load of sediment shoots straight out into the bay, rapidly extending the delta front. Waves, which reshape the fronts of deltas that are exposed to them, rarely get very big in the short fetch and shallow water of Missisquoi Bay, so the sediment tends to stay where the river puts it.

The present delta includes not only the three main distributaries out at the delta front, but the subsidiary distributary known as Dead Creek, some abandoned distributaries such as Maquam and Black creeks in the southern part of the refuge, and an abandoned main channel now called Charcoal Creek. Some of these waterways were used by smugglers carrying potash, used in England's woolen mills, north to Montreal during the war of 1812, when there was a trade embargo with England and Canada. These same waterways now provide canoeists with pathways into many of the different kinds of wetland habitat found on the delta.

The present and recently abandoned distributaries have built levees, strips of high ground formed by sediment deposition when the river floods over its banks. The 1- to 2- foot elevation of the levee soil surface above the surrounding marshes means that the soils are above water and well-aerated during most of the growing season, so the levees support productive swamp forests dominated by silver maple (*Acer saccharinum*) and green ash (*Fraxinus pennsylvanica*), with occasional swamp white oak (*Quercus bicolor*). Close to the riverbank where the light gets in, the understory may consist of little more than dense stands of ostrich fern (*Matteuccia pensylvanica*), the source of the edible fiddleheads that are sometimes sold in grocery stores, while in shadier areas sensitive fern (*Onoclea sensibilis*), stinging nettles (*Urtica dioca*), and a host of other herbaceous species are dominant.

Levees subside slowly after a channel is abandoned, so that along the older channels such as Charcoal and First creeks, they may be marked by a line or just occasional clumps of dead, weathered trees. Much of this mortality dates to a period of repeated and prolonged flooding in the late 1970s, which killed trees in swamp forests all around Lake Champlain.

The wildlife refuge provides breeding habitat for about 80 bird species, with numerous others stopping by during migration. Shad Island, outlined by the delta front and two distributary channels, hosts a great blue heron (*Ardea herodias*) rookery with several dozen pairs of birds occupying big, messy stick nests in the skeletons of dead swamp maples. While access to the rookery is restricted, with a good pair of binoculars or a spotting scope it is possible to watch and listen to—and sometimes smell—the birds and their nesting from the delta-front wetlands.

Lurking deeper in the marshes are more secretive birds such as American bittern (*Botaurus lentiginosus*), snipe (*Gallinago gallinago*), Virginia rail (*Rallus limicola*), and marsh wren (*Cistothorus palustris*), all more often heard than seen. Mallards (*Anas platyrhynchos*) and black ducks (*Anas rubripes*) congregate and feed along the delta front and in larger pools all over the refuge. Ring-necked ducks (*Aythya collaris*) can sometimes be seen in summer, and numerous other duck species stop by during migration.

Northern harriers (*Circus cyaneus*) ride low over the tops of the marshes with a characteristic V-winged teetering flight; a bright white rump over a long tail is a distinctive field mark. There are at least eight nesting sites for osprey (*Pandion haliae-*

tus) in and around the refuge, and the birds are often seen circling over the river or the bay in search of fish. Flooded marshes are also important nursery areas for a wide range of fish species, and anglers take primarily warm-water species like northern pike and large and small-mouth bass from the refuge waters.

The delta front is the place to see black terns (*Chlidonias niger*), flying fast and low over the water, making quick drops and turns to snatch insects from the air and water surface. Black terns are a species of inland lakes and marshes, including the Great Lakes, and Lake Champlain marks the eastern edge of their range. The Missisquoi Delta is one of only two breeding areas for this species in Vermont, but here they are locally abundant. They sometimes roost on logs that are anchored in the shallow bottom of the delta front, also a favorite haunt of ring-billed gulls (*Larus delawarensis*), which face upwind in neat rows, along the length of the log.

Deltas

Deltas form wherever a sediment-laden river runs into a lake or ocean, and can take a variety of shapes depending on the character of the river and the receiving waters. The water slows down suddenly as it enters the relatively still water of the bay, causing the river to drop most of the sediment that it is carrying. Over time, deltas build outward, and as the river tends to block its own channel with deposited sediment, it forks and builds new channels around the barrier. Deltas may be strongly modified by wave action along the delta front.

The refuge also supports two turtle species that are at the eastern edge of their ranges here, the map turtle (*Graptemys geographica*) and the Eastern spiny soft-shell (*Trionyx spinferus*). Map turtles bask warily on logs along the riverbanks; more often than not you'll just glimpse the motion as they drop into the water. They have bold yellow streaks on head, legs, and tail, and a slightly keeled shell with intricate light markings on a dark background that suggest a detailed map. The Eastern spiny soft-shell basks mainly on mud banks and has an olive green, leathery, and nearly round shell marked with scattered black rings. They typically reach dinner-plate size. A pointy, flat-tipped nose and bold, black-lined eye streaks are also good field marks.

Along the river channel, belted kingfishers (*Ceryle alcyon*) roost on branches overhanging the water, drop suddenly and strike the water surface with a splash, and rise again to a feeding perch. The riverbank swamp forests are also home to a wide variety of songbirds including numerous species of warblers.

Other, less appreciated forms of wildlife are abundant throughout the summer months: mosquitoes and deer flies. Chemical repellents deter the former, but for the latter there is no better defense than a swift slap.

Directions: Take Exit 21 off I-89, and follow VT 78 through the town of Swanton and north along the west bank of the Missisquoi River. Missisquoi National Wildlife Refuge headquarters is on the left about 5 miles from the highway exit.

Activities: Canoeing, hiking, bird and wildlife-watching, blueberry picking, fishing.

Mount Independence State Historic Site

Mount Independence is Vermont's newest state historic site.

Ref: Mount Independence State Historic Site Map

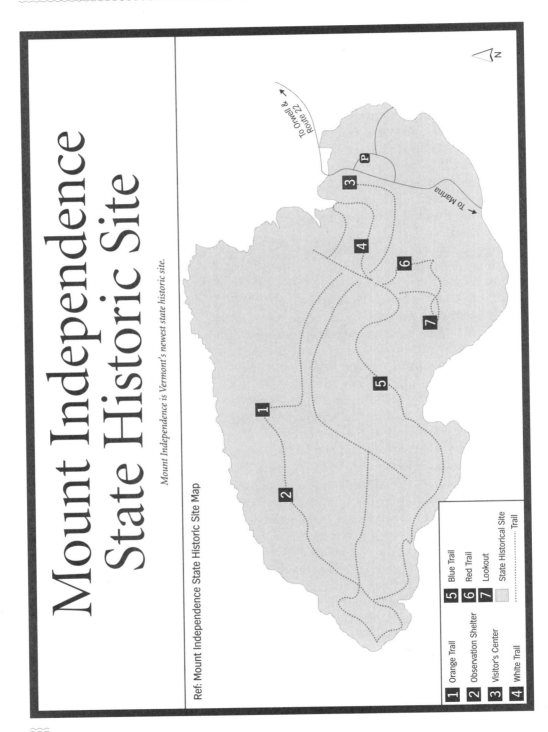

1	Orange Trail	5	Blue Trail
2	Observation Shelter	6	Red Trail
3	Visitor's Center	7	Lookout
4	White Trail		State Historical Site
		....	Trail

To Orwell & Route 22

To Marina

Facilities: Outhouses are available in summer at the headquarters parking area; boat ramps, short nature trails.

Dates: Open year-round.

Fees: None.

Closest town: Swanton, 2 miles.

For more information: Missisquoi National Wildlife Refuge, PO Box 163, Swanton, VT 05488. Phone (802) 868-4781.

Museums and Historic Sites

No visit to the Champlain Valley is complete without dipping into the region's historic past. Lake Champlain is home to the nation's best-preserved collection of Revolutionary War shipwrecks and other artifacts. Vermont was also an important stop in the Underground Railroad that helped escaping slaves north to the safety of Canada. And one of the nation's foremost agricultural estates, built in 1886 with Vanderbilt railroad money and landscaped by Frederick Law Olmstead, still stands as a monument to the genteel life of the wealthy in the nineteenth century.

The pleasure of visiting all these museums and historic sites is that each offers walking tours or hikes through landscapes that give the visitor a sense of traveling back in time to eighteenth- and nineteenth-century Vermont.

MOUNT INDEPENDENCE

[Fig. 9] Vermont's newest state historic site, Mount Independence, with its sister fortification Fort Ticonderoga, played a decisive role in the Revolutionary War. The fortifications on the mountaintop, overlooking the narrows on Lake Champlain, are credited with turning the British back in October 1776 after the Redcoat victory in the Battle of Valcour.

In 1776, Benedict Arnold, who would later gain notoriety as America's first traitor, came to Lake Champlain determined to build a fleet to keep the British from using the lake as a travel corridor from their camps in Canada to the north. The British were also busily building boats, or hauling disassembled boats around the rapids at Chambly, on the Richelieu River, and reassembling them upstream at St. Jean. Hopelessly outnumbered, Arnold lost the ensuing battle of Valcour, but while the British withdrew into Canada, the American troops overwintered at the lakeshore forts, with considerable losses to the winter cold and smallpox. Some of the men wrote letters and kept diaries, which are accessible on a computer database at the visitor center.

The battles fought on Lake Champlain have left another legacy for history buffs. The bottom of Lake Champlain is littered with Revolutionary War boats dating from the ill-fated Battle of Valcour. Many of these artifacts, including a 3,000 pound cannon, have been recovered and are displayed at Mount Independence.

Outside the visitor center, 7 miles of trails of varying lengths wander through more than 400 acres of pasture and woodland. The area is underlain by limestone and dolomite and supports a range of unusual and rare plant species, including climbing fumatory (*Adlumia fungosa*), four-leaved milkweed (*Asclepias quadrifolia*), narrow blue-eyed grass (*Sisyrinchium angustifolium*) and yellow oak (*Quercus muhlenbergii*). The visitor center has free maps of a self-guided historic tour of the area. The trails, which are all easy walking, take visitors past various remains and fortifications.

Directions: The Mount Independence State Historic Site is 5.5 miles off VT 22A in Orwell. From the junction of VT 73 and VT 22A in Orwell, continue west on VT 73 to the first fork in the road. Take the left hand fork, leaving VT 73. At the next fork, bear right and the road will turn to dirt and parallel Lake Champlain. Continue on this road until it forks again, and take a sharp left-hand turn toward a small marina. The parking lot for the site is on the left at the top of the hill. All trails leave from the site's visitor center.

Activities: Hiking, photography.

Facilities: Visitor center and hiking trails; a dock for boaters is available down the road at Buoy 39 Marina in Catfish Bay. A nearby private cruise boat, the M/V Carillon, operates from May 1 to the end of October from Larrabee's Point and docks at Mount Independence and Fort Ticonderoga.

Dates: Late May—mid-Oct.

Fees: There is a charge for admission at Mount Independence; children under 14 are free. There is a charge for a two-hour cruise on M/V Carrillon.

For more information: Mount Independence State Historic Site, phone (802) 759-2412; the private cruise ship M/V Carillon, Teachout's Lakehouse Store and Wharf, PO Box 64A Shoreham, VT 05770. Phone (802) 897-5331. For general historic site information, the State of Vermont Division of Historic Preservation, 135 State Street, Drawer 33, Montpelier, VT 05633-1201. Phone (802) 828-3051.

🏛 LAKE CHAMPLAIN MARITIME MUSEUM

[Fig. 10(3)] Located next to the exclusive Basin Harbor Club, this rapidly growing museum includes a working replica of Benedict Arnold's Revolutionary War gunboat Philadelphia and countless Revolutionary War artifacts pulled from the bottom of Lake Champlain. There's an open-air boat-building exhibit, a blacksmith's forge, and an old, one-room schoolhouse made of the local Panton stone, a beautiful dark-gray limestone. One building houses quirky old boats, from an enormous ice boat dating from the turn of the century to several canvas lake canoes. A must for history buffs and people curious about the early maritime history of Lake Champlain.

Directions: The museum is 7 miles northwest of Vergennes. From Vergennes, take VT 22A south across Otter Creek. Take the third right off VT 22A onto Panton Road. Continue west on Panton Road for 1 mile and turn right onto Basin Harbor Road. Continue along Basin Harbor Road for 6 miles to the entrance of the museum on the right after passing through the gates of the Basin Harbor Club.

Lake Champlain's Underwater Historic Preserves

Vermont has six underwater historic preserves, marked with yellow buoys so divers can find them easily. Divers must register for the season before they dive on the wrecks. Contact the Vermont Division for Historic Preservation at (802) 828-3051, the Burlington Community Boathouse at (802) 865-3777, or the Lake Champlain Maritime Museum at (802) 475-2022.

Here's a description of the shipwrecks:

The Phoenix, in 60 to 110 feet of water on the northern face of Colchester Shoal Reef. The second commercial steamboat on Lake Champlain, launched in 1815, burned and sank on September 4, 1819, in a suspicious fire.

Burlington Horse Ferry, near the Burlington breakwater in 50 feet of water. Discovered in 1983, made famous in a *National Geographic* story in June 1988. Horse ferries were used extensively on Lake Champlain in the 1830s and 1840s.

General Butler, in 40 feet of water 75 yards west of the southern end of the Burlington breakwater. A schooner-rigged sailing canal boat built in 1862; sank on December 9, 1876, in a powerful winter storm.

A.R. Noyes Coal Barge, north of the Coast Guard's navigational buoy on Proctor Shoal off Oakledge Park, in 65 to 80 feet of water. Sank October 17, 1884, when a number of canal boats broke loose from their steam tug.

Diamond Island Stone Boat, in 12 to 25 feet of water near the south side of Diamond Island off Kingsland Bay in Ferrisburgh. A nineteenth century wooden canal boat that transported cargo through the lake and the Champlain Canal; sank with a load of quarried stone.

O.J. Walker, a schooner-rigged sailing canal boat, sits upright with masts, booms and ship's wheel all present, in 65 feet of water in Burlington Bay. Sank with a load of bricks and tile en route from Mallet's Bay to Shelburne, May 11, 1895.

An additional historic preserve, the wreck of the *Champlain II*, lies on the New York side of the lake.

Activities: Museum exhibits, workshops, and special events.

Facilities: 12 buildings, the gunboat Philadelphia II, store, open-air boat-building shop, conservation laboratory, restrooms, picnic tables.

Dates: Early May to mid-October.

Fees: There is a charge for admission, except for children under age 6.

For more information: Lake Champlain Maritime Museum, 4472 Basin Harbor Road, Vergennes, VT 05491 Phone (802) 475-2022.

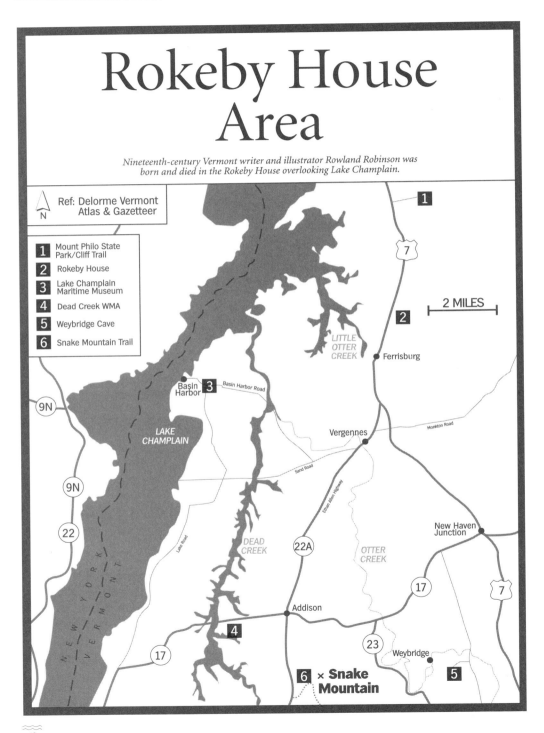

Rokeby House Area

Nineteenth-century Vermont writer and illustrator Rowland Robinson was born and died in the Rokeby House overlooking Lake Champlain.

Ref: Delorme Vermont Atlas & Gazetteer

1 Mount Philo State Park/Cliff Trail
2 Rokeby House
3 Lake Champlain Maritime Museum
4 Dead Creek WMA
5 Weybridge Cave
6 Snake Mountain Trail

2 MILES

LITTLE OTTER CREEK

Ferrisburg

Basin Harbor
Basin Harbor Road

LAKE CHAMPLAIN

Vergennes

Monkton Road

Sand Road

Ethan Allen Highway

New Haven Junction

Lake Road

DEAD CREEK

22A

OTTER CREEK

17

7

Addison

23

Weybridge

SNAKE Mountain

NEW YORK
VERMONT

ROKEBY HOUSE

[Fig. 10(2)] Nineteenth-century Vermont writer and illustrator Rowland Robinson was born and died in this Ferrisburg house overlooking Lake Champlain. Robinson wrote 10 books, but his fame—and Rokeby's—comes from his role helping slaves escape to freedom in Canada along the Underground Railroad. There's some debate about how many slaves actually passed through Vermont, fueled by the fact that there were never any records kept and written accounts in newspapers or letters are scarce. Vermont's fervent opposition to slavery is clearly documented, however, since the state outlawed the practice in its constitution in 1777, and in 1837, Vermont Representative William Slade introduced the first bill in Congress that proposed to abolish slavery.

At Rokeby, period letters explode the commonly held beliefs that slaves were smuggled northward in false-bottomed hay wagons and hidden during the day in barns and cellars. The Robinsons, who were Quakers, apparently hired fugitive slaves to work their 1,000 acre farm, and fugitives also attended school.

The museum's eight rooms house furniture and memorabilia from four generations of Robinsons. Outbuildings include a combined icehouse and milkhouse that was characteristic of the early 1900s; a granary from the 1850s with specialized construction to permit ventilation; and a slaughterhouse and shop from the 1890s, complete with a 4-foot diameter wooden wheel mounted overhead to give the farmer enough mechanical advantage to hoist an animal carcass high enough for butchering.

Directions: 1.5 miles north of Ferrisburg on VT 7. From the four corners in town, go north on VT 7 and look for the museum on the right, or east side of the road, on the corner of Robinson Road where it meets VT 7.

Activities: Visitor center, hiking trails on the grounds, guided tours.

Facilities: A main building with three outbuildings, restrooms.

Dates: Open May 20—mid-October, Thursday through Sunday.

Fees: There is a charge for admission.

For more information: Rokeby Museum, 4334 Route 7, Ferrisburg, VT 05456. Phone (802) 877-3406

SHELBURNE FARMS

[Fig. 11(1)] This 1,400-acre estate was built beginning in 1886 by Lila Vanderbilt Webb and W. Seward Webb, who constructed it with Lila's $10 million inheritance from her railroad baron father. In its day, it was home to the largest barn in America, the Breeding Barn, where Dr. Webb bred Hackney horses. These are not barns in the classic sense, but beautiful Victorian structures with designs that so blend with the landscape you don't have any sense of the building's true size until you go inside. Part of the charm is the landscaping, designed by Frederick Law Olmsted of Central Park fame. Now Shelburne Farms is open to the public as a working farm and environmental education center with hiking trails that meander through the grounds. The Webb home on Lake Champlain is an inn and restaurant, furnished with the Webb family's

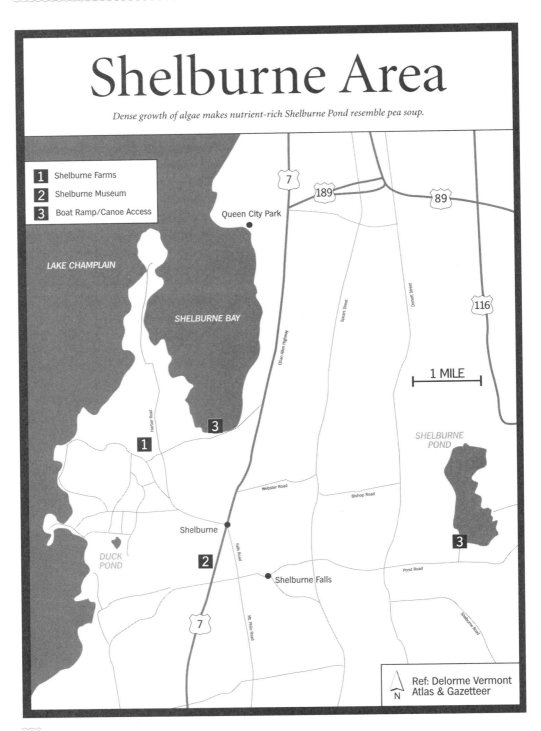

Shelburne Area

Dense growth of algae makes nutrient-rich Shelburne Pond resemble pea soup.

1 Shelburne Farms
2 Shelburne Museum
3 Boat Ramp/Canoe Access

LAKE CHAMPLAIN

Queen City Park

SHELBURNE BAY

1 MILE

SHELBURNE POND

Harbor Road

Ethan Allen Highway

Spear Street

Dorset Street

7

189

89

116

3

1

Webster Road

Bishop Road

Shelburne

DUCK POND

Falls Road

2

3

Shelburne Falls

Pond Road

Mt. Philo Road

7

Shelburne Road

N
Ref: Delorme Vermont
Atlas & Gazetteer

furniture, books, and considerable artwork collection that make guests feel as if they have been transported to a late-1800s country estate.

Directions: In Shelburne, about 1.5 miles northwest of the village toward Lake Champlain. At the traffic light on VT 7 in the center of town, turn west onto Harbor Road. Stay on Harbor Road for 2 miles. At the stop sign, Shelburne Farms entrance is on the left.

Activities: Hiking, photography, tours.

Facilities: Barn with children's farmyard, small cheese factory, retail store, 8-mile trail network, formal gardens, inn and restaurant.

Dates: Year-round activities, with hiking trails and shop open daily year-round. Tours, children's farmyard, inn, and restaurant open daily from the end of May to mid-Oct.

Fees: There is a charge for access to hiking trails and the children's farmyard, and a tour.

For more information: Shelburne Farms, 1611 Harbor Road, Shelburne VT 05482. Phone (802) 985-8686.

SHELBURNE MUSEUM

[Fig. 11(2)] This outdoor museum is a world-class collection of Americana on 45 acres right in Shelburne Village. With 37 early American buildings and the 220-foot-long, 900-ton Lake Champlain sidewheeler ferry, the Ticonderoga, it has come a long way from its beginnings in 1947. Electra Havermeyer Webb and her husband, J. Watson Webb, started the museum to house the Webb family's collection of antique carriages and sleighs.

Electra Webb had a penchant for collecting odd bits of Americana, and with sugar refinery money from her parents, she had the funds to indulge her tastes. Her family donated impressionist paintings, but Electra Webb sought out the commonplace made beautiful: duck decoys and cigar store Indians, weathervanes and old quilts and dolls. Children will especially enjoy the working merry-go-round, the collection of wooden horses and other carousel animals, and the two hand-carved sets of miniature circus figures on parade, with literally hundreds of pieces that took two amateur carvers their lifetimes to create. Although there are no hiking trails as such, walking the grounds is a full-day's job, and in fact, an admission ticket is good for a two-day visit.

Directions: On VT 7 in downtown Shelburne. From the traffic light in the center of town, travel south on VT 7 about 0.6 mile; the entrance to the museum is well marked and on your right as you travel south.

Facilities: 37 exhibit buildings, cafeteria, restrooms, shops, children's hands-on exhibit area.

Dates: Open daily, mid-May—late Oct.

Fees: There is a charge for admission (except for children under age 6); tickets are good for two consecutive days.

For more information: Shelburne Museum, PO Box 10, Shelburne, VT 05482. Phone (802) 985-3346.

Taconic Mountains

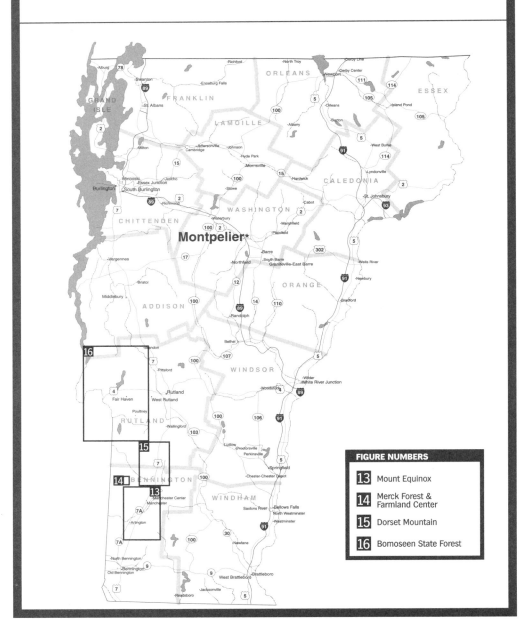

FIGURE NUMBERS

13	Mount Equinox
14	Merck Forest & Farmland Center
15	Dorset Mountain
16	Bomoseen State Forest

Taconic Mountains

The rounded, steep-sided hills of the Taconic Mountains are quite unlike the ridges and broad domes of the Green Mountains. These hills look exotic–and in a biological and geologic sense, they are. The rich flora has strong ties not only to the southern Appalachians but also to the deciduous forests of eastern Asia, with dozens of genera in common. The bedrock originated from lumps of seafloor schists and slates transported westward by thrust faulting during the Taconic orogeny, and later isolated by erosion to form a single large klippe. Underneath the thrust fault are the limestones and marbles of the Valley of Vermont, making for rich soils and diverse flora on the steep lower eastern slopes.

The marble pillars of the Equinox Hotel in Manchester and the abundance of slate roofs throughout the Taconic region show that all this good rock has been put to good use. The eastern slopes of the Taconics have for years been the major source

[*Above:* Natural Bridge, a 4-foot-wide bedrock bridge, is on the slopes of Netop Mountain]

of white marble not only in the state, but also in the entire Northeast. On the western side of the range, numerous flooded quarry pits and enormous piles of shattered slate are the result of a century and a half of slate mining.

Shaftsbury State Park

[Fig. 13(10)] Man-made Lake Shaftsbury is fed by groundwater springs that once surfaced in a wet meadow. In the nineteenth century the water was bottled and sold under the name Vermont Healing Springs. By the turn of the century, a first generation dam had been built and the healthful water was used to float logs and power a sawmill. By the Roaring Twenties, the present earth and concrete dam that holds back Lake Shaftsbury was built, and summer folk stayed in cottages on the lakeshore and bathed, canoed, and fished in the healthful water, much as they do now. The private resort operated until 1974, when the area became a state park.

The Healing Springs Nature trail circles the lake, exploring the natural and human history of the lakeshore woods and wetlands. Along the western shore of the lake it takes the high road along the top of an esker that separates cattail marshes and shrub swamps from the open waters of the lake.

Directions: Take Exit 3 off of US 7 in East Arlington. Go west on VT 313 about 2 miles and turn left on VT 7A. The state park entrance is on the left, about 3 miles from the junction.

Activities: Picnicking, camping (groups only), hiking, swimming, fishing.

Facilities: Group camping area with 15 lean-tos, picnic area, swimming beach, snack bar, boat rentals, restroomss.

Dates: Mid-May through Labor Day.

Fees: There are fees for camping and day use.

Closest town: Arlington, 4 miles.

For more information: Shaftsbury State Park, RD 1, Box 266, Shaftsbury, VT 05262. Phone (802) 375-9978 (summer). Vermont Department of Forests, Parks, and Recreation, 317 Sanitorium Road, West Wing, Pittsford, VT 05763-9358. Phone (802) 483-2001 (winter).

Fisher-Scott Memorial Pines

[Fig. 13(9)] Hidden on a side road off US 7A, this 13-acre grove of old-growth Eastern white pines (*Pinus strobus*) is an amazing sight. Trees tower 140 feet overhead, and the largest tree is 42 inches in diameter—almost 11 feet around. Although forest historians don't really know what the state's forests looked like before Europeans settled here, the Fisher-Scott grove gives at least a hint of what some parts of it might have been like, with large white pines towering over a mixed forest of hardwoods and softwoods. The grove is both a state natural area and a National Natural Landmark.

Although the dominant species here is clearly white pine, the forest is quite diverse, with American beech (*Fagus grandifolia*), red maple (*Acer rubrus*), red and white oak (*Quercus rubra* and *Q. alba*), and Eastern hemlock (*Tsuga canadensis*) all in the understory waiting to replace the pines when they fall or die, as they will eventually.

Still, the sandy soil here makes it easier for the pines to continue to dominate the forest, because they thrive in this soil type. The key is the tree's root system: Instead of just one tap root, white pine usually grows with three to five large roots spreading out and down into the soil. Other tree species have a harder time competing in the dry soils.

Ghostly Flowers

Pine sap (*Monotropa hypopitys*), the closely related Indian pipe (*M. uniflora*), and several related species have waxy looking white, yellow, or reddish stems and flowers, and are leafless except for a few pale bracts along the stem. These unusual plants are considered saprophytes; like fungi, they obtain energy for growth from the decay of the organic matter in the soil. But they don't do this on their own. The roots of these species are invaded by threads of fungi, forming a mutualistic knot known as a mycorrhiza that occurs in most upland flowering plants, green or otherwise. The fungi likely do the decaying, but in this case it is unclear what benefit, if any, the plant provides for the fungus.

The flat-topped, steep-sided landform where the pines are found looks to be a kame terrace, left in this small valley when the glaciers were here more than 12,000 years ago. The terrace formed on the edge of the glacier where it pressed up against the hillside; running water filled the space between the glacier and the hill with sediments of all sizes, from large cobbles to fine silts and sands.

Though the gauzy shade of the pines reduces the number of understory plants, partridgeberry (*Mitchella repens*) and blueberry (*Vaccinium* spp.) do survive in the relatively low light. The waxy yellow stems of pinesap (*Monotropa hypopitys*) show up in midsummer.

Directions: From Arlington at the junction of VT 313 and US 7A, go 2.9 miles north on US 7A. Turn left onto Red Mountain Road. Climb a short hill 0.2 mile and look carefully on your left, or south side, for a very small parking spot. The trail opening is faintly visible, but a boulder with a plaque marking the area as a National Natural Landmark is set in the woods (although not visible from the road), so there is no mistaking the access trail.

Activities: Hiking, picnicking.

Facilities: None.

Dates: Open year-round.

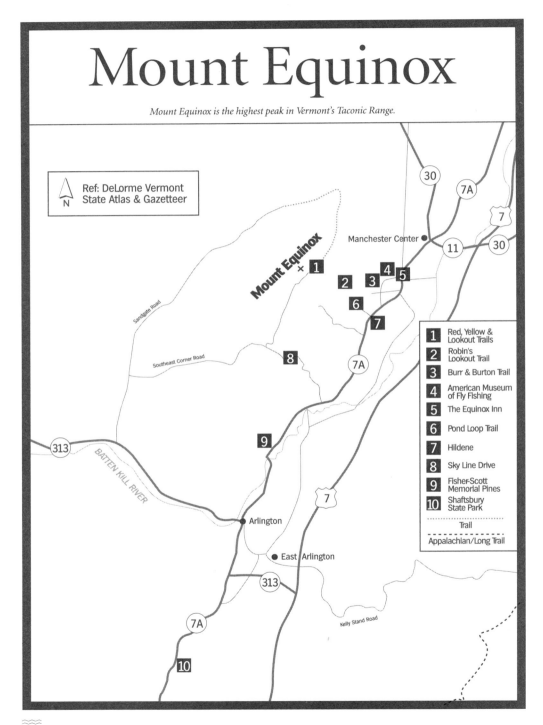

Mount Equinox

Mount Equinox is the highest peak in Vermont's Taconic Range.

Ref: DeLorme Vermont State Atlas & Gazetteer

N

30
7A
7
Manchester Center
11
30

Mount Equinox

1
2
3
4
5
6
7
8
7A

313
BATTEN KILL RIVER

9

7

Arlington

East Arlington

313

7A

Kelly Stand Road

Sandgate Road
Southeast Corner Road

1	Red, Yellow & Lookout Trails
2	Robin's Lookout Trail
3	Burr & Burton Trail
4	American Museum of Fly Fishing
5	The Equinox Inn
6	Pond Loop Trail
7	Hildene
8	Sky Line Drive
9	Fisher-Scott Memorial Pines
10	Shaftsbury State Park

.... Trail
– – – – – Appalachian/Long Trail

10

Fees: None.

Closest town: Arlington, 3 miles.

For more information: Vermont Department of Forests, Parks, and Recreation, 317 Sanitorium Road, West Wing, Pittsford, VT 05763-9358. Phone (802) 483-2314.

Mount Equinox

[Fig. 13] With its long ridgeline and steep slopes, Mount Equinox, the highest peak in Vermont's Taconic Range, makes a stunning green backdrop for the town of Manchester. It is a mecca for botanists who come because of the rich northern hardwood forests that blanket the lower slopes below 2,600 feet, and the rare grasses and plants that grow in several remote areas on the mountain. An old-growth area of red spruce (*Picea rubens*) and yellow birch (*Betula alleghaniensis*) can be found near the Burr and Burton Trail in the transition zone between 2,600 feet and 3,000 feet.

Mount Equinox's 3,825-foot-high summit is tough Cambrian-age phyllites and schists, but below about 2,600 feet, its slopes are limestones and marbles which north of here are mined for building and sculpture stone. These easily eroded rocks explain Mount Equinox's steep sides: Weathering has chewed away the lower slopes at a much faster rate than it does the resistant summit cap.

The rich northern hardwood forests contain uncommon species such as wood millet (*Milium effusum*), Goldie's fern (*Thelypteris goldiana*), and squawroot (*Conopholis americana*), a leafless parasite on tree roots, usually oaks. A variety of birds and wildlife abounds, in part because of the seeps and springs that dot the eastern face of the mountain. Among the more unusual birds reported from this area is the yellow-bellied flycatcher (*Epidonax flaviventris*), which is more common in spruce-fir forests to the north.

At lower elevations, look for mourning warblers (*Oporornis philadelphia*), which were spotted nesting here in 1997, along with veerys (*Catharus fuscescens*), black-throated blue warblers (*Dendroica caerulescens*), and scarlet tanagers (*Piranga olivacea*), among others. High in the sky, look for broad-winged hawks (*Buteo platypterus*), and along the summit ridge, listen for the globally rare Bicknell's thrush (*Catharus bicknelli*).

Three areas on the mountainside have special ecological significance and are occasionally open to visitors during workshops or guided tours. Deer Knoll, at about 1,500 feet elevation, and Table Rock, at about 2,700 feet elevation, are open areas with unusual plant assemblages. Ecologists don't know exactly why the two areas continue to be bare of trees, but some possible explanations include drought or periodic fires. Both areas are home to the Vermont endangered Richardson's sedge (*Carex richardsonii*) and the scirpus-like sedge (*Carex scirpoidea*).

Cook Hollow is the third area of ecological significance. High ledges in the hollow support several rare alpine plants, including roseroot stonecrop (*Sedum rosea*), a threatened species in Vermont. Cook Hollow is generally closed to hikers because of its sensitivity and because the steep ledges are potentially dangerous.

Unlike most of Vermont's other large mountains, Mount Equinox is privately owned, but much of the land has been protected by the Equinox Preservation Trust, a nonprofit group formed by the Equinox Resort Associates, which owns the resort at the base of the mountain. Conservation easements have been signed over to the Vermont Land Trust and The Nature Conservancy, and the Vermont Institute of Natural Science has its Taconic Field School here and offers workshops and guided hikes. Bennington College and the Burr and Burton Academy also collaborate with the Preservation Trust in conducting research and using the mountain as an outdoor classroom.

Directions: From Manchester Center at the junction of VT 7A and VT 30, go south on VT 7A approximately 1 mile to Manchester village. One cluster of hiking trails begins from behind the Burr and Burton Academy, which is approximately 0.3 mile from VT 7A off Seminary Street, just north of the Equinox. Trails for mountain-biking, horseback riding, and cross-country skiing begin south of the Equinox off VT 7A. Turn right onto Taconic Road and go to the end, where you turn left onto Prospect Street. Go south a short distance and then go right on Pond Road, a dirt road that leads to a gate and trailheads.

Activities: Hiking, cross-country skiing, mountain bike riding, horseback riding, snowshoeing, bird-watching.

Facilities: Trails, auto road.

Dates: Open year-round, activity depends on season.

Fees: There is a charge for the auto road and to ski on the cross-country trails.

Closest town: Manchester, 1 mile.

For more information: Equinox Preservation Trust, Route 7A, Manchester Village, VT 05254. Phone (802) 362-4700. Vermont Institute of Natural Science Taconic Field School, PO Box 46, 109 Union Street, Manchester Village, VT 05254. Phone (802) 362-4374.

THE EQUINOX

[Fig. 13(5)] One of Vermont's first inns, the 1,100-acre Equinox resort grew out of a tiny facility, Marsh Tavern, which first opened in 1769. More than 200 years later, the original tavern is still in use as one of the resort's restaurants, but chances are, the original owner, William Marsh, wouldn't recognize the place.

The Equinox's history spans numerous owners, a stint as mountain resort boast-ing its own bottled spring water, a brush with fame when Mrs. Abraham Lincoln and her two sons vacationed there, and now, a reincarnation as an elegant mountain resort, complete with a spa, golf course, and superb network of cross-country ski trails on the flanks of Mount Equinox. In the summer, the ski trails are open for hiking, mountain biking, and horseback riding. Marble sidewalks lead to Georgiancolumned porches, the 183 rooms feature such special touches as framed Audubon prints, and guests can learn how to hunt with falcons at the resort's British School of Falconry or take lessons at the resort's Land Rover off-road driving school.

Directions: From Manchester Center at the junction of VT 7A and VT 11/30, go south on VT 7A approximately 1 mile to Manchester village and the resort on the west side of the road.

Activities: Hiking, cross-country skiing, snowshoeing, horseback riding, golf, other special activities organized by the resort.

Facilities: Inn, restaurants, ski trails, hiking trails, golf course, spa.

Dates: Open year-round.

Fees: There is a charge to stay at the resort and use the golf course and other facilities.

Closest town: Manchester, 1 mile.

For more information: The Equinox, Historic Route 7A, Manchester Village, VT 05254. Phone (800) 362-4747.

🌌 SKY LINE DRIVE

[Fig. 13(8)] This 5.2-mile paved road winds its way to the summit of Mount Equinox and its views of Manchester Village. On clear days, the horizon is a panorama of peaks in New York, New Hampshire, and Massachusetts, as well as the rest of the Taconic Range in Vermont. Set in a deep valley to the west and visible from Skyline Drive is the nation's first Carthusian monastery. Carthusian monks live in seclusion, and no visitors are allowed at the monastery, which was built to last for centuries out of special 9.5-foot-long granite blocks brought from the Rock of Ages quarry in Barre. The Carthusian Foundation owns the summit and the toll road and leases the mountaintop inn to a business for operation.

Equinox also has a place in Vermont's fledgling efforts to develop alternative energy sources; in 1989, two wind turbines have began generating electricity from atop Little Equinox, the second highest knob on the summit ridgeline. The towers were considered an experiment by Green Mountain Power, the utility that operated them, but were later removed in favor of 11 wind towers installed near Searsburg in 1997 (*see* page 89).

RED FOX
(*Vulpes vulpes*)
Notorious for preying on chickens, the red fox feeds mainly on small mammals and birds.

Directions: From Manchester Center at the junction of VT 7A and VT 11/30, go south on VT 7A approximately 4 miles to the Sky Line Drive entrance on the right.

Activities: Sight-seeing, hiking, picnicking, bird-watching.

Facilities: Auto road, hiking trails, picnic tables, inn and restaurant on summit.

Dates: Road and inn open May 1 to Nov. 1, trails open year-round.

Fees: There is a charge to use the road and stay at the inn.

Closest town: Arlington, 3 miles.

For more information: Equinox Sky Line Drive, RD2 Box 2410, Arlington, VT 05250. Phone (802) 362-1114.

HIKING TRAILS IN THE MOUNT EQUINOX AREA
RED, YELLOW AND LOOKOUT TRAILS

[Fig. 13(1)] This trio of trails loops like a long necklace from the Mount Equinox summit to intersections with Sky Line Drive along its most spectacular stretch, the saddle between Little Equinox and Mount Equinox's main summit. From the inn at the summit, 0.5-mile Lookout Trail goes north to Lookout Rock, with its almost dizzying view of Manchester and the Green Mountains to the east. While red spruce (*Picea rubens*) can be found in the forests below, the summit is almost exclusively balsam fir (*Abies balsamea*), with an understory of starflower (*Trientalis borealis*), goldthread (*Coptis groenlandica*), twinflower (*Linnaea borealis*), and blue bead lily (*Clintonia borealis*). The strange green stringy substance hanging from the tree branches is old-man's beard (*Usnea* spp.), a lichen that finds its way into boreal bird nests such as the ones built by the Blackburnian warbler (*Dendroica fusca*).

Although you won't see them, red-backed voles (*Clethrionomys gapperi*) make their home in the coniferous forests on and below the summit area. You're more likely to see sign of a snowshoe hare (*Lepus americanus*), which will leave its button-shaped scat in piles in the forest. In snow, the 3-inch-long snowshoe-shaped impressions of the hind feet are unmistakable.

The Red and Yellow trails share a single path until they reach a small seep about halfway across the mountainside; sphagnum moss and round-leaved sundew (*Drosera rotundifolia*) mark the spring's location. Below the seep is an old landslide scar stretching down the mountainside, partially grown in with mountain ash (*Sorbus americana*), birches (*Betula* spp.), and other high elevation early successional species.

After the seep, the trails diverge with the Yellow Trail taking the higher, shorter route to the Sky Line Drive. The Red Trail takes a lower, longer path to the road past several more seeps and through paper birch glades (*Betula papyrifera*) carpeted with New York fern (*Thelypteris noveboracensis*).

Directions: From the summit parking area of the Skyline Drive, look for signs showing trailheads for all three trails.

Trail: Lookout Trail, 0.5 mile one-way; Red Trail, 2 miles one-way; Yellow Trail, 1.5 miles one-way.

Degree of difficulty: Moderate.

Surface and blaze: Rough footpath, difficult to follow in places. Red and yellow blazes.

For more information: Equinox Sky Line Drive, RD2 Box 2410, Arlington, VT 05250. Phone (802) 362-1114.

BURR AND BURTON TRAIL

[Fig. 13(3)] The main route up Mount Equinox, the Burr and Burton Trail, climbs through a rich northern hardwood forest of maple (*Acer saccharum*), beech (*Fagus grandifolia*), and red oak (*Quercus rubra*), with a sprinkling of white ash (*Fraxinus americana*), basswood (*Tilia americana*), and bitternut hickory (*Carya cordiformis*).

TROUT LILY
(*Erythronium americanum*)

Under this rich mix of hardwoods, look for maidenhair fern (*Adiantum pedatum*), wild ginger (*Asarum canadense*), Goldie's fern (*Dryopteris goldiana*), wood millet (*Milium effusum*), blue cohosh (*Caulophyllum thalictroides*), Dutchman's breeches (*Dicentra cucullaria*), large-flowering bellwort (*Uvularia grandiflora*), and round-leaved dogwood (*Cornus rotundifolia*).

As the slope steepens, the size of the trees increases: Loggers had a difficult time here. At about 2,600 feet, the trail passes through a large red spruce (*Picea rubens*) and yellow birch (*Betula alleghaniensis*) grove believed to contain old growth.

Using the Burr and Burton Trail as their main access, staff with the Vermont Institute of Natural Science's Taconic Field School have scoured the mountain for wildlife such as ermine (*Mustela erminea*), bobcat (*Felis rufus*) and gray fox (*Urocyon cinereoargenteus*), the last of which is gradually increasing its population in the state.

The trail is steep and rough, but it offers hikers a glimpse of local history along with its unusual natural features. A spur trail roughly halfway up the mountain leads to the main Equinox Spring, which resort owners bottled and once piped to the Equinox Inn, where as late as 1920 it could bubble into a fountain in the resort's dining room.

Directions: From Manchester Village center, take Seminary Street 0.3 mile to West Union Street and turn left. Take the first right off West Union into the Burr and Burton Seminary facility. Climb the hill and look for a parking lot next to a small athletic field. The trailhead leaves from the southwest corner of the athletic field.

Trail: 2.9 miles one-way.

Degree of difficulty: Strenuous.

Surface and blaze: Rough footpath. Blue blazes.

For more information: Equinox Preservation Trust, Route 7A, Manchester Village, VT 05254. Phone (802) 362-4700. Vermont Institute of Natural Science Taconic Field School, PO Box 46, 109 Union Street, Manchester Village, VT 05254. Phone (802) 362-4374.

ROBIN'S LOOKOUT TRAIL

[Fig. 13(2)] This short and steep trail was opened as a alternative for picnickers who traditionally used the Deer Knoll or Table Rock natural areas, now closed, to savor lunch with a view. Robin's Lookout gives spectacular vistas of Equinox Pond, the Batten Kill Valley, and the Green Mountains to the east. It's a hike well worth the effort at any time of the year, but the calcium-rich soils that underlie much of the lower slopes of Mount Equinox virtually guarantee profuse spring wildflowers. On the Robin's Lookout Trail, spring beauty (*Claytonia caroliniana*) and several species of violets (*Viola* spp.) complement the showy white flowers of bloodroot (*Sanguinaria canadensis*) and deep purple of jack-in-the-pulpit (*Arisaema atrorubens*).

Directions: Go south of the Equinox resort on US 7A to Taconic Road and turn right. Go to the end and turn left onto Prospect Street. Go south a short distance and then go right on Pond Road, a dirt road that leads to a gate and trailhead.

Trail: 0.75 mile round-trip.

Elevation: 300-foot elevation gain.

Degree of difficulty: Easy.

Surface and blaze: Woods path. Green blazes.

For more information: Equinox Preservation Trust, Route 7A, Manchester Village, VT 05254. Phone (802) 362-4700.

POND LOOP TRAIL

[Fig. 13(6)] Equinox Pond was built some time before 1880 by Franklin Orvis, who operated the first Equinox Hotel beginning in 1853. Orvis decided he needed a trout pond for his guests, and had a 10-acre pond specially constructed in a drainage fed by three mountain streams. Equinox Pond is still a good place to fish, but most visitors come to savor its fine setting. The Pond Loop is an easy walk that passes in part through century-old Eastern white pines (*Pinus strobus*) planted as part of a government program to reclaim old fields.

Directions: Go south of the Equinox resort on US 7A to Taconic Road and turn right. Go to the end and turn left onto Prospect Street. Go south a short distance and then go right on Pond Road, a dirt road that leads to a gate and trailhead.

Trail: 0.75 mile loop.

Elevation: 1,150 feet. Limited elevation change.

Degree of difficulty: Easy.

Surface and blaze: Woods road. Red blazes.

For more information: Equinox Preservation Trust, Route 7A, Manchester Village, VT 05254. Phone (802) 362-4700.

HILDENE

[Fig. 13(7)] Manchester made a great impression on President Abraham Lincoln's family. His wife stayed at the Equinox with her two sons two years before Lincoln was assassinated and planned to return with the entire family. Had President Lincoln survived that fateful night at the Ford Theater in 1865, Vermont might well have been able to boast that Abraham Lincoln slept here.

Nonetheless, Abraham Lincoln's family later spent summers in Vermont, at Hildene, a magnificent 24-room Georgian Revival mansion just south of Manchester Village. The structure dates from the turn of the century, when it was built for Robert Todd Lincoln, the president's oldest son. The family retained the house and grounds until 1975, when the nonprofit Friends of Hildene opened the 400-acre property to the public. Nature trails in summer turn into 15 km (10 miles) of cross-country ski trails in the winter. In the summer, visitors can tour the mansion, which retains its original furnishings, including a 1,000 pipe Aeolian organ built in 1908, as well as family photographs and memorabilia.

Directions: From Manchester Center at the junction of US 7A and VT 11/30, go south on US 7A 2 miles to the entrance.

Invasion of the Honeysuckle

Alien invaders sound as if they ought to be nasty, ugly plants or animals. But in many cases, it is their beauty that causes people to introduce them where they don't belong. Such is the case of Morrow's honeysuckle (*Lonicera morrowii*), a Japanese shrub brought to North America in 1869 by a plant collector. The plants were established in Harvard University's Arnold Arboretum, but within just a few decades they had escaped. Now they are found in Ontario, Quebec, and 25 eastern states, including Vermont.

When Morrow's honeysuckle arrived in Vermont in the early 1930s, it found particularly fertile ground on the eastern flanks of Mount Equinox, where land had been cleared for sheep farming and for timber. Honeysuckle can be spread by birds, which eat the shrub's berries and defecate intact seeds. People also planted honeysuckle as ornamental shrubs, to attract birds, and as hedgerows.

Now, the plant is creeping up the flanks of Mount Equinox, colonizing areas that were pasture or old fields when the plant first arrived in Vermont, and taking advantage of recreational trails cut into the forests. Like other invading plants, honeysuckle has the ability to displace native species by robbing natives of water, light, or nutrients. For conservationists, Morrow's honeysuckle poses an as-yet unsolved problem in their quest to protect the rich and rare assemblage of plants on Mount Equinox.

Activities: Mansion tours, nature walks, cross-country skiing, workshops, and exhibitions.

Facilities: Mansion, formal gardens, nature trails.

Dates: Open mid-May to Oct. with special winter tours Dec. 26, 27, and 28; cross-country ski trails open in winter.

Fees: There is a charge.

Closest town: Manchester, 2 miles.

For more information: Friends of Hildene, PO Box 377, Manchester Village, VT 05254. Phone (802) 362-1788.

Merck Forest & Farmland Center

This 3,130-acre environmental education center includes 28 miles of multi-use trails, as well as secluded cabins and shelters hidden in the second growth forest.

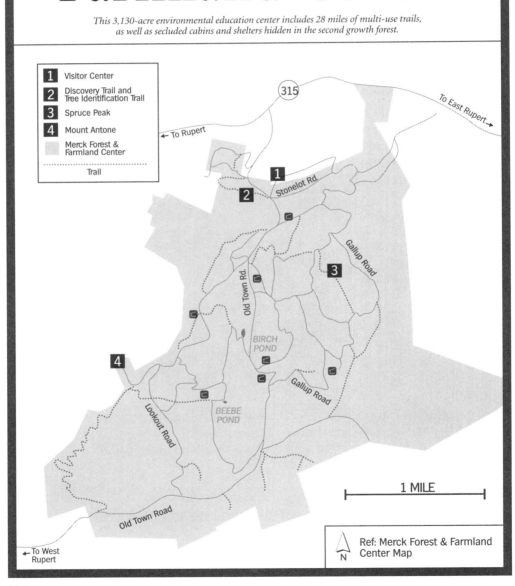

1 Visitor Center
2 Discovery Trail and Tree Identification Trail
3 Spruce Peak
4 Mount Antone
Merck Forest & Farmland Center
Trail

315
← To Rupert
To East Rupert →

Stonelot Rd.
Gallup Road
Old Town Rd.
BIRCH POND
Gallup Road
Lookout Road
BEEBE POND
Old Town Road

1 MILE

N
Ref: Merck Forest & Farmland Center Map

← To West Rupert

Merck Forest and Farmland Center

[Fig. 14] There aren't many places in Vermont where you can ski to a remote cabin with a view—and have it all to yourself. The Merck Forest and Farmland Center offers just that. The 3,130-acre environmental education center includes 28 miles of multiuse trails (but mountain bikes are not permitted), and secluded cabins and shelters hidden in the second-growth forest. A working farm, complete with Belgian draft horses that take people for sleigh rides in the winter, rounds out the estate.

As its name implies, the center was started by George Merck, president of the pharmaceutical firm that bears his family's name, although it was family money, not company money, that bought the initial 2,000-acre parcel. Much like railroad magnate and Woodstock resident Frederick Billings, Merck made the initial purchase thinking he could establish a model farm and forest preserve. Before Merck died in 1957, he achieved his goal, establishing a nonprofit conservation center that was then called the Vermont Forest and Farmland Center.

The marriage of a working forest and farm make for a pleasing patchwork of fields and deep woods; in some places, clear-cuts for aspen (*Populus tremuloides*) encourage populations of ruffed grouse (*Bonasa umbellus*) and turkey (*Meleagris gallopavo*). Some areas are managed as a Christmas tree farm, by planting balsam fir (*Abies balsamea*), or for red oak (*Quercus rubra*) to be harvested at some future date. The center also has about 1,650 taps in sugar maples (*Acer saccharum*) for maple syrup production. There are non-native trick trees, too: Merck conducted some experiments when he was managing the forests, planting both European larch (*Larix decidua*) along with its North American native cousin, tamarack (*Larix laricina*) to see which variety deer preferred.

Elsewhere, the mostly hardwood-dominated forests are a rich environment for wildlife and birds. Many of the common woodland warblers have been spotted here, including parula warblers (*Parula americana*), cerulean warblers (*Dendroica cerulea*), and black-throated blue and black-throated green warblers (*Dendroica caerulescens* and *D. virens*).

Deer (*Odocoileus virginianus*) are abundant, and it's not unusual to see a moose (*Alces alces*) cross a trail or clearing. The occasional Eastern hemlock (*Tsuga canadensis*) groves are a good place to look up—for porcupines (*Erethizon dorsatum*), which love to gnaw on hemlock needles and bark. They typically start at the top of the tree and work their way down, giving the tree a strange, flat-topped appearance that is unmistakable.

Directions: From Manchester Center at the junction of VT 7A and VT 11/30, go north roughly 8 miles on VT 30 to VT 315 in East Rupert. Turn west on VT 315 and go approximately 2.4 miles to the Merck access road (with large sign) on the left, or south side of VT 315. Take the access road approximately 0.5 mile to the center headquarters and parking.

Activities: Hiking, hunting, cross-country skiing, snowshoeing, horseback riding, educational workshops, self-guided nature trails.

Facilities: 5 cabins, 6 shelters, 11 tent sites, trails, shop, interpretive center.
Dates: Open year-round.
Fees: There is a charge for cabins, shelters, and tent sites.
Closest town: East Rupert, 2 miles.
For more information: Merck Forest and Farmland Center, Route 315, Rupert Mountain Road, PO Box 86, Rupert, VT 05768. Phone (802) 394-7836.

HIKING TRAILS IN THE MERCK FOREST AND FARMLAND CENTER
MOUNT ANTONE

[Fig. 14(4)] At 2,610 feet, Mount Antone is the highest peak in the Merck Forest and provides good views to the east of the Adirondacks, and to the northeast of the center's barn, Dorset Peak, and Woodlawn Mountain. The Merck Forest's trails double as logging roads and ski trails in the winter, and while there is one direct way to reach the summit via Antone Road, it's possible to link side trails for a trip to Birch Pond, a lovely swimming hole in a small clearing about halfway between the mountain's summit and the trailhead. The visitors center has detailed maps of the trail network.

Directions:. The trail leaves from the main gate next to the Merck visitor center.
Trail: 2.5 miles one-way on the direct trail.
Elevation: 1,800 feet to 2,610 feet.
Degree of difficulty: Moderate.
Surface and blaze: Old woods road, no blaze.

SPRUCE PEAK

[Fig. 14(3)] An easier hike than Mount Antone, Spruce Peak offers good views all its own of the surrounding forests and Mount Antone to the west. The trail follows logging roads through the expansive pastures above the center's barn and into a second-growth hardwood forest, finally picking up the sharp ridge with its namesake trees clustered around the summit. The visitor center has detailed maps of the trail network.

Directions: The trail leaves from the main gate next to the Merck visitor center.
Trail: 1.5 miles one-way.
Elevation: 1,800 feet to 2,585 feet.
Degree of difficulty: Easy.
Surface and blaze: Old woods road, no blaze.

DISCOVERY TRAIL AND TREE IDENTIFICATION TRAIL

[Fig. 14(2)] These two short nature hikes, which leave from the visitor center, are especially good for children curious about the forest. The Discovery Trail passes the center's Christmas tree plantation; the Tree Identification Trail identifies 12 trees and passes through one of George Merck's experimental forests, planted with European and native larch (*Larix decidua* and *L. laricina*).

Directions: The trail leaves from the main gate next to the Merck visitor center.

Trail: Discovery Trail, 0.75 mile round-trip; Tree Identification Trail 0.25 mile round-trip.

Elevation: No elevation change.

Degree of difficulty: Easy.

Surface and blaze: Woods road, no blaze.

Batten Kill River

[Fig. 13] Ask where the best trout fishing can be found in Vermont and chances are you'll be referred to the Batten Kill, where there are wild brook trout (*Salvelinus fontinalis*), especially in the river's upper reaches, near East Dorset. On the lower reaches of the river, where it winds through Sunderland and Arlington on its way southwest to New York, brown trout (*Salmo trutta*) are the most plentiful fish, although in recent years, fish population numbers have begun to drop, for reasons biologists can't determine.

The Batten Kill is beautiful, and it has wild trout, but it also has history. Charles Orvis founded the fishing-tackle company that still bears his name in Manchester on the Batten Kill in 1856.

The state manages the Batten Kill as a native fishery, stocking only Dufresne Pond, a 12-acre lake formed on the river just north of Manchester Depot. A section of the river between the Benedict Crossing bridge and the Rochester (West Mountain) bridge is managed as an area where only artificial lures and dry flies may be used, with a slot limit prohibiting the taking of brookies and brown trout between 10 inches and 14 inches long.

Anglers aren't the only ones enjoying the Batten Kill's clear, cold water. In recent years, the Batten Kill has become increasingly popular with canoeists and people riding inner tubes, chiefly from the Water Street bridge on VT 313 in Arlington to the New York state line roughly 6 miles west where the river is mostly quickwater. North of Arlington, the river has

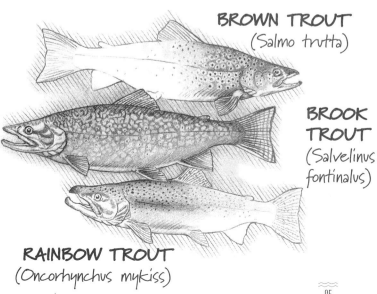

BROWN TROUT
(Salmo trutta)

BROOK TROUT
(Salvelinus fontinalus)

RAINBOW TROUT
(Oncorhynchus mykiss)

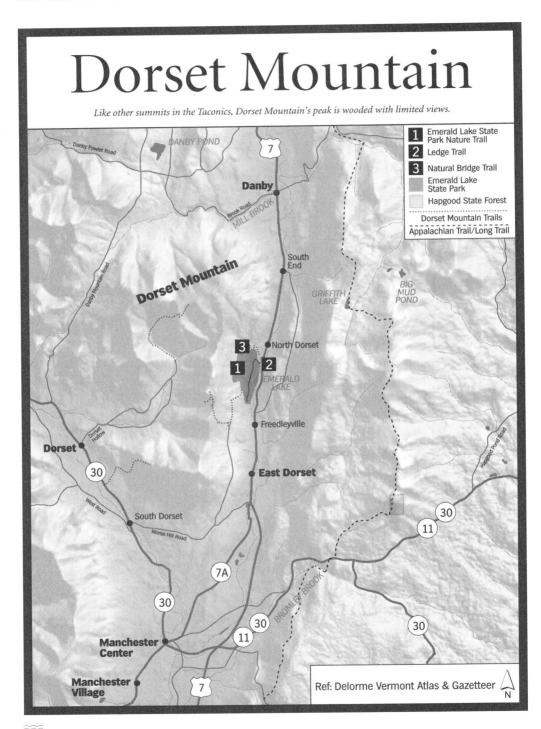

Dorset Mountain

Like other summits in the Taconics, Dorset Mountain's peak is wooded with limited views.

1 Emerald Lake State Park Nature Trail
2 Ledge Trail
3 Natural Bridge Trail
Emerald Lake State Park
Hapgood State Forest
Dorset Mountain Trails
Appalachian Trail/Long Trail

Danby Pawlet Road
DANBY POND
7
Danby
Brook Road
MILL BROOK
South End
GRIFFITH LAKE
BIG MUD POND
Dorset Mountain Road
Dorset Mountain
3 North Dorset
1 **2**
EMERALD LAKE
Freedleyville
Dorset Hollow
Dorset
30
Hapgood Pond Road
West Road
South Dorset
East Dorset
Morse Hill Road
30
11
7A
BROMLEY BROOK
30
30
11
30
30
Manchester Center
Manchester Village
7

Ref: Delorme Vermont Atlas & Gazetteer
N

some Class II rapids, and north of Manchester, the river is often too narrow and shallow in summer to run.

Directions: Numerous accesses from River Road off US 7A in Manchester, and from VT 313 between Arlington and the New York border.

Activities: Fishing, canoeing, bird-watching.

Facilities: Canoe put-ins.

Dates: Open year round, trout season typically second Saturday in Apr. to last Sunday in Oct.

Fees: There is a charge for a Vermont fishing license.

Closest town: Manchester, Arlington.

For more information: Vermont Fish and Wildlife Department, 363 River Street, North Springfield, VT 05150-9726. Phone (802) 886-2215.

AMERICAN MUSEUM OF FLY FISHING

[Fig. 13(4)] Ernest Hemingway, Daniel Webster, Bing Crosby, and Presidents Eisenhower and Hoover all have at least two things in common: They enjoyed fly fishing, and their tackle is on display at the American Museum of Fly Fishing. But the high-profile items are easily outclassed by the collections of colorful hand-tied flies, hand-built and commercial rods, and paintings and sketchbooks of some of the stars of the fly-fishing world.

Directions: The museum is in Manchester Village, next to the Equinox Hotel.

Dates: Year-round, weekdays only Nov. through Apr.

Fees: There is a charge.

For more information: The American Museum of Fly Fishing, PO Box 42, Manchester, VT 05254. Phone (802) 362-3300.

Dorset Mountain

[Fig. 15] The Taconic klippe is an island of ancient rock overlying the complex mix of younger rocks that make the Champlain Valley. In southern Vermont, the Precambrian gneiss that forms the core of the Green Mountains is a kind of mainland, separated from the Taconics by a narrow band of valley rocks. Dorset Mountain, which divides the town of Dorset, is a nearly detached peninsula of Taconic rocks that squeezes the valley rocks into a narrow band, just 1.5 miles wide by Emerald Lake State Park.

The several summits of Dorset Mountain form a rough semicircle around southwest-flowing Metawee Creek in Dorset Hollow and, like many other Taconic summits, are wooded with no or limited views. Three summits are accessible by rather informal trails. Adventuresome types can approach the others by exploring old logging roads out of Dorset Hollow. The real attractions in hiking here are the rich flora and odd formations, such as the Natural Bridge near Emerald Lake State Park, that are characteristic of this marble-rich area.

Vermont Marble Company's Imperial Marble Quarry extends deep under the north flank of the mountain, extracting the lightly veined white marble for which the region is famous. The quarry is not open to the public, but its products can be seen at the Vermont Marble Exhibit in Proctor.

DORSET MOUNTAIN TRAILS

[Fig. 15] The unmarked and unmaintained trails to Dorset Peak, Mount Aeolus, and Owl's Head are described in the Green Mountain Club's *Day Hiker's Guide to Vermont*. Each has its attractions: The trail to the main summit of Dorset Peak crosses the debris from flooding and landslides that hit Dorset Hollow in 1976; the Mount Aeolus Trail passes the gated entrance to Mount Aeolus Cave, a hibernaculum for bats; and the Owl's Head Trail passes through an old marble quarry. All showcase the rich flora associated with the varied geology and relatively warm and moist climate of southern Vermont.

Trail: Dorset Peak, 3.4 miles one-way; Mount Aeolus, 2.7 miles one-way; Owl's Head, 2.2 miles one-way.

Elevation: Dorset Peak, 1,410 to 3,730 feet; Mount Aeolus, 1,380 to 3,230 feet; Owl's Head, 1,220 to 2,480 feet.

Degree of difficulty: Moderate to strenuous.

Surface and blaze: Old roads and footpath. Unmarked trails.

VERMONT MARBLE EXHIBIT

[Fig. 15] Nine miles north of Dorset, the town of Proctor takes up a 3.5-mile stretch of the Valley of Vermont, like a jigsaw puzzle piece cut out of the town of Pittsford to the north, and the northern reaches of Rutland and West Rutland to the south. There must have been some interesting politicking behind the establishment of that boundary, and the town bears the name of the man behind it all, Redfield Proctor, who made his fortune on the clean white marble quarried in the hills overlooking the town.

The construction of rail lines through the valley in 1849 to 1852, which allowed transportation of marble to distant markets, put Mr. Proctor in the right place at the right time, and his Vermont Marble Company was a Rockefeller-like consolidation of numerous small quarries in the region. The company provided the Corinthian columns of the Supreme Court building in Washington, D.C. Today it is the only major marble producer in the state, with most of its white marble coming from the Imperial Quarry on Dorset Mountain.

The marble exhibit provides a fascinating look at the history and present day uses of marble. Exhibits include a film on the history of the company, a geology exhibit, a sculpture gallery, and a sculpture workshop with artists in residence. One large hall displays polished slabs of marble from Vermont and all over the world, which come in a variety of colors, with colorful names to match. These include the dark gray marbles of the Lake Champlain Islands, which bear abundant fossils of coral, crinoids, brachiopods, and cephalopods. Verde Antique, a beautiful, veined, dark green rock, is actually a form of serpentinite that is geologically and mineralogically unrelated to marble (*see* page 245, Belvidere Mountain). It is quarried in Rochester and other points along the eastern front of the Green Mountains.

Directions: Take Exit 6 from US 4 in West Rutland, go east on Business US 4 about 3 miles and turn left on VT 3. In Proctor, about 5 miles up VT 3, turn left over the marble bridge, then bear right to the exhibit.

Facilities: Exhibits, restrooms, cafeteria, gift shop, outdoor marble market.

Dates: Open year-round.

Fees: There is a charge.

Closest town: Proctor.

For more information: Vermont Marble Exhibit, 62 Main Street, Proctor, VT 05765. Phone (802) 459-2300.

The Limestone Landscape

Most caves are formed by underground streams that flow through cracks in limestone or marble and slowly dissolve the rock. Although calcite will dissolve slowly in pure water with a pH of 7, the presence of acid accelerates the process. Carbon dioxide in the air dissolves in rainwater to form carbonic acid, so even before the days of acid rain, natural rain had a pH of about 5.6. Organic matter from decaying plants can also add acid to water flowing over and through the soil.

In landscapes where limestone and related rocks are the dominant bedrock type, this process of solution weathering produces deep caves. As cave systems grow, their roofs can collapse to form surface sinkholes like the one that is used as the main entrance to Carlsbad Caverns in New Mexico. In very old limestone landscapes, solution weathering removes so much of the rock that it leaves beehive-shaped limestone mountains, called hums, like those seen in photographs and paintings from parts of southern China. The peculiar landforms found in limestone landscapes are collectively called karst topography, after a limestone region in eastern Europe.

The Taconic Mountain landscape does not qualify as karst topography because the surface rock is not limestone and it is too young to have developed sinkholes and hums. But the rounded shapes of the Taconic hills are suggestive of what may become the distant future for this corner of Vermont.

Emerald Lake State Park

[Fig. 15] The low divide between the Batten Kill River and Otter Creek is just 1 mile south of Emerald Lake. The latter stream, which at 100 miles is Vermont's longest river, comes tumbling off the west slopes of Mount Tabor as a vigorous young mountain stream, hits the valley floor at Emerald Lake, and begins its leisurely journey north along the Valley of Vermont to Lake Champlain which, at around 100 feet above sea level, is just 700 feet lower than Emerald Lake. This is the narrowest part of the Valley of Vermont, with verdant slopes rising directly from the western shore of the lake and just across US 7 from the eastern shore.

In fall and especially spring, the Valley of Vermont funnels forest birds through its narrow waist, making Emerald Lake a birder's hotspot for migrant songbirds. Summer residents include barred owl (*Strix varia*), yellow-throated and warbling vireo (*Vireo flavifrons* and *Vireo gilvus*), least and great crested flycatchers (*Empidonax minimus* and *Myriarchus crinitus*) and Louisiana waterthrush (*Seiurus motacilla*).

The campground is perched on a kame terrace above the valley floor, with many sites right at the foot of a steep, cobbled slope with a rich flora. Traffic noise from US 7 does reach the campground but usually settles down in the evening. Higher up on the same slope, an old county road slices through the woods, and past old stone walls, home sites, and a marble quarry.

Directions: From the junction of US 7 and VT 7A in East Dorset, go north on VT 7 approximately 3.5 miles to the park entrance on the left.

Activities: Camping, picnicking, swimming, canoeing, fishing, hiking, horseback riding, mountain biking.

Facilities: 69 campsites, 36 lean-tos, picnic area, swimming beach, snack bar, boat rentals, restrooms.

Dates: Mid-May to mid-Oct.

Fees: There are fees for camping and day use.

Closest town: East Dorset, 3 miles.

For more information: Emerald Lake State Park, 374 Emerald Lake Lane, East Dorset, VT 05253. Phone (802) 362-1655 (summer). Vermont Department of Forests, Parks, and Recreation, 317 Sanitorium Road, West Wing, Pittsford, VT 05763-9358. Phone (802) 483-2001 (winter).

EMERALD LAKE STATE PARK NATURE TRAIL

[Fig. 15(1)] This trail makes a loop on the slopes above the day-use area of the park, with numbered stations and a trail guide, available at the entrance station, that discusses the ecology of fields, forests, and streams.

Trail: 0.7-mile loop.

Elevation: Around 800 feet.

Degree of difficulty: Easy.

Surface and blaze: Footpath. Numbered posts.

LEDGE TRAIL

[Fig. 15(2)] Beginning on the park entrance road just past the entrance station, this trail crosses US 7 via a railway underpass, and ascends to a ledge with views of Emerald Lake, its southern wetland, and the steep east slopes of Netop Mountain.

Trail: 0.6 mile one-way.

Elevation: 800 to 1,000 feet
Degree of difficulty: Moderate.
Surface and blaze: Rocky footpath. Blue blazes.

THE NATURAL BRIDGE TRAIL

[Fig. 15(3)] On a small, steep stream plunging down the slopes of Netop Mounatin, a narrow marble gorge is spanned by a 4-foot-wide bedrock bridge. The marble of the gorge varies from buff-colored to gray and has been sculpted both by abrasion, where the running water uses sediment as grit to grind away at the rock, and solution, where the water dissolves the calcite that is the major mineral in marble. Abrasion creates the overall shape of the gorge and some features like potholes, while solution works on the cracks and faces to create new textures at a finer scale.

The stream probably once flowed over the natural bridge, but water flowing through cracks in the rock dissolved a small tunnel through the rock, which eventually widened enough for the whole stream to flow through it to begin forming the gorge under the bridge. Upstream from the bridge the gorge narrows to a tight, sinuous slot, with less than 1 foot between the walls in some places. Below the gorge the stream plunges into a pothole then cascades down another 10 feet into a broad pool, where the gorge abruptly widens to form a V-shaped valley.

In broader parts of the gorge, the walls are draped with the long, limp fronds of bulblet fern (*Cystopteris bulbifera*). In the woods near the gorge, plants such as spikenard (*Aralia racemosa*), blue cohosh (*Caulophyllum thalictroides*), and maidenhair fern (*Adiantum pedatum*) indicate rich soil conditions. Along the old county road, look for wood betony (*Pedicularis canadensis*), which has a basal rosette of hairy, fernlike leaves and a short, dense spike of yellow flowers. It is a semiparasite that uses its roots to absorb nutrients from the roots of other plants.

Directions: On the access road to Emerald Lake State Park, continue straight ahead up the hill instead of turning into the park entrance. Park at the state park or in a dirt parking area past the last house. The trail follows a steep logging road on the right-hand side of the stream, passing three junctions with other roads before reaching the old county road. Turn right on the old county road, then right and downhill along the stream to the bridge.

COMMON GARTER SNAKE
(*Thamnophis sirtalis*)

Trail: 1.4 miles one-way.
Elevation: 500 to 1,900 feet.
Degree of difficulty: Moderate.
Surface and blaze: Old road, rocky in places. Blue blazes.

Lake Saint Catherine State Park

[Fig. 16(7)] Lake Saint Catherine has a big and sometimes noisy central section where a southerly wind can whip up whitecaps in short order. The open lake waters have views of the steep west slopes of the Taconic Mountains to the east and lower rolling hills to the west.

To the south the lake narrows enough to pass under a road bridge, then swells again to form its south bay, known as Little Lake (or pond on some maps), with quieter and calmer waters for canoeists. The southern reach of the connecting channel is bordered by open bog, dominated by knee-high masses of leatherleaf (*Chamaedaphne calyculata*) and groves of stunted black spruce (*Picea mariana*) and tamarack (*Larix laricina*) growing in the ubiquitous peat mosses (*Sphagnum* spp.). There are clumps of numerous other bog shrubs, including sheep laurel (*Kalmia angustifolia*), pale laurel (*K. polifolia*), bog rosemary (*Andromeda glaucophylla*), black chokeberry (*Aronia melanocarpa*), and sweet gale (*Myrica gale*). Two insectivorous plants, round-leaved sundew (*Drosera rotundifolia*) and northern pitcher plant (*Sarracenia purpurea*), are abundant, as are cranberries (*Vaccinium macorcarpon* and *V. oxycoccos*). North and east of the bog and along the south shore of the lake there are extensive shrub swamp and maple-ash swamp communities, with abundant highbush blueberry (*Vaccinium corymbosum*) in some areas. All the lakeshore wetlands are on private property but their margins can be explored by canoe.

In addition to the boat ramp in the park, there are ramps on the west shore near the bridge over the narrows, and one on the east shore of Little Lake. The big lake is the place for lake and rainbow trout (*Salvelinus namaycush* and *Oncorhynchus mykiss*), while Little Lake and the lake shallows offer the full range of warm-water fish.

Directions: From the junction of VT 31 and VT 30 in Poultney, take VT 30 south approximately 3 miles. The park entrance is on the right.

Activities: Camping, picnicking, swimming, boating, fishing.

Facilities: 51 campsites, 10 lean-tos, picnic area, beach, snack bar, restrooms, boat rentals.

Dates: Mid-May to mid-Oct.

Fees: There are fees for camping and day use.

Closest town: Poultney, 3 miles.

For more information: Lake Saint Catherine State Park, RD 2, Box 1775, Poultney, VT 05764. Phone (802) 287-9158 (summer); Vermont Department of Forests,

Parks, and Recreation, 317 Sanitorium Road, West Wing, Pittsford, VT 05763-9358. Phone (802) 483-2001 (winter).

BIG TREES NATURE TRAIL

[Fig. 16(6)] The last farmer to work the fields and pastures that became Lake St. Catherine State Park must have let a few red oaks (*Quercus rubra*) and others trees grow, their boughs spreading in the pasture and perhaps providing shade for cows on a summer day or a springtime run of sap to sweeten pancakes. Those big trees now stand surrounded by their progeny and those of other species that have found shelter in their shade, forming a diverse second-growth forest in the rich soils of the valley bottom. The numbered posts on this trail help identify 11 common species, including distinctive valley specialists like shagbark hickory (*Cary ovata*) and musclewood (*Carpinus caroliniana*). The well-written guide pamphlet, available at the State Park entrance station, describes the Native American, colonial, and more modern uses of the wood, fruits, and other products of the trees. The numbers run out, but the trail continues through forests and old fields. Botanists-in-training can look for tree species that are not numbered, such as black birch (*Betula lenta*) and hop hornbeam (*Ostrya virginiana*), or explore the productive old field area at the end of the trail for shrubs and wildflowers.

Trail: 0.3 mile one-way, or continue as 1.1 mile loop.

Elevation: 500 feet. Limited elevation change.

Degree of difficulty: Easy.

Surface and blaze: Rocky footpath. Blue blazes.

DELAWARE AND HUDSON RAIL TRAIL

[Fig. 16(5)] In its heyday, the Delaware and Hudson railroad carted roofing slate– 3,400 freight cars worth in 1890–down the Hudson River to New York City and beyond. A gradual waning of the slate market ended with the last run of the railway in 1983 and the opening of a new chapter in its history. Now cyclists, equestrians, hikers, skiers, and snowmobilers can cruise nearly 20 miles of the old rail bed in Vermont. On some sections the forest has closed in, arching over the pathway, other reaches form an elevated pathway across pastures and wetlands, and still others pass old slate quarries or over 100-foot-long bridges. The Vermont stretch of the railway is divided into two sections, from Castleton to Poulney and West Pawlet to West Rupert. The intervening section is in New York State and is not open to public use. VT 153 and VT 30 alongside Lake Saint Catherine, or back roads west of the lake can be used to close the roughly 13-mile gap between the two sections.

Directions: The rail trail crosses numerous main and side roads, but parking is unavailable on many of these. The north end is in Castleton: from Rutland, take US 4 west to exit 5, then VT 4A west to Castleton. Turn left on South Street to Castleton State College. The trail begins as a narrow path off of South Street, just past the college Information and Safety Building, where there is public parking. The rail trail also crosses

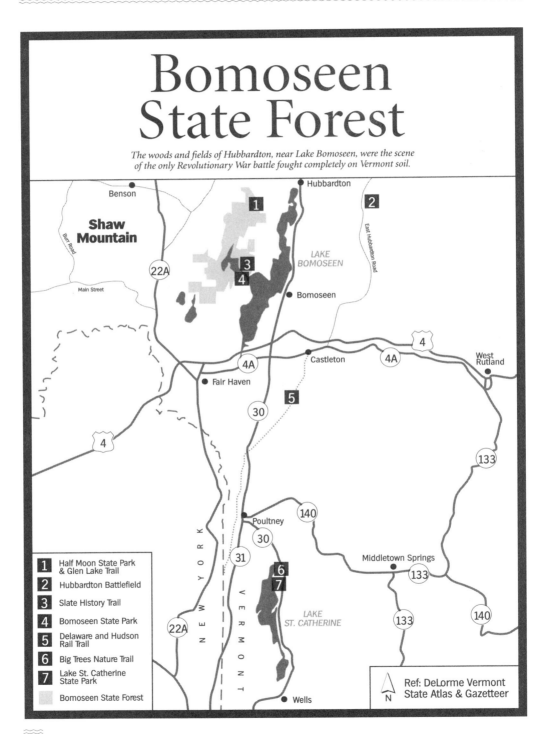

Bomoseen State Forest

The woods and fields of Hubbardton, near Lake Bomoseen, were the scene of the only Revolutionary War battle fought completely on Vermont soil.

Benson

Hubbardton

1

2

Shaw Mountain

Burr Road

22A

Main Street

LAKE BOMOSEEN

3
4

East Hubbardton Road

Bomoseen

4

4A

Castleton

4A

West Rutland

Fair Haven

5

30

4

133

30

140

Poultney

31

Middletown Springs

6
7

133

133

LAKE ST. CATHERINE

133

140

NEW YORK

VERMONT

22A

1	Half Moon State Park & Glen Lake Trail
2	Hubbardton Battlefield
3	Slate History Trail
4	Bomoseen State Park
5	Delaware and Hudson Rail Trail
6	Big Trees Nature Trail
7	Lake St. Catherine State Park
	Bomoseen State Forest

Wells

N

Ref: DeLorme Vermont State Atlas & Gazetteer

VT 140 in the town of Poultney before reaching the New York Border. It can be picked up again off of VT 153 in West Pawlet, or at its southern terminus in West Rupert.

Trail: Northern section, 9.3 miles one-way; southern section, 10.5 miles one-way.

Elevation: 400 to 500 feet.

Degree of difficulty: Easy.

Surface and blaze: Cinders, gravel, and stone.

For more information: Vermont Department of Forests, Parks, and Recreation, 317 Sanitorium Road, West Wing, Pittsford, VT 05763-9358. Phone (802) 483-2001.

Bomoseen State Forest

[Fig. 16] Seven-mile-long Lake Bomoseen is Vermont's third largest lake, and like many other lakes in the state, its shorelines are heavily developed. On busy summer weekends its waters are churned by powered craft of every kind from little fishing skiffs and jet skis to big power boats pulling water skiers. But the lake also has quiet moods, when the low, blue hills along the west shore are graced by a warm sunset or a morning mist floats over the summer-warm waters. Bomoseen State Forest takes up 3,000 acres of the hilly ground west of the lake. Two state parks with campgrounds are threaded together by 8 miles of trails that run past quiet upland lakes and along old quarry roads.

🦫 BOMOSEEN STATE PARK

[Fig. 16(4)] This small state park is located between the big waters of Lake Bomoseen and the smaller waters of Glen Lake. The latter has a 5-mph speed limit and, except for a few houses at the southern end, is undeveloped. The big lake is stocked with brook and brown trout (*Salvelinus fontinalus* and *Salmo trutta*), and both lakes have plenty of warm-water fish as well.

The speedboats stay out of the shallow waters of the north end of Lake Bomoseen, where there about 275 acres of marsh and shrub swamps that have formed since the lake level was raised by a dam built in the 1930s. The lakeward edges and shallow channels in these wetlands can be explored by canoe or kayak. A number of threatened and rare plant species are found in the marshes, many of them inconspicuous to the untrained eye, including two species of bladderwort (*Utricularia* spp.). These rootless, floating aquatic plants, of which there are also some common species, use hollow bladders about the size of a sesame seed to capture and digest zooplankton for nutrients. Patient birders may be rewarded by the harsh calls or even a glimpse of a least bittern (*Ixobyrchus exilis*) or other more common, but secretive marsh birds such as marsh wrens (*Cistothorus palustris*) or Virginia rails (*Rallus limicola*).

Directions: Take Exit 3 off of US 4 in Fair Haven. Go north on Scotch Hill Road to West Castleton, about 4 miles. Bear right toward Lake Bomoseen; the park entrance is a short distance straight ahead.

Activities: Camping, picnicking, swimming, boating, fishing, mountain biking.

Facilities: Campground with lean-tos, picnic area, beach, snack bar. There are boat ramps to the north and south.

Dates: Mid-May to mid-Oct.

Fees: There are fees for camping and day use.

Closest town: Fair Haven, 5 miles.

For more information: Bomoseen State Park, RR1, Box 2620, Fair Haven, VT 05743. Phone (802) 265-4262 (summer); Vermont Department of Forests, Parks, and Recreation, 317 Sanitorium Road, West Wing, Pittsford, VT 05763-9358. Phone (802) 483-2001 (winter).

HALF MOON STATE PARK

[Fig. 16(1)] Half Moon Pond is just big enough to be worth putting a canoe on. The shallow water is thick with aquatic vegetation, including yellow water lily (*Nuphar variegatum*), pondweeds (*Potamogeton* spp.), and, unfortunately, the invasive water milfoil (*Myriophyllum spicatum*). No motors are allowed on the pond, but the shore can be busy and a little noisy when the campground is full. Catch it on a quiet evening and you may be able to watch beaver (*Castor canadensis*) as they fan out from the lodge near the northern end in search of water lily roots and other foods.

Directions: On VT 30 in Hubbardton, at the north end of Lake Bomoseen, go north about 0.5 mile and turn left on Hortonville Road. After about 2.7 miles, turn left on Black Pond Road. The park entrance is 1.7 miles farther on the left.

Activities: Camping, limited swimming, boating, hiking.

Facilities: Campground with lean-tos, canoe put-in, boat rentals.

Dates: Mid-May to early Sept.

Fees: There is a charge for camping and day use.

Closest town: Hubbardton, 5 miles.

For more information: Half Moon State Park, RR1 Box 2730, Fair Haven, VT 05743. Phone (802) 273-2848 (summer); Vermont Department of Forests, Parks, and Recreation, 317 Sanitorium Road, West Wing, Pittsford, VT 05763-9358. Phone (802) 483-2001 (winter).

GLEN LAKE TRAIL

[Fig. 16(1)] The 4.5-mile Glen Lake Trail samples the upland pine, hemlock, and oak-hickory forests and pond shore wetlands between Half Moon Pond and Moscow Pond, then follows old slate mine roads to and around Glen Lake. Moscow Pond is more meadow than open water, with acres of dense grasses and sedges growing around the silvered stubs of trees drowned when beaver raised the water level. In summer the pond basin rings with the guttural twang of green frogs (*Rana clamitans*) and the swelling baritone of bullfrogs (*Rana catesbiana*). As the trail leaves Moscow Pond for Glen Lake it passes through a wet glade with a dense growth of both the common ostrich fern (*Matteuccia struthiopteris*) and the uncommon narrow-leaved spleenwort (*Athyrim pycnocarpon*), both over 3 feet tall. An overlook above Glen Lake has views to the south and east.

Directions: The northern end of the trail leaves from the Half Moon State Park campground, and the southern end is by the Glen Lake Dam, near the entrance to Bomoseen State Park.

Trail: 4.5 miles one-way.

Elevation: 500 to 700 feet.

Degree of difficulty: Moderate.

Surface and blaze: Old road and rocky footpath. Blue blazes.

An old slate mill in Bomoseen State Forest.

SLATE HISTORY TRAIL

[Fig. 16(3)] The area between Glen Lake and Lake Bomoseen was once a company town, complete with row houses occupied by immigrant workers and a store that took company scrip. The 12-page Slate History Trail guidebook, available at the Bomoseen Sate Park entrance station, will lead you past piles of slate rubble, a flooded quarry, the ruins of the row houses, and the remains of an old mill, with the carved datestone still standing proudly atop a roofless and overgrown end wall. The company store and the supervisors' houses, beautifully built of stacked slate, are now private residences but can be seen near the park entrance.

Trail: 0.5-mile loop.

Elevation: Around 500 feet.

Degree of difficulty: Easy.

Surface and blaze: Road and footpath. Numbered slate diamonds.

HUBBARDTON BATTLEFIELD

[Fig. 16(2)] The woods and fields of Hubbardton, near Lake Bomoseen, were the scene of the only Revolutionary War battle fought completely on Vermont soil. It was a desperate rearguard action that preceded the Battle of Bennington by about five weeks. The American forces had chosen to abandon Fort Ticonderoga and Mount Independence rather than face up to the overwhelming firepower of British Gen. Burgoyne's army, which had set up cannon on the hills above the forts. A British force pursued the retreating Americans south but ran into startling resistance at Hubbardton. For a few precious hours, a small American force, including a detachment of the Green Mountains Boys under Col. Seth Warner, held the British at bay while the main force continued its retreat.

Slate Country

The west slope of the Taconic Mountains is slate country. There are open pits and scrap piles all over the landscape, and most of the buildings in the towns and villages–from big civic buildings like the town halls and libraries right down to humble cottages–have slate roofs.

Slate is a metamorphic rock derived from mild alteration of sedimentary rocks, like shale, which develop from deep-water silt and clay deposits. The horizontal pressure from mountain building causes the platy clay minerals to line up in the thin layers that allow the slate to be split up in fine sheets. Even minor irregularities in the slate make it unusable, so that up to 85 percent of the rock removed from the ground winds up in waste piles. Unlike tailings from some other types of mines, these are not toxic, but because the coarse rock particles do not hold water well, they can still be a challenge for plant communities to colonize.

With the rise of slate production in the 1840s, there was an influx of Welshmen armed with practical experience in quarrying. Names like Jones, Lloyd, and Evans are still found on mailboxes in the region, which still claims one of the highest concentrations of people of Welsh descent in the country.

Their job done, the rear guard melted away with minimal casualties.

The state historic site includes a marble monument and a museum with a diorama of the battle, and sponsors annual summer re-enactments of Revolutionary War tactics.

Directions: Take Exit 5 off of US 4 in Castleton. Go approximately 7 miles north on East Hubbardton Road. The state historic site is on the right, just north of the village of East Hubbardton.

Facilities: Restrooms, gift shop, museum.

Dates: Open mid May through mid-Oct., re-enactments on one weekend in July.

Fees: There is a charge.

For more information: Vermont Division of Historic Preservation, 135 State Street, Drawer 33, Montpelier, VT, 05633. Phone (802) 828-3051.

Shaw Mountain

[Fig. 16] Like the west-facing cliffs of Snake Mountain and Mount Philo farther north in the Champlain Valley, Shaw Mountain is a klippe, with older summit rocks thrust over the younger shales of the valley. But there is a crucial difference: The summit plateau, cliffs, and talus of Shaw Mountain are made of limestone, rather than the generally more acid quartzite that makes up the northern summits. The high pH of the soils developed from limestone, combined with the warmth of the west-facing slopes, make for nutrient-rich but dry growing conditions that support a unique flora. Some 25 rare and threatened plant species are known to occur on Shaw

Mountain, ranging from chinquapin oak (*Quercus muhlenbergii*), growing near the northern limit of its range, to wall-rue (*Asplenium ruta-muraria*), a tiny fern that grows in seeps on limestone cliffs. The Vermont State Heritage Program recognizes this as one of the most diverse and important natural areas in the state.

A rough-and-ready trail goes over a small hill and crosses a bridge over a shrub wetland connected to nearby Root Pond, then circles the summit area of the mountain, passing through a young, dry, oak-hickory-hop hornbeam (*Quercus* spp.-*Carya* spp.-*Ostrya virginiana*) forest. The fertile soils support high rates of decomposition and earthworm activity, so unlike most other forest soils in the state there is no litter layer—the leaves that fall to the ground in autumn are completely decomposed and mixed into the upper layers of the soil by the end of the following summer. In parts of the forest, there is almost no shrub layer; the trees grow out of a carpet of fire sedge (*Carex pensylvanica*), with scattered clumps of wildflowers, including the rare panicled and large-bracted tick-trefoils (*Desmodium paniculatum* and *D. cuspidatum*). The hickory nuts and acorns produced by the trees are an important food source for a wide variety of animals, including white-tailed deer (*Odocoileus virginanus*), black bear (*Ursus americanus*), gray squirrels (*Sciurus caroliniensis*), and wild turkeys (*Meleagris gallopavo*).

The trail passes close to the edge of the west-facing limestone ledges, but to see what's on and below them you're on your own. The wall-rue and two species of cliff-brake (*Pellaea* spp.) grow on the cliffs while the talus below has both open and forested sections with a variety of rare shrubs, grasses, and wildflowers. Ravens (*Corvus corax*) nest on the ledges and are often seen and heard in the area.

The return leg of the trail descends the gradual eastern slope of the mountain, passing near the northernmost of several vernal pools. These pools, formed in pockets in the bedrock, fill up with water in the spring and gradually dry up through the summer. Because there are no permanent predator populations in them, vernal pools are important breeding grounds for terrestrial frogs and salamanders, including wood frogs (*Rana sylvatica*), gray treefrogs (*Hyla versicolor*), spring peepers (*Hyla crucifer*), and spotted salamanders (*Ambystoma maculatum*).

Directions: From the junction of VT 22A and VT 144 in Benson, go 0.9 mile south on VT 22A and turn right on Mill Pond Road. Continue west 1.1 miles, through the crossroads by the small store in Benson, and turn left on Park Hill Road, then after 0.6 mile turn right on Money Hole Road. After passing Root Pond Road, look for a small pullout on the left with a Nature Conservancy sign, about 1.7 miles from Park Hill Road.

Trail: 2.4-mile loop.

Elevation: 400 to 700 feet.

Degree of difficulty: Moderate.

Surface and blaze: Unimproved footpath. Thinly marked with blue, white, or blue and white blazes.

For more information: The Nature Conservancy, 27 State Street, Montpelier, VT 05602. Phone (802) 229-4425.

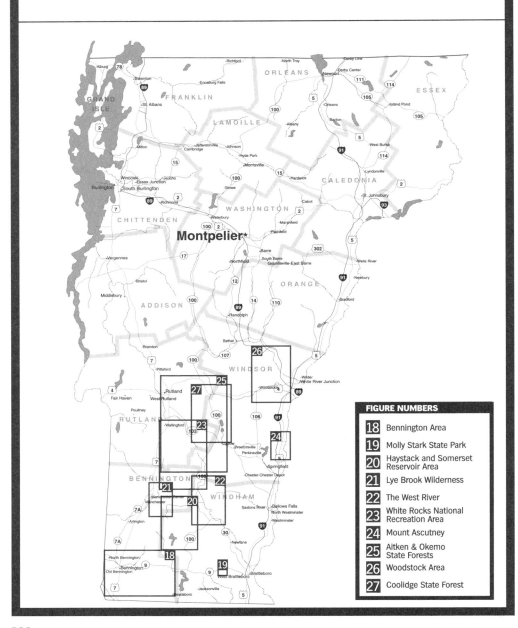

Southern Green Mtns.

FIGURE NUMBERS

18	Bennington Area
19	Molly Stark State Park
20	Haystack and Somerset Reservoir Area
21	Lye Brook Wilderness
22	The West River
23	White Rocks National Recreation Area
24	Mount Ascutney
25	Aitken & Okemo State Forests
26	Woodstock Area
27	Coolidge State Forest

Southern Green Mountains

During the Taconic and Acadian orogenies, the complex mélange of rocks found in the Champlain Valley and the northern Green Mountains were pushed over billion-year-old basement rocks that were formed during an earlier cycle of mountain building, the Grenville orogeny. In the southern Green Mountains a great fold of the ancient basement rock comes to the surface, forming a broad plateau dotted with small lakes and wetlands, many of them near or above 2,000 feet in elevation. Standing above these are the higher ridges and domes of the bigger southern summits like Stratton and Killington.

The ancient gneisses and schists of the plateau have no calcite, the mineral that sweetens the soil by various degrees over much of the rest of the state. The combination of high elevation and generally acid soil brings spruce-fir and beech-birch-maple forests—and animals that live in them—down to the Massachusetts border.

[*Above:* The White Rocks National Recreation Area is a great destination for backcountry recreation]

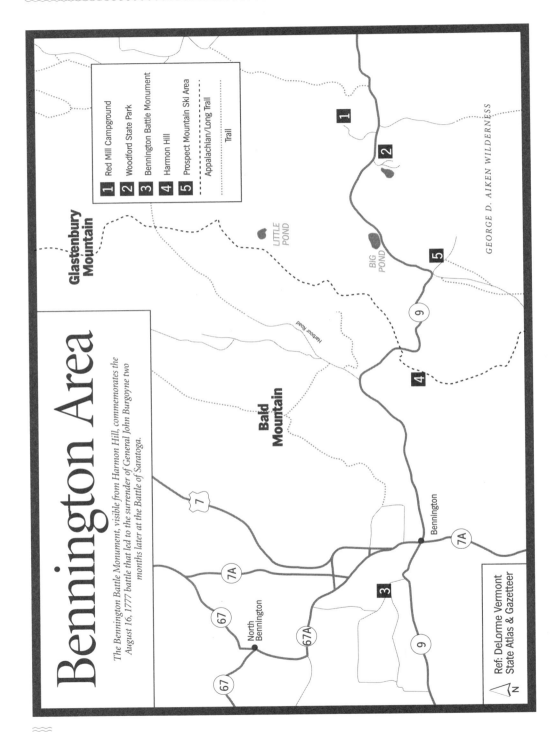

Bennington Area

The Bennington Battle Monument, visible from Harmon Hill, commemorates the August 16, 1777 battle that led to the surrender of General John Burgoyne two months later at the Battle of Saratoga.

Legend:

1 Red Mill Campground
2 Woodford State Park
3 Bennington Battle Monument
4 Harmon Hill
5 Prospect Mountain Ski Area

Appalachian/Long Trail

Trail

Glastenbury Mountain

GEORGE D. AIKEN WILDERNESS

LITTLE POND

BIG POND

Bald Mountain

Harbour Road

Bennington

North Bennington

Ref: DeLorme Vermont State Atlas & Gazetteer

N

Like the thumb on a mittened hand, a smaller fold of basement rock again comes to the surface in the eastern piedmont between Woodstock and Townshend. Hanging off the tip of the thumb, granite that cooled in the core of a 120-million-year-old volcano forms Mount Ascutney, looming above the Connecticut River. Although not really part of the Green Mountains, Ascutney and other piedmont sites to the south are included in this chapter.

To the west, the plateau drops off sharply into the Valley of Vermont, bordered by the hard band of Cheshire Quartzite that marks the western front of the range from Massachusetts to Quebec.

Although little of the high-elevation land was farmed, it was logged extensively, and post-logging fires sterilized the soils in some areas like The Burning in Lye Brook Wilderness. Although several large areas of the Green Mountain National Forest have been designated as wilderness areas and are now roadless, they were once threaded by logging roads and railroads, many of which are now used as trails. Flood control and hydroelectric dams constructed over the years since the 1927 flood have created new freshwater lakes and wetlands.

The Long Trail and the Appalachian Trail share a common treadway through the southern Green Mountains. Near Gifford Woods State Park, just north of US 4, the Long Trail continues north while the Appalachian Trail veers east to head for the hills of New Hampshire.

Bennington

▨ HARMON HILL

[Fig. 18(4)] Just 12 miles north of the Vermont-Massachusetts border, the broad, open summit of Harmon Hill gives northbound Long/Appalachian trail hikers their first sweeping views of Vermont. Day hikers can take the Long/Appalachian Trail south from VT 9.

The chunky white quartzite blocks that form the summit were once beach sands in the 550 million-year-old sea that lapped the western side of Vermont. Similar quartzite beds fringe the western edge of the Appalachians as far south as Tennessee. As the quartzite weathers, the quartzite forms an almost pure white sand topped by rich, dark humus, the formation of which is augmented by the Forest Service's periodic burning of the area to keep the summit open.

The burning has helped create openings dominated by bracken fern (*Pteridium aquilinum*) and raspberries (*Rubus idaeus*). Those willing to travel the extra distance down the southern side of the hill into a mixed forest of red spruce (*Picea rubens*) and yellow birch (*Betula alleghenesis*) will find pink lady slipper (*Cypripedium acaule*) and Indian cucumber root (*Medeola virginiana*).

The summit offers a fine view to the west of the town of Bennington, with the 306-foot-tall obelisk of the Bennington Battle Monument appearing as a stark white needle against the green haystacks of the Taconic Mountains.

Directions: From Bennington, go east on VT 9 approximately 4.5 miles to the trailhead on the south side of the road. Parking is on the north side of the road.

Trail: 1.7 miles one-way.

Elevation: 1,360 feet to 2,325 feet.

Degree of difficulty: Moderate/strenuous.

Surface and blaze: Wooded footpath with section of steep stone steps. White blazes.

For more information: Green Mountain Club, 4711 Waterbury-Stowe Road, Waterbury Center, VT 05677. Phone (802) 244-7037.

BENNINGTON BATTLE MONUMENT

[Fig. 18(3)] The Bennington Battle Monument, clearly visible from Harmon Hill on the Long/Appalachian Trail, commemorates the August 16, 1777 battle in which mostly untrained Colonial forces under Gen. John Stark routed the disciplined army of British Gen. John Burgoyne. Although the battle was fought 5 miles to the northwest, just over the border in New York, the immediate British objective was a supply depot at the monument site in Bennington. Denied those supplies, Burgoyne surrendered his entire force two months later at the Battle of Saratoga.

The monument houses a diorama of the battle. The observatory, accessible by 412 stone steps or a steel elevator, has slotted stone windows with sweeping views of the town and surrounding Green Mountain and Taconic summits.

Directions: From the junction of US 7 and VT 9 in Bennington, go west on VT 9 about 1 mile. Turn right on Monument Avenue and follow it to the state historic site.

Facilities: Visitor center, restrooms, gift shop.

Dates: Mid-Apr. to mid-Oct.

Fees: There is an entrance fee.

For more information: Bennington Battle Monument, 15 Monument Circle, Old Bennington, VT 05201. Phone (802) 447-0550. Vermont Division of Historic Preservation, 135 State Street, Drawer 33, Montpelier, VT 05633. Phone (802) 828-3051.

GLASTENBURY MOUNTAIN

[Fig. 18] From the summit fire tower on Glastenbury Mountain, it's said you can see more wilderness than from any other vantage point in the state of Vermont. Once you've made the long climb to the summit and had a chance to feast your eyes on the view, that statement is hard to dispute.

To the east, Somerset Reservoir glows like a new dime in the sun, framed by the Mount Snow-Haystack massif. The rumpled green hills of the Berkshires lie to the south, the Taconics to the west, and the long ridgelines of Mount Equinox and

Stratton Mountain to the north. In a summer haze, it's easy to imagine the wilderness goes on forever.

The steady climb to Glastenbury along the Long/Appalachian Trail passes through an amazing beech (*Fagus grandifolia*) forest, where trees have been gnarled and somewhat stunted, probably by wind. Atop the ridge, red spruce (*Picea rubens*), heart-leaved paper birch (*Betula papyrifera* var. *cordifolia*), and balsam fir (*Abies balsamea*) turn the trail into a fragrant green tunnel, populated by birds of high-elevation coniferous forests, including Swainson's thrushes (*Catharus undulatus*), yellow-rumped warblers (*Dendroica coronata*), Cape May warblers (*D. Tigrina*), brown creepers (*Certhia americana*), solitary vireos (*Vireo solitarius*) and white-throated sparrows (*Zonothrichia albicollis*).

The rock type here is the oldest found in the Green Mountain State, billion-year-old rocks that are part of the central core of North America. They are mainly gneisses, banded rocks that have been cooked and crushed in the intense pressures and temperatures from the Acadian and Taconic orogenies, as well as the Grenville orogeny, the region's first mountain-building event, more than 1 billion years ago.

Visiting Glastenbury requires ambition: It's roughly 10 miles from the nearest road. Fortunately, Goddard Shelter, one of the Long Trail's most charming shelters, sits on Glastenbury's shoulder just 0.3 mile from the summit, making an overnight trip an attractive option.

Directions: From Bennington, go east on VT 9 approxomately 5.2 miles to the trailhead. Parking is on the north side of the road.

Trail: 10.1 miles one-way; a link-up with the West Ridge Trail (*see* Bald Mountain, page 89) makes a 21.8-mile loop possible.

Elevation: 1,306 feet to 3,748 feet.

Degree of difficulty: Strenuous.

Surface and blaze: Rocky footpath. White blazes.

For more information: Green Mountain National Forest, Manchester Ranger District, 2538 Depot Street, Manchester Center, VT 05255. Phone (802) 362-2307. Green Mountain Club, 4711 Waterbury-Stowe Road, Waterbury Center, VT 05677. Phone (802) 244-7037.

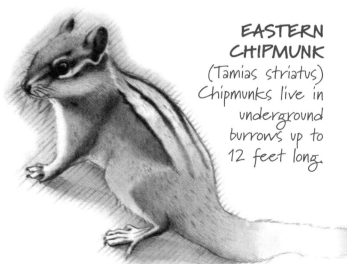

EASTERN CHIPMUNK (Tamias striatus) Chipmunks live in underground burrows up to 12 feet long.

RED MILL CAMPGROUND

[Fig. 18(1)] This simple campground makes for a convenient and affordable place to stay while exploring area hiking trails near Bennington or bushwhacking in the George D. Aiken Wilderness Area to the south. Bring binoculars; a small wetland bisects the campground and makes for good birding.

Directions: From Bennington at the junction of VT 9 and US 7, go east on VT 9 for approximately 10 miles. Red Mill Campground is on the north, or left side of the road.

Activities: Primitive camping, bird-watching.

Facilities: 31 tent sites, pit toilets, hand water pumps.

Dates: Open mid-May to mid-Oct.

Fees: None.

Closest town: Searsburg, 2 miles.

For more information: Green Mountain National Forest, Manchester Ranger District, 2538 Depot Street, Manchester Center, VT 05255-9733. Phone (802) 362-2307.

GEORGE D. AIKEN WILDERNESS AREA

[Fig. 18] The George D. Aiken Wilderness is something of an anomaly in the Green Mountain National Forest; its 5,060 acres are virtually without trails. Only one other wilderness area, Bristol Cliffs (*see* page 183), shares this distinction. Consequently, the George Aiken delivers what it promises: wilderness.

The wilderness was named for the late Sen. George Aiken of Vermont, who fought in Congress to expand the National Wilderness Preservation System to the eastern United States.

Few hikers visit this high plateau because the lack of trails, combined with the wetness of much of the terrain, make summertime travel extremely difficult. Those willing to bushwhack and swat the healthy blackfly and mosquito populations, however, will find an area rich with animal signs in and around beaver ponds and meadows.

Beaver meadows form when beavers abandon a pond, usually because they've exhausted the supply of the trees and other preferred foods in and around the pond, leaving dams to deteriorate and eventually drain. One of the highest concentrations of beaver meadows in the southern Greens is in the George Aiken Wilderness.

The spongy mat of rich organic matter left behind when a beaver pond drains is typically colonized by a sedge (*Carex stricta*) and a grass (*Calamagrostis canadensis*), along with a mix of other grasses and sedges. Shrubs also invade, typically meadowsweet (*Spirea alba*), alder (*Alnus incana*), and sweet gale (*Myrica gale*).

The beaver ponds and meadows attract animals and birds that use the area for food or nesting. Moose (*Alces alces*) are regular spring visitors as they come to feed on young shoots and green vegetation. Mink (*Mustela vison*), river otter (*Lutra canadensis*), and fisher (*Martes pennanti*) are also present.

When beavers first flood an area, the flooding kills trees, which then become places for wood ducks (*Aix sponsa*) and other cavity-nesters to use. Newer beaver ponds can also be good places to fish for brook trout (*Salvelinus fontinalis*).

The forests here—dominated by sugar maple (*Acer saccharum*), yellow birch (*Betula alleghaniensis*), American beech (*Fagus grandifolia*), black cherry (*Prunus serotina*), and white ash (*Fraxinus americana*)— are typical of the second-growth hardwoods that blanket much of lower elevations in the national forest. Wetter areas near ponds or meadows are typically colonized by a mix of red spruce (*Picea rubens*), balsam fir (*Abies balsamea*), and red maple (*Acer rubrum*).

The oldest trees date from 1870, but the Hoosick Lumber Company had cleared much of the hardwoods in the area by the early 1920s. By the end of that decade, the softwoods were gone, too, harvested by an area business called the Metal Edge Company.

Both operations were selective, taking only the most valuable trees, leaving a forest devoid of many of the earliest successional species that typically colonize cleared areas, such as paper birch (*Betula papyrifera*).

While summer travel is difficult, winter is a different matter. The area receives some of the heaviest snowfall in Vermont, a product in part of its elevation of about 2,500 feet on a high plateau where winter storm tracks concentrate. Cross-country skis open the wilderness area in a way that foot travel can't. But skiers need good map and compass skills, because the thick forests and lack of any distinctive high points or views can make it easy to get lost.

Directions: From Bennington at the junction of VT 9 and US 7, go east on VT 9 for 10 miles past the entrance for Red Mill Campground on Forest Road 72. Look for Forest Road 74 on the south side of the road. Turn right onto Forest Road 74 and choose a parking spot along the road, which extends approximately 1.5 miles south along the eastern boundary of the wilderness. There are no trailheads, and the road is not plowed in winter.

Activities: Bushwhacking, fishing, snowshoeing, cross-country skiing.

Facilities: None.

Dates: Open year-round.

Fees: None.

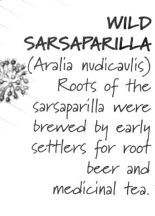

WILD SARSAPARILLA (Aralia nudicaulis) Roots of the sarsaparilla were brewed by early settlers for root beer and medicinal tea.

Closest town: Searsburg, 2 miles.

For more information: Green Mountain National Forest, Manchester Ranger District, 2538 Depot Street, Manchester Center, VT 05255-9733. Phone (802) 362-2307.

PROSPECT MOUNTAIN SKI AREA

[Fig. 18(5)] Opened in the 1930s as a downhill ski area, Prospect Mountain is now solely devoted to cross-country skiing. At 2,250 feet, the area holds the distinction of being the highest elevation cross-country ski resort in Vermont. Elevation makes a difference in the Green Mountain State when it comes to snow: it may be raining in nearby Bennington but snowing on Prospect Mountain. The area grooms 18 miles (30 km) of trails and offers easy winter access to the adjacent 5,060-acre George Aiken Wilderness Area in the Green Mountain National Forest.

Directions: From Bennington, take VT 9 east 7 miles to the resort on the south side of the road.

Activities: Cross-country skiing.

Facilities: Base lodge, restaurant, gift shop, ski shop, 30 km groomed trails.

Dates: Winter season.

Fees: There is a charge to use the trails.

Closest town: Woodford, 1 mile.

For more information: Prospect Mountain Ski Area, HCR 65, Box 760, Woodford, VT 05201. Phone (802) 442-2575.

WOODFORD STATE PARK

[Fig. 18(2)] Surrounded by the Green Mountain National Forest and bounded on one side by the George Aiken Wilderness Area, Woodford State Park's 400 acres are a bit of civilization among the wilds.

Like its surroundings, the park is on a high plateau colonized by a mixed forest of American beech (*Fagus grandifolia*), sugar maple (*Acer saccharum*), yellow birch (*Betula alleghaniensis*), red spruce (*Picea rubens*), and balsam fir (*Abies balsamea*). The neighboring unbroken forests, ponds, and beaver meadows make the area good habitat for otter (*Lutra canadensis*), deer (*Odocoileus virginianus*), moose (*Alces alces*), and black bear (*Ursus americanus*).

The shallow 23-acre Adams Reservoir was first created in the early 1800s to power area sawmills. It was rebuilt by the state in 1969. Wetland plants such as leatherleaf (*Chamaedaphne calyculata*) and round-leaved sundew (*Drosera rotundifolia*) colonize the reservoir's shallow boggy shoreline.

Directions: From Bennington, take VT 9 east approximately 10 miles to Woodford State Park on the south, or right side of the road.

Activities: Hiking, fishing, boating, camping, picnicking.

Facilities: 83 campsites, 20 lean-tos, restrooms, beach, picnic area, rental boats, hiking trails.

Dates: Open mid-May to mid-Oct.

Fees: There is a charge for day use and camping.

Closest town: Woodford, 3 miles.

For more information: Woodford State Park, HCR 65, Box 928, Bennington, VT 05201. Phone (802) 447-7169 (summer). Vermont Forests, Parks and Recreation Department, 317 Sanitorium Road, West Wing, Pittsford, VT 05763-9358. Phone (802) 483-2314

The Searsburg Wind Farm

Look due west from the old fire tower on Mount Olga and on a ridge that dominates the skyline, you'll see a line of wind turbines standing in stark silhouette against the sky. In winds of 10 to 29 miles per hour, the 11 towers on Mt. Waldo can generate up to six megawatts, enough power for about 2,000 houses, making this the largest wind power project in the eastern United States. It's hard to appreciate the scale of them from 8 miles away: the towers are almost 200 feet high, and the three-pronged fiberglass blades are 132 feet in diameter and weigh about 2 tons. Green Mountain Power is using the experimental wind farm to evaluate advanced wind technology, developed in friendlier climes, in Vermont's harsh winters. The facility is closed to visitors except during occasional open houses.

BALD MOUNTAIN

[Fig. 18] With its ever-growing crown of conifers, Bald Mountain is no longer quite so bald, but it is still a pleasant destination via a trail that leaves from within Bennington city limits. Views from the summit are limited, but several vantage points along the way allow for views south of Bennington, the Taconic Range, and Mount Greylock in Massachusetts. It's also possible to continue on from Bald Mountain up to Glastenbury Mountain via the challenging West Ridge Trail, making for an enjoyable two-day backpacking loop with fine views.

Directions: For the western branch of the Bald Mountain Trail, from the junction of VT 9 and US 7 in Bennington, go east on VT 9 approximately 1 mile to Branch Street. Turn left, or north, on Branch Street and go about 0.8 mile to limited trailhead parking. For the eastern branch of the Bald Mountain Trail, from the junction of VT 9 and US 7 in Bennington, go east on VT 9 approximately 4 miles to the Woodford Hollow Road. Turn left and go approximately 0.8 mile on Woodford Hollow Road; limited parking is available.

Trail: 4.1 miles one-way on western branch of the Bald Mountain Trail; 2 miles one-way on eastern branch of the Bald Mountain Trail; 7.8 miles one-way from Bald Mountain summit on West Ridge Trail to Glastenbury Mountain.

Elevation: 800 feet to 2,857 feet.

Degree of difficulty: Moderate.

Surface and blaze: Rocky footpath, can be difficult to follow especially along the trail's western branch. Blue blazes.

For more information: Green Mountain National Forest, Manchester Ranger

Molly Stark State Park

Molly Stark is remembered for rounding up a corps of volunteers to cross the state and bail out her husband, General John Stark, during the Revolutionary War.

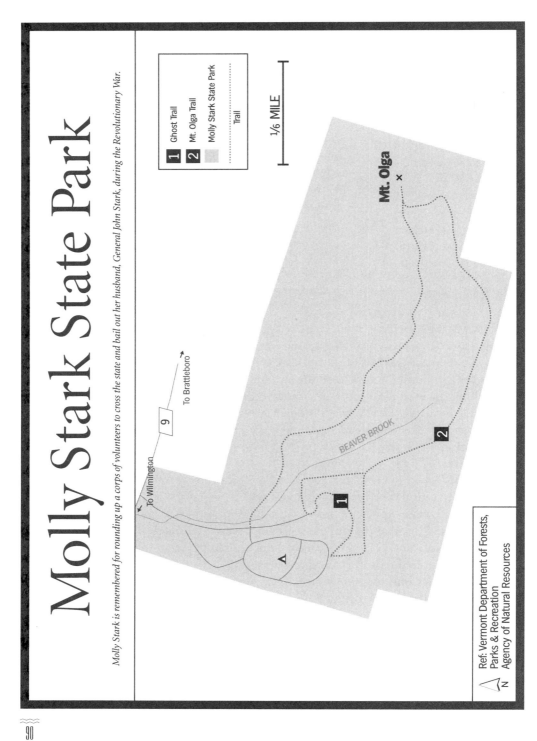

To Brattleboro

9

To Wilmington

1

2

BEAVER BROOK

Mt. Olga
×

Ghost Trail — 1

Mt. Olga Trail — 2

Molly Stark State Park

Trail

1/6 MILE

N

Ref: Vermont Department of Forests,
Parks & Recreation
Agency of Natural Resources

District, 2538 Depot Street, Manchester Center, VT 05255. Phone (802) 362-2307. Green Mountain Club, 4711 Waterbury-Stowe Road, Waterbury Center, VT 05677. Phone (802) 244-7037.

Molly Stark State Park

[Fig. 19] In Vermont, Molly Stark is fondly remembered as woman enough to get on her horse, round up a corps of volunteers, and send them across the state to bail out her husband, General John Stark, at the Battle of Bennington during the Revolutionary War. Their route was along the lines of today's VT 9, dubbed the Molly Stark Trail, which rounds the north shoulder of Mount Olga, the modest physiographic centerpiece of Molly Stark State Park.

Although it stands apart from the main southern reach of the Green Mountains and looks like a small piedmont foothill, Mount Olga is made of the same rock formations that make up the high ridges of the northern and central Green Mountains. To the north these bands of rock span up to 25 miles, but here they are compressed into a few miles, sandwiched between the gneiss core of the southern Green Mountains and the metamorphosed volcanic rocks of the piedmont.

Directions: From the junction of VT 100 and VT 9 in Wilmington, go east on VT 9 about 3 miles. The park entrance is on the right.

Activities: Camping, picnicking, hiking.

Facilities: 23 campsites, 11 lean-tos, picnic area, restrooms, playground, hiking trails.

Dates: Mid-May to mid-Oct.

Fees: There is a charge for camping and day use.

Closest town: Wilmington, 3 miles.

For more information: Molly Stark State Park, 705 Route 9 East, Wilmington, VT 05363. Phone (802) 464-5460 (summer). Vermont Department of Forests, Parks, and Recreation, RR 1 Box 33, North Springfield, VT 05150-9726. Phone (802) 885-8855 (winter).

MOUNT OLGA TRAIL

[Fig. 19(2)] The loop trail to Mount Olga ascends through northern hardwood forest and descends through dense conifer forest of hemlock (*Tsuga canadensis*) and white pine (*Pinus strobus*). This varied habitat makes for good forest bird-watching, and the summit is a good place to spot hawks migrating along the Green Mountain front in autumn. The summit has an old but sound fire tower, high enough to get well

NORTHERN PARULA
(*Parula americana*)
Parula means "little titmouse," which refers to the bird's active foraging through foliage for insects.

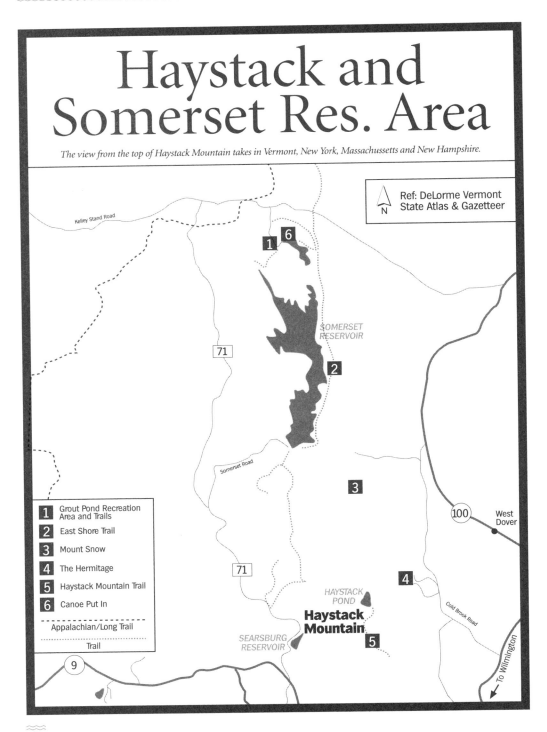

Haystack and Somerset Res. Area

The view from the top of Haystack Mountain takes in Vermont, New York, Massachussetts and New Hampshire.

Ref: DeLorme Vermont State Atlas & Gazetteer

Kelley Stand Road

SOMERSET RESERVOIR

71

71

Somerset Road

100 West Dover

HAYSTACK POND

Haystack Mountain

SEARSBURG RESERVOIR

Cold Brook Road

To Wilmington

9

1 Grout Pond Recreation Area and Trails

2 East Shore Trail

3 Mount Snow

4 The Hermitage

5 Haystack Mountain Trail

6 Canoe Put In

---------- Appalachian/Long Trail

.... Trail

above the trees for broad views of rolling blue hills and broad summits in three states, including the impressive line of wind turbines on nearby Waldo Mountain in Searsburg.

Trail: 1.7-mile loop.

Elevation: 1,900 to 2,415 feet.

Degree of difficulty: Easy to moderate.

Surface and blaze: Rocky footpath. Blue blazes.

Haystack and Somerset Reservoir

MOUNT SNOW

[Fig. 20(3)] Mount Snow and neighboring Haystack Mountain form a 9-mile ridge on the eastern edge of the Green Mountains in southern Vermont. The east slopes of the ridge are dominated by Vermont's second largest ski area, Mount Snow, which includes separate trail systems on both mountains. The ski trails extend to the summit of Mount Snow but leave Haystack's slightly lower summit untouched. In summer, the ski area also offers 45 miles of mountain bike trails, along with a climbing wall, BMX and skate park, and hiking center with 40 miles of trails.

Directions: From the junction of VT 9 and VT 100 in Wilmington, go north on VT 100 through the village of West Dover; the turnoff to the resort is on the left.

Activities: Downhill and cross-country skiing, hiking, mountain biking.

Facilities: Extensive ski and summer resort with numerous lifts, a variety of accommodations, and activity centers.

Dates: Open year-round.

Fees: There is a charge for trail access and all activities.

Closest town: West Dover, 3 miles.

For more information: Mount Snow, Route 100, Mount Snow, VT 05356. Phone (800) 246-7669.

THE HERMITAGE

[Fig. 20(4)] The Hermitage is a country inn in grand style, centered on an eighteenth-century farmhouse. It offers first-class accommodations and dining, a cross-country ski center with 30 miles (50 km) of groomed ski touring trails in winter, and sporting clays (a refined version of skeet shooting) and guided release hunting for pheasant and partridge in summer and autumn.

Directions: From the junction of VT 9 and VT 100 in Wilmington, go north on VT 100. Turn left at 2.5 miles onto Coldbrook Road; the Hermitage is 3 miles up on the left.

Activities: Cross-country skiing, sporting clays, release hunting.

Frogs in Winter

Along with the rushing of swollen streams and the cheery songs of robins (*Turdus migratorius*), one of the harbingers of springtime in Vermont is the deafening chorus of spring peepers (*Hyla crucifer*), which gather in vegetation by shallow vernal pools to breed. Another is the dry, ducklike "chuk" of wood frogs (*Rana sylvatica*), which can be seen by the hundreds, floating on the waters of woodland ponds, often before the ice is completely gone. These two species, along with the gray tree frog (*Hyla versicolor*), share an unusual adaptation to the winter rigors of the north country: freezing tolerance. Unlike their amphibian brethren that hibernate in the unfrozen mud at the bottom of ponds, these species hibernate in the upper layers of the soil, where they assume the demeanor of a frog-shaped rock. Studies have shown that about one-third of the total body water in these frogs freezes solid, while the remainder is prevented from freezing by accumulation of glycerol, a kind of alcohol, in the body tissues. Freezing kills other species of frogs. Because soils usually thaw and warm sooner than ponds, the freezing-tolerant species can begin breeding well ahead of amphibians still in suspended animation in the cold mud at the bottom of ponds–and perhaps before many avian predators have arrived from points south.

Facilities: Inn, cross-country ski center with rentals and instruction.

Dates: Open year-round.

Fees: There is a charge for facility use and for cross-country ski trail access.

Closest town: Wilmington, 5.5 miles.

For more information: The Hermitage, Box 457, Coldbrook Road, Wilmington, VT 05363. Phone (802) 464-3511.

HAYSTACK MOUNTAIN TRAIL

[Fig. 20(5)] While the Mount Snow Hiking Center offers access to the ridgetop and Haystack Mountain, along with equipment and advice (for a fee), the traditional route up Haystack runs up through the woods along its southern ridge. The view from the top takes in nearby summits of the Green and Taconic mountains in New York and Vermont, Mount Greylock in the Massachusetts Berkshires, and Mount Monadnock and other peaks in southeastern New Hampshire.

Much of the trail, except the final 0.4-mile pitch to the summit, is used as a cross-country ski and snowmobile trail in winter. The 3-mile Deerfield Ridge Trail, used mainly in winter, connects the summit areas of Haystack Mountain and Mount Snow. A spur trail leads to Haystack Pond, a lovely subalpine lake.

The lake and the stunted forests along the ridge top are a good place to look and listen for mountain birds such as rusty blackbirds (*Euphagus carolinus*), ruby-crowned kinglets (*Regulus calendula*), yellow-bellied flycatcher (*Empidonax flaviventris*), blackpoll warblers (*Dendroica striata*), and Swainson's and Bicknell's thrushes (*Catharus ustulatus* and *C. bicknelli*).

Directions: From the traffic light in Wilmington, take VT 9 about 1.1 miles west and turn right on Haystack Road (paved). Turn left at about 2.4 miles, following a sign for Clubhouse and Chimney Hill roads, then turn right on Binney Brook Road (dirt) at 2.5 miles. At 3.5 miles, turn right on Upper Dam Road, then turn left at 3.6 miles. The trail is on the right at 3.8 miles; park along the road.

Trail: 2.4 miles one-way

Elevation: 2,600 to 3,425 feet.

Degree of difficulty: Moderate.

Surface and blaze: Old road and rocky footpath. Blue and orange plastic or blue paint blazes.

SOMERSET RESERVOIR

[Fig. 20] Just north of the busy year-round resort of Mount Snow, 5-mile-long Somerset Reservoir offers canoeists and fishermen a relatively quiet getaway. Its 16 miles of shoreline can keep a paddler wondering what's around the next bend for at least a full day. The reservoir is managed by the New England Power Company, which prohibits camping on the shoreline but maintains a picnic area on Streeter Island near the northern end of the reservoir. There is primitive and sheltered camping nearby at the Green Mountain National Forest Grout Pond Recreation Area.

The reservoir is set among rolling hills along the eastern edge of the Green Mountains, with views of nearby Mount Snow to the south and Stratton Mountain to the north. Several bays have wetland pockets with their associated wildlife. It is the southernmost common loon (*Gavia immer*) nesting site in the state. The power company maintains high water levels through the breeding season but may draw the reservoir down in late summer. Vermont is one of only a handful of states with no confirmed breeding records for bald eagles (*Haliaeetus leucocephalus*), and Somerset Reservoir is one of only a few sites in the state where they have been seen regularly in recent years. The lake supports chain pickerel (*Esox niger*), smallmouth bass (*Micropterus dolomieui*), and other warm-water fish in its extensive shallows, and brook trout (*Salmo fontinalis*) in the deeper waters.

Directions: From Wilmington, go west on VT 9 about 6 miles and turn right on Somerset Road, a 9-mile gravel road that ends at the parking and picnic area by the dam at the southern end of the reservoir. Canoeists can also carry in to the northern arm of the reservoir 0.8 mile from Grout Pond.

Activities: Canoeing, fishing, hiking, cross-country skiing, snowshoeing, wildlife-watching, picnicking.

Facilities: Boat ramp, picnic areas with outhouses.

Dates: The access road is open year-round.

Fees: None.

Closest town: Wilmington, 15 miles.

For more information: New England Power Company, Bellows Falls, VT 05101. Phone (802) 463-3226.

EAST SHORE TRAIL

[Fig. 20(2)] This trail follows an old railroad bed along the east shore of Somerset Reservoir, and is also used by cross-country skiers as a stretch of the Catamount Trail (*see* page 304) in winter, continuing north to Grout Pond and south to Mount Snow. The trail begins in the picnic area near the dam and skirts several coves along the lakeshore, with opportunities for study of lakeshore and wetland vegetation and wildlife.

Trail: 4.2 miles one-way.

Elevation: 2,100 feet, limited elevation change.

Degree of difficulty: Easy.

Surface and blaze: Old road with log bridges over the wet spots. Yellow blazes; blue plastic diamonds mark the Catamount Trail.

GROUT POND RECREATION AREA

[Fig. 20(1)] Just north of Somerset Reservoir, 86-acre Grout Pond, a Green Mountain National Forest Recreation Area, is an end-of-the-road quiet water hideaway for canoeists and hikers, with a striking variety of shallow water and shoreline vegetation. There is no boat ramp, but a short carry allows canoe access. Only electric motors are allowed on the pond. Twelve miles of trails used for hiking and ungroomed cross-country skiing form a series of loops in the woods and hills around the pond. Two lean-tos and several tent sites (one wheelchair accessible, four with canoe access) scattered along the shore and some trails provide overnight options. Camping is allowed in designated sites only. Winter visitors can use the caretaker's cabin. The Catamount Trail (*see* page 304) Vermont's end-to-end cross-country ski trail, passes along the west shore of the pond, connecting south to Somerset Reservoir and north to the Stratton area.

Grout Pond is surrounded by hardwood forests, with clumps of spruce, fir, and hemlock near the shore. The shoreline is bordered by a dense and diverse shrub community that hangs far enough over the water to make for convenient botanizing, and even a little berry picking, from a canoe seat. Mountain holly (*Nemopanthus mucronata*) and withe-rod (*Viburnum nudum*) are especially abundant, with arrow-wood (*V. recognitum*), highbush blueberry (*Vaccinium corymbosum*), sheep laurel (*Kalmia angustifolia*), Labrador tea (*Ledum groenlandicum*), sweet gale (*Myrica gale*), red-berried elder (*Sambucus racemosa*), and bush honeysuckle (*Diervilla lonicera*) filling the gaps. The berries produced by many of these shrubs attract flocks of cedar waxwings (*Bombycilla cedrorum*) and numerous other birds and small mammals.

On rocks and partially submerged logs near the shore, round-leaved sundew (*Drosera rotundifolia*), an insectivorous plant, grows alongside marsh St. Johnswort (*Triadenum fraseri*) and water horehound (*Lycopus americanus*). In some of the shallow bays, there is a variety of floating and emergent plants, including pipewort (*Eriocaulon septangulare*), swamp horsetail (*Equisetum fluviatile*), water arum (*Calla*

Fish Consumption Advisories

In response to high levels of mercury found in sample fish, the Vermont Department of Health has joined several other northeastern states in advising people not to eat fish taken from some lakes, and to limit consumption of some species statewide. The state recommends that no one should eat any fish except brown bullhead (*Ictalurus nebulosus*) taken from the Deerfield Chain Lakes, including Grout Pond and Somerset, Harriman, Sherman, and Searsburg reservoirs. In other lakes, limits are set by species, with separate limits for pregnant women and children. High risk species are walleye (*Stizostedion vitreum*), chain pickerel (*Esox niger*), and lake trout (*Salvelinus namaycush*).

The limits are based on standards set by the Environmental Protection Agency, which some people charge is overly cautious. Contaminant concentrations in the water are extremely low, and pose no risk to swimmers, but mercury and other contaminants accumulate in animal tissues and are passed from prey to predator. As a result they are biomagnified, with many times higher concentrations found in animals higher up in the food chain–in some cases, concentrations high enough to cause problems in reproductive and nervous systems.

The drainage basins of Deerfield Chain are mainly on Precambrian gneiss of the southern Green Mountains, which tends to make them more acid than many other Vermont lakes, and some of these lakes also have extensive wetlands on their shores. Both of these factors may contribute to converting mercury from its relatively harmless elemental form to methylmercury, the form that enters the food chain.

For current information on fish consumption advisories in Vermont, contact the Vermont Department of Health, 108 Cherry Street, Burlington, VT 05402. Phone (802) 863-7200.

palustris), three-way sedge (*Dulichium arundinaceum*), pondweeds (*Potamogeton* spp.), yellow water lily (*Nuphar variegatum*), and tapegrass (*Valisneria americana*).

Beaver (*Castor canadensis*) have dammed the southern outlet of the pond, creating a ghost forest of silvered conifer trunks with ample nesting cavities for tree swallows (*Tachycineta bicolor*), wood ducks (*Aix sponsa*), and other birds, and shallow water habitat for aquatic plants and insects. Although there are no breeding records, loons (*Gavia immer*), which nest on Somerset Reservoir, are frequent visitors, often flying in during the early morning hours to haunt the pond with their mournful and eerie calls.

Directions: From VT 100 in Wardsboro, go west on Kelley Stand Road (West Wardsboro-Arlington Road) 6 miles and turn left onto a gravel road that goes 1 mile to the north end of the pond. The access road is not plowed in winter, but there is a winter parking area at the turnoff on Kelley Stand Road.

Activities: Camping, canoeing, hiking, fishing, cross-country skiing.

Facilities: Picnic area, cabin (winter only), 2 lean-tos, primitive campsites, outhouses, water from hand pump.

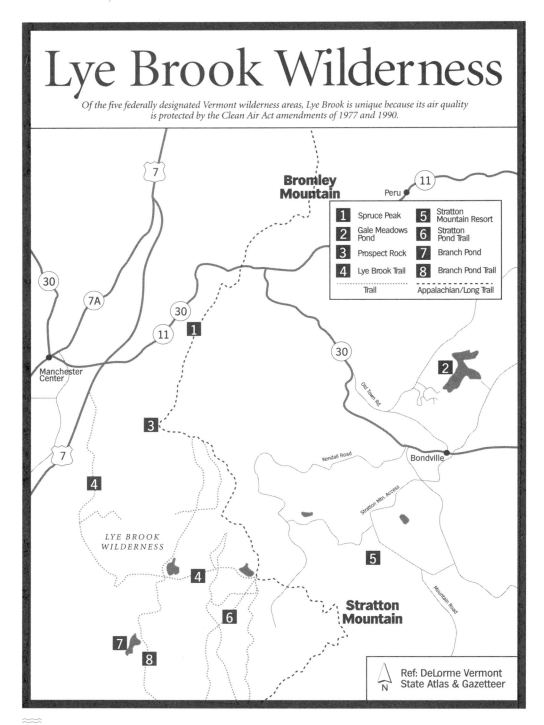

Lye Brook Wilderness

Of the five federally designated Vermont wilderness areas, Lye Brook is unique because its air quality is protected by the Clean Air Act amendments of 1977 and 1990.

Bromley Mountain

Peru

1 Spruce Peak	**5** Stratton Mountain Resort		
2 Gale Meadows Pond	**6** Stratton Pond Trail		
3 Prospect Rock	**7** Branch Pond		
4 Lye Brook Trail	**8** Branch Pond Trail		
········· Trail	— — Appalachian/Long Trail		

Manchester Center

Old Town Rd

Kendall Road

Bondville

Stratton Mtn. Access

LYE BROOK WILDERNESS

Stratton Mountain

Mountain Road

Ref: DeLorme Vermont
State Atlas & Gazetteer

N

Dates: Open year-round; Kelley Stand Road between Arlington and Grout Pond is not plowed in winter.

Fees: Voluntary fee for camping.

Closest town: West Wardsboro, 10 miles.

For more information: Green Mountain National Forest, Manchester Ranger District, 2538 Depot Street, Manchester Center, VT 05255. Phone (802) 362-2307.

GROUT POND TRAILS

[Fig. 20(1)] **Trail:** 12 miles total, loops of 1.5 to 7 miles.

Elevation: 1,700 feet, limited elevation change.

Degree of difficulty: Easy; easy to moderate cross-country skiing.

Surface and blaze: Old road and footpath. Blue diamonds.

Lye Brook Wilderness

[Fig. 21] Lye Brook Wilderness may be wild now, but it was once home to intensive human activity: Logging railroads chuffed through the 15,680 acre wilderness area and kilns were fired to turn the plentiful wood supply to charcoal and make potash. Clues to this past land use are still faintly visible as you walk the wilderness. Earthen mounds in the wilderness's northern region hide evidence of 150-year-old charcoal kilns, and the flat easy hiking along the northern third of the Lye Brook Trail follows an old railroad bed.

The forest itself gives evidence of its past, too. What's here now is the mix of trees that grew back after heavy logging in the early 1900s and a large lightning-caused fire that occurred at about the same time. When foresters look at these lands, they see a forest in transition, with red spruce (*Picea rubens*) in the understory ready to take over when the relatively short-lived paper birch and balsam fir eventually decline.

In spite of their relatively young age, the forests have matured to the extent that they are home to species that need large undisturbed woods. Bobcat (*Lynx rufus*) and black bear (*Ursus americanus*) are common here, and pine marten (*Martes americana*), extirpated in Vermont in the early 1900s, are being reintroduced. The western part of the wilderness is a good place to find wild turkey (*Meleagris gallopavo*), although the wily birds won't likely let you see them unless they want you to.

Much of Lye Brook Wilderness sits on a high plateau, as the Green Mountains go, at about 2,500 feet, on billion-year-old gneiss and quartzite that underlies much of the southern third of the Green Mountain range. The elevation and weathering properties of the rock–and the fact that amongst the gneiss and quartzite are calcium-rich inclusions—make for a thick second-growth deciduous forest of sugar maple (*Acer saccharum*), American beech (*Fagus grandifolia*), white ash (*Fraxinus americana*), black cherry (*Prunus serotina*), and birch (*Betula papyrifera* and *B. alleghaniensis*).

Lye Brook Air Quality

The federal government lists Lye Brook Wilderness as a Class I Air Quality area, which gives it special protection under the Clean Air Act. A Class I designation is intended to provide for as pristine an area as possible and to protect views; probably the most well-known Class I Air Quality area is the Grand Canyon.

While Lye Brook Wilderness doesn't have quite the views of the Grand Canyon, its keepers take the responsibility of its air quality designation seriously. Air quality near the wilderness is continuously monitored by the Vermont Forest Ecosystem Monitoring Cooperative, a unique partnership of representatives from federal and state agencies, college and university scientists, and environmental organizations.

Conducting air quality monitoring in a federal wilderness area isn't easy, however. Monitoring stations must actually be located outside the wilderness boundary because its federal designation does not allow machinery or other permanent man-made objects.

Consequently the main monitoring station for Lye Brook is actually to the west, on Little Equinox Mountain. An air sampler at about 3,000 feet collects samples that are analyzed for particulates, such as sulfur, nitrogen, carbon, zinc, lead, and mercury. Another machine, called a nephelometer, is used in summer to measure concentrations of pollutants that affect visibility.

The information from the monitoring site has been used by the State of Vermont to make a case to the federal Environmental Protection Agency for stronger regulations, so that Lye Brook is in compliance with the Clean Air Act. And when a power company wanted to build a coal-fired power plant in Halfmoon, New York, directly upwind of Lye Brook ,Vermont officials used the Lye Brook information to demonstrate the power plant would severely affect the wilderness area. The permit for the power plant was subsequently denied.

In 1903 a fire razed the forests in what is now the southwestern part of Lye Brook Wilderness and left one of the most intriguing (and inaccessible) habitats in all of the Green Mountain National Forest.

Known as The Burning, this area lies on a plateau, and almost imperceptible changes in elevation make a difference in the moisture available for plant growth, and thus the plant communities found here.

Those areas that are slightly higher and drier than their surroundings host a heath barren covered by a thick blanket of shrubs, including lowbush blueberry (*Vaccinium angustifolium*), sheep laurel (*Kalmia angustifolia*), rosebud azalea (*Rhododendron prinophyllum*), and wintergreen (*Gaultheria procumbens*). Red spruce (*Picea rubens*) saplings, mountain holly (*Nemopanthus mucronata*), and withe-rod (*Viburnum nudum*) are scattered throughout this shrub thicket.

Areas that are slightly lower than their surroundings are wetter, and depending upon topographical gradients and the amount of drainage, host bog or poor fen communities. Bogs form where drainage is limited, and are characterized by a thick mat of peat moss (*Sphagnum* spp.) with leatherleaf (*Chamaedaphne calyculata*) as the dominant shrub, along with bog laurel (*Kalmia polifolia*), a sedge (*Carex trisperma*), cottongrass (*Eriophorum spissum*), and scattered black spruce (*Picea mariana*). At least one bog that is 5 acres in size has been identified in the southwestern part of The Burning.

In areas where seeps or small streams can bring nutrients to poorly and moderately drained areas, fens form. Gray birch (*Betula populifolia*), sheep laurel (*Kalmia angustifolia*), and red spruce saplings (*Picea rubens*) are spread throughout areas where the dominant plant is commonly a sedge (*Carex paupercula*) or in some areas, a quaking mat of peat moss (*Sphagnum* spp.). Velvet-leaf blueberry (*Vaccinium myrtilloides*), Labrador tea (*Ledum groenlandicum*), and cinnamon fern (*Osmunda cinnamomea*) also abound.

Roughly 20 percent of the wilderness is coniferous forest, interspersed with lush meadows created by the area's large beaver (*Castor canadensis*) population. Look for star-nose moles (*Condylura cristata*) in wet areas where they may cross trails.

In the areas dominated by conifers, balsam fir (*Abies balsamea*), red spruce (*Picea rubens*), and large-diameter yellow birch (*Betula alleghaniesis*) line the trails, with an understory of hobblebush (*Viburnum alnifolium*), red trillium (*Trillium erectum*), goldthread (*Coptis trifolia*), and an occasional Indian cucumber (*Medeola virginiana*).

Although much of the wilderness area is on a raised plateau, deep ravines cut into the northern and western fringes of the plateau. The most spectacular, and inaccessible, is Downer Glen, colonized by a rich mixed forest of red spruce, Eastern hemlock (*Tsuga canadensis*), sugar maple (*Acer saccharum*), basswood (*Tilia americana*), and white ash (*Fraxinus americana*). Ferns and forest plants blanket the forest floor, with silvery spleenwort (*Athyrium thelypteroides*), lady fern (*A. filix-femina*), wood nettle (*Laportea canadensis*), and blue cohosh (*Caulophyllum thalictroides*), among others. Botanists have also found Goldie's fern (*Dryopteris goldiana*), which is a state rare plant. Some of the older trees in Downer Glen have diameters greater than 36 inches, giants indeed in a high-elevation Vermont site, with its cooler temperatures and poor growing conditions.

While Vermont has five federally designated wilderness areas, Lye Brook is unique because its air quality is also protected by the Clean Air Act amendments of 1977 and 1990. Protecting the air quality in Lye Brook has been a challenge for state and federal officials because Vermont is downwind of the Midwest and its coal-burning power plants, which cause acid rain. The first mile of Lye Brook is the first and only area in Vermont believed to have been made so acidic by acid rain that fish no longer can live there.

Directions: There are five access areas around the perimeter of the wilderness, two from the north and three from the south. Access from the Manchester area is from spur roads off the East Manchester Road and VT 11/30. From the south, the wilderness is accessible from the Arlington-West Wardsboro Road from individual trailheads.

Activities: Hiking, cross-country skiing, snowshoeing, bushwhacking, fishing.

Facilities: Hiking trails, 2 primitive shelters.

Dates: Open year-round.

Fees: None.

Closest town: Manchester Center, 2 miles.

For more information: Green Mountain National Forest, Manchester Ranger District, 2538 Depot Street, Manchester Center, VT 05255-9733. Phone (802) 362-2307. Green Mountain Club, 4711 Waterbury-Stowe Road, Waterbury Center, VT 05677. Phone (802) 244-7037.

LYE BROOK TRAIL

[Fig. 21(4)] One of the most popular trails in the wilderness area, the first few miles of the Lye Brook Trail's northern section follow an old logging railroad bed and consequently are fairly flat. Add to that the fact that Lye Brook Falls, one of the highest waterfalls in Vermont, is only 2.3 miles from the trailhead, and it's easy to see why hikers come here in great numbers.

At its southern extension, the 9.7-mile trail links to Bourn Pond, another popular destination, in part because the pond is stocked by the state. The trail then passes scenic Stratton Pond (another heavily used area) and ends at a link to the Long/Appalachian Trail.

Directions: From Manchester Center at the junction of VT 7A and VT 11/30, go east 1.9 miles on VT 11/30 and turn right on East Manchester Road. Continue 1.2 miles and turn left on Glen Road. Bear left at the next fork and look for trailhead parking.

Trail: 9.7 miles one-way.

Elevation: 1,000 feet to 2,600 feet.

Degree of difficulty: Moderate.

Surface and blaze: Wide footpath, narrowing and in some places difficult to find as it gets farther from the road. Blue blazes.

For more information: Green Mountain National Forest, Manchester Ranger District, 2538 Depot Street, Manchester Center, VT 05255-9733. Phone (802) 362-2307. Green Mountain Club, 4711 Waterbury-Stowe Road, Waterbury Center, VT 05677. Phone (802) 244-7037.

BRANCH POND TRAIL

[Fig. 21(8)] In spite of its name, the Branch Pond Trail actually leads to Bourn Pond and Little Mud Pond, passing Branch Pond along the way. The trail traverses the eastern edge of the Lye Brook Wilderness on its way north to a junction with the

Long/Appalachian Trail, traveling through extensive areas of fine, but buggy, beaver meadows. Hikers should prepare for the possibility of wet feet and for difficult river and brook crossing after heavy rains or snowmelt.

Bourn Pond is a popular destination, in part because there is both a tenting area and a shelter on the pond. But it also draws hikers because of its beautiful remote feel and the boggy vegetation that fills some of its bays. Much like Branch Pond to the south, these mats are dominated by leatherleaf (*Chamaedaphne calyculata*), with occasional speckled alder (*Alnus incana*), meadowsweet (*Spirea alba*), marsh cinquefoil (*Potentilla palustris*), northern pitcher plant (*Sarracenia purpurea*), and round-leaved sundew (*Drosera rotundifolia*).

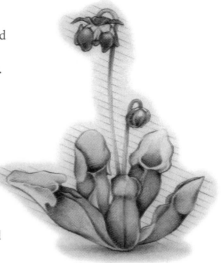

PITCHER PLANT
(Sarracenia sp.)

Directions: From the south, take the Arlington-West Wardsboro Road (known locally as the Kelly Stand Road) approximately 7.5 miles east from Arlington, or approximately 11 miles west from West Wardsboro to the trailhead and parking on the north side of the road. Parking is also available at the end of Forest Road 70, which is approximately 2 miles west of the Branch Pond Trailhead. Take Forest Road 70 about 2.4 miles to the end of the road and a spur trail to the Branch Pond Trail and canoe portage to Branch Pond.

Trail: 8.3 miles one-way.

Elevation: 2,279 feet to 2,980 feet.

Degree of difficulty: Strenuous.

Surface and blaze: Rocky footpath, wet in places. Blue blazes.

For more information: Green Mountain National Forest, Manchester Ranger District, 2538 Depot Street, Manchester Center, VT 05255-9733. Phone (802) 362-2307. Green Mountain Club, 4711 Waterbury-Stowe Road, Waterbury Center, VT 05677. Phone (802) 244-7037.

▒ BRANCH POND

[Fig. 21(7)] This tiny pond, not quite 40 acres, offers probably one of the easiest opportunities in Vermont to explore a fen. Much of the periphery, and many of the pond's small bays are filled with the kinds of plants commonly associated with a fen. Fens are similar to bogs and share some of the same plant and animal species, but fens are generally more nutrient-rich, because fens have a spring or stream that brings in water, whereas bogs have only one water source—rainfall.

Just a two-minute paddle from the Branch Pond put-in on its southeastern end

The yellow lady's slipper (Cypripedium calceolus) depends on insects for pollination.

brings canoeists to a floating mat of sphagnum moss laced with bog buckbean (*Menyanthes trifoliata*), northern pitcher plant (*Sarracenia purpurea*), leatherleaf (*Chamaedaphne calyculata*), and blue flag (*Iris versicolor*). Dwarf, twisted tamarack (*Larix laricina*) and black spruce (*Picea mariana*) poke up through the sphagnum here and there.

Elsewhere around the perimeter look for steeplebush (*Spirea alba*), northern arrow-wood (*Viburnum recognitum*), and swamp winterberry (*llex verticillata*). In one of the northernmost bays, bladderwort (*Utricularia cornuta*) can be found in great clumps, making for a stunning sight when they produce their pea-like yellow flower in the spring. Beaver (*Castor canadensis*) have been busy at work in the area, with several beaver lodges attesting to their success.

Branch Pond is fabulous habitat for cedar waxwings (*Bombycilla cedrorum*), which travel in flocks to places such as this to feed on berries and socialize. Their distinctive keening whistle can be heard long before they are seen. Diving ducks, such as hooded mergansers (*Lophodytes cucullatus*) also use the pond.

Eastern chipmunks (*Tamais striatus*) and red squirrels (*Tamiasciurus hudsonicus*) are plentiful in the mostly coniferous forest surrounding the pond, and it's a good bet that moose (*Alces alces*) come here in the spring and fall to browse on the wetland plants. Wetland-loving mammals, such as mink (*Mustela vison*) and river otter (*Lutra canadensis*) can also be found here.

Though the pond is an easy day trip from the Manchester area, there are several well-used campsites on the pond's perimeter for canoeists who want to use Branch Pond as a base for exploring the Lye Brook Wilderness.

Directions: Take the Arlington-West Wardsboro Road (known locally as the Kelley Stand Road) approximately 6.9 miles east from East Arlington, or approximately 10 miles west from West Wardsboro to Forest Road 70. Take Forest Road 70 roughly 2.4 miles to the end of the road. The canoe portage to Branch Pond is on the west side of the road.

Trail: 0.3-mile portage one-way.

Elevation: Minimal change.

Degree of difficulty: Easy.

Surface and blaze: Rocky footpath. Blue blazes.

For more information: Green Mountain National Forest, Manchester Ranger District, 2538 Depot Street, Manchester Center, VT 05255-9733. Phone (802) 362-2307

PROSPECT ROCK

[Fig. 21(3)] An old jeep road, now used as a hiking trail, gives access to Prospect Rock on the northern fringe of the Lye Brook Wilderness. While Prospect Rock is no giant—it's only 2,079 feet high—its location makes for spectacular views of Manchester Valley, Mount Equinox, and Downer Glen.

The trail passes through rich northern hardwood forests of birch, beech, maple, and red oak (*Quercus rubra*), making for an especially fine hike on a fall day, when the yellow, red, scarlet, and brown of the different species turn the woods into an impressionist painting.

Directions: From Manchester Center at the junction of VT 7A and VT 11/30, go east on VT 11/30 (Depot Street) for approximately 1.5 miles to East Manchester Road. Go right on East Manchester Road and take an immediate left onto Rootville Road. Go 0.5 mile to limited parking, making sure not to block private driveways and the unmaintained remainder of Rootville Road (which is the footpath to Prospect Rock).

Trail: 1.5 miles one-way.

Elevation: 1,060 feet to 2,079 feet.

Degree of difficulty: Strenuous.

Surface and blaze: Abandoned roadway, rocky and washed out in places. No blazes.

For more information: Green Mountain National Forest, Manchester Ranger District, 2538 Depot Street, Manchester Center, VT 05255-9733. Phone (802) 362-2307. Green Mountain Club, 4711 Waterbury-Stowe Road, Waterbury Center, VT 05677. Phone (802) 244-7037.

SPRUCE PEAK

[Fig. 21(1)] Not far from Manchester, a short hike to the summit of Spruce Peak offers good views of the Manchester valley and the Taconic range to the west. It travels through a lovely hardwood forest where hikers should look for turkey (*Meleagris gallopavo*), ruffed grouse (*Bonasa umbellus*), and red fox (*Vulpes fulva*). Moose (*Alces alces*) frequent the area; look at shoulder height for bark scraped off of mountain ash (*Sorbus americana*). During the winter, moose browse on the bark, but because they only have lower incisors, they scrape the bark off with strong, upward motions.

Just 0.4 mile south of the Spruce Peak summit is Spruce Peak Shelter, with space for 16. It was built by the Brattleboro section of the Green Mountain Club in cooperation with the U.S. Forest Service. There is no charge to stay at the shelter, and there is a reliable water supply nearby.

Directions: From Manchester Center at the junction of US 7A and VT 11/30, take VT 11/30 east approximately 5.8 miles. Parking is on the north side of the road across from the trailhead and is marked by a Forest Service sign.

Trail: 2.2 miles one-way.

Elevation: 1,870 feet to 2,028 feet.
Degree of difficulty: Easy to moderate.
Surface and blaze: Rocky footpath. Blue blazes.
For more information: Green Mountain National Forest, Manchester Ranger District, 2538 Depot Street, Manchester Center, VT 05255-9733. Phone (802) 362-2307. Green Mountain Club, 4711 Waterbury-Stowe Road, Waterbury Center, VT 05677. Phone (802) 244-7037.

Stratton Mountain

[Fig. 21] On a rainy summer day in 1909, Vermont schoolteacher James P. Taylor sat on the side of Stratton Mountain, frustrated that there was no trail to the summit. Taylor had hiked in Germany, through the Black Forest, and he knew what pleasure could be had traveling for days on end through the woods.

That frustration, legend has it, is what spurred Taylor to found the Green Mountain Club in 1910. The group spent the next two decades building the Long Trail, Vermont's end-to-end hiking trail.

Stratton's claim to fame extends to an even longer hiking trail. Benton MacKaye, a forester and planner who in 1921 was the first to call for the Appalachian Trail, the 2,025-mile hiking trail that stretches from Maine to Georgia, credited Stratton Mountain with his epiphany.

MacKaye often told the story of climbing to the top of a tree to get a better view of Stratton's summit. "I felt as if atop the world, with a sort of 'planetary feeling,'" he later wrote. "Would a footpath someday reach far southern peaks from where I was then perched."

In 1937, trail workers cut the last swath for MacKaye's dream—the Appalachian Trail.

MINK
(Mustela vison)
Like other members of the weasel family, which includes the skunk, the mink emits a pungent odor when provoked.

Stratton's magic extends to this day. Numerous hiking trails climb to its cone-shaped peak, and the north side of the mountain sports a downhill ski area. High-elevation Stratton Pond and its shelters attract more overnight visitors than perhaps any other spot on the Long/Appalachian Trail, save for Mount Mansfield, Vermont's highest peak.

Hikers come for the panoramic views from a historic fire tower on the summit. The tower was first built in 1914 (it's been revamped several times since) and has been nominated to the National Register of Historic Places. From the tower, Mount Snow, Somerset Reservoir, Glastenbury Mountain, and Mount Equinox are visible nearby; on good days it's possible to see Mount Ascutney and Mount Monadnock in New Hampshire far to the west.

Directions: From the north, take VT 30 to Bondville. At the center of town, turn south on Stratton Mountain Road and go 11 miles, past the Stratton maintenance area, and take the first right after that, marked by a sign that says "to Route 100." Go 4 miles to the first stop sign and turn right. Go 3 miles to the end of this road, which is in the town of Stratton. Look for the town hall on the right. Turn right on the Kelley Stand Road, also known as the Arlington-West Wardsboro Road. Go 6.3 miles on Kelley Stand Road to the AT/LT trailhead and parking. From the south, take the Arlington-West Wardsboro Road (also known as the Kelley Stand Road) approximately 11 miles east from East Arlington, or approximately 8 miles west from West Wardsboro to the AT/LT trailhead. The trailhead to Stratton Pond is 1.1 miles west of the AT/LT trailhead on Kelley Stand Road.

Activities: Hiking, mountain biking, cross-country skiing, snowshoeing, fishing.

Facilities: 3 shelters, hiking trails.

Fees: None.

Dates: Open year-round.

For more information: Green Mountain National Forest, Manchester Ranger District, 2538 Depot Street, Manchester Center, VT 05255-9733. Phone (802) 362-2307. Green Mountain Club, 4711 Waterbury-Stowe Road, Waterbury Center, VT 05677. Phone (802) 244-7037.

STRATTON MOUNTAIN RESORT

[Fig. 21(5)] People have been skiing Stratton Mountain for 35 years, but things have changed radically in that time. Like many Vermont ski areas, Stratton has expanded its operation to provide year-round activities, from golf to horseback riding to tennis and year-round music and food festivals. But the centerpiece of the area is skiing and snowboarding. Ninety trails, 12 lifts, 2 halfpipes in a snowboard park, and a new gladed skiing area with nearly complete snowmaking coverage guarantees good skiing.

Stratton also has the distinction of being the ski area where Jake Burton Carpenter, one of the early pioneers of snowboarding, first worked in the 1980s. Carpenter went on to found Burton Snowboards, the largest snowboard manufacturer in the country. While working as a bartender at Stratton, Carpenter came up with his snowboard design based

A male spruce grouse claps its wings during short flights as part of its courtship display.

on a child's ski toy called a snurfer.

Directions: From I-91, take Exit 2 to VT 30 north. Go 38 miles to Bondville. From Bondville center, just next to the post office, turn left, or south, onto Stratton Mountain Road. The resort is 4 miles south on the Stratton Mountain Road.

Activities: Skiing, snowboarding, snowshoeing, cross-country skiing, hiking, mountain biking, golf, tennis, horseback riding, music and food festivals.

Facilities: Base lodge, rental properties, hotel, shops, ski and snowboarding school, snowmaking equipment, golf course, tennis courts, childcare center.

Fees: There is a charge for use of the facilities and ski trails.

Dates: Open year-round.

For more information: Stratton Mountain Resort, RR1, Box 145, Stratton Mountain, VT 05155-9406. Phone (800) 787-2886.

⛰ STRATTON MOUNTAIN VIA THE LONG/APPALACHIAN TRAIL.

[Fig. 21] One of the more popular day hikes in the southern Green Mountains, the Long/Appalachian Trail makes a steady climb through maple-beech-birch forest and then climbs through a thick spruce-fir forest near Stratton's summit cone, where the globally rare Bicknell's thrush (*Catharus bicknelli*) nests. Bird biologists believe Stratton is near the southern limit of the thrush's habitat. The habitat, more typical of northeastern Vermont, is also welcoming to bay-breasted warblers (*Dendroica castanea*), which are rare in this part of the state. Stratton is a prime spot for black-backed woodpeckers (*Picoides arcticus*) and boreal chickadees (*Parus hudsonicus*).

The mountain's lower-elevation northern hardwood forests are home to one of the state's larger populations of black bear (*Ursus americanus*), though the animals are reclusive and difficult to see. The population here has been studied more than any other black bear population in Vermont, as part of an agreement with Stratton Mountain Corporation. A complicated deal was worked out in the late 1980s requiring the ski company to study the bears and determine their habitat requirements before expanding the trail network and facilities.

Directions: From the north, take VT 30 to Bondville. At the center of town, turn south on Stratton Mountain Road and go 11 miles, past the Stratton maintenance area, and take the first right after that, marked by a sign that says "to Route 100." Go 4 miles to the first stop sign and turn right. Go 3 miles to the end of this road, which is in the town of Stratton. Look for the town hall on the right. Turn right on the Kelley Stand Road, also known as the Arlington-West Wardsboro Road. Go 6.3 miles on Kelley Stand Road to the AT/LT trailhead and parking. From the south, take the Arlington-West Wardsboro Road (also known as the Kelley Stand Road) approximately 11 miles east from East Arlington, or approximately 8 miles west from West Wardsboro to the AT/LT trailhead.

COMMON LOON
(Gavia immer)
The loon can swim long distances underwater or with its eyes and bill under the surface before diving below.

Trail: 3.8 miles one-way.

Elevation: 2,230 feet to 3,936 feet..

Degree of difficulty: Strenuous.

Surface and blaze: Rocky footpath. White blazes.

For more information: Green Mountain National Forest, Manchester Ranger District, 2538 Depot Street, Manchester Center, VT 05255-9733. Phone (802) 362-2307. Green Mountain Club, 4711 Waterbury-Stowe Road, Waterbury Center, VT 05677. Phone (802) 244-7037.

STRATTON POND TRAIL

[Fig. 21(6)] Great fishing, easy hiking, and lovely views make Stratton Pond the most heavily used location on the 100-mile section of Appalachian Trail that runs through Vermont. A 1.4-mile loop trail circles Stratton Pond, with good views from Stratton View Shelter, on the west side of the pond.

Virtually all of the forests the trail traverses have been logged. Look for stumps amongst the second-growth forests of American beech (*Fagus grandifolia*), birch (*Betula alleghaniesis* and *B. papyrifera*), and maple (*Acer saccharum*). There are softwood stands mixed among the hardwoods, especially around the numerous wet areas on the trail. Biologically, the wet areas are the most fascinating. It's possible to find fresh droppings of mink (*Mustela vison*), which hunt and fish in the wet spots along the trail. Look for their 1.5- to 2-inch-long scats on raised areas like stumps, logs, or rocks. The scat looks braided and is slender, about 0.25 inch in diameter. Listen for rusty blackbirds (*Euphagus carolinus*) and Lincoln's sparrows (*Melospiza lincolnii*) near wet areas and the pond.

Directions: Take the Arlington-West Wardsboro Road (also known as the Kelley Stand Road) approximately 10 miles east from East Arlington, or approximately 9.1 miles west from West Wardsboro to the Stratton Pond trailhead. Parking is on the same side of the road as the trailhead.

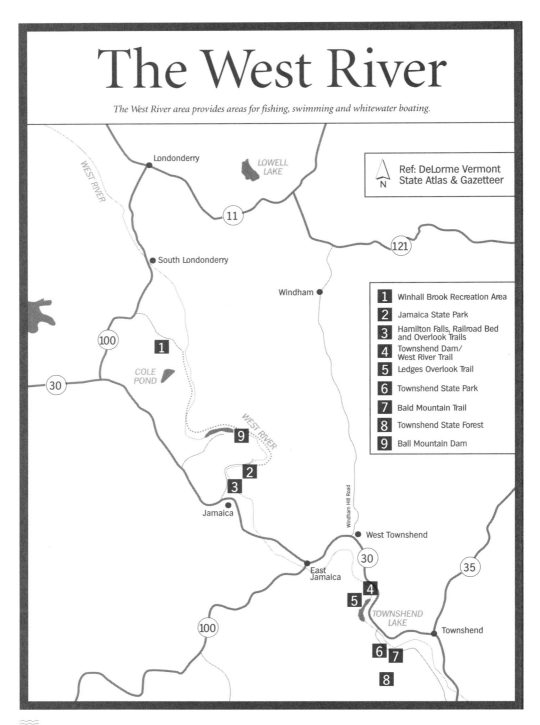

The West River

The West River area provides areas for fishing, swimming and whitewater boating.

Londonderry

LOWELL LAKE

WEST RIVER

11

121

N
Ref: DeLorme Vermont
State Atlas & Gazetteer

South Londonderry

Windham

100

1

COLE POND

30

WEST RIVER

9

2

3

Jamaica

Windham Hill Road

West Townshend

30

35

East Jamaica

100

4

5

TOWNSHEND LAKE

Townshend

6 7

8

1	Winhall Brook Recreation Area
2	Jamaica State Park
3	Hamilton Falls, Railroad Bed and Overlook Trails
4	Townshend Dam/ West River Trail
5	Ledges Overlook Trail
6	Townshend State Park
7	Bald Mountain Trail
8	Townshend State Forest
9	Ball Mountain Dam

Trail: 3.9 miles one-way; loop trail around the pond another 1.1 miles.
Elevation: 2,400 feet to 2,600 feet.
Degree of difficulty: Easy to moderate.
Surface and blaze: Rocky footpath, wet in places. Blue blazes.
For more information: Green Mountain National Forest, Manchester Ranger District, 2538 Depot Street, Manchester Center, VT 05255-9733. Phone (802) 362-2307. Green Mountain Club, 4711 Waterbury-Stowe Road, Waterbury Center, VT 05677. Phone (802) 244-7037.

The West River

[Fig. 22] The West River drains over 423 square miles of the eastern Green Mountains and Vermont piedmont, a large area for its relatively brief (46-mile) length, making this a short but powerful river. The West River Railroad, built in 1892, connected the towns and farms along the river to Brattleboro and the world, but never turned much of a profit before its demise in the 1927 flood. Consequently the Army Corps of Engineers has tamed the river with two flood control dams. Spring and fall releases from the Ball Mountain Dam by Jamaica State Park provide for excellent Class III and IV whitewater paddling and national caliber races. It was once an important spawning stream for Atlantic salmon (*Salmo salar*) and is now part of the Connecticut River salmon restoration project.

▒ THE WEST RIVER TRAIL

[Fig. 22(4)] The Windham Regional Commission is developing a 16-mile trail along the West River, using some of the "36 miles of trouble" that locals once called the West River Railroad, as well as sections of old roadbed and new footpath where dams have put the railroad bed under water. At present, the trail runs from Townshend Dam to West Townshend, takes a break, then runs from Jamaica State Park, over Ball Mountain Dam, through Winhall Brook Campground, and north into South Londonderry, comprising several of the trails described for these areas in the sections below. It traverses undisturbed rich hardwood forests along the river and sections where irregular flooding by the dams has created open parklike areas. In future years the commission hopes the trail will offer a continuous route that is rich with the human and natural history of the area.

Trail: Planned 16 miles one-way; currently a 1.2-mile section from Townshend Dam to West Townshend and a 9-mile section from Jamaica State Park to South Londonderry are open.
Elevation: About 500 to 1,000 feet.
Degree of difficulty: Moderate.

Surface and blaze: Old railroad and roadbed, footpath. Intermittently marked with green on lavender West River Trail train logo.

For more information: U.S. Army Corps of Engineers, Townshend Lake Office, Route 30, Box 2800, Townshend, VT 05353. Phone (802) 365-7703.

TOWNSHEND STATE FOREST AND PARK

[Fig. 22(8)] Bald Mountain in Townshend State Forest overlooks the deep valley of the West River in the foothills just east of the higher summits of the southern Green Mountain plateau. It occurs in an area where four major rock formations that span 25 miles in the northern Green Mountains are compressed into a narrow band about 2 miles wide. All four formations are predominantly schists and phyllites and difficult to distinguish in the field, but each has a unique geologic history that can be traced to a particular kind of submarine sedimentary deposit. The forests on the mountain are dominated by hemlock and northern hardwoods growing in acid till soils derived mainly from rocks of the gneiss plateau to the northwest.

Townshend State Park [Fig. 22(6)], at the southern edge of the state forest along the West River, provides a campground and picnic area. The road to the state park passes the 130-year old Scott Covered Bridge, at 276 feet the longest in the state, now closed to vehicles but open to pedestrians.

Directions: From the junction of VT 30 and VT 35 in Townshend, go 2 miles north on VT 30, turn left and cross a bridge over the spillway of the Townshend Dam. Turn left at a T intersection and go downstream past the Scott Covered Bridge. Continue downstream to the state park entrance, 1.4 miles from VT 30.

Activities: Camping, hiking, picnicking, fishing.

Facilities: 30 campsites, 4 lean-tos, picnic area and shelter, restrooms, hiking trails, swimming and boating nearby.

Dates: Early May to mid-Oct.

Fees: There is a charge for camping and day use

Closest town: Townshend, 3.4 miles.

For more information: Townshend State Park, Rt. 1, Box 2650, Townshend, VT 05353. Phone (802) 365-7500 (summer). Vermont Department of Forests, Parks, and Recreation, RR 1 Box 33, North Springfield, VT 05150-9726. Phone (802) 885-8855 (winter).

BALD MOUNTAIN TRAIL

[Fig. 22(7)] The loop trail on Bald Mountain makes a nice half-day hike, with summit views of Stratton and Bromley mountains in Vermont and Mount Monadnock in New Hampshire. If the loop is done clockwise, the descent is steeper than the ascent. On the ascending leg, the trail travels along a stream with a series of small cascades and pools, and passes through an alder (*Alnus incana*) swamp about 0.25 mile below the summit.

Trail: 3.5-mile loop.

Elevation: 600 to 1,680 feet.
Degree of difficulty: Moderate.
Surface and blaze: Old road and rocky footpath, blue blazes.

TOWNSHEND LAKE

[Fig. 22] Just up the river from Townshend State Park, the U.S. Army Corps of Engineers has built a flood control dam that holds back enough water to make for fine swimming, boating, and fishing for both warm- and cold-water fish. As part of an Atlantic salmon (*Salmo salar*) restoration project, migrating salmon are trapped below the dam, trucked around, and released in the river above the lake. A 10 horse-power limit on boat motors helps keep the lake quiet. A recreation area on the west shore has a picnic area, a wide beach, and a short trail. In rare extreme flood events, as occurred in 1987, the dam is used to store up to 11 billion gallons of water, enough to raise the lake level 75 feet and put the entire recreation area under water.

Directions: From the junction of VT 30 and VT 35 in Townshend, go 2 miles north on VT 30, turn left across a bridge over the spillway of the dam, then continue across the dam and turn right on the recreation area access road.

Activities: Swimming, boating, fishing, hiking.

Facilities: Picnic area, picnic shelters, restrooms, beach, boat ramp.

Dates: Mid-May through mid-Sept.

Fees: None.

Closest town: Townshend, about 2.5 miles.

For more information: U.S. Army Corps of Engineers, Townshend Lake Office, Route 30, Box 2800, Townshend, VT 05353. Phone (802) 365-7703.

LEDGES OVERLOOK TRAIL

[Fig. 22(5)] From the Townshend Lake access road, this trail ascends to a ledge overlooking the lake and West River valley, then continues through a hop hornbeam (*Ostrya virginiana*) glade before descending back to the road.

Trail: 1.7-mile loop.

Elevation: 500 to 750 feet.

Degree of difficulty: Moderate.

Surface and blaze: Old road, footpath, and ledge.

JAMAICA STATE PARK

[Fig. 22(2)] In Jamaica State Park, the West River makes a wild, 2.5-mile reverse S-bend in a deep, steep-walled valley. When the river is up, this reach provides some of the best Class III to IV paddling in the state, with more Class II to III water below the state park. During scheduled releases from the Ball Mountain Dam on the last weekends of April and September, it is the site of national-level canoe and kayak races, and the river can be run in medium to high water at other times of year. The state park provides a boat shuttle on release weekends, otherwise it's a long carry

CEDAR WAXWING
(Bombycilla cedrorum)

over Ball Mountain Dam or up the old railroad bed along the river.

The state park campground is near Salmon Hole, a great swimming hole with a small beach. It was the site of an ambush and massacre of a British detachment during the French and Indian War. Brook and brown trout (*Salvelinus fontinalis* and *Salmo trutta*) lurk in this and other pools along the river. Although Atlantic salmon (*Salmo salar*) are being restored to the West River, it is now illegal to take any anadromous (sea-run) salmon in Vermont.

Directions: From the junction of VT 100 and VT 30 in East Jamaica, take VT 100/30 north approximately 3.5 miles to Jamaica and turn right; there is a sign for the park at the turnoff.

Activities: Camping, picnicking, hiking, swimming, fishing, whitewater canoeing and kayaking.

Facilities: 61 campsites, 18 lean-tos, picnic area, picnic shelter, playground, restrooms, hiking trails.

Dates: Early May to mid-Oct.

Fees: There is a charge for camping and day use.

Closest town: Jamaica, 1 mile.

For more information: Jamaica State Park, Box 45, Jamaica, VT 05343. Phone (802) 874-4600 (summer). Vermont Department of Forests, Parks, and Recreation, RR 1 Box 33, North Springfield, VT 05150-9726. Phone (802) 885-8855 (winter).

RAILROAD BED TRAIL

[Fig. 22(3)] The walk up the old railroad bed provides access to the West River for swimming, fishing, and whitewater boating in season. A series of interpretive signs along the trail offer insight into the natural and social history of the river and surrounding forests. About 0.5 mile up from the campground the trail passes the Dumplings, a group of big, water-smoothed boulders on the north side of the river that make for one of the most challenging rapids on the river. This trail doubles as a section of the West River Trail.

The trail ends at the impressive Ball Mountain Dam, a 265-foot-high earth fill dam built mainly from schist blasted out of the hillside on the south side of the river. The West River Trail continues up the face of the dam, across the top, and along the south-west side of the river to Winhall Brook Campground and South Londonderry. The dam is also accessible by a road that leaves VT 100 about 2 miles north of Jamaica.

After a walk along the wild river, the sight of the dam, its 250-foot-tall concrete control structure, the blasted rock face, and the irregularly flooded area behind it is at once disturbing and fascinating. As a flood control structure, most of the time the dam holds back only 40 feet or so of water, so the lake behind the dam is disproportionately small. The shoreline is a kind of ecological disaster zone, because even the hardiest riparian communities are not well-adapted to deep and irregular flooding on rocky slopes. A 1987 flood filled the lake until it was more than 200 feet deep and 6 miles long, extending almost to South Londonderry, and water flowed over the spillway of the dam for the first time since the dam was completed in 1961. The high water mark of this event can still be seen as a line of debris on the upstream face of the dam and a horizontal dent in the forests on the steep slopes above the reservoir. The same event scoured and re-shaped the river channel below the dam, perhaps causing the big landslides on the south wall of the valley just below the dam.

BLACK FLY
(Simulium spp.)
Found near running water, these biting flies are the curse of human visitors to the mountains and forests.

Trail: 3 miles one-way.
Elevation: Around 800 feet.
Degree of difficulty: Easy.
Surface and blaze: Old railroad bed. No blazes.

HAMILTON FALLS TRAIL

[Fig. 22(3)] Hamilton Falls is a steep, dramatic cascade cut into the hard schist that lines Cobb Brook. At 125 feet, it is one of the state's highest waterfalls, and the rock around it is sculpted into potholes and two long chutes. The sunny pools at the base of the falls provide fine and reasonably safe swimming. There is another tempting pool in a pothole at the top of the 50-foot-high main cascade, but swimming here and climbing on the slippery rocks along the cascade can be dangerous. Several people have died here over the years.

The Hamilton Falls Trail follows a steep old road, used to carry goods between West Windham and the railway, along the steep slopes above Cobb Brook. The brook dances and falls from pool to pool in a shady ravine below the trail, inviting exploration on a hot day. A short trail bears left off the main trail to the base of the falls. The easiest way to the top is to stay on the road until it intersects West Windham Road by a sawmill, then turn left towards the brook and left again on a road trace to the top of the falls, where a state natural area sign offers both welcome and warning.

Trail: 1 mile one-way from the Railroad Bed Trail; 3.5 miles from the parking area.
Elevation: 800 to 1,600 feet.
Degree of difficulty: Moderate.
Surface and blaze: Rocky road bed, blue blazes.

OVERLOOK TRAIL

[Fig. 22(3)] The Overlook Trail provides an alternate route on the hike to or from Ball Mountain Dam or Hamilton Falls. It climbs to a series of overlooks on Little Ball Mountain, with views of the West River and the surrounding hills.

Directions: The trail begins in the southern loop of the campground, near Hackberry lean-to, and joins the Railroad Bed Trail about 0.6 mile from the parking and picnic area.

Trail: 2 miles one-way.

Elevation: 800 to 1,300 feet.

Degree of difficulty: Moderate.

Surface and blaze: Old road and rocky footpath, blue blazes.

WINHALL BROOK RECREATION AREA

[Fig. 22(1)] Along both shores of Winhall Brook near its confluence with the West River, the U.S. Army Corps of Engineers operates an extensive campground and recreation area with plenty of open ground and fishing and swimming access to both the brook and the river. There is a short hiking trail in the woods near the campground. Like the Townshend Lake Recreation Area downstream, this one will go under water during extreme floods.

Directions: From the junction of VT 11 west and VT 100 in Londonderry, go south on VT 100, through South Londonderry, about 4 miles and turn left on Winhall Station Road. The entrance to the recreation area is about 1 mile in.

Activities: Camping, swimming, fishing, picnicking.

Facilities: 111 campsites, limited hookups, lean-tos, picnic area, restrooms.

Dates: Late May through early Sept.

Fees: There is a charge for camping.

Closest town: Londonderry, 5 miles

For more information: U.S. Army Corps of Engineers, Ball Mountain Lake Office, 25 Ball Mt. Lane, Jamaica, VT 05343. Phone (802) 874-4881.

GALE MEADOWS POND

[Fig. 21(2)] Halfway between Stratton and Bromley mountains, with views of both, Gale Meadows Pond lies in a broad basin west of Ball Mountain Reservoir. It is a shallow pond with rich wetland and aquatic communities, known and loved by local canoeists, birders, and anglers. A 5 mph speed limit helps keep the pond quiet for humans and wildlife alike.

The southwestern end of the pond has marsh and shrub communities dominated by cattail (*Typha latifiolia*), sedges (*Carex* spp. and *Scirpus* spp.), and speckled alder (*Alnus incana*). The pond margins are lined with yellow water lilies (*Nuphar variegatum*) and other emergent and floating aquatic species, making great beaver (*Castor canadensis*), mink (*Mustela vison*), and duck habitat. The northern end has peatland communities with groves of tamarack (*Larix laricina*). Standing dead trees provide nest cavities for tree swallows (*Tachiceneta bicolor*). Wood duck (*Aix sponsa*), hooded merganser (*Lophodytes cucullatus*), American bittern (*Botaurus lentiginosus*), goshawk (*Accipiter gentilis*), and saw-whet owl (*Aegolius acadicus*) also nest here.

Directions: From the junction of VT 100 and VT 30 northwest of Jamaica, go west on VT 30 about 2 miles and take a sharp right onto River Road. At 0.8 mile from the main road, bear left onto Gale Meadows Road, then bear left again after another 0.9 mile onto the side road to the boat ramp and parking area.

Activities: Canoeing, fishing, bird-watching.

Facilities: None.

Dates: Year-round.

Fees: None.

Closest town: Jamaica, 8 miles.

For more information: Vermont Department of Fish and Wildlife, RR 1 Box 33, North Springfield, VT 05150. Phone (802) 886-2215.

Bromley Mountain

[Fig. 21] Bromley Mountain marks the beginning of a transition in the structure of the Green Mountains, from the broad plateau to the south toward the more organized ridges of the central part of the range. The rock is still Precambrian basement rock, but in this case the summit is formed of quartzite and schists rather than the banded gneiss that forms most of the plateau. Hapgood State Forest encloses the summit, while much of the remainder falls in the Green Mountain National Forest.

Bromley Mountain Ski Area occupies the southeastern slopes of the mountain, with lifts extending right to the summit, where a cafeteria disturbs or refreshes hikers, depending on their expectations and outlook. An observation platform offers views of the busy slopes of Stratton Mountain to the south, the wild peaks in the Peru Peak Wilderness to the north, and the nearby Taconic Mountains and distant hills of New Hampshire to the west and east. The summit ski lift is open for sight-seeing in the fall.

Directions: From the junction of US 7 and VT 30/11 in Manchester, take VT 11 east about 6 miles to the ski area entrance on the left.

Activities: Hiking, downhill skiing, alpine slide, and other rides.

Facilities: Downhill ski area with lodging and dining, summit cafeteria with restrooms.

Dates: Open during ski season, weekends Memorial Day to mid-June, daily mid-June to mid-Oct. Summit chairlift open late Sept. through early Oct.; other lifts open for ski season or for summer activities.

Fees: There is a charge to use lifts and facilities.

Closest town: Manchester, 7 miles.

For more information: Bromley Mountain, Box 1130, Manchester Center, VT 05255. Phone (802) 824-5522.

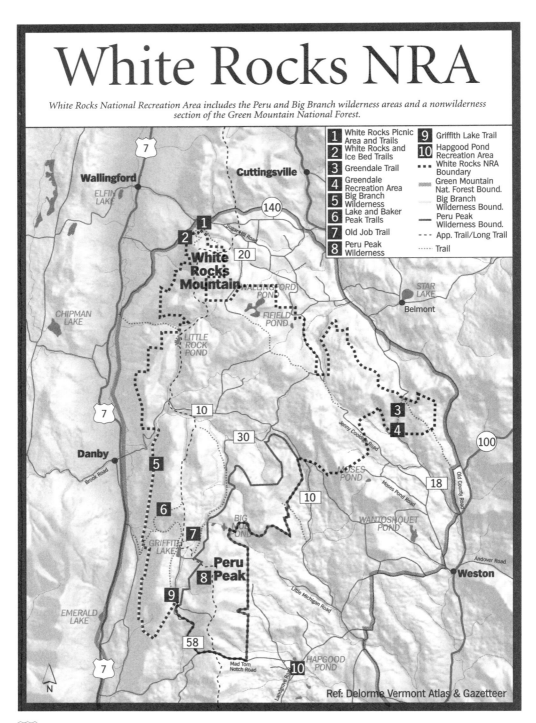

White Rocks NRA

White Rocks National Recreation Area includes the Peru and Big Branch wilderness areas and a nonwilderness section of the Green Mountain National Forest.

1 White Rocks Picnic Area and Trails
2 White Rocks and Ice Bed Trails
3 Greendale Trail
4 Greendale Recreation Area
5 Big Branch Wilderness
6 Lake and Baker Peak Trails
7 Old Job Trail
8 Peru Peak Wilderness
9 Griffith Lake Trail
10 Hapgood Pond Recreation Area
▪▪▪ White Rocks NRA Boundary
Green Mountain Nat. Forest Bound.
Big Branch Wilderness Bound.
Peru Peak Wilderness Bound.
- - - App. Trail/Long Trail
⋯⋯⋯ Trail

Ref: Delorme Vermont Atlas & Gazetteer

🪨 LONG/APPALACHIAN TRAIL OVER BROMLEY MOUNTAIN

[Fig. 21] A 5-mile section of the Long/Appalachian Trail passes over Bromley Mountain, so the summit can be reached as a day hike from either VT 30/11 to the south or Mad Tom Notch to the north. There is camping at the Green Mountain Club's Bromley Tenting Area and Mad Tom Shelter, or off the trail as allowed by Green Mountain National Forest primitive camping regulations.

Directions: From the junction of US 7 and VT 30/11 in Manchester, take VT 30/11 east about 4.5 miles to the Long/Appalachian Trail crossing and parking. For Mad Tom Notch, continue east on VT 11 another 4 miles to the village of Peru and turn left on Landgrove Road. At 1 mile, turn left on North Road, continue another 0.7 mile, and turn left on Mad Tom Notch Road (Forest Road 21); the Long/Appalachian Trail crossing and parking are at the height of land, about 2.5 miles up.

Trail: 2.7 miles one-way from VT 30/11, or 2.5 miles one-way from Mad Tom Notch.

Elevation: 1,800 feet at VT 11/30; 3,260 feet at the summit; 2,450 feet at Mad Tom Notch.

Degree of difficulty: Moderate.

Surface and blaze: Old road, rocky footpath, and ski trail; white blazes

White Rocks National Recreation Area

[Fig. 23] White Rocks National Recreation Area includes the Peru and Big Branch wilderness areas and a nonwilderness section of the Green Mountain National Forest that is managed primarily for backcountry recreation. The area is traversed by a few Forest Service roads and a 20-mile section of the Long/Appalachian Trails; with numerous other trails giving access to the peaks and ponds of the southern Green Mountain plateau.

🪨 HAPGOOD POND RECREATION AREA

[Fig. 23(10)] Though it lies outside the White Rocks National Recreation area boundary, the Green Mountain National Forest campground at Hapgood Pond makes a good base for day hikes in the recreation area and on nearby Bromley Mountain. The day-use area includes two picnic areas with log shelters built by the Civilian Conservation Corps in the 1930s, open play areas, a swimming beach, a canoe access, and a wheelchair-accessible fishing pier. An 0.8-mile trail circles the small pond.

Directions: From the junction of US 7 and VT 30/11 in Manchester, take VT 30/11 east about 8.5 miles to the village of Peru and turn left on Landgrove Road. At a four-way intersection, continue straight on Hapgood Pond Road, and turn left on the access road to the recreation area, about 2 miles from Peru.

Activities: Camping, picnicking, swimming, fishing, hiking.

Facilities: 21 drive-in campsites, 4 walk-in campsites, picnic area, vault toilets, swimming beach, wheelchair-accessible fishing pier, canoe access, hiking trail.

Dates: Open Memorial Day to Labor Day.

Fees: There are fees for camping and day use.

Closest town: Peru, 2 miles.

For more information: Hapgood Pond Recreation Area, General Delivery, Peru, VT 05152 (summer). L&L Inc., 747 E. 1000 S., Orem, UT, 84097-7259. Phone (801) 226-3564 (winter).

PERU PEAK WILDERNESS

[Fig. 23(8)] The Long/Appalachian Trail traverses the southern leg of this wilderness, while Pete Parent Peak and the surrounding forests, brooks, and ponds in the northern section are left for hardy bushwhackers to share with the deer, beaver, and black flies. Two 3,000-foot peaks provide views and solitude for on-trail hikers. Overnight hikers can approach these peaks from the Griffith Lake Area to the northwest.

LONG/APPALACHIAN TRAIL TO STYLES AND PERU PEAKS

[Fig. 23] **Directions:** From the junction of US 7 and VT 30/11 in Manchester, take VT 11 east about 8.5 miles to the village of Peru and turn left on Landgrove Road. At 1 mile, turn left on North Road, continue another 0.7 mile, and turn left on Mad Tom Notch Road (Forest Road 21); the Long/Appalachian Trail crossing and parking are at the height of land, about 2.5 miles up.

Trail: 1.6 miles one-way to Styles Peak, 3.3 miles one-way to Peru Peak.

Elevation: Mad Tom Notch, 2,450 feet, Styles Peak 3,394 feet, Peru Peak, 3,429 feet.

Degree of difficulty: Moderate.

Surface and blaze: Rocky footpath, white blazes.

GRIFFITH LAKE

[Fig. 23] The Peru and trailless Big Branch wildernesses are separated by a narrow corridor, traversed by the Old Job Trail which meets its southern end at Griffith Lake. The Big Branch Wilderness sections of the Long/Appalachian and Old Job trails form a 10.4-mile loop over scenic Baker Peak. The lake can also be reached by an easy, unnamed trail (here called the Griffith Lake Trail) from Forest Road 58 to the south, which makes an easy ski-in in the winter. Parts of these trails are used by snowmobiles. There is a tenting area at Griffith Lake, Peru Peak Shelter is nearby, and the Old Job and Big Branch shelters are to the north. The lake makes a nice base camp for exploration of both the Big Branch and Peru Peak wildernesses.

Directions: Access by trail as described below.

Activities: Hiking, cross-country skiing, camping, swimming.

Facilities: Primitive campground with outhouses.

Dates: Open year-round.

Fees: There is a fee for camping in summer.

Closest town: Peru, 6.2 miles by trail and road.

For more information: Green Mountain National Forest, Manchester Ranger

District, 2538 Depot Street, Manchester Center, VT 05255-9733. Phone (802) 362-2307. Green Mountain Club, 4711 Waterbury-Stowe Road, Waterbury Center, VT 05677. Phone (802) 244-7037.

OLD JOB TRAIL

[Fig. 23(7)] **Directions:** From the village of Danby on US 7, turn east on Forest Road 10, cross the Long/Appalachian Trail at 3.2 miles, continue another 3.7 miles, and turn right on Forest Road 30. There is a parking area at the end of the road, 2.3 miles in. The trail extends both south, intersecting the Long/Appalachian Trail at Griffith Lake, and north, joining the Long/Appalachian Trail at Big Branch Shelter 1 mile south of Forest Road 10.

Trail: 3.4 miles to Griffith Lake, 2 miles to Big Branch Shelter.
Elevation: 1,470 to 2,600 feet.
Degree of difficulty: Easy.
Surface and blaze: Old road, blue blazes.

GRIFFITH LAKE TRAIL

[Fig. 23(9)] **Directions:** From the junction of US 7 and VT 30/11 in Manchester, take VT 11 east about 8.5 miles to the village of Peru and turn left on Landgrove Road. At 1 mile, turn left on North Road, continue another 0.7 mile, and turn left on Mad Tom Notch Road (Forest Road 21), then right after about 2.5 miles onto Forest Road 58. Park at the end of the road.

Trail: 2 miles one-way.
Elevation: Around 2,600 feet.
Degree of difficulty: Easy.
Surface and blaze: Old road, blue blazes.

▨ BIG BRANCH WILDERNESS

[Fig. 23(5)] For hikers, the focal point of the Big Branch Wilderness is Baker Peak, which, in spite of its smallish size, has dramatic views of the pastoral depths of the Otter Creek valley, the Taconic Mountains, Dorset Peak, and other summits to the south, east, and west. The peak straddles the boundary between the 400- to 500- million-year old Cambrian and Ordovician carbonate and quartzite rocks of the valley and the billion-year-old gneiss and schist at the core of the Green Mountains.

LAKE AND BAKER PEAK TRAILS

[Fig. 23(6)] The Lake and Baker Peak trails, together with a short section of the Long/Appalachian Trail, combine to make a fine day hike with a two-way section at the bottom and a loop at the top. The upper loop is also accessible from Griffith Lake via the Long/Appalachian Trail. The Lake Trail begins in rich forests over carbonate rocks near the valley floor, then ascends steep slopes underlain by Cheshire Quartzite, exposed in numerous ledges along the trail.

Directions: From Danby, take US 7 south 2.1 miles, turn left on South End Road, and continue 0.5 mile to a parking area at the Lake Trail head.

Trail: 8.1 miles round-trip from South End Road, 4.9 mile loop from Griffith Lake.
Elevation: 800 to 2,850 feet; Griffith Lake is 2,600 feet.
Degree of difficulty: Baker Peak Trail is strenuous, other sections are moderate.
Surface and blaze: Rocky footpath. Blue blazes.

GREENDALE RECREATION AREA

[Fig. 23(4)] This is a small Green Mountain National Forest campgound and picnic area on the northeastern side of the White Rocks National Recreation Area. Most of the sites are near Greendale Brook, the site of fish habitat improvements and introduction of Atlantic salmon (*Salmo salar*) fry as part of the Connecticut River Atlantic salmon restoration effort. Rocks and logs in streams provide protection from both predators and the swift current, and are essential for the survival of young fish.

Directions: From the junction of VT 100 and VT 11 in Londonderry, go north on VT 100 through the village of Weston. About 3 miles north of Weston, turn left on Greendale Road (Forest Road 18) and follow it 2 miles to the campground.
Activities: Camping, picnicking, fishing, hiking.
Facilities: 10 campsites, vault toilets, picnic area, drinking water pump.
Dates: Open year-round, but access road is not plowed in winter.
Fees: Fee for camping.
Closest town: Weston, 5 miles.
For more information: Green Mountain National Forest, Manchester Ranger District, 2538 Depot Street, Manchester Center, VT 05255-9733. Phone (802) 362-2307.

GREENDALE TRAIL

[Fig. 23(3)] This short trail begins at a beaver pond just past the campground and ends in some open meadows.

Trail: 1.5 miles one-way.
Elevation: 1,600 to 2,200 feet.
Degree of difficulty: Easy.
Surface and blaze: Old road. Unblazed.

WALLINGFORD POND

[Fig. 23] Hidden away behind White Rocks Mountain, this remote mountain pond is divided into three bays that make for a long shoreline and a variety of wetland communities. Rich marshes are home to marsh birds, waterfowl, and frogs, and make good summer habitat for moose (*Alces alces*). There are also boggy stretches. While much of the shoreline is guarded by alder (*Alnus incana*) thickets, a half dozen primitive campsites are well-spaced around the shore.

Directions: From the junction of US 7 and VT 140 in Wallingford, take VT 140 east about 2.4 miles and turn right on Sugar Hill Road. After about 2 miles, turn right on Wallingford Pond Road, and go about another 2 miles to the access road on the right. The 0.2-mile access road is too rough and muddy for low-slung vehicles, but there is a parking area before the turnoff.

Activities: Canoeing, camping, bird-watching, fishing.

Dates: The road is not plowed in winter.

Fees: None.

Closest town: Wallingford, 7 miles.

For more information: Green Mountain National Forest, Manchester Ranger District, 2538 Depot Street, Manchester Center, VT 05255-9733. Phone (802) 362-2307.

TIMBER RATTLESNAKE
(*Crotalus horridus*)

WHITE ROCKS PICNIC AREA AND TRAILS

[Fig. 23(1)] The White Rocks Recreation Area takes its name from the dramatic triangular peak and ledges of White Rocks Mountain at its northern end. The white- to buff-colored rock is Cheshire Quartzite, a tough metamorphic sandstone that forms other cliffs along the western front of the Green Mountains, including Rattlesnake Cliffs near Lake Dunmore and Bristol Cliffs farther north (*see* page 183).

Underneath the ledges are some of the most extensive open talus slopes in the state—steep and unstable piles of boulders that have fallen from the cliffs above. In winter, ice accumulates deep in the spaces between the boulders and can last until late summer. The desert-dry and warm expanse of open boulders contrasts with the cool air flowing out of the base of the talus slope to form a range of microenvironments and associated plant communities. Two trails begin at the White Rocks Picnic Area near Wallingford.

Directions: From the junction of US 7 and VT 140 in Wallingford, take VT 140 east about 2.4 miles and turn right on Sugar Hill Road. Take the first right, which is the access road to White Rocks Picnic Area.

Activities: Picnicking, hiking.

Facilities: Picnic tables, vault toilets, drinking water from a hand pump.

Dates: Open year-round.

Fees: None.

Closest town: Wallingford, 3 miles.

For more information: Green Mountain National Forest, Manchester Ranger District, 2538 Depot Street, Manchester Center, VT 05255-9733. Phone (802) 362-2307.

WHITE ROCKS AND ICE BEDS TRAILS

[Fig. 23(2)] The White Rocks Trail ascends to an open ledge with a dramatic view of the cliffs and talus. From the ledge, the Ice Beds Trail continues over a dry ridge and down to the toe of one of the talus slopes.

From the viewpoint and others along the Ice Beds Trail you can see a phenomenon common to all talus slopes. The momentum of the biggest boulders carries them to the bottom of the slope, while smaller rocks tend to stop higher up, so in general the boulders get smaller toward the top of the slope. The very top of the slope may be filled in by fine mineral and organic material sifting in from above, creating pockets

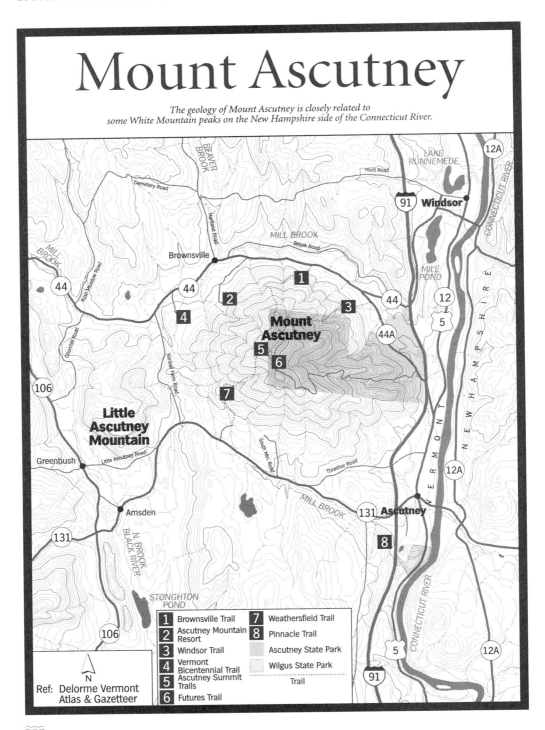

Mount Ascutney

*The geology of Mount Ascutney is closely related to
some White Mountain peaks on the New Hampshire side of the Connecticut River.*

Legend:

1. Brownsville Trail
2. Ascutney Mountain Resort
3. Windsor Trail
4. Vermont Bicentennial Trail
5. Ascutney Summit Trails
6. Futures Trail
7. Weathersfield Trail
8. Pinnacle Trail

Ascutney State Park
Wilgus State Park
Trail

Ref: Delorme Vermont Atlas & Gazetteer

of soil that support trees and shrubs in a band along the base of the ledges. Bristly sarsaparilla (*Aralia hispida*), chokeberry (*Aronia melanocarpa*), blueberries (*Vaccinium* spp.), and huckleberries (*Gaylussacia dumosa*) grow in cracks and pockets of soil on the dry ledges at the ridgetop, while forests of hemlock, birch, and red spruce occupy the cool, north-facing slopes.

From the ridge, the trail drops into a cool hemlock ravine and follows a small brook upstream toward the talus. Check the temperature of the water as you approach the talus. Near the base of the slope, the water runs well below 40 degrees Fahrenheit, a sign of the melting ice above. You can explore for ice among the boulders at the base of the slope, but by late summer it has retreated deeper into the talus so it's not always easy to find. Mats of rock polypody (*Polypodium virginianum*), a small, simple fern, grow on the tops of boulders near the bottom and sides of the slope. You may be tempted to explore up the talus slope, but you should do so carefully.

Common ravens (*Corvus corax*) nest on the cliffs, but attempts to get peregrine falcons (*Falco peregrinus*) re-established here have so far failed. The viewpoints on the Ice Beds Trail provide fine vantages for watching hawks during migration.

Trail: 0.3 mile one-way to viewpoint; 0.8 mile one-way to ice beds.

Elevation: About 1,100 to 1,500 feet.

Degree of difficulty: Moderate.

Surface and blaze: Rocky footpath with some open ledge. Blue blazes.

WHITE ROCKS MOUNTAIN

[Fig. 23] The Keewaydin Trail ascends the slopes of White Rocks Mountain and joins the Long/Appalachian Trail just north of the White Rocks Cliff Trail, a spur trail that leads 0.2 mile down to the top of the cliffs for views of the talus below and summits to the north and west. For through hikers, Greenwall Shelter on the Long/Appalachian Trail just north of the Keewaydin Trail, makes a good overnight base for exploration of the White Rocks area.

Trail: 1.3 miles one-way to the viewpoint on White Rocks Mountain.

Elevation: 1,100 to 2,400 feet.

Degree of difficulty: Moderate.

Surface and blaze: Rocky footpath, blue blazes.

Ascutney

ASCUTNEY STATE PARK

[Fig. 24] Like a neglected younger sibling, Mount Ascutney stands alone above the rumpled hills of the Connecticut River valley, well apart from the southern peaks of the Green Mountains. Its geology is nearly unique among Vermont's mountains, and more closely related to that of some White Mountain peaks on the other side of the

Mount Ascutney is a premier launch site for expert hang glider pilots.

river. Although it is not really a Green Mountain, it is included here because of its proximity to Woodstock.

During the Mesozoic Era, the supercontinent Pangaea, which was stitched together by mountain-building events like the ones that built the Appalachians, began to fall apart. Like the messy collisions that formed the continent, the breakup was not a tidy process. Along with the main rift that became today's Atlantic Ocean, there were smaller, subsidiary tears that were active for a time, but failed to widen further. The red rocks of the Connecticut River valley in central Connecticut mark one of these zones.

Associated with the great continental divorce, northern New England saw a new wave of volcanic activity, lasting from about 225 to 120 million years ago. Magma from the mantle welled up into cracks and weaknesses created by stretching of the crust. This event was a dramatic final chapter in the geologic history of New Hampshire, creating surface lava flows and deep bodies of rock, known as the White Mountain magma series, that are a 100 million years or more younger than any other rocks in the state. In Vermont, this volcanic invasion is more of a footnote, because relatively little magma leaked across the old suture line between the former edge of the continent and the volcanic island arc that collided with it to cause the Taconic orogeny. Mount Ascutney is one of only four small bodies of White Mountain rocks in the state, and at about 120 million years old, is among the youngest rocks in the region.

Over the last 125 million years, culminating in the repeated glaciation of the Pleistocene era, weather and water have worn away most of the surface layers of the old volcanoes. In New Hampshire, there are fragments of the surface flows remaining on the tops of a few mountains. But the inner cores of these volcanoes remain as round or oblong bodies of granitic rock, sometimes forming a series of partial concentric rings known as ring dikes. As a body of magma burns its way upward toward the surface, a circle of the overlying rock may collapse, and fresh magma invades the surrounding fracture to form a ring dike. Chunks of the surrounding rock, called xenoliths (literally "stranger-rocks"), altered by contact with the hot magma, are often found embedded in the younger plutonic rock. As the rock cools, cracks that form as it contracts are filled by more magma to form linear dikes that may cut across several different rock types.

Mount Ascutney has an inner core of granite, surrounded by a complex of similar rock types lumped together as syenite, a finer-grained plutonic rock, with partial rings of other volcanic rock types embedded in it. Little Ascutney, to the west of the main peak, is a large body of gabbro and diorite, rocks that contain less silica than granite, with another small body of syenite inside.

Ascutney's summit is accessible by a toll road that begins at the state park entrance, ascending 2,250 feet in 3.8 miles. A 0.8-mile trail covers the final 350 vertical feet from the parking area to the summit. Unlike the toll roads on many other peaks in the region, the Ascutney road is open to bicycles, but the summit trails are not. The state park has a small campground at the base of the mountain, and picnic areas near the summit and at a viewpoint partway up the toll road. One of the four main hiking trails up the mountain begins in the campground.

The combination of road access to the summit and the precipitous west slopes make Ascutney a premier launch site for expert hang glider pilots. On good flying days you can watch them assemble their colorful gliders and take off from the west peak, a short walk from the parking area. They can spend hours in the air, circling in updrafts to soar over the summit, then heading east over the Connecticut River to land far away in New Hampshire.

Directions: From Exit 8 on I-91, go east on VT 131 approximately 0.3 mile and turn left on VT 5, through Ascutney village. Bear left on VT 44A; the park entrance is about 1.5 miles from the junction on the left.

Activities: Picnicking, hiking, bicycling, sight-seeing on toll road, hang-gliding.

Facilities: 30 campsites, 10 lean-tos, picnic areas, restrooms, toll road, hiking trails, hang glider launch site.

Dates: Mid-May to mid-Oct.

Fees: There are fees for camping, day use, and the toll road.

Closest town: Ascutney, 2.5 miles.

For more information: Ascutney State Park, Box 186, HCR 71, Windsor, VT 05089. Phone (802) 674-2060 (summer). Vermont Department of Forests, Parks, and Recreation, RR 1 Box 33, North Springfield, VT 05150-9726. Phone (802) 885-8855 (winter).

ASCUTNEY SUMMIT TRAILS

[Fig. 24(5)] An open observation tower on the main summit has 360-degree views of mountains in four states, but the views are compromised by two telecommunications towers, bristling with dishes and antennae. A network of trails links together various viewpoints on the minor summits and ledges of the mountain, all within about 0.75 mile of the summit and away from the distractions of the main summit. A map of the Ascutney trail system is available at the state park. The Ascutney Trails Association, which maintains many of the trails on the mountain, publishes an excellent guidebook to the mountain that includes detailed descriptions of the trails and lots of mountain lore.

Trail: Round trips or loops of 1.4 to 3 miles.

Elevation: 2,500 to 3,144 feet.

Degree of difficulty: Easy to moderate, some short, rough stretches.

Surface and blaze: Rocky footpath and ledge, blue or white blazes.

For more information: Ascutney Trails Association, PO Box 147, Windsor, VT, 05089.

FUTURES TRAIL

[Fig. 24(6)] Beginning only a few hundred feet above the Connecticut River, this is the longest way up the mountain, climbing over 2,500 feet to the summit. A short side trail leads to a rusting steam donkey, a steam-powered winch used to haul logs on steep terrain.

Directions: The trailhead is by campsite 22 in Ascutney State Park.

Trail: 4.6 miles one-way.

Elevation: 560 to 3,144 feet.

Degree of difficulty: Strenuous.

Surface and blaze: Rocky footpath and old logging roads. Blue blazes.

WINDSOR TRAIL

[Fig. 24(3)] This trail follows a brook past a small cascade before climbing into spruce-fir forest on the upper slopes of the mountain. A side loop goes to a log shelter with an indoor fireplace. An alternate route, the Blood Rock Trail, passes over a broad ledge exposed by a 1925 landslide.

Directions: The trailhead is 1.5 miles northeast of the state park entrance on VT 44A.

Trail: 2.7 miles one-way.

Elevation: 630 to 3,144 feet.

Degree of difficulty: Strenuous.

Surface and blaze: Rocky footpath. White blazes.

BROWNSVILLE TRAIL

[Fig. 24(1)] This trail follows the old quarry access road and crosses the tailings of the old Norcross granite quarry, one of four quarries on the mountain that exported rock as far away as New York City and Canton, Ohio. The fallen booms and cables used to move the granite blocks are still there. The trail follows a ridge over the north summit, joining the Windsor Trail 0.3 mile below the summit. The trailhead is about 1 mile from the Windsor trailhead, so the two can be done as a 7-mile loop.

Directions: From Ascutney State Park, follow VT 44A north until it joins VT 44 from Windsor, then continue on VT 44 west about 1 mile to trail parking on the left.

Trail: 3.2 miles one-way to the summit.

Elevation: 750 to 3,144 feet.

Degree of difficulty: Moderate, with some rough sections.

Surface and blaze: Rocky footpath. White blazes.

WEATHERSFIELD TRAIL

[Fig. 24(7)] Ascutney's unique geology comes to the fore on this trail, which passes the top of Crystal Cascade, formed along the line of contact between the schist of the surrounding lowlands and the body of syenite that forms the main mass of the mountain. Upstream from the cascade, xenoliths of the schist can be found embedded in the syenite. Below Crystal Cascade the trail crosses a smaller cascade and, upstream from that, a mossy gorge carved along an easily eroded basalt dike. The trail visits a couple of quiet lookouts before emerging at the hang glider port on the west peak.

Directions: From Exit 8 on I-91, take VT 131 west about 2 miles and turn right on Cascade Falls Road. Bear left at a fork then right into a parking area.

Trail: 2.9 miles one-way to summit.

Elevation: 1,090 to 3,144 feet.

Degree of difficulty: Strenuous.

Surface and blaze: Rocky footpath and ledge. Blue-and-white blazes.

VERMONT BICENTENNIAL TRAIL

[Fig. 24(4)] This trail in the West Windsor Town Forest, on the west slopes of Ascutney, falls well short of the summit, instead ascending an old road to the abandoned Mower granite quarry. Side trails lead to two small cascades and a viewpoint.

Directions: From Ascutney State Park, take VT 44A north to VT 44 west and continue past Ascutney Mountain Resort and through the village of Brownsville. About 0.75 mile past the village, turn left on Coaching Lane Road. Bear right at a fork, then turn right up a short access road to a parking area.

Trail: 2 miles one-way.

Elevation: 1,000 to 1,700 feet.

Degree of difficulty: Moderate.

Surface and blaze: Old road and rocky footpath. Yellow blazes.

ASCUTNEY MOUNTAIN RESORT

[Fig. 24(2)] Extending 1,500 feet up the northwest slope of the mountain, Mount Ascutney's ski area offers excellent skiing on a modest scale. Like other ski areas, it has expanded its facilities to include a variety of summer and winter family activities, including guided hikes up the mountain.

Directions: From Exit 8 on I-91, go east on VT 131 approximately 0.3 mile and turn left on VT 5, through Ascutney village. Bear left on VT 44A and continue west

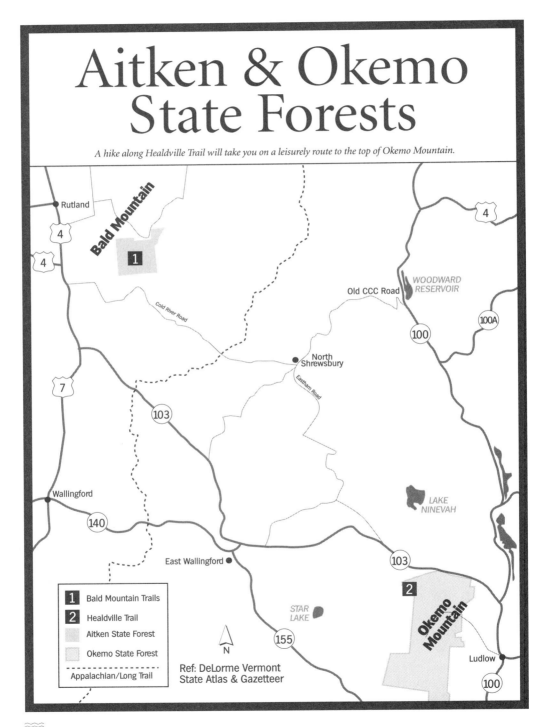

Aitken & Okemo State Forests

A hike along Healdville Trail will take you on a leisurely route to the top of Okemo Mountain.

Rutland

Bald Mountain

4

4

4

1

Cold River Road

Old CCC Road

WOODWARD RESERVOIR

100

100A

North Shrewsbury

Eastham Road

7

103

Wallingford

140

East Wallingford

LAKE NINEVAH

103

STAR LAKE

2

Okemo Mountain

Ludlow

100

155

N

1 Bald Mountain Trails
2 Healdville Trail
Aitken State Forest
Okemo State Forest
- - - - Appalachian/Long Trail

Ref: DeLorme Vermont
State Atlas & Gazetteer

after it joins VT 44 west. The ski area entrance is on the left about 2 miles west of the junction of VT 44 and VT 44A.

Activities: Downhill skiing, indoor and outdoor fitness activities and games.

Facilities: Lifts and base lodge, fitness and family centers.

Dates: Open during winter ski season; fitness facilities open year-round.

Fees: There are fees for skiing and use of other facilities.

Closest town: Windsor, 4 miles.

For more information: Ascutney Mountain Resort, PO Box 694, Brownsville, VT 05037. Phone (800) 243-0011.

WILGUS STATE PARK

[Fig. 24] Vermont's only state park on the Connecticut River has a small campground with sites near the river, a picnic area, canoe access to the river, a nature trail with signs identifying trees along the river, and a short hike to a hilltop with views over the river valley into New Hampshire.

Directions: From Exit 8 on I-91, go east on VT 131 approximately 0.3 mile, then south on US 5 approximately 1 mile to the park entrance on the left.

Activities: Camping, canoeing, fishing, hiking.

Facilities: 19 campsites, 6 lean-tos, group camping area with 3 lean-tos, picnic area, playground, restrooms, hiking trail, canoe access.

Dates: Open Mid-May to mid-Oct.

Fees: There are fees for camping and day use.

Closest town: Ascutney, 1.5 miles.

For more information: Wilgus State Park, Box 196, Ascutney, VT 05030. Phone (802) 674-5422 (summer). Vermont Department of Forests, Parks, and Recreation, RR 1 Box 33, North Springfield, VT 05150-9726. Phone (802) 885-8855 (winter).

PINNACLE TRAIL

[Fig. 24(8)] **Directions:** The trail begins on the west side of US 5 just north of the entrance to Wilgus State Park.

Trail: 1.3-mile loop from the campground area.

Elevation: 300 to 600 feet.

Degree of difficulty: Easy.

Surface and blaze: Old road and footpath. Blue blazes.

Aitken State Forest

[Fig. 25] At just 2,090 feet, Bald Mountain in Aitken State Forest is dwarfed by nearby peaks in the Green Mountains. But the three-trail network on the mountain leads to a series of lookouts with views of the bigger peaks and the Otter Creek valley below. The oak-hickory forests on the south slopes and northern hardwood forests on other aspects host a wide variety of forest birds, including several warbler species and the Vermont state bird, the hermit thrush (*Catharus guttatus*). The ledges are good places to watch for hawks during migration.

Directions: From the junction of US 7 and US 4 west in Rutland, go south on VT 7 about 0.4 mile, turn left on Killington Avenue, and follow it to its end. Turn right on Town Line Road, then bear left at a fork onto Notch Road. Park along the roadside near Tamarack Notch Camp, about 1.4 miles up Notch Road.

Activities: Hiking, bird-watching.

Facilities: None.

Dates: Open year-round.

Fees: None.

Closest town: Rutland, 3 miles.

For more information: Vermont Department of Forests, Parks, and Recreation, RR 1 Box 33, North Springfield, VT 05150-9726. Phone (802) 885-8855.

BALD MOUNTAIN TRAILS

[Fig. 25(1)] **Trail:** Loops of 2.9, 3.4 or 4.1 miles

Elevation: 1,400 to 2,090 feet.

Degree of difficulty: Moderate.

Surface and blaze: Old road and rocky footpath, blue blazes.

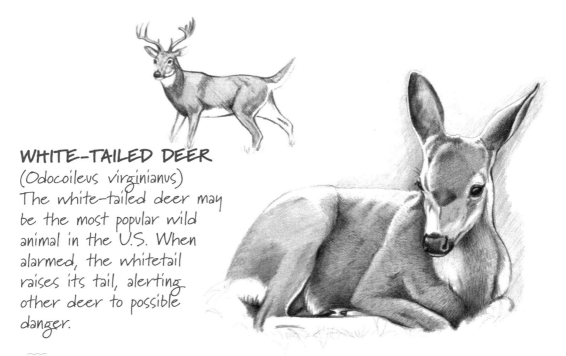

WHITE-TAILED DEER
(Odocoileus virginianus)
The white-tailed deer may be the most popular wild animal in the U.S. When alarmed, the whitetail raises its tail, alerting other deer to possible danger.

Okemo State Forest

[Fig. 25] Okemo Mountain is a prominent peak on the eastern edge of the southern Green Mountain plateau. Okemo Ski Area dominates its eastern slopes, while most of the rest of the mountain is undeveloped state forest land. A paved road and 0.5-mile trail provide automotive access to the summit, or a challenging hill climb for cyclists. The 2.9-mile Healdville Trail takes a more leisurely route to the top. A summit fire tower gives views of Mount Ascutney, Killington Peak, and other summits in the Green and Taconic mountains.

Directions: From Ludlow village, go north on VT 100/103 about 0.25 mile and turn left on Okemo Mountain Road. This continues past the ski area to a parking area 0.5 mile below the summit.

Activities: Hiking, sight-seeing, downhill skiing.

Facilities: Full service downhill ski area with restaurants and lodging.

Dates: Lodging available year-round. Other activities are seasonal.

Fees: There are fees for the lifts; the road is free.

Closest town: Ludlow, 0.25 mile.

For more information: Okemo Mountain Resort, 77 Okemo Ridge Road, Ludlow, VT 05149. Phone (802) 228-4041. Vermont Department of Forests, Parks, and Recreation, RR 1 Box 33, North Springfield, VT 05150-9726. Phone (802) 885-8855.

HEALDVILLE TRAIL

[Fig. 25(2)] While the road and a short trail have provided access to Okemo's summit for years, the Healdville Trail, completed in 1993, is young enough that it is not found in some of Vermont's older guidebooks. From the hamlet of Healdville on the north side of the mountain, the trail makes a leisurely climb through second-growth hardwood forest.

Trail: 2.9 miles one-way.

Elevation: 1,400 to 3,343 feet

Degree of difficulty: Moderate.

Surface and blaze: Graded and rocky footpath. Blue blazes.

BLACK SPRUCE
(Picea mariana)
Growing up to 40 feet tall, the black spruce is identified by its four-sided, blue-green needles and purple-brown cones.

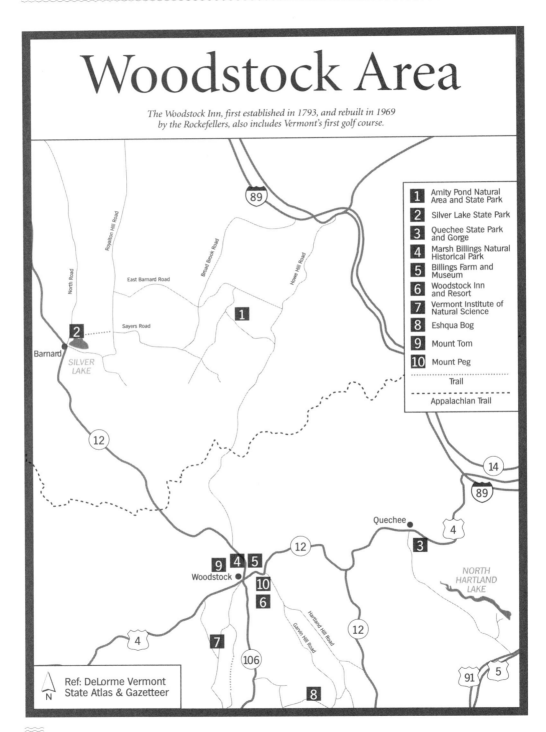

Woodstock Area

The Woodstock Inn, first established in 1793, and rebuilt in 1969 by the Rockefellers, also includes Vermont's first golf course.

1 Amity Pond Natural Area and State Park
2 Silver Lake State Park
3 Quechee State Park and Gorge
4 Marsh Billings Natural Historical Park
5 Billings Farm and Museum
6 Woodstock Inn and Resort
7 Vermont Institute of Natural Science
8 Eshqua Bog
9 Mount Tom
10 Mount Peg
········· Trail
- - - - - Appalachian Trail

Rogaton Hill Road
North Road
East Barnard Road
Broad Brook Road
Howe Hill Road
Sayers Road
Barnard
SILVER LAKE
Woodstock
Quechee
NORTH HARTLAND LAKE
Hartland Hill Road
Garvin Hill Road
Ref: DeLorme Vermont State Atlas & Gazetteer
N

Woodstock

▒ MARSH BILLINGS NATIONAL HISTORICAL PARK

[Fig. 26(4)] Newly opened in 1998, the Marsh-Billings National Historical Park is the first national park in the country to have a specific focus on the history and evolution of land conservation in North America. The 555-acre park was given to the people of the United States by Laurance and Mary Rockefeller, whose summer mansion is included as part of the park.

The park is named after the two men whose early land conservation efforts are responsible for the forests that can now be seen while walking the grounds. George Perkins Marsh grew up on the property in the early 1800s; he later wrote *Man and Nature*, a treatise on the need for land stewardship first published in 1864. *Man and Nature* was one of the first English-language books to describe the damage done by widespread and poorly planned land-clearing for agriculture or forestry. Frederick Billings, who made his fortune in western railroads, bought Marsh's homestead in 1869. He also read Marsh's book and established a professionally managed forest on the property, as well as a dairy farm that was run according to scientifically based management principles. The dairy farm is now the Billings Farm and Museum just across the River Road and is owned by the Rockefellers' nonprofit Woodstock Foundation.

While the park's name celebrates Billings and Marsh, it is the Rockefellers who most come to life here. Laurance and Mary Rockefeller summered in their Woodstock mansion for 44 years and decided in 1993 to donate their Woodstock lands and residence to the National Park Service. Mary died in April 1997 and in January 1998 Laurance Rockefeller renounced the lifetime lease he had on the house. The park opened in June of that same year.

The house is thick with Rockefeller furnishings and memorabilia, including 541 pieces of artwork and photographs, many of which document nearly two centuries of shifting perceptions of America's landscape. Included in the collection are works by landscape artists Thomas Cole, Asher B. Durand, and Albert Bierstadt. What's most impressive, however, is the sheer number of everyday household items that were left by Rockefeller, from bed quilts to books to televisions and boom boxes. The completeness of the collection is so detailed and intimate, it makes a visitor feel as if Rockefeller had just stepped out for a moment to view his estate.

Some of the Rockefeller holdings are as momentous as the famous silver spike that marked the crossing of the Northern Pacific Railroad into Montana in 1880 (Billings owned the Northern Pacific, and Mary Rockefeller was his granddaughter) and several Tiffany stained glass windows. Others are as mundane as Laurance Rockefeller's 1969-1970 season's ski pass for Suicide Six Ski Area, and the loose change he carried in his pockets and collected in ceramic bowls on a dresser in his study.

It is the forests that will most draw hikers' and skiers' attention. Fifty forest stands of single species and mixed plantations make a checkerboard on Mount Tom's slopes, and more than 20 miles of carriage roads wind through them. Eleven of the 50 stands date from Billings' original efforts, and forest historians believe these are the oldest continuously managed forest stands in the United States.

Left on its own, Mount Tom would be colonized by the northern hardwood trio, sugar maple, beech, and yellow birch. Billings and his descendants planted a number of European species, however, in part because there were no established guidelines for using native species when the trees were first planted in the 1880s. The most prominent plantations are of Norway spruce (*Picea abies*), including the largest Norway spruce in the state (46 inches in diameter, and 126 feet tall), European larch (*Larix decidua*), and Scots pine (*Pinus sylvestris*). Some of the native plantations include white pine (*Pinus strobus*) and red pine (*Pinus resinosa*). Some of the red oak (*Quercus rubra*) are thought to be old growth, and a few hemlocks (*Tsuga canadensis*) on the flanks of Mount Tom, along the trail called Gully View, are as much as 400 years old.

Because the forest stands here have been managed for more than a century, undergrowth is limited, giving the stands a parklike feel. Four species of fern found on the property are either endangered species in Vermont, or uncommon. Moonwort (*Botrychium lunaria*) and male fern (*Dryopteris filix-mas*) are both state-listed endangered species. Goldie's fern (*Dryopteris goldiana*), and narrow-leaved glade fern (*Asplenium angustifolia midix*) are considered uncommon, as is late coralroot (*Corallorhiza odontorhiza*), a saprophytic member of the orchid family.

In the summer, the trails offer endless possibilities for day hikes, and in the winter, the Woodstock Ski Touring Center (another Rockefeller holding) maintains the roads and the area's footpaths for cross-country skiing.

Directions: From I-89, take Exit 1 to US 4 west. Go 13 miles to Woodstock Village. In Woodstock, turn north (right) onto VT 12, cross the iron bridge over the Ottauquechee River. Bear right onto River Road and take first right to Billings Farm and Museum parking lot (which is also the parking lot for the park).

Activities: Hiking, cross-country skiing, guided tours.

Facilities: Museum buildings, restrooms, hiking trails.

Dates: Open May to Oct.

Fees: There is a fee for guided tours.

Closest town: Woodstock.

For more information: Marsh-Billings National Historical Park, PO Box 178, Woodstock, VT 05091. Phone (802) 457-3368.

MOUNT TOM
[Fig. 26(9)] **Trail:** More than 20 miles of carriage roads for hiking and skiing.

Elevation: 700 to 1,300 feet.

Degree of difficulty: Easy hiking, easy to moderate cross-country skiing.

Surface and blaze: Old road, unblazed.

BILLINGS FARM AND MUSEUM

[Fig. 26(5)] Through museum exhibits and actual farming practices, the Billings Farm and Museum portray rural farming life in east-central Vermont in the late 1800s. The farm was originally established by the railroad magnate Frederick Billings when he bought the Marsh estate in 1869. It is owned now by Laurance and Mary Rockefeller's Woodstock Foundation, which is working in cooperation with the Marsh-Billings National Historic Park to offer an integrated view of the Billings estate.

When Billings first established his farm, he saw the rolling farmland as a perfect showcase for the newly emerging field of scientific agriculture. Among other efforts, Billings brought milk cows from the Isle of Jersey to Vermont to demonstrate their superior qualities as milkers.

So careful and complete were Billings's efforts that a century later, all the farm's business records are archived and available for research purposes.

The 1890s farmhouse was built for Frederick Billings's farm manager, George Aitken, as a business office, creamery, and apartment. All have been restored to their 1890s appearance as part of a living-history exhibit. Other outbuildings for hogs and sheep, pastures, a beautiful heirloom garden, and museum exhibits complete the 88-acre establishment.

Directions: From I-89, take Exit 1 to US 4 west. Go 13 miles to Woodstock Village. In Woodstock, turn north (right) onto VT 12, cross the iron bridge over the Ottauquechee River. Bear right onto River Road and take the first right to the Billings Farm and Museum parking lot.

Activities: Picnicking, bird-watching.

Facilities: Museum buildings, heirloom gardens, shop, restrooms, dairy bar, picnic area.

Dates: Open May to Oct..

Fees: There is an admission fee.

Closest town: Woodstock.

For more information: Billings Farm and Museum, PO Box 489 Woodstock, VT 05091. Phone (802) 457-2355.

WOODSTOCK INN AND RESORT

[Fig. 26(6)] No visit to the historic village of Woodstock is complete without a stop at the Woodstock Inn, first established in 1793 (though not in the present building) on the Woodstock Green. The resort, yet another Laurance and Mary Rockefeller holding, includes Vermont's first golf course, built in 1895; 75 kilometers of cross-country ski trails on mounts Tom and Peg as part of the Woodstock Ski Touring Center; and a health-and-fitness center. Three miles from the inn is the

Suicide Six Ski Area, first opened in 1937 and not far from the location of the first ski tow in the United States.

Though Rockefeller built the Woodstock Inn's current structure in 1969—the inn built in 1891 was beyond repair when Rockefeller took over the resort—the building fits nicely into its historic surroundings. Look carefully as you walk the green and visit Woodstock's other establishments: There are no power lines in town. Not long after the Rockefellers bought the resort, they paid to bury all the power lines in the village to preserve its quaint New England feel.

Directions: From I-89, take Exit 1 to US 4 west. Go 13 miles to Woodstock Village and the green in the center of town.

Activities: Hiking, cross-country skiing, downhill skiing, snowshoeing, horseback riding, golf.

Facilities: Inn, tavern, golf course, cross-country ski trails, downhill ski area, fitness center.

Dates: Inn open year-round, activities determined by seasons and weather.

Fees: There is a charge for trail, ski area, and golf course use, and to stay at the inn.

Closest town: Woodstock.

For more information: Woodstock Inn and Resort, Fourteen the Green, Woodstock, VT 05091-1298. Phone (802) 457-1100.

MOUNT PEG

[Fig. 26(10)] An easy woods walk or moderate ski tour, Mount Peg nonetheless rewards its visitors with a stunning view of neighboring (and more challenging) Mount Tom, with its scenic ledges, and at a distance, Killington Mountain and Mount Ascutney frame the horizon. Much like the manicured forests on Mount Tom, Mount Peg has been managed intensively as a tree farm, and the trail actually passes through an apple orchard.

Directions: From I-89, take Exit 1 to VT 4 west. Go 13 miles to Woodstock Village. In Woodstock, go west on US 4 to the junction of VT 106 and head south on VT 106 (also called South Street). Take the first left onto Cross Street, then the next right onto Golf Avenue. Parking for the trailhead is just before the intersection with Maple Avenue in a small, paved lot on the left.

Trail: 1.5 miles round-trip.

Elevation: 710 feet to 1,060 feet.

Degree of difficulty: Easy.

Surface and blaze: Well maintained footpath. Yellow blazes.

For more information: Woodstock Inn and Resort, Touring Center, Woodstock, VT 05091. Phone (802) 457-2114.

VERMONT INSTITUTE OF NATURAL SCIENCE

[Fig. 26(7)] Founded in 1972, the Vermont Institute of Natural Science fills many roles. It offers elementary school programs, publishes quarterly state bird records, and operates the Vermont Raptor Center, a veterinary clinic for wounded birds that welcomes visitors to view birds too injured to survive in the wild. The center offers an unparalleled opportunity to see up-close hawks and owls from all over the country that are usually only seen on the wing. From the tiny saw-whet owl (*Aegolius acadicus*) to the enormous great gray owl (*Strix nebulosa*), from bald and golden eagles (*Haliaeetus leucocephalus* and *Aquila chrysaetos*) to peregrine falcons (*Falco peregrinus*), more than two dozen species are represented at the raptor center. The only nonraptors in the collection, ravens (*Corvus corax*), are fascinating to watch, as they have well-developed social behaviors including a variety of odd vocal sounds.

OSPREY
(*Pandion haliaetus*)
Also known as the fish hawk, the osprey hovers over water before plunging in feetfirst to grasp the fish with its talons.

The Gordon Welchman Nature Trail, a 1.5-mile walk, and the 0.9-mile Communities Trail, including a loop around a pond, both leave from the center. Trail guides are available to borrow at the trailhead for use or to purchase.

Directions: From I-89, take Exit 1 to US 4 west. Go 13 miles to Woodstock Village and green. Staying on US 4 and passing through the center of town, look for Church Hill Road and signs for the institute on the left. Take a left on Church Hill Road and go approximately 1.5 miles to the institute and the Vermont Raptor Center.

Activities: Hiking, bird-watching.

Facilities: Museum, raptor center, nature shop, hiking and nature trails.

Dates: Open year-round.

Fees: There is a charge for the museum and raptor center.

Closest town: Woodstock, 2 miles.

For more information: Vermont Institute of Natural Science, Church Hill Road, Woodstock, VT 05091. Phone (802) 457-2779.

ESHQUA BOG

[Fig. 26(8)] With its dramatic display of showy lady's slippers (*Cyperipedium reginae*) in June and July, Eshqua Bog is a must-see for wildflower lovers. A boardwalk and trail through this 40.8 acre bog and natural area make for easy access, and a short loop trail that does a figure eight through the bog takes visitors through upland habitat as well as the fascinating microhabitats that make up this unusual natural area.

Technically, Eshqua Bog is considered a fen, because a small stream brings nutrients into the area. Like bogs, fens are formed by the accumulation of peat, the mostly unde-composed remains of sphagnum mosses, sedges, or other plant material, which forms a water-saturated, fibrous mat. A bog is fed primarily or exclusively by rainwater, so that acid generated by peat mosses and other plants accumulate, and there is no source of new nutrients. In a fen, groundwater or surface water flows through the peat, rinsing out some of the acid and bringing in fresh dissolved nutrients. Although the water in a fen is less acid and has higher nutrient availability than in a bog, it is still more acid and lower in nutrients than in other wetland types or in upland soils. Fens generally tend to have higher plant diversity than bogs. Eshqua Bog is no exception.

In spite of Eshqua Bog's relatively rich nutrient status (especially compared to a true bog), you'll still find round-leaved sundew (*Drosera rotundifolia*) and northern pitcher plants (*Sarracenia purpurea*). Both are insectivorous plants that satisfy their need for nitrogen by attracting insects to their leaves and capturing them so they can be digested for nutrients.

Look for Labrador tea (*Ledum groenlandicum*), purple avens (*Geum rivale*), and, clumped in the middle of the southern end of the bog, a grove of black spruce (*Picea mariana*) and tamarack (*Larix laricina*).

The presence of purple avens and bloodroot (*Sanguinaria canadense*), found near the small, intermittent stream that feeds the area, gives hints about the bedrock here. Scattered through the bedrock schists and quartzites, once muds and sands in the Iapetus Ocean more than 400 million years ago, are pockets of limestone. The limestone lends its calcium to the area, fueling plant diversity.

Be they bogs, fens, or marshes, wetlands are always a rich area for bird life. At Eshqua Bog, listen for common yellowthroats (*Geothlypis trichas*), probably the easiest wetland bird to identify, along with tree swallows (*Tachycineta bicolor*) and Eastern kingbirds (*Tyrannus tyrannus*).

Directions: From I-89, Exit 1, take US 4 west 10.4 miles to Woodstock Village. Just before US 4 enters Woodstock Village proper, where the road takes a sharp 90-degree turn to the right, turn left onto Hartland Hill Road. Go 1.2 miles to Garvin Hill Road on right. Follow Garvin Hill Road, which is dirt, 1.3 miles to limited trailhead parking. The bog is on the right.

Trail: 0.5 mile one-way.

Elevation: No elevation change.

Degree of difficulty: Easy.

Surface and blaze: Boardwalk and footpath.

For more information: The Nature Conservancy, Vermont Field Office, 27 State Street, Montpelier, VT 05602-2934. Phone (802) 229-4425. The New England Wild-flower Society, 180 Hemenway Road, Framingham, MA 01701. Phone (508) 877-7630.

NORTH HARTLAND LAKE

[Fig. 26] Vermont's mountainous landscape is a double-edged sword: It gives the Green Mountain State its great beauty, but the steep mountains and associated rainfall and snow make valley villages susceptible to flooding. In 1927 and again in 1936, disastrous flooding impelled the state and federal government to find ways to control the torrents. Flood control dams and other structures, roughly a half dozen of them, eventually sprouted on the larger tributaries of Vermont's major rivers, the Winooski and the Connecticut.

The North Hartland Dam, built by the Army Corps of Engineers between 1958 and 1961, is one of those structures. The dam, built at a cost of $7.3 million, makes a 215-acre lake, the upper reaches of which contain the spectacular Quechee Gorge, a 165-foot deep, sheer-sided vale through which flows the Ottauquechee River.

The area is popular—nearly 100,000 people visited the lake in 1997, mainly to take advantage of its swimming area—in part because there aren't many natural lakes within an easy drive. But the river is also stocked with rainbow trout (*Oncorhyncus myskiss*), and fishing for yellow perch (*Perca flavescens*) and largemouth bass (*Micropterus salmoides*) is good, at least good enough to attract great blue heron (*Ardea herodias*), which are not uncommon.

A self-guided nature trail leads hikers through a mixed forest of Eastern white pines (*Pinus strobus*), hemlock (*Tsuga canadensis*), American beech (*Fagus grandifolia*), and red maple (*Acer rubrum*) interspersed with occasional white oak (*Quercus alba*) and red oak (*Quercus rubra*). The crazy patchwork comes in part from the fact that trees are invading an area that was once a farmer's field, abandoned nearly 50 years ago when the federal government took ownership of the land.

Look carefully at the soils here—or better yet, feel them. They are silky soft, fine sands, part of a large lake deposit dumped by the Ottauquechee into glacial Lake Hitchcock, the lake that formed in the Connecticut River valley 12,000 years ago or more when a huge mound of glacial debris dammed the river just outside of Hartford, Connecticut. Elsewhere in the Ottauquechee Valley, particularly just north of Quechee Gorge, these glacial lake sediments are more than 200 feet thick. The fine sands aren't particularly nutrient-rich, but they are great to dig in. Innumerable small mammal holes pock the soil along the nature trail, as does a coyote (*Canis latrans*) den found near the end of the nature trail.

Directions: From Exit 11 off I-89, go south on US 5 approximately 4.4 miles to Clay Hill Road on the right, just before US 5 goes under the interstate bridge. Turn right on Clay Hill Road and go 1.1 miles to the dam access road on the right. The access road, is approximately 1 mile long. To access the interpretive trail, take the left fork off the access road toward the beach and before the dam.

Activities: Boating, fishing, picnicking, swimming, hunting.

Facilities: Picnic sites, playground, boat launch, restrooms, swimming area, interpretive trail.

Dates: Open year-round.

Fees: There is an entry fee.

Closest town: North Hartland, 1 mile.

For more information: US Army Corps of Engineers, North Hartland Lake, PO Box 55, North Hartland, VT 05052-0055. Phone (802) 295-2855.

QUECHEE STATE PARK AND GORGE

[Fig. 26(3)] Quechee Gorge speaks of ghosts: An old mill pond is a reminder of Vermont's brief heyday as a woolen mill capital, and the 165-foot-deep gorge itself is a ghost of a vastly larger kind. About 13,000 years ago, after the glaciers had melted that were north of here, a long, narrow water body called Lake Hitchcock formed along the Connecticut River, dammed by an enormous pile of debris left by the glacier's passing. The debris dam was near the present location of Hartford, Connecticut. The Ottauquechee River drained into Lake Hitchcock and as the river flowed, it dumped its load of sediments into the lake, eventually building a delta roughly 200 feet thick and burying its former riverbed.

Then the glacial debris dam in Connecticut broke. The release of water must have been a truly fantastic event, and the evidence of it is carved into the landscape here at the gorge. As the waters flowed south, they cut into the lake bottom sediments, sometimes cutting down to the old riverbeds, and sometimes not. At Quechee Gorge, the rapidly eroding river chewed down through the Ottauquechee's 200-foot-thick delta, hit bedrock, and kept eroding. The result is Quechee Gorge.

There's a final kind of ghost found at Quechee Gorge: Five of Vermont's rarer plants that once colonized the gorge environs have disappeared. The bedrock here is a calcium-rich schist derived from 400-million-year-old shallow sea sediments that formed when Vermont was the continent's east coast, and steep walls near fast water tend to be good places for rare plants. As late as 1930, two ferns (*Woodsia glabella* and *W. alpina*), a gentian (*Halenia deflexa*), a thimbleweed (*Anemone multifida*), a lily (*Tofieldia glutinosa*), and a fleabane (*Erigeron hyssopifolius*) were easily found by botanists. Now, only the fleabane can be found, and that only with some searching.

Botanists don't know why these five other rare plants have disappeared over the past 60 years. Some plants, like the thimbleweed, need very specific habitat, specifically limy cliffs that are sprayed by water. But others may have disappeared because of other, hard-to-detect changes in microclimate or in climate as a whole. No one knows.

The best place to see the gorge is from the US 4 bridge, which crosses directly over one of the most dramatic views straight down to river 165 feet below. A footpath to the north side of US 4 takes hikers 0.5 mile down to the river proper through a varied forest of hardwoods and, in one area, a hemlock forest. The state maintains a small campground 0.5 mile east of the gorge off US 4.

Directions: From I-89, take Exit 1 to US 4 west. Go approximately 3 miles west to the suspension bridge over the gorge; the campground is 0.5 mile east of the bridge.

Activities: Hiking, picnicking, camping.

Facilities: 47 tent/trailer sites, 7 lean-tos, restrooms, showers, playground, hiking trail along the gorge.

Dates: Gorge open year-round, campground open mid-May to Oct.

Fees: There is a fee for camping.

Closest town: Quechee, 1.5 miles.

For more information: Queechee State Park, 190 Dewey Mills Road, White

Wild ginger (Asarum canadense) has an acrid taste. However, the stems can be boiled in sugar water, and the decoction can be used in the place of sugar.

River Junction, VT 05001. Phone (802) 295-2990 (summer).Vermont Department of Forests, Parks and Recreation, RR1 Box 33, North Springfield, VT 05150. Phone (802) 885-8855 (winter).

AMITY POND NATURAL AREA AND STATE PARK

[Fig. 26(1)] A Woodstock couple, Elizabeth and Dick Brett, deeded this 184-acre parcel to the state of Vermont in 1969 with the strict condition that no machinery be used in the area, except for maintenance and emergency reasons. The land was once cut over and cleared for pasture; Now, second-growth forests and a red pine (*Pinus resinosa*) plantation are transforming the landscape. The fields are kept open in places, inviting white-tailed deer (*Odocoileus virginianus*), red fox (*Vulpes fulva*) and snowshoe hare (*Lepus americanus*), among other mammals. The fields are also a good place to listen for woodcock (*Scolopax minor*) in the spring when the birds are mating.

The openings, whether natural or maintained, make for fine views: From Amity Pond, for example, it's possible to see Mount Ascutney, Killington and Pico peaks.

Directions: From Woodstock, take VT 12 north 1.2 miles to South Pomfret Road. Bear right, and follow this road for 4.7 miles, bearing right at the South Pomfret Post Office. Look for Howe Hill Road and turn left, toward Sharon. Go 0.3 mile on Howe Hill and turn left onto East Barnard Road. The access is on the left approximately 2.3 miles up on this road; park on the right at the road's crest.

Activities: Hiking, cross-country skiing.

Facilities: Hiking trails, two shelters.

Dates: Open year-round.

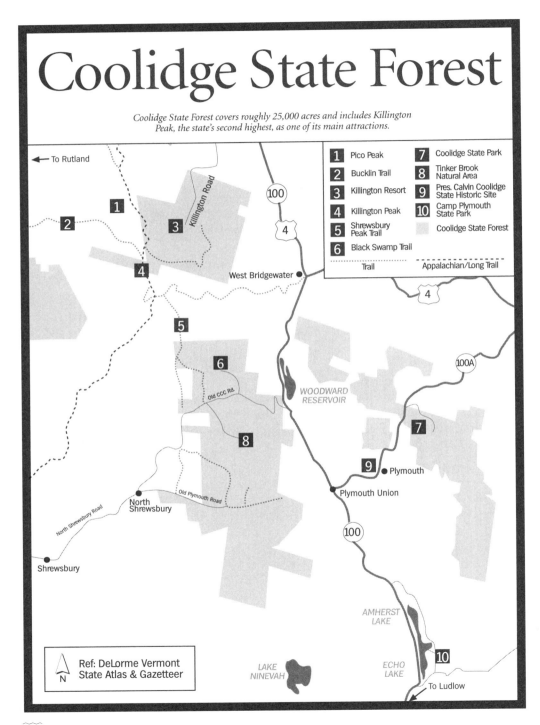

Coolidge State Forest

Coolidge State Forest covers roughly 25,000 acres and includes Killington Peak, the state's second highest, as one of its main attractions.

1 Pico Peak		**7** Coolidge State Park	
2 Bucklin Trail		**8** Tinker Brook Natural Area	
3 Killington Resort		**9** Pres. Calvin Coolidge State Historic Site	
4 Killington Peak		**10** Camp Plymouth State Park	
5 Shrewsbury Peak Trail		Coolidge State Forest	
6 Black Swamp Trail			

········· Trail   - - - - Appalachian/Long Trail

To Rutland

Killington Road

100

4

West Bridgewater

4

5

6

Old CCC Rd.

WOODWARD
RESERVOIR

100A

8

7

9 • Plymouth

Old Plymouth Road

North
Shrewsbury

Plymouth Union

North Shrewsbury Road

100

Shrewsbury

AMHERST
LAKE

N
Ref: DeLorme Vermont
State Atlas & Gazetteer

LAKE
NINEVAH

ECHO
LAKE

10

To Ludlow

Fees: None.

Closest town: Pomfret, 2 miles.

For more information: Vermont Department of Forests, Parks, and Recreation, RR1 Box 33, North Springfield, VT 05150. Phone (802) 886-2215.

SILVER LAKE STATE PARK

[Fig. 26(2)] This a good base camp for explorations eastward toward the White and Connecticut rivers, westward into the Green Mountains, and south to the Ascutney area. The campsites are set back from the lakeshore, where there is a picnic area and beach. The lake is shallow and supports mainly warm-water species such as northern pike (*Esox lucius*) and largemouth bass (*Micropterus salmoides*), with stocked rainbow and brown trout (*Oncorhynchus mykiss* and *Salmo trutta*) in the deeper water.

Directions: From exit 3 on Interstate 89, go west on VT 107 to Bethel, then continue on VT 107/12 about 2 miles and turn right on VT 12 south. In the village of Barnard, turn left on Hill Road; the state park entrance is on the right.

Activities: Camping, picnicking, fishing.

Facilities: Campground, lean-tos, picnic area, picnic shelter, beach, snack bar, restrooms boat rentals.

Dates: Mid-May to mid-Sept.

Fees: There are fees for camping and day use.

Closest town: Barnard, 0.1 mile.

For more information: Silver Lake State Park, Barnard, VT 05031. Phone (802) 234-9451 (summer). Vermont Department of Forests, Parks, and Recreation, RR 1 Box 33, North Springfield, VT 05150-9726. Phone (802) 885-8855 (winter).

Coolidge State Forest

[Fig. 27] Calvin Coolidge, the 30th president of the United States and a resident of Vermont in his early years, lends his name to the long ridge of mountains in central Vermont that includes the state's second highest peak, Killington. The Coolidge State Forest, now roughly 25,000 acres, has been pieced together, year after year, to protect the mountain peaks that make up the backbone of south-central Vermont. Adjacent to the forest is the 1,857-acre Plymsbury Wildlife Management Area, which is managed with the state forest for black bear (*Ursus americanus*) habitat.

The jewel in the crown is the 4,235-foot-high Killington Peak, most well known for the ski area on its northern slope. There's more than skiing, however. Killington's high-altitude spruce-fir forests, along with those of its neighboring peaks, are packed with unusual plants and birds.

Among the forest's treasures is Parker's Gore, obtained by the state in 1997 in a land swap with Killington Resort. This 2,948-acre area is some of the most important black bear habitat in the region. Several large stands of American beech (*Fagus grandifolia*) have been identified by biologists as crucial fall feeding habitat, and wetlands in the gore provide the succulent early spring vegetation that bears need just after they emerge from their winter sleep.

Bushwhackers can tackle the 3,840-foot-high Mendon Peak, one of the few trailless high-elevation summits in Vermont. The forest also includes Tinker Brook Natural Area, a small area of old-growth red spruce and hemlock on the steep slopes bordering Tinker Brook, and Cooper Lodge, which, at 3,850 feet, is the highest shelter on the Long/Appalachian Trail.

Directions: From the junction of US 4 and US 7 in Rutland, go east on US 4 approximately 7 miles to trailhead parking for hiking trails, and for ski area access.

Activities: Hiking, downhill and cross-country skiing, snowboarding, snowshoeing, hunting, fishing, bird-watching, mountain-biking, primitive camping.

Facilities: Hiking trails, 3 shelters, downhill and cross-country ski trails, conference center and hotel.

Dates: Open-year round.

Fees: There is a fee to use the ski resort's facilities.

Closest town: Rutland, 7 miles.

For more information: Vermont Department of Forests, Parks, and Recreation, RR 1 Box 33, North Springfield, VT 05150-9726. Phone (802) 885-8855. Phone (802) 483-2314.

BLACK BEAR
(Ursus americanus)
This bear grows to
300 pounds.

▓ HIKING TRAILS IN COOLIDGE STATE FOREST
KILLINGTON PEAK VIA THE LONG/APPALACHIAN TRAIL

[Fig. 27(4)] As the second highest peak in the Green Mountains, Killington Peak commands an impressive view. All the major summits in the Green Mountain range seem to march away from the summit, from Glastenbury Mountain in the south to Mount Mansfield in the north. To the west are the Taconics; and Mount Ascutney stands solo in the southeast. On clear days, the White Mountains in New Hampshire frame the eastern skyline, as do Lake Champlain and the Adirondacks to the west.

Killington's summit makes it worthwhile to shift your focus to the near-at-hand, too. The peak is covered by a 1-acre rock outcrop of 800-million-year-old coarse-grained schist that splinters and fractures at weaknesses in its mica layers. The craggy rocks are so inhospitable that only one higher plant, hoary sedge (*Carex canescens*) is able to grow here. Where foot traffic hasn't erased them from the rocks, map lichen (*Rhizocarpon geographicum*) and other crustose lichens cover many of the rock faces.

Just below the outcrop, on the western side of the peak, is an area of subalpine krummholz, one of only 10 in the state. Stunted balsam fir (*Abies balsamea*) and occasional heart-leaved paper birch (*Betula papyrifera* var. *cordifolia*) and mountain ash (*Sorbus americana*) make up the bulk of this community. The krummholz thicket is ideal nesting habitat for the globally rare Bicknell's thrush (*Catharus bicknelli*).

The spruce-fir forest below the krummholz is typical of high-elevation forests of this type elsewhere in Vermont, with two exceptions. Northern mountain ash (*Sorbus decora*), a relative of the mountain ash known from less than five sites in the state, has been found growing occasionally in Killington's spruce-fir forest. Small-flowered rush (*Luzula parviflora*), also uncommon, is widely scattered along the summit trail and along the Long/Appalachian Trail for about 0.5 mile south of Cooper Lodge.

As the Long/Appalachian Trail and side trails traverse the spruce-fir forest, look in the understory for Bartram's shadbush (*Amelanchier bartramiana*), skunk currant (*Ribes glandulosum*), and red-berried elder (*Sambucus pubens*). The common sedges are brownish sedge (*Carex brunnescens*) and hoary sedge (*Carex cannescens*), intermingled with goldthread (*Coptis trifolia*), intermediate woodfern (*Dryopteris intermedia*), Canada mayflower (*Maianthemum canadense*), and wood sorrel (*Oxalis acetosella*).

The berry-bearing plants found in the spruce-fir forests provide food for Bicknell's, Swainson's, and hermit thrushes (*Catharus bicknelli, C. guttatis*, and *C. ustulatus*). There are numerous seed-eating and insectivorous birds as well, including white-throated sparrows (*Zonotrichia albicollis*), dark-eyed juncoes (*Junco hyemalis*), golden-crowned and ruby-crowned kinglets (*Regulus satrapa* and *R. calendula*), and blackpoll, yellow-rumped, and magnolia warblers (*Dendroica magnolia, D. coronata*, and *D. striata*). Although small mammal information is lacking for the Killington area, state records show in 1934, biologists trapped long-tailed shrew (*Sorex dispar*) at about 4,000 feet on the mountain.

Directions: From the junction of US 4 and US 7 in Rutland, take US 4 east approximately 9.3 miles to trailhead parking on the south side of the road.

Trail: 5.6 miles one-way.

Elevation: 2,150 feet to 4,241 feet.

Degree of difficulty: Strenuous.

Surface and blaze: Rocky footpath. White blazes.

For more information: Green Mountain Club, 4711 Waterbury-Stowe Road, Waterbury Center, VT 05677. Phone (802) 244-7037. Appalachian Trail Conference, New England Regional Office, One Lyme Common, PO Box 312, Lyme, NH 03768. Phone (603) 795-4935.

BUCKLIN TRAIL

[Fig. 27(2)] If the Long /Appalachian Trail is the main highway to Killington's summit, then the Bucklin Trail is the sleepy back road approach. The trail, named for a family in Killington, climbs the western side of Killington Peak, passing the Green Mountain Club's Cooper Lodge, and then scrambles to the summit. Expect intermittent views of Pico Peak from the steady summit climb that characterizes the last leg of the trail.

Directions: From the junction of US 4 and US 7 in Rutland, go east on US 4 approximately 5 miles to Wheelerville Road. Turn south on Wheelerville Road and go roughly 3.9 miles to the trailhead on the left side of the road.

Trail: 3.5 miles one-way.

Elevation: 1,786 feet to 4,241 feet.

Degree of difficulty: Strenuous.

Surface and blaze: Rocky footpath. Blue blazes.

For more information: Green Mountain Club, 4711 Waterbury-Stowe Road, Waterbury Center, VT 05677. Phone (802) 244-7037.

PICO PEAK VIA THE LONG/APPALACHIAN TRAIL

[Fig. 27(1)] Although Killington Resort owns the 3,957-foot-high summit, two arms of the Coolidge State Forest frame Pico Peak. A new route for the Long/Appalachian Trail in this region brings the Long/Appalachian Trail to the west of Pico, with a spur trail to the summit. Despite all its ski area development, Pico's summit continues to draw hikers who are attracted by the historic nature of the area. The first record of a trail over the summit dates from an 1893 U.S. Geological Survey map. By 1910 and the formation of the Green Mountain Club, that trail had more or less disappeared in the undergrowth. In 1913 a crew working on the first sections of the Long Trail, the state's end-to-end hiking trail, cut the footpath north from Killington, across Pico Peak, as far as Mount Horrid. Since then, the trail has doubled as the Appalachian Trail and more or less held to this treadway in the Coolidge Range, until a new route for the trail was selected in 1996 as a way to provide permanent protection for both the Long and Appalachian rails while accommodating ski area development.

Much like Killington to the south, Pico's southern and western summit slopes are covered with a dense area of krummholz, thick with stunted balsam fir (*Abies balsamea*), heart-leaved paper birch (*Betula papyrifera* var. *cordifolia*), and mountain ash (*Sorbus americana*). Just south of the trailhead, near Sherburne Pass in the low-elevation hardwood forest, botanists have found a patch of wild millet (*Milium effusum*), which is uncommon in Vermont. Between Sherburne Pass and Pico Camp, some sugar maples and American beeches have been found to be between 200 and 300 years old. Roughly 1 mile from the trailhead is Sink Hole Brook, which literally disappears into a hole in the ground along the trail.

Because of the good views both from Pico summit and from overlooks along the route, the trail tends to be heavily used.

Directions: From the junction of US 4 and US 7 in Rutland, take US 4 east approximately 9.3 miles to trailhead parking on the south side of the road.

Trail: 2.9 miles one-way.

Elevation: 2,150 feet to 3,957 feet.

Degree of difficulty: Moderate.

Surface and blaze: Rocky footpath. White blazes; blue blazes for Pico Link.

For more information: Green Mountain Club, 4711 Waterbury-Stowe Road, Waterbury Center, VT 05677. Phone (802) 244-7037. Appalachian Trail Conference, New England Regional Office, One Lyme Common, PO Box 312, Lyme, NH 03768. Phone (603) 795-4935.

SHREWSBURY PEAK TRAIL/BLACK SWAMP TRAIL

[Fig. 27(5), Fig. 27(6)] The stunted spruce-fir forest near the summit of 3,720-foot Shrewsbury Peak offers prime habitat for the globally rare Bicknell's thrush (*Catharus bicknelli*). Birders will delight in trying to spot other typical species for this habitat, such as Swainson's thrush (*Catharus ustulatus*), yellow-bellied flycatcher (*Empidonax flaviventris*), blackpoll warbler (*Dendroica striata*), and winter wren (*Troglodytes troglodytes*). The summit has good views to the south and east of Mounts Ascutney, Kearsarge, and Monadnock, and Ludlow, Bromley, and Stratton mountains. Hikers wishing to make a loop hike can continue on the Shrewsbury Peak Trail after it crests the summit to pick up the Black Swamp Trail. The trail drops into Parker's Gore, one of the more wild parts of the Coolidge State Forest and home to a healthy population of black bear (*Ursus americanus*). Look for semicircles of black claw marks on the smooth gray trunks of beech trees, left by bears as they climb the trees for beech nuts. They feed by bending branches in toward the trunk, often breaking them. Because bears use wetlands near the Black Swamp Trail for spring foraging, the trail is generally closed until July 1.

Directions: From the junction of US 4 and VT 100 in West Bridgewater, go south on VT 100 approximately 3 miles to the Old CCC Road (closed in the winter). Go west on the Old CCC Road approximately 2 miles to the trailhead for the Black Swamp Trail on the right, or north side of the road. Continue on the Old CCC Road

BLACK-THROATED BLUE WARBLER
(Dendroica caerulescens)
A black face and white spot on the wing over a blue body identify this warbler.

another 1.5 miles beyond the Black Swamp trailhead to find the Shrewsbury Peak Trailhead, also on the right.

Trail: 1.8 miles one-way to Shrewsbury Peak via Shrewsbury Peak Trail; 2.1 miles one-way on Black Swamp Trail to summit.

Elevation: 2,200 feet to 3,720 feet.

Degree of difficulty: Moderate.

Surface and blaze: Rocky footpath. Blue blazes.

For more information: Vermont Department of Forests, Parks and Recreation, RD 2, Box 2161, Pittsford, VT 05763. Phone (802) 483-2314.

TINKER BROOK NATURAL AREA

[Fig. 27(8)] On the steep, rocky slopes that tumble down the north side of Burnt Mountain to Tinker Brook is a 45-acre forest of old-age red spruce (*Picea rubens*) and Eastern hemlock (*Tsuga canadensis*). Some of the trees in the natural area are thought to be more than 200 years old. The old-growth red spruce measure as much as 20 inches in diameter, and the hemlocks more than 3 feet.

One of the more unusual features of Tinker Brook is the quantity and size of striped maple (*Acer pensylvanicum*), an understory tree. Some of striped maples in this forest have trunks more than 6 inches in diameter. Above the steepest part of the ravine, where the slopes are more level, is an older northern hardwood forest with yellow birch (*Betula alleghaniensis*), sugar maple (*Acer saccharum*), beech (*Fagus grandifolia*), and white ash (*Fraxinus americana*). The understory in the hardwoods is much richer than in the old-growth spruce-hemlock forest below; look for Canada mayflower (*Maianthemum canadense*), painted and red trillium (*Trillium undulatum* and *T. erectum*), blue cohosh (*Caulophyllum thalictroides*), and great-spurred, round-leaved, and northern white violet (*Viola selkirkii, V. rotundifolia,* and *V. pallens*).

Directions: From the center of North Shrewsbury, take the Old Plymouth Road east roughly 2.3 miles to a pull-out near the trailhead on the north side of the road. A developed parking area can be found about 0.8 mile west of the trailhead on the paved portion of Old Plymouth Road.

Activities: Hiking, snowshoeing, cross-country skiing, fishing, hunting, primitive camping.

Facilities: Hiking trail, 1 shelter.

Dates: Open year-round.

Fees: None.

Closest town: North Shrewsbury, 2.3 miles.

For more information: Vermont Department of Forests, Parks and Recreation, RD 2, Box 2161, Pittsford, VT 05763. Phone (802) 483-2314.

KILLINGTON RESORT

[Fig. 27(3)] The largest ski resort in the East, Killington Resort covers six mountains with a 77-mile trail system, plus neighboring Pico Mountain, with its own 18-mile system. Killington was one of the first ski areas in America to provide snow-making, has the longest ski trail and steepest mogul run in the East, and most years in Vermont it is the first ski area to open and the last to close for the season. Though the emphasis is on skiing, the resort is building its four-season appeal, in part by hosting a hiking center, which rents equipment and sells maps.

Directions: From the junction of US 4 and US 7 in Rutland, go east on US 4 approximately 10 miles to the ski area access road; the resort is approximately 4 miles south on the road.

Activities: Hiking, downhill and cross-country skiing, snowboarding, snowshoeing, bird-watching, mountain-biking.

Facilities: Hotel and conference center, hiking center, restaurants, rental and retail shops, 33 lifts, 205 trails, 2 gondolas.

Dates: Open year-round.

Fees: There is a charge for resort use.

Closest town: Sherburne, 5 miles.

For more information: Killington Resort, Killington Road, Killington, VT 05751. Phone (802) 422-3333 or (800) 621-6867.

COOLIDGE STATE PARK

[Fig. 27(7)] The Depression-era Civilian Conservation Corps had a hand in constructing nearly all of Vermont's early recreational facilities, including some of the first ski trails on Mount Mansfield. The hand of the CCC can be seen here too: The corps constructed 19 log lean-tos, hewed out of massive timbers and seemingly built to last a century.

The ghost village of Plymouth Five Corners lies to the south of the park's facilities. It once hosted a mill and rock crusher erected by prospectors hoping to find gold in Buffalo Creek (which flows through nearby Camp Plymouth State Park, see page 153). Bushwhackers may find old cellar holes and stone foundations along the streams in the southern part of the park.

A number of short hiking trails loop through the area, including a 1-mile climb to a vista just below the summit of the 2,174-foot-high Slack Hill. Maps are available at the park ranger's office.

Directions: From Plymouth Union at the junction of VT 100 and VT 100A, go north on VT 100A approximately 2 miles to the park entrance on the right.

Activities: Camping, hiking, bird-watching, picnicking, bushwhacking, hunting.

Facilities: 25 campsites, 35 lean-tos, picnic area with shelters, playground, hiking trails, restrooms.

Dates: Open mid-May to Oct.

Fees: There is a charge for day use and camping.

Closest town: Plymouth, 1 mile.

For more information: Coolidge State Park, HCR 70 Box 105, Plymouth, VT 05056 Phone (802) 672-3612 (summer).Vermont Department of Forests, Parks and Recreation, RR1 Box 33, North Springfield, VT 05150. Phone (802) 885-8855 (winter).

🏛 CAMP PLYMOUTH STATE PARK

[Fig. 27(10)] California wasn't the only state to have a gold rush: In 1855, prospectors who had returned to Vermont from the 1849 gold rush found traces of gold in a small stream outside of Plymouth. That stream was Buffalo Brook, in the middle of Camp Plymouth State Park. For 30 years miners continued to find small quantities of gold in the stream, which originated as placer gold left in the outwash from the glaciers.

People still pan for gold in Buffalo Brook and sometimes even find gold. But most people come to the park to enjoy Echo Lake and the surrounding land. The lake is known for its perch (*Perca flavescens*) and smallmouth and largemouth bass (*Micropterus dolomieui* and *M. salmoides*) fishery. A short hiking trail brings hikers to a vista of the lake and passes an old cemetery that includes the remains of Amos Pollard, a Vermonter who farmed here before gold was found in Buffalo Brook.

In its previous incarnation, before the state purchased the land in 1984, the park was a Boy Scout camp. Two cabins left from Boy Scout camp days have been converted into fully furnished cottages for rent by the week.

Directions: From the junction of VT 100 and VT 103 in Ludlow, go north on VT 100 approximately 4.5 miles to a right turn just before Echo Lake. Turn right, or east, and go 1 mile to a crossroad and turn left. Go 1 mile north along the east side of Echo Lake to the park.

Activities: Group camping, hiking, boating, fishing, picnicking, gold panning, hunting.

Facilities: Two fully furnished cottages, group camping area with 6 lean-tos, tent sites, pit toilets, picnic shelter, playground, boat rentals.

Dates: Open mid-May through Oct.

Fees: There is a charge to use the facilities.

Closest town: Ludlow, 6.5 miles.

For more information: Camp Plymouth State Park, Rt. 1 Box 489, Ludlow, VT 05149. Phone (802) 672-3612 (summer). Vermont Department of Forests, Parks and Recreation, RR1 Box 33, North Springfield, VT 05150. Phone (802) 885-8855 (winter).

PRESIDENT CALVIN COOLIDGE STATE HISTORIC SITE

[Fig. 27(9)] Vermont's rolling green hills and picturesque farms often evoke another century, but the little village of Plymouth, President Calvin Coolidge's birthplace, truly remains nearly un-changed since the early 1900s.

A historic district around Coolidge's homestead includes a cheese factory built in 1890 that is still making cheese today, a one-room schoolhouse, a farm, an 1840s Congregational church, and the requisite family graveyard, this one containing six generations of Coolidges, including the president.

Vice President Coolidge was vaca-tioning at his Plymouth family home when he learned that President Warren Harding had died. Coolidge was given the presidential oath of office by his father, a notary public, on August 3, 1923, and the rest is, as they say, history.

A crab spider feeds on a syrphid fly.

Directions: From West Bridgewater at the junction of US 4 and VT 100, go south on VT 100 approximately 5 miles to Plymouth Union at the junction of VT 100A. Go north on VT 100A through Plymouth Notch to the well-marked entrance on the west side of the road.

Activities: Sight-seeing.

Facilities: Visitor center, gift shop, museum, restrooms.

Dates: Open late May through mid-Oct.

Fees: There is a fee for the museum.

Closest town: Plymouth.

For more information: Vermont Division for Historic Preservation, 135 State Street, Drawer 33, Montpelier, VT 05633-1201. Phone (802) 828-3051 (winter); (802) 672-3773 (summer).

Central Green Mtns.

FIGURE NUMBERS

29	Chittenden Area
30	Moosalamoo
31	Breadloaf Wilderness
32	Bristol Area
33	Monroe Skyline
34	Camel's Hump State Park

Central Green Mountains

From Sherburne Pass northward, the main ridge of the Green Mountains gets longer and leaner, culminating in the 10-mile straightaway of Lincoln Mountain. The section of the Long Trail known as the Monroe Skyline flows over every bump and knob on that ridge, remaining above 3,250 feet for 8 miles. It takes a short break at Appalachian Gap, then makes a final run over the ice- and fire-scoured schists of Camel's Hump before the plunge to the Winooski River, the lowest point on the Long Trail.

To the east, the lower, parallel ridge of the Northfield Mountains confines the upper White and Mad rivers into narrow, intermittent floodplains, leaving little room for farming. On the west side, the ridge falls away to the rolling lowlands of the Champlain Valley. Running parallel to the Green Mountain front is a layer of quartzite, a massive rock that forms ridges and cliffs along much of the length of Vermont, including the dramatic Bristol Cliffs and Rattlesnake Point near Lake Dunmore, a haunt of the pere-

[*Above:* No Vermont mountain is more eaily recognized than Camel's Hump]

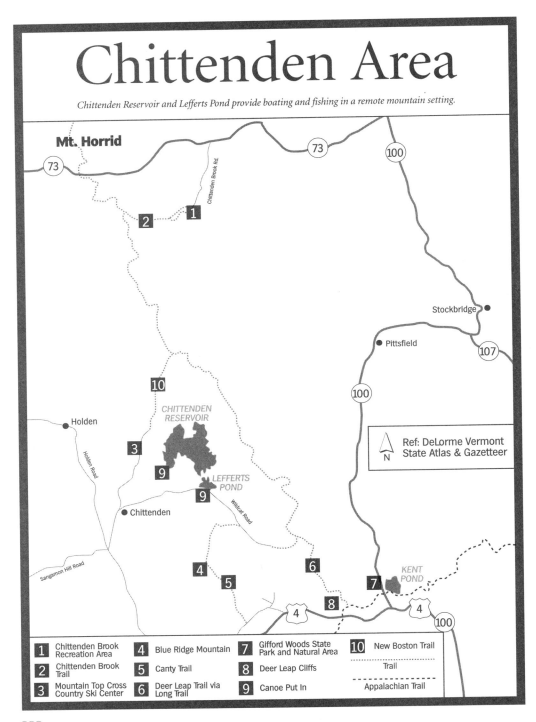

Chittenden Area

Chittenden Reservoir and Lefferts Pond provide boating and fishing in a remote mountain setting.

Mt. Horrid

73

Chittenden Brook Rd.

73

100

1

2

Stockbridge

Pittsfield

107

10

CHITTENDEN
RESERVOIR

Holden

100

3

9

LEFFERTS
POND

Holden Road

9

Wildcat Road

Chittenden

Sangamon Hill Road

4

6

KENT
POND

5

7

8

4

100

Ref: DeLorme Vermont
State Atlas & Gazetteer
N

1 Chittenden Brook Recreation Area	**4** Blue Ridge Mountain	**7** Gifford Woods State Park and Natural Area
2 Chittenden Brook Trail	**5** Canty Trail	**8** Deer Leap Cliffs
3 Mountain Top Cross Country Ski Center	**6** Deer Leap Trail via Long Trail	**9** Canoe Put In

10 New Boston Trail

.... Trail

— · · — Appalachian Trail

grine falcon (*Falco peregrinus*). The schist, glacial scouring, and elevation of the summits makes for low-diversity spruce-fir forests on thin, acid soils. In the valleys you're likely to run into limy bedrock and deep deposits of till and outwash that support fine hardwood forests, often with a fair variety of ferns, wildflowers, and wildlife.

In the lower two-thirds of this region, most of the higher-elevation areas fall in the Green Mountain National Forest, which includes the Breadloaf and Bristol Cliffs wilderness areas. North of Lincoln Gap, the state takes over with Camel's Hump State Park.

Chittenden Area

BLUE RIDGE MOUNTAIN

[Fig. 29(4)] Blue Ridge Mountain stands apart from the main range of the Green Mountains, which is dominated by Killington Peak to the east. This gives it a unique vantage, with views of Killington and the White Mountains of New Hampshire on one side, and the depths of the Otter Creek valley and the green wall of the Taconic Mountains on the other. The rock here is the billion-year-old Precambrian gneiss and quartzite that make up Killington Peak and other summits of the southern Green Mountains.

CANTY TRAIL

[Fig. 29(5)] The Canty Trail ascends the mountain from the south, taking a rocky line alongside a small cascading brook before curving west to the south summit. Continue southwest to an outcrop a short way past the main summit for more viewpoints.

Directions: From Rutland go 6 miles east on US 4, turn north on Turnpike Road and go 0.7 mile to a gated wood road on the left. The trail follows the road past Tall Timbers Camp.

Trail: 2.4 miles one-way.

Elevation: 1,800 feet to 3,278 feet.

Degree of difficulty: Moderate.

Surface and blaze: Rocky footpath. Blue blazes.

DEER LEAP CLIFFS

[Fig. 29(8)] It's an easy hike to the big views from the top of the Deer Leap Cliffs, where there is also rock climbing. You can hike one-way to the lookout via the Long and Deer Leap trails, or make a loop by continuing over Deer Leap Mountain and return via the Long Trail. The Green Mountain Club's Tucker-Johnson Shelter is 0.5 mile past the northern junction of the Deer Leap and Long trails.

DEER LEAP TRAIL VIA LONG TRAIL

[Fig. 29(6)] **Directions:** From Rutland take US 4 east to the height of land in Sherburne Pass. There is trail parking on the south side of the road, and the trail ascends east of the cliffs on the north side of the road.

Trail: 1.1 miles one-way to Deer Leap Lookout; or 3.5 mile loop over Deer Mountain.
Elevation: 2,150 feet to 2,580 feet (lookout) or 2,782 feet (Deer Leap Mountain).
Degree of difficulty: Easy.
Surface and blaze: Rocky footpath and ledge. White or blue blazes.

GIFFORD WOODS STATE PARK AND NATURAL AREA

[Fig. 29(7)] Gifford Woods Natural Area preserves a 7-acre stand of hardwood forest dominated by sugar maple (*Acer saccharum*), American beech (*Fagus grandifolia*), and yellow birch (*Betula alleghaniensis*), with smaller amounts of other species including white ash (*Fraxinus americana*), American basswood (*Tilia americana*), black cherry (*Prunus serotina*), and hop hornbeam (*Ostrya virginiana*). While the area was never cut over completely, it was used as a sugarbush, or a place where trees are tapped for maple syrup production, in the nineteenth century. Consequently, it may have been modified extensively, so botanists don't consider it undisturbed old growth. One hemlock (*Tsuga canadensis*) in the stand is more than 400 years old. The herbaceous flora includes some 17 ferns and clubmosses, including the uncommon rattlesnake fern (*Botrychium virginianum*) and Goldie's fern (*Dryopteris goldiana*), and 64 flowering plant species.

The Appalachian Trail passes through the state park, which also has a campground and a boat ramp on Kent Pond. A 0.7-mile loop trail travels through northern hardwoods around the campground. There are no trails in the old growth, but visitors are free to wander among the big trees.

Directions: From the junction of VT 4 and VT 100 in Sherburne, go 0.4 mile north on VT 100. The campground is on the west side of VT 100, and the old-growth area is on the east side, just north of the boat ramp parking area on Kent Pond.

Activities: Short walks, bird-watching, picnicking, camping, boating, fishing.

Facilities: 27 campsites, 21 lean-tos, restrooms, showers, picnic area, playground, boat ramp.

Dates: Open mid-May to mid-Oct..

Fees: There is a charge for camping.

Closest town: Sherburne, 3 miles.

For more information: Gifford Woods State Park, HC 65, Killington, VT 05751. Phone (802) 775-5354 (summer). Vermont Department of Forests, Parks, and Recreation, RR 1 Box 33, North Springfield, VT 05150-9726. Phone (802) 885-8855 (winter).

CHITTENDEN RESERVOIR AND LEFFERTS POND

[Fig. 29] Set in a broad basin ringed by 2,000- to 3,000-foot summits, these two lakes provide boating and fishing in a remote mountain setting. The 674-acre reservoir is owned by the Central Vermont Public Service Company, which uses the water for power generation, resulting in some water-level fluctuation. There is a boat ramp on the southwestern bay, and a carry-in canoe put-in on the southeastern bay, near Lefferts Pond. Motorboats are limited to 15 horsepower.

Half-mile-long Lefferts Pond is a wildlife management area with extensive wetlands on the eastern and southern shores, home to beaver (*Castor canadensis*), muskrat (*Ondatra zibethicus*), mink (*Mustela vison*), otter (*Lutra canadensis*), and several waterfowl species including wood duck (*Aix sponsa*). The wetlands of the pond are also a good place to look and listen for wetland birds like American bittern (*Botaurus lentiginosus*) and snipe (*Gallinago gallinago*), bullfrogs (*Rana catesbiana*), and green frogs (*Rana clamitans*). There is no boat ramp, but there are canoe put-ins on the north and south shores.

Chittenden Reservoir has fishing for largemouth bass (*Micropterus salmoides*), northern pike (*Esox lucius*), stocked trout (*Salmo* spp.), and walleye (*Stizostedion vitreum*), while Lefferts Pond supports warm-water species only.

Directions: From Rutland, go 4 miles east on route 4 to Mendon, and turn left toward East Pittsford. Continue straight through East Pittsford, turn right at a T intersection, and continue to the village of Chittenden. Take Chittenden Dam Road 2 miles to the boat ramp on the reservoir. For the canoe put-ins, bear right off of the dam road onto Wildcat Road 1.2 miles out of Chittenden, then turn left onto an unimproved access road (closed in winter and mud season) which ends at a parking area between the lakes. There is also canoe access to Lefferts Pond directly off Wildcat Road where it passes near the pond.

Activities: Boating, canoeing, fishing, wildlife-watching.

Facilities: Boat ramp.

Dates: Open May through Nov.

Fees: None.

Closest town: Pittsford, 6 miles.

For more information: Central Vermont Public Service Company, 77 Grove Street, Rutland, VT 05701. Phone (802) 773-2711.

MOUNTAIN TOP CROSS-COUNTRY SKI CENTER

[Fig. 29(3)] With 40 miles (65 km) of trails groomed for both classical and skate skiing, and 28 miles (45 km) more single-track or backcountry, Mountain Top is one of Vermont's best cross-country ski areas. The trail system is centered on the privately owned Mountain Top Inn, with many trails in the Green Mountain National Forest, and stretches from the shores of Chittenden Reservoir at 1,500 feet to the eponymous summit at over 2,000 feet. The area around the reservoir is promising ground for wildlife tracking. There is a log cabin warming hut near the top, and the open fields and hill slopes have views of the Green Mountains and the reservoir. The Catamount Trail (*see* page 304) passes through Mountain Top's trail system. The inn doubles as an equestrian center in both summer and winter.

Directions: From Rutland, go 4 miles east on VT 4 to Mendon, and turn left toward East Pittsford. Continue straight through East Pittsford, turn right at a T intersection, and continue to the village of Chittenden. From Chittenden, take Mountain Top Road about 1.8 miles to Mountain Top Inn.

Activities: Cross-country skiing, snowshoeing, ice skating, sleigh rides, horseback riding.

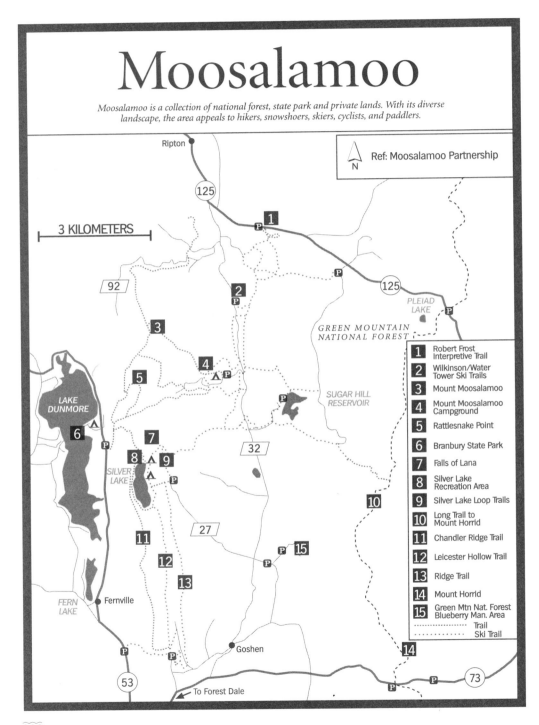

Moosalamoo

Moosalamoo is a collection of national forest, state park and private lands. With its diverse landscape, the area appeals to hikers, snowshoers, skiers, cyclists, and paddlers.

Ripton

125

N

Ref: Moosalamoo Partnership

3 KILOMETERS

92

1 Robert Frost
Interpretive Trail

2 Wilkinson/Water
Tower Ski Trails

3 Mount Moosalamoo

4 Mount Moosalamoo
Campground

5 Rattlesnake Point

6 Branbury State Park

7 Falls of Lana

8 Silver Lake
Recreation Area

9 Silver Lake Loop Trails

10 Long Trail to
Mount Horrid

11 Chandler Ridge Trail

12 Leicester Hollow Trail

13 Ridge Trail

14 Mount Horrid

15 Green Mtn Nat. Forest
Blueberry Man. Area

.... Trail

·············· Ski Trail

PLEIAD
LAKE

GREEN MOUNTAIN
NATIONAL FOREST

SUGAR HILL
RESERVOIR

LAKE
DUNMORE

SILVER
LAKE

FERN
LAKE

Fernville

Goshen

53

To Forest Dale

73

Facilities: Full-service inn and restaurant, ski and snowshoe rentals, ski school.

Dates: The ski season generally runs from mid-Dec. through late March, and the inn is open year-round.

Fees: There is a trail fee, but inn guests use the trails free.

Closest town: Chittenden, 1.8 miles.

For more information: Mountain Top Inn, Mountain Top Road, Chittenden, VT 05737. Phone (800) 445-2100.

CHITTENDEN BROOK RECREATION AREA

[Fig. 29(1)] The Green Mountain National Forest Chittenden Brook Recreation Area includes an off-the-beaten-track campground and a 7.3-mile (12-km) network of hiking and cross-country ski trails. The Chittenden Brook Trail connects the campground to the Long Trail, and the 2.3-mile Brandon Gap ski trail connects it to Brandon Gap, avoiding the steep ground along the ridge. The 2.5-mile access road to the campground is not plowed in winter, but some trails begin within 0.6 mile of VT 73, where there is winter parking.

Directions: From the junction of VT 100 and VT 73 in Rochester, travel west 5 miles on VT 73, then turn south on Forest Road 45. The campground is 2.5 miles from VT 73.

Activities: Camping, hiking, cross-country skiing, fishing.

Facilities: Campground with washrooms and nonflush vault toilets, ungroomed cross-country ski trails.

Dates: Camping May to mid-Nov.

Fees: There is a charge for camping.

Closest town: Rochester, 8.5 miles.

For more information: Green Mountain National Forest Rochester Ranger District, RR 2, Box 35, Rochester, VT 05767. Phone (802) 767-4261.

CHITTENDEN BROOK TRAIL

[Fig. 29(2)] **Directions:** This trail begins at the trail parking area 0.6 mile off VT 73 on Forest Road 45 and passes near a beaver pond before ascending to the Long Trail between Farr Peak and Goshen Mountain. The Green Mountain Club Sunrise shelter is 1.4 miles north from the Chittenden Brook's junction with the Long Trail.

Trail: 3.7 miles one-way.

Elevation: 1,400 to 2,951 feet.

Degree of difficulty: Moderate.

Surface and blaze: Old road and rocky footpath. Blue blazes.

Moosalamoo

[Fig. 30] Moosalamoo is a collection of national forest, state park, and private lands that provides ample opportunities for hikers, snowshoers, skiers, cyclists, and paddlers. It straddles the geologic contact between the limy Paleozoic rocks of the Valley of Vermont and the acid Precambrian core of the Green Mountains, and covers elevations from 569-foot Lake Dunmore to 3,366-foot Gillespie Peak on the Long Trail. This diversity in the landscape results in a corresponding diversity of plant and animal communities.

For more information: Moosalamoo Partnership, Brandon Area Chamber of Commerce, PO Box 267, Brandon, VT 05733. Phone (800) 448-0707.

MOUNT HORRID

[Fig. 30(14)] The 700-foot Great Cliff of Mount Horrid forms the northern wall of Brandon Gap, an ice-carved passage across the main spine of the Green Mountains between Brandon and Rochester. The cliff is a well-established nesting area for peregrine falcon (*Falco peregrinus*), which can be observed from a parking area on VT 73. The view of the cliffs from below is almost as good as the view from the top. The broken gneiss of the cliffs falls away to a steep, forested talus slope with a beaver pond at its base. The Long Trail climbs steeply to a short side trail that ends at a cliff top overlook. The side trail to the overlook is closed when peregrine falcons are nesting on the cliffs, usually from May through mid-August.

Directions: From the junction of VT 73 and VT 53 in Forest Dale, take VT 73 5.2 miles east to the height of land in Brandon Gap. The Long Trail parking lot is on the south side of the highway, and a scenic viewpoint of the cliff with interpretive signs is 0.3 mile east.

LONG TRAIL TO MOUNT HORRID

[Fig. 30(10)] **Trail:** 0.7 mile one-way.

Elevation: 2,180 to 2,800 feet.

Degree of difficulty: Strenuous.

Surface and blaze: Rocky footpath, log steps. White blazes.

GREEN MOUNTAIN NATIONAL FOREST BLUEBERRY MANAGEMENT AREA

[Fig. 30(15)] The old fields and ledgy slopes of Moosalamoo make for good berries of all kinds, but at its blueberry management area, Green Mountain National Forest officials use prescribed burns every three to five years to keep an abandoned downhill ski area open for berries, mainly one or more species of lowbush blueberries (*Vaccinium* spp.), These species favor dry ground and survive and grow vigorously after fire. Raspberries and blackberries (*Rubus* spp.) and wild cherries (*Prunus* spp.) are also found in some spots. Berry production is weather-dependent and is usually best after a wet midsummer period. The berries start to ripen in mid-July, with good picking extending as late as the end of August.

As humans are not the only animals to enjoy a good blueberry, this and other berry-rich areas are good places to see a variety of birds, from robins (*Turdus migratorius*) to ruffed grouse (*Bonasa umbellus*); and mammals, from chipmunks (*Tamias* striatus) to black bear (*Ursus americanus*). The open hillsides also give spectacular views of the surrounding country, including the Green, Taconic, and Adirondack mountains.

Directions: From the junction of VT 73 and VT 53 in Forest Dale, take VT 73 about 1.6 miles east and turn left toward the village of Goshen on Capen Hill Road. Go approximately 0.4 mile to Goshen and take Forest Road 32 north about 1.7 miles. Turn right on Flora White Road, then left after 0.6 mile on Forest Road 224. There are two small parking areas on the left side of the road, about 0.5 mile from the turn-off.

Activities: Berry picking, bird- and wildlife-watching.
Facilities: None.
Dates: Berry picking mid-July through Aug.
Fees: None.
Closest town: Goshen, 2.8 miles.
For more information: Green Mountain National Forest Middlebury Ranger District, RD 4 Box 1260, Middlebury, VT 05753. Phone (802) 388-4362.

ROUND-LEAF SUNDEW
(*Drosera rotundifolia*)
Insects attracted to a sweet sticky fluid on the tips of the sundew's hairy leaves become stuck among the hairs that bend like tentacles to smother the victim.

🔲 BRANBURY STATE PARK

[Fig. 30(6)] This small state park on the east shore of Lake Dunmore makes a great base camp for outings in the Moosalamoo area. The 3.3-mile-long lake has summer residences along most of its shoreline, and it is heavily used by motorboats, making it less than ideal for canoeists. There is fishing for both warm-water fish and stocked lake trout (*Salvelinus namaycush*) and brook trout (*S. fontinalus*). The park has a lakefront day-use area with a swimming beach, plenty of picnic tables, and acres of lawn.

Directions: From the junction with US 7 and VT 53 between Middlebury and Brandon, take VT 53 3.5 miles south. The state park entrance is on the right.

Activities: Camping, picnicking, hiking, swimming, boating, fishing.
Facilities: 39 camp sites, 6 lean-tos, showers, restrooms, showers, swimming beach, boat rentals.
Dates: Open mid-May to mid-Oct.
Fees: There are fees for camping and day use.
Closest town: Salisbury, 6 miles.
For more information: Branbury State Park, RR 2 Box 2421, Brandon, VT 05733. Phone (802) 247-5925 (summer). Vermont Department of Forests, Parks, and Recreation, 317 Sanitorium Road, West Wing, Pittsford, VT 05763-9358. Phone (802) 483-2001 (winter).

MOUNT MOOSALAMOO CAMPGROUND

[Fig. 30(4)] This small, out-of-the-way forest campground is well away from the bustle around Lake Dunmore. Hiking trails connect it to Mount Moosalamoo and the Silver Lake area.

Directions: From the junction of VT125 and VT 116 in East Middlebury, take VT 125 about 6 miles east and turn south on Forest Road 32 (Ripton-Goshen Road). Turn right on the campground access road 3.2 miles from VT 125.

Activities: Camping, hiking.

Facilities: Campground, nonflush vault toilets.

Dates: Open mid-May to mid-Oct..

Fees: There is a fee for camping.

Closest town: Ripton, 4.2 miles.

For more information: USFS Middlebury Ranger District, RD #4, Box 1260, Middlebury, VT 05753. Phone (802) 388-4362.

SILVER LAKE RECREATION AREA

[Fig. 30(8)] There is no open road access to Lake Dunmore's little sister, a small, quiet-water lake accessible to hikers and canoeists rugged enough to make the 0.6-mile carry-in on the Goshen Trail. The lake is now a part of a small-scale, vintage hydroelectric scheme that collects water from streams above Silver Lake and moves it in under- and above-ground pipes over 2 miles, through Silver Lake, to a small brick powerhouse on VT 53, just south of Branbury State Park.

The Green Mountain National Forest Silver Lake Recreation Area provides primitive camping and picnicking sites under hemlocks and hardwoods along the east shore. The Silver Lake Loop Trail skirts the shoreline of the lake and intersects the longer Chandler Ridge and Leicester Hollow trails. Interpretive signs along the trail comment on flora, fauna, and the lake's history as the site of a 60-room hotel used for religious camp meetings. Day hikers can combine a loop around the lake with a visit to the Falls of Lana or Rattlesnake Cliffs.

The lake lies in a little valley between

Peregrine Falcon

The peregrine falcon (*Falco peregrinus*) is one of the Endangered Species Act's success stories. It was extirpated in Vermont and virtually throughout the conterminous U.S. due to indiscriminate use of DDT, but it has been widely reestablished through a captive breeding and release program. In 1997, there were 16 territorial pairs in Vermont with 9 successful breeding pairs, all on cliffs and ledges. Three young were fledged by a pair at Mount Horrid. Falcons are swift aerial predators, and can take other birds on the wing. Flying at speeds of over 60 mph and stooping (diving) at speeds up to 175 mph, peregrines favor a wide variety of robin-to duck-sized birds. Breeding pairs engage in spectacular courtship flights, wheeling, looping, and diving along cliff faces while calling to one another.

the quartzite Chandler Ridge to the west and schistlike graywacke of the Green Mountains to the east. In between the two there is a narrow band of marble that makes for an interesting twist in the local ecology. The more easily eroded marble forms a natural line of weakness for Leicester Hollow Brook, a small stream that runs southward from a height-of-land just south of Silver Lake. It also makes for locally sweet, rich soil conditions along the Leicester Hollow Trail. One sign of this is American basswood (*Tilia americana*), mixed in with the usual crew of northern hardwoods: beech, birch, and maple. But the ferns and wildflowers in the understory are the real indicators—maidenhair fern (*Adiantum pedatum*), bulblet bladder fern (*Cystopteris bulbifera*), blue cohosh (*Caulophyllum thalictroides*), wild leeks (*Allium tricoccum*), and herb robert (*Geranium maculatum*) are all good indicators of relatively rich soil conditions. Much of the trail is lined with dense growth of stinging nettle (*Laportea canadensis*).

AMERICAN CRANBERRY (*Vaccinium macrocarpon*)

The high and dry quartzite of Chandler Ridge provides a striking contrast to Leicester Hollow. Here the hardwoods are joined or in places dominated by red oak (*Quercus rubra*), white oak (*Quercus alba*), and hop hornbeam (*Ostrya virginiana*), all indicators of relatively dry, warm, and usually acid soil conditions, as are bracken fern (*Pteridium aquilinum*), blueberries (*Vaccinium* spp.), huckleberries (*Gaylussacia baccata*), and trailing arbutus (*Epigaea repens*). Another trail, the Ridge Trail, travels through typical moist upland hardwood forest over Green Mountain graywacke east of Leicester Hollow.

The Chandler Ridge, Leicester Hollow, and Ridge trails can be combined to make loops of up to about 8.5 miles from the Silver Lake Campground or from the Leicester Hollow trailhead in Forest Dale. The Silver Lake and Leicester Hollow trails are open to mountain bikes, and the 2.2 mile Minnie Baker Trail, also open to bicycles, can be used as a cutoff back to VT 53, making an 11.3 mile road and trail loop from the Silver Lake trail parking area.

Directions: Silver Lake is accessible by trail only. From Forest Dale and the junction of VT 53 and VT 73, go east on VT 73 1.7 miles, then turn left on Forest Road 32 through Goshen. After another 2.7 miles, turn left on Forest Road 27 and park at its end for the trailhead to the Goshen Trail (0.6 mile, easy), which provides the shortest way to the lake.

Activities: Camping, canoeing, swimming, fishing, hiking, mountain biking.

Facilities: Camp and picnic sites with tables, outhouses.

Dates: Open year-round.

Fees: None.

Closest town: Salisbury, 7.5 miles.

For more information: Green Mountain National Forest Middlebury Ranger District, RD 4, Box 1260, Middlebury, VT 05753. Phone (802) 388-4362.

SILVER LAKE AND SILVER LAKE LOOP TRAILS [FIG. 30(9)]

Directions: From Forest Dale at the junction of VT 73 and VT 53, go north on VT

WOOD FROG
(Rana sylvatica)

53 approximately 4.6 miles to the trailhead, a shady parking lot on the east side of the road, 0.6 mile south of the Branbury State Park entrance.

Trail: 1.5 miles one-way to Silver Lake; 2.5-mile interpretive loop around the lake.

Elevation: 800 feet to 1,250 feet.

Degree of difficulty: Easy.

Surface and blaze: Old road, unblazed but obvious.

LEICESTER HOLLOW, CHANDLER RIDGE, AND RIDGE TRAILS

[Fig. 30(12), Fig. 30(11), Fig. 30(13)] These three trails can be accessed from the Leicester Hollow trailhead. The Chandler Ridge Trail leaves the Leicester Hollow Trail 0.4 miles from the trailhead, and the Ridge Trail leaves the Leicester Hollow Trail 0.3 miles from the trailhead.

Directions: From Forest Dale at the junction of VT 73 and VT 53, go east 0.8 mile on VT 73 to Brandon Town Road 40 (a dirt road) at the Churchill House Inn. Turn left on the road, and go 0.6 mile to the end, where there is parking.

Trail: Leicester Hollow Trail, 4.6 miles one-way; Chandler Ridge Trail, 3.5 miles one-way; Ridge Trail, 3.9 miles one-way.

Elevation: 1,250 feet to 1,600 feet.

Degree of difficulty: Moderate.

Surface and blaze: Old road and rocky footpath. Blue blazes.

FALLS OF LANA, RATTLESNAKE POINT, AND MOUNT MOOSALAMOO

Three trails lead to the Falls of Lana—two from the Branbury State Park Campground on the north side of Sucker Brook and one from a trail parking area on VT 53 on the south side of the brook, 0.2 mile south of the park entrance. The rough trail up the southern side of the brook follows a penstock or intake pipe for the hydroelectric station, making it an unattractive route, but the trail offers a view up the falls and is one way to make a loop of it. The Silver Lake Trail (see above) also passes by the top of the falls. Along Sucker Brook near the top of the falls there is a hike-in picnic area with tables in the shade of tall hemlocks.

The Falls of Lana [Fig. 30(7)] is a series of 10- to 15-foot cascades in a steep chute, ending in a broad green pool. The bedrock is massive Cheshire Quartzite, the same rock that makes up Bristol Cliffs to the north and the White Rocks cliffs to the south. Here the stream has dug in along a weak zone in the rocks, where the joints are closely spaced. The name is a play on the name of General Wool, whose men discovered the falls in 1850 when the general was fresh from a tour of duty in Mexico—llana is the Spanish word for wool.

The steep slopes around and below the falls are dominated by Eastern hemlock

Berry Natural History

Berries eaten by humans–blueberries (*Vaccinium* spp.), raspberries (*Rubus* spp.), and the like–are a small fraction of the many different kinds of fleshy fruits in Vermont's flora. Some berries, like those of nightshade (*Solanum dulcamara*) or baneberry (*Actaea rubra*) are poisonous to humans, and others we may find tasteless (dogwoods, *Cornus* spp.), sour (choke cherry, *Prunus virginiana*), or otherwise bad-tasting, but they are all eaten safely by birds or other animals.

While berries vary widely in their nutritional content, they represent a significant energy investment for the parent plant. The return on the investment comes in the form of seed dispersal. Birds and other dispersers may digest the fleshy part of the berry while the seed survives the quick passage through their simple guts. In the final event, the seeds are carried far from the parent plant, and deposited with a little fertilizer for an added boost.

Not all fruit-eating animals act as dispersers; those that crush or chew the seeds or have complex digestive systems, usually mammals, may be seed predators, effectively destroying seeds rather than dispersing them.

Blueberries and other sweet berries are usually consumed in summer as a ready source of energy. Some fall berries, notably dogwoods, have relatively high fat contents and are important foods for migrating birds. Lower-quality fruits from species such as winterberry holly (*Ilex verticillata*) and sumac (*Rhus* spp.) may be ignored by migrant species, but are an important survival resource for winter resident birds such as pine grosbeaks (*Piniciola enucleator*) and cedar waxwings (*Bombycilla cedrorum*).

(*Tsuga canadensis*), a species that produces deep shade, discouraging undergrowth. Add to this lack of undergrowth the soil compaction caused by heavy foot traffic as people try to reach and view the cascades, and it becomes difficult to tell where the trail isn't. Nearest the falls there are open quartzite ledges with pockets of lowbush blueberry (*Vaccinium* spp.) and mats of rock polypody (*Polypodium virginianum*).

From the falls you can continue up the brook and pick up the trails to Rattlesnake Point [Fig. 30(5)] and Mount Moosalamoo. The Rattlesnake Cliff Trail provides a moderate route through forests dominated by hemlock or beech. The steep Aunt Jenny Trail provides a more direct but strenuous route to Rattlesnake Point. Like Mount Horrid, the cliffs below Rattlesnake Point provide nest sites for peregrine falcon (*Falco peregrinus*), so that the Aunt Jenny and the side trails to the lookouts are closed from as early as mid-April until as late as August 1. The closure dates vary from year-to-year, and state officials remove signs and trail blockages when the young birds are off the nest. When open, the cliffs, also composed of Cheshire Quartzite, have lovely views of Lake Dunmore, the Adirondacks, and the Champlain Valley.

The Oak Ridge Trail (7.1 miles, moderate) runs from Rattlesnake Point over Mount Moosalamoo [Fig. 30(3)] to VT 125 in Ripton. For the first 0.5 mile or so, as it skirts the top of the cliffs, the Oak Ridge Trail passes through a dry ridgetop forest dominated by red oak (*Quercus rubra*), with patches of huckleberry (*Gaylussacia baccata*), beaked hazelnut (*Corylus cornuta*), trailing arbutus (*Epigaea repens*), wintergreen (*Gaultheria procumbens*), and other dry ground species in the understory. In late spring, look for the pink, trumpet-shaped flowers of pink azalea (*Rhododendron nudiflorum*) in the area around the trail junction. Mount Moosalamoo has views to the south and east. You can use the Moosalamoo (2.3 miles, easy) and North Branch (2.2 miles, easy) trails to loop back to Silver Lake from near the summit. From Branbury State Park this makes for an 8.7-mile day, or a 7.7-mile loop from Moosalamoo Campground.

Trail: 0.7 miles one-way to Falls of Lana; 2.3 miles one-way to Rattlesnake Point. Loops of 1.4 to 8.7 miles can be made using connecting trails.

Elevation: 600 feet to 900 feet (falls), 1,700 feet (Rattlesnake Point), or 2,659 feet (Mount Moosalamoo).

Degree of difficulty: Easy to moderate, except the Aunt Jenny Trail, which is strenuous.

Surface and blaze: Old road, rocky footpath, and ledge. Blue blazes.

ROBERT FROST INTERPRETIVE TRAIL

[Fig. 30(1)] Robert Frost spent 23 summers in the Ripton area, and the mountains, brooks, and hill farms in the area were a source of inspiration and imagery for his poetry. This short interpretive trail presents Frost's poems linked to the natural history of the old field and woods that it loops through. The Green Mountain National Forest keeps the field open by prescribed burning, making for both good berry-picking in late summer and views of the surrounding hills, including 2,513-foot Robert Frost Mountain to the northwest. The first 0.3 mile of the trail, as far as a bridge over a small brook, is wheelchair friendly.

Directions: From the junction of VT 125 and VT 116 in East Middlebury, take VT 125 east about 7 miles. The parking area is on the right.

Trail: 1-mile loop.

Elevation: 1,280 feet to 1,320 feet.

Degree of difficulty: Easy.

Surface and blaze: Graded trail, boardwalks, and smooth footpath. Metal interpretive signs.

WINTER SPORTS IN MOOSALAMOO

[Fig. 30(2)] The rolling upland terrain of Moosalamoo lends itself well to cross-country and backcountry skiing, snowshoeing, and wildlife tracking. Anyone who's had a grouse explode from the snow under their ski tips, followed the tracks of a fox on the trail of a snowshoe hare, or seen tree bark stripped by moose or deer knows that wildlife can, in some ways, be more visible in winter than in summer.

In Moosalamoo, three privately run touring centers and two small Green Mountain National Forest trail systems are interconnected by the Catamount and other trails to form a network of over 100 miles of trails, with opportunities to push the limits further by using the Long Trail and hiking trails around Mount Moosalamoo.

The Blueberry Hill Inn's ski touring center has 31 miles (50 km) of groomed cross-country ski trails on both private land and the Green Mountain National Forest, including a loop that ascends to 2,600 feet on nearby Romance Mountain. The Rikert Ski Touring Center, on the Breadloaf Campus of Middlebury College in Ripton, has 26 miles (40 km) of groomed trails. The Churchill House Inn adds another 15 miles (24 km) of groomed trails to the network. The Wilkinson (5.2 miles, 8.3 km) and Water Tower (4.9 miles, 7.8 km) trail systems are

TRAILING ARBUTUS
(Epigaea repens)
The state flower of Massachusetts, the trailing arbutus has fragrant spring flowers.

small, ungroomed, free Green Mountain National Forest ski areas near Ripton. Across VT 125 in Ripton, the 3-mile (4.8 km) Norske Trail connects the Middlebury Snow Bowl, a small downhill ski area, to the Rikert Ski Touring Center.

Directions: From the junction of VT 73 and VT 53 in Forest Dale, take VT 73 1.6 miles east and turn left toward the Village of Goshen at the southern end of the road to find Forest Road 32. Or, from the junction of VT 125 and VT 116 in East Middlebury, take VT 125 about 6 miles east and turn right onto the northern end of Forest Road 32. Blueberry Hill Inn is on Forest Road 32, about 2.8 miles north of Goshen or 5.4 miles south of VT 125. The Rikert Ski Touring Center is on VT 125, about 9 miles east of East Middlebury. The Churchill House Inn is on VT 73, 1 mile west of Forest Dale. For the Wilkinson and Water Tower systems, there is a winter parking area on Forest Road 32 about 4.8 miles south of VT 125. There is also winter parking 0.3 mile off of VT 125 on Forest Road 67, which turns right off of VT 125 about 1 mile east of the Rikert Ski Touring Center.

Activities: Cross-country skiing, snowshoeing.

Fees: There are trail fees at touring centers with groomed trails. The Green Mountain National Forest Trails are free.

For more information: Blueberry Hill Inn, RR 3, Goshen, VT, 05733. Phone (800) 448-0707. Churchill House Inn, RR3 Box 3265, Brandon, VT 05733. Phone (802) 247-3300. Rikert Ski Touring Center, Middlebury College, Middlebury, VT 05753. Phone (802) 388-2759. Green Mountain National Forest, Middlebury Ranger District, RD 4, Box 1260, Middlebury, VT 05753. Phone (802) 388-4362.

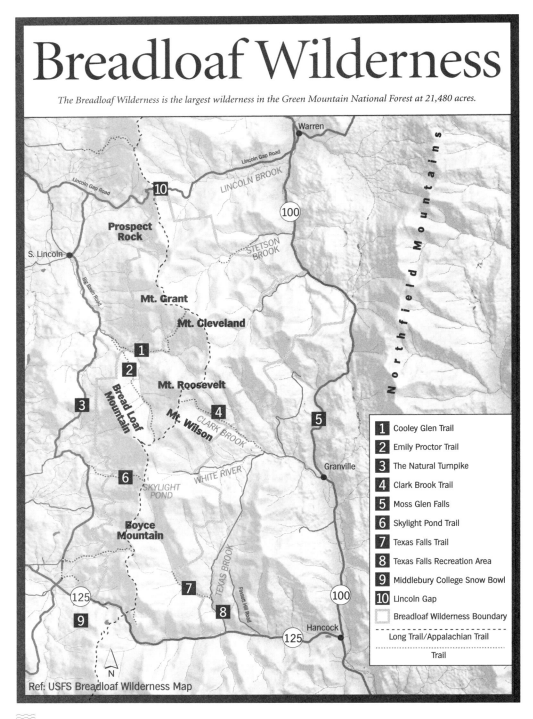

Breadloaf Wilderness

The Breadloaf Wilderness is the largest wilderness in the Green Mountain National Forest at 21,480 acres.

Warren

Lincoln Gap Road

LINCOLN BROOK

Lincoln Gap Road

10

100

Prospect Rock

S. Lincoln

STETSON BROOK

Big Basin Road

Mt. Grant

Mt. Cleveland

1

2

Mt. Roosevelt

Bread Loaf Mountain

3

Mt. Wilson

4

CLARK BROOK

5

Granville

6

WHITE RIVER

SKYLIGHT POND

Boyce Mountain

125

7

TEXAS BROOK

Fassett Hill Road

100

8

9

Hancock

125

N

Northfield Mountains

1	Cooley Glen Trail
2	Emily Proctor Trail
3	The Natural Turnpike
4	Clark Brook Trail
5	Moss Glen Falls
6	Skylight Pond Trail
7	Texas Falls Trail
8	Texas Falls Recreation Area
9	Middlebury College Snow Bowl
10	Lincoln Gap
	Breadloaf Wilderness Boundary
	Long Trail/Appalachian Trail
	Trail

Ref: USFS Breadloaf Wilderness Map

Breadloaf Wilderness

[Fig. 31] At 21,480 acres, the Breadloaf Wilderness is the largest federally protected primitive area in the Green Mountain National Forest. Seventeen miles of the Long Trail (*see* page 302) traverse 11 peaks above 3,000 feet in elevation, between two spectacular mountain gaps—Middlebury Gap to the south and Lincoln Gap to the north. Along the way, there are superb vistas to be had from a number of peaks, particularly Bread Loaf Mountain, and Mounts Wilson, Roosevelt, Cleveland, and Grant. What's most striking about the views is the simplicity of the landscape itself. Roads are nearly invisible, and the pale green pastels of pastureland melt into the rich emeralds of hilltop forests. These are views that will please in any season but are especially breathtaking in autumn when the hills are afire with hues of red, orange, and yellow.

But it's not just the views that make the Breadloaf Wilderness so special. A wilderness area, in the words of the federal Wilderness Act of 1964, is a place where "man himself is a visitor who does not remain." The Breadloaf Wilderness won federal protection in 1984, and nature has been busy in the 15 years since logging has ceased.

Trout lilies (*Erythronium americanum*) and spring beauties (*Claytonia virginica*) grow so thickly in the thin brown trace of trails that they crowd stepping stones in the paths. Ruffed grouse (*Bonasa umbellus*) drum as the songs of hermit thrushes (*Catharus guttatus*) and winter wrens (*Troglodytes troglodytes*) fill the air. The persistent cry of the great crested flycatcher (*Myiarchus crinitus*) and the chattering of goldfinches (*Carduelis tristis*) punctuate the early morning cacophony of birdsong.

Underfoot is much the same rock that underlies the spine of the Green Mountains as they march north of here: a Cambrian-age chlorite-biotite schist. The schists were first laid down as sediments in a shallow sea and were strongly metamorphosed in the Acadian orogeny, the mountain-building event that lifted the Green Mountains skyward. But there are surprises, too, particularly a tongue of calcium-rich schists and quartzites, also Cambrian in age, that ride the eastern shoulder of Bread Loaf Mountain and promise more of Vermont's calcium-loving plants, including blue cohosh (*Caulophyllum thalictroides*), bulblet fern (*Cystopteris bulbifera*), early yellow violet (*Viola rotundifolia*), squirrel corn (*Dicentra canadensis*), hepatica (*Hepatica americana*), and wild leeks (*Allium tricoccum*).

Most of the wilderness is second-growth hardwood forests, but above 2,500 feet, the spruces (*Picea rubens*) and balsam fir (*Abies balsamea*) take over in the familiar transition of low-elevation deciduous species to the hardier evergreen summit species. Particularly striking is the abrupt transition of forest types on Mount Grant: From afar, the peak appears to wear a cap of dark green coniferous forests on its summit. Likely the sudden transition is linked more to the logging history of the area than the natural history, and is due to loggers' inability to cut all the way to the summit. Because trees were so valuable around the turn of the century, they would have cut as much as they could before giving up.

This wilderness has its own "Presidential Range," a series of peaks named after the nation's leaders. From the south, the first is 3,745-foot Mount Wilson, named for Woodrow Wilson, the 28th president. Next is 3,528-foot Mount Roosevelt, named for Theodore, the 26th president. The Long Trail then passes into the town of Lincoln, which, in spite of its location, was not named for Abraham. Instead, the town's name honors Maj. Gen. Benjamin Lincoln (1733-1810), a farmer from Hingham, Massachusetts, who served in the Revolutionary War as the head of the Massachusetts Militia, which fought in the Battle of Bennington. The last presidential peak is 3,482-foot Mount Cleveland, named for Grover Cleveland, who was the 22nd and 24th president. The ridge top forests along this section of the Long Trail were severely damaged by an ice storm in early January, 1998 that left the trail virtually impassible until Green Mountain Club trail crews cleared it the following summer.

While presidents may be celebrated by their hilltop names, the real hero of the Breadloaf Wilderness is Col. Joseph Battell, a wealthy nineteenth-century business-man who bought mountain summits much as some people buy artwork. Battell was horrified at how lumber companies were stripping mountains of their trees. In his day, Vermont was 75 percent cleared land, either from logging or for agriculture. His response was to buy the summits he wanted to protect. Mountain historians Guy and Laura Waterman quote Battell as saying "(People) go to Europe and pay $10,000 for a painting and hang it up in their home where none but their friends can see it; I buy a mountain for that money and it is hung up where everybody can see and enjoy it."

In what is now Breadloaf Wilderness, Battell bought Grant, Roosevelt, Bread Loaf, and Boyce Peak. When he died in 1915, he deeded much of his 31,000 acres of holdings to Middlebury College.

Although Battell's inclinations were toward preservation of the natural world, his legacy extends into the arts. Battell's posthumous gift also included the Bread Loaf Campus of Middlebury College, which is located in Middlebury Gap just west of the wilderness area boundary. In 1919, four years after Battell bequeathed his inn to the college, the trustees decided to get out of the inn business and founded the Bread Loaf School of English for graduate students. Two years later, poet Robert Frost gave the first of many readings at the new school, and the Bread Loaf Writers' Conference began to take shape.

For two weeks in August, the yellow-and-green buildings with ample porches and fabulous views are crawling with big name writers and lots of wannabes. Frost was probably the most well-known emeritus (his summer house was just down the road), but others include Wallace Stegner, Sinclair Lewis, Carson McCullers, Archibald MacLeish, John Gardner, and John Irving (who lives not-so-nearby in southern Vermont, in the town of Dorset).

Directions: From Middlebury, go south on VT 7/125 to East Middlebury, approximately 3 miles. Continue east on VT 125 9 miles to the top of Middlebury Gap, and access to the

Long Trail. Other hiking trails on forest roads are signed along VT 125. To enter the northern portion of the wilderness, from the town center of Bristol, go east on VT 116 approximately 1.5 miles out of town to a junction with the Lincoln Road. Go straight on the Lincoln Road, which will turn into Main Street, and then the Lincoln Gap Road, approximately 6.5 miles to the top of Lincoln Gap.

Activities: Hiking, fishing, cross-country skiing, snowshoeing.

Facilities: Hiking trails, 4 shelters, picnic area with nature trail.

Dates: Open year-round.

Fees: There is a fee for shelter use at Skyline Lodge.

Closest town: Middlebury, 11 miles.

For more information: Middlebury Ranger District, Green Mountain National Forest, RD 4 Box 1260, Middlebury, VT 05753. Phone (802) 388-4362. Green Mountain Club, 4711 Waterbury-Stowe Road, Waterbury Center, VT 05677. Phone (802) 244-7037.

The Ice Storm of 1998

Wind storms, floods, insects and disease shape and trim Vermont's forests as surely as any logger's chainsaw. But the great ice storm of January 1998 was the worst in Vermont's recorded history, and had a profound effect on the state's forests.

An aerial survey of Vermont's 4.5 million acres of forests, conducted by the Forests, Parks and Recreation Department in the spring after the storm, found 300,000 acres were severely damaged, with trees having lost more than 50 percent of their crowns or branches. Another 400,000 acres were moderately damaged, with trees losing 10 to 50 percent of their branches.

The opened canopy damage lets more light penetrate to the forest floor, stimulating the growth of some plants, likely at the expense of their more shade tolerant but less competitive neighbors. The fallen trees and broken branches also provide a big dose of coarse woody debris on the forest floor, which may take years to decompose completely, in the meantime providing hiding places for small mammals and a complete habitat for insects and fungi that attack dead wood.

In Vermont's populated areas, most of the damage was down low, along the Champlain Valley, where a pocket of cold air sat for three days while warm air aloft dropped rain. Ice crusted some areas more than three inches thick, and did millions of dollars of damage to urban trees and power lines. In the Lake Champlain Islands and further north in the Montreal area, some residents went without electric power for as long as three weeks.

Temperatures at elevations between 2,000 and 3,000 feet were also just right for ice formation. Trees in places like the Green Mountain National Forest's Breadloaf Wilderness were coated with as much as three inches of ice. In one 2.3-mile section of Long Trail, just south of the Breadloaf Wilderness, trail workers counted 426 trees across the trail, or a downed tree every 28 feet.

🕸 SKYLIGHT POND TRAIL

[Fig. 31(6)] One of the best ways to sample the Breadloaf Wilderness is to visit Skylight Pond and the Green Mountain Club's Skyline Lodge. The moderate climb on the Skylight Pond Trail to the pond and Skyline Lodge starts on an old logging road but then begins a steady climb through rich northern hardwood forests, grading into ridgetop spruce-fir forests. Wood sorrel (*Oxalis acetosella*) grows in extensive patches along the upper reaches of the trail and is one of several forest floor species found abundantly in both transition hardwoods and spruce-fir forests. The lodge overlooks a high mountain beaver pond with an impressive dam and lodge. Lurking in a marshy area among the usual suite of pondside plants is the insect-eating sundew (*Drosera rotundifolia*).

The lodge sits just above the pond. It was named to commemorate the governing board of the Middlebury Mountain Club, which built the original structure in 1955. In 1987, helicopters chattered over the wilderness area as cedar logs, cement, and other construction materials were dropped at the site so that the Green Mountain Club and the U.S. Forest Service could replace the old shelter.

The Skylight Pond Trail can also be used as an access for the 3,835-foot Bread Loaf Mountain, 1.2 miles north of the lodge and pond along the Long Trail. A spur trail just off the wooded summit of Bread Loaf offers vast views west to the Champlain Valley, Lake Champlain, and the Adirondacks. Just 0.1 mile south of the junction of the Long Trail and the side trail to Skylight Pond is another viewpoint to the southwest from just below the summit of Battell Mountain.

Directions: From East Middlebury and the junctions of VT 125 and VT 116, head east approximately 6 miles on VT 125 to Forest Road 59. Go 3.6 miles to trailhead parking on the right side of the road.

Trail: 2.6 miles one-way; from lodge via Long Trail to Bread Loaf Mountain, 1.2 miles one-way.

Elevation: 2,000 feet to 3,350 feet at Skyline Lodge, or 3,835 feet at Bread Loaf Mountain.

Degree of difficulty: Moderate; hike to Bread Loaf Mountain has some strenuous sections.

Surface and blaze: Woods road grading into narrow footpath. Blue blazes; white blazes on Long Trail.

🕸 COOLEY GLEN AND EMILY PROCTOR TRAILS

[Fig. 31(1), Fig. 31(2)] The Cooley Glen and Emily Proctor trails make for an enjoyable overnight loop hike traversing the Breadloaf Wilderness's Presidential ridge, with an overnight stay at either Cooley Glen Shelter or Emily Proctor Shelter. Hikers willing to undertake the strenuous ridge walk will be rewarded with good views to the south and east from Mount Wilson and Mount Roosevelt. The Emily Proctor Shelter also commands good views to the north across a branch of the New

Haven River, the Green Mountains, and the northern Champlain Valley.

Directions: From the town center of Bristol, go east on VT 116 approximately 1.5 miles out of town to a junction with the Lincoln Road. Go straight on the Lincoln Road, which will turn into Main Street in the center of Lincoln village. Go approximately 2.2 miles to Gerry Road; take a right and go 1.5 miles to Big Basin Road on the left. Take a left onto Big Basin Road (which grades into Forest Road 54) and follow it to Forest Road 201 on the left. The single trailhead for both trails is at the end of Forest Road 201, about 0.5 mile from its junction with Forest Road 54.

Trail: 12.8-mile loop.

Elevation: 1,650 feet to 3,528 feet.

Degree of difficulty: Strenuous.

Surface and blaze: Narrow footpath with some steep and rocky sections. Blue blazes on side trails, white blazes on the Long Trail.

CLARK BROOK TRAIL

[Fig. 31(4)] The Clark Brook Trail meanders through a northern hardwood forest along its namesake, a tributary of the White River on the eastern side of the wilderness. It offers a route to the summit of Mount Roosevelt, with good views of the bucolic upper White River valley.

Directions: From VT 100 in Granville, and 4.5 miles north of the junction of VT 100 with VT 125, take Forest Road 55 approximately 2 miles to the trailhead and parking.

Trail: 3.4 miles one-way.

Elevation: 1,600 feet to 3,528 feet.

Degree of difficulty: Moderate.

Surface and blaze: Old logging road grading into narrow footpath. Blue blazes; last 0.4 mile on Long Trail, white blazes.

TEXAS FALLS RECREATION AREA

[Fig. 31(8)] Texas Falls tumbles down a 5-foot-wide gorge into four deep emerald pools that glow in the filtered sunlight. This 700-foot-long section of the Hancock Branch of the White River is shaded by a thick canopy of hemlocks (*Tsuga canadensis*), while yellow birch (*Betula alleghanesis*), maples (*Acer* spp.), and white ash (*Fraxinus americana*) dot the hillside overlooking the falls. A Cambrian-age schist, the bedrock here is particularly suited for sculpturing and pothole formation. The 1.2-mile Texas Falls Nature Trail [Fig. 31(7)] makes an easy loop through a fine display of spring wildflowers: red and painted trillium (*Trillium erectum* and *T. undulatum*), blue-bead lily (*Clintonia borealis*), starflower (*Trientalis borealis*), and twisted stalk (*Streptopus roseus*). For those willing and able to identify them, as many as 20 different mosses and liverworts colonize the sloping rocks of the lower gorge, including *Hylocomnium splendens*, *Pogonatum alpinum*, and *Ceratodon purpureus*. None, however, are rare.

Directions: From Hancock at the junction of VT 100 and VT 125, go west on VT 125 approximately 3.1 miles to a sign for Texas Falls Recreation Area. The parking area is 0.5 mile up on the right, with additional parking another 0.3 mile away at the picnic area.

Activities: Hiking, picnicking.

Facilities: Picnic tables, nonflush vault toilets, nature trail.

Dates: Open year-round

Fees: None.

Closest town: Hancock, 5 miles.

For more information: Green Mountain National Forest, Rochester Ranger District, RR2 Box 35, Rochester, VT 05767. Phone (802) 767-4261.

MOSS GLEN FALLS

[Fig. 31(5)] As VT 100 winds its way south from the Mad River valley town of Warren, it drops into Granville Gulf, a 6-mile scenic drive through a deep ravine where old hemlocks (*Tsuga canadensis*) line the roads and filter the sunlight even on the brightest of days. In 1928, marble magnate and former governor Redfield Proctor donated the scenic lands around Granville Gulf to the state as a special scenic reservation.

Just as the road emerges from the deepest part of the ravine, Deer Hollow Brook tumbles over a sheer rock face at Moss Glen Falls. A wheelchair-accessible boardwalk travels through a sugar maple (*Acer saccharum*) and American beech (*Fagus americana*) forest to a viewing platform at the base of the falls. The falls tumbles down a 30-foot rock face of Cambrian-age schist into a lovely shallow pool. Hemlocks frame the steep cliffs around the falls. In the late spring, look for large beds of mountain twisted stalk (*Streptopus amplexifolius*), blue-bead lily (*Clintonia borealis*), and Canada mayflower (*Maianthemum canadense*). There is a historical record, but no recent one, of hairy wood mint (*Blephilia hirsuta*), a rare woodland mint in Vermont that has been located in only one other spot in the state.

Directions: From Warren, go south on VT 100 about 6 miles to roadside parking on the right.

Trail: 0.1 mile from roadside parking to falls.

Elevation: Level.

Degree of difficulty: Easy.

Surface and blaze: Wheelchair-accessible boardwalk.

THE NATURAL TURNPIKE

[Fig. 31(3)] The literally dozens of numbered forest roads in the Green Mountain National Forest invite exploration by mountain bike in a way that paved roads just can't. Probably the most enjoyable of these roads is the Natural Turnpike, Forest Road 54, which travels through a narrow gap near the headwaters of the New Haven River. A trip from Middlebury Gap, taking VT 125, near the Robert Frost Interpretive

Trail, to South Lincoln and back makes for a pleasant half-day ride of about 20.8 miles through lovely wooded mountains.

Directions: From the junction of VT 125 and VT 116 in East Middlebury, go east on VT 125 about 7.5 miles to Forest Road 59 on the left. Go 4.8 miles along FR 59, passing a large meadow maintained by the Forest Service as a wildlife feeding area. At a three-way junction, take a right onto FR 54, and continue north. Look for a large beaver pond on the right about 1.5 miles from the junction of FR 54 and FR 59. Continue down the hill and along the New Haven River to South Lincoln, approximately 3.6 miles beyond the beaver pond.

Trail: 10.4 miles one-way.

Elevation: Begin at 1,436 feet at VT 125, climb to 2,030 feet at the height-of-land, drop to 1,292 feet at South Lincoln.

Degree of difficulty: Moderate.

Surface and blaze: Gravel forest road with paved sections at either end. Brown U.S. Forest Service road signs.

MIDDLEBURY COLLEGE SNOW BOWL

[Fig. 31(9)] As its name implies, this small (by Vermont standards) ski area was intended for Middlebury College students, but it's open to the public. The resort faces into the Breadloaf Wilderness, with views of Burnt Hill, Boyce and Battell mountains. Best of all, because most skiers frequent the larger resorts, the lift lines here tend to be short, and the cost of a ticket cheaper than most.

Directions: From East Middlebury at the junction of VT 125 and VT 116, go east on VT 125 for approximately 10 miles. The resort is on the south side of the road.

Activities: Alpine skiing, snowshoeing, hiking.

Facilities: 3 lifts, 14 trails, snowmaking.

Dates: Winter season, depending on snow.

Fees: There is a charge.

Closest town: East Middlebury, 10 miles.

For more information: Middlebury College Snow Bowl, Middlebury, VT 05753. Phone (802) 388-4356.

PAPER BIRCH
(Betula papyrifera)

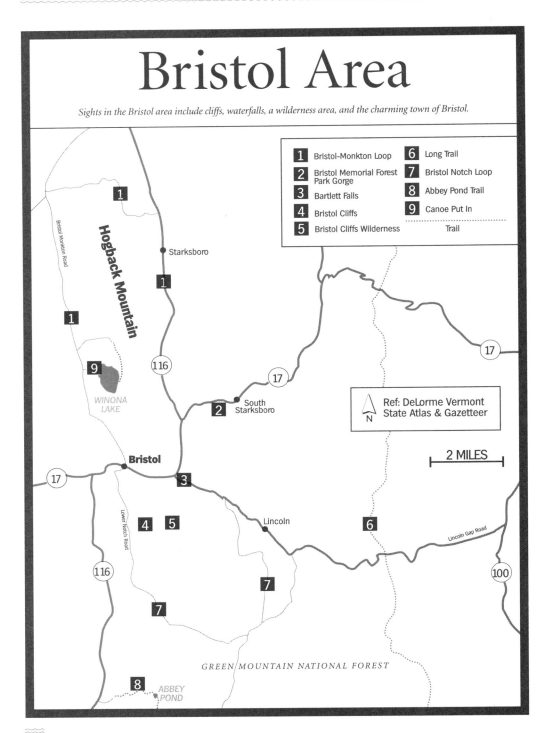

Bristol Area

Sights in the Bristol area include cliffs, waterfalls, a wilderness area, and the charming town of Bristol.

1 Bristol-Monkton Loop

2 Bristol Memorial Forest Park Gorge

3 Bartlett Falls

4 Bristol Cliffs

5 Bristol Cliffs Wilderness

6 Long Trail

7 Bristol Notch Loop

8 Abbey Pond Trail

9 Canoe Put In

.... Trail

Bristol Monkton Road

Hogback Mountain

Starksboro

WINONA LAKE

116

17

South Starksboro

Bristol

Lower Notch Road

Lincoln

Lincoln Gap Road

116

100

GREEN MOUNTAIN NATIONAL FOREST

ABBEY POND

Ref: DeLorme Vermont State Atlas & Gazetteer
N

2 MILES

Bristol Area

[Fig. 32] Look east over the rooftops of Bristol's charming turn-of-the-century main street and you'll see a ridge high enough to postpone a December sunrise until sometime after coffee break. As the Green Mountains were formed, layers of rock were warped into great folds so that, in the area around Bristol, the originally flat-lying layers now nearly stand on end, with hard, erosion-resistant quartzite rock to the east and younger, softer dolomite to the west. The dolomite and other soft rocks to the west were excavated by stream and glacial erosion, leaving the quartzite standing high as a dramatic forested ridge with a steep west face, interrupted by small ledges behind the town. Bristol Cliffs, just south of town, is an extensive cliff and talus area that stands out as a stark white patch, visible from US 7 near Vergennes or even as far off as the Adirondacks.

The New Haven River emerges from the hills at Bartlett Falls on the east side of town, then makes a bouldery run alongside East Street before dropping out of sight along the south side of town. Over twelve thousand years ago, ice still filled the central Champlain Valley. In place of today's river, an ice-melt-swollen torrent raged out of the hills and dumped its sediment load in the gap between the ice and the mountain front, rapidly forming a kame terrace, which forms the level foundation of Bristol village.

As Lake Vermont dropped, the river cut back down through the terrace on the south side of town and formed a floodplain at a lower level, now the site of a sawmill. Parts of the terrace are more boulder and cobble than sand and gravel, testament to both the power of the water and the tremendous volumes of sediment it was carrying.

Visitors coming in from the east can't help but notice Bristol Rock, a large rock by the road with the Lord's Prayer engraved in white-painted, 6-inch letters. The engraving was funded in 1891 by a Buffalo, New York, doctor and former Starksboro resident who, as a teenager, drove logs down a dangerous mountain road that came into the valley bottom near the rock, a journey perilous enough that the sight of the rock was a cause for thankful prayer. A more down-to-earth version of the story has it that the prayer was to serve as an antidote to the creative curses of log drivers straining to get their teams out of a nearby mud hole.

WATERFALLS AND GORGES
BARTLETT FALLS

[Fig. 32(3)] On the east side of Bristol, the New Haven River sluices through a gorge cut through the hard quartzite, then rides over broad, open ledges in a series of cascades and pools before going under a bridge and making its run through the town. The falls make for fine sunning and swimming on hot summer days, and the rush and tumble of the water makes this a pleasant place to explore at other times of year. Venturesome types will want to explore upstream into the gorge, which has 30-foot walls and a 12-foot waterfall at its head.

Quartzite is formed from intertidal beach sand and usually has no lime in it, but around Bartlett Falls there are limy layers at the geologic top of the formation, where it gives way to very limy dolostone, formed in a shallow, tropical, subtidal environment. Botanists have noted several limestone-loving mosses on the walls of the gorge.

It is also a home for a common gorge fern, the bulblet fern (*Cystopteris bulbifera*), which has long, narrow, drooping lacy fronds with "bulblets" along the main leaf stalk. These are neither seeds nor spores, but are produced asexually, and when they fall off, they can take root and start a new fern that is genetically identical to the parent.

Directions: From the traffic light in Bristol, take VT 116 N / VT 17 E (East Street) 1.6 miles to a bridge over the New Haven River. Immediately after the bridge, turn right onto Lincoln Road, then park along the roadside and pick up one of many paths down to the river.

Activities: Swimming, river shore walking and scrambling.

Facilities: None.

Dates: Open year-round.

Fees: None.

Closest town: Bristol, 1.5 miles.

For more information: Addison County Chamber of Commerce, 2 Court Street, Middlebury, VT 05753. Phone (802) 388-7951,

BRISTOL MEMORIAL FOREST PARK GORGE

[Fig. 32(2)] Established as a memorial to World War II and Korean War veterans, this small park includes a modest stone monument and a deep, shady waterfall and gorge that dates back at least 10,000 years. Although it is not generally used for swimming, the deep shade of the hemlocks along the sides of the gorge along with the mere sight of cool, cascading water can be refreshing on a hot day. There is a picnic table near the parking area to make this a good lunch stop.

A short (100 yards) trail from the parking area will guide you over steep ledges alongside a series of small cascades to a wooden bridge over the gorge. Above the gorge the creek tumbles over a 15-foot waterfall, then takes a sharp right turn and runs between the nearly vertical walls of the gorge, which are about 40 feet high where the creek breaks out again into an open stream bed. The rock is a hard, fine-grained schist, part of a complex of similar rocks that makes up the bulk of the Green Mountains.

Steep-walled gorges like this one are usually formed where running water finds a weakness in the rock, such as a dike or seam of softer rock or an area where the joints in the rock are closely spaced. The carving was likely begun under the retreating ice sheet, where meltwater collects and flows under the ice to the glacier front.

Directions: From Bristol, take VT 116 north 3.4 miles, turn right on VT 17, and continue 1.8 miles to a parking area on the right, marked by a sign with a red cross on a blue background.

Activities: A short walk by a waterfall and gorge, picnicking.

Facilities: Picnic tables and a barbecue pit, trail.

Dates: Open during the snow-free season (parking area not plowed).

Fees: None.

Closest town: Bristol, 5.2 miles

For more information: Addison County Chamber of Commerce, 2 Court Street, Middlebury, VT 05753. Phone (802) 388-7951.

Moss Glen Falls.

🦫 SHORT HIKES NEAR BRISTOL
BRISTOL LEDGES

[Fig. 32(4)] At just 2.8 miles round-trip from the Bristol village green, this is good digestive walk for a summer evening, after an early dinner at one of the local eateries. The ledges offer good views over the rooftops of Bristol to the Champlain Valley and beyond to the Adirondack High Peaks. The ledges are at the southern end of the long, straight ridge of Hogback Mountain, made of the erosion-resistant Cheshire quartzite that also forms Bristol Cliffs, a few miles south. This same rock is found in a narrow discontinuous band in western Vermont from Quebec to Massachusetts and on across the border in both directions. The Bristol Ledges, also known as Deer Leap, offer a piecemeal exposure of this rock formation, which originated 550 million years ago as deep, sandy beach deposits along the pre-Appalachian east coast of North America.

Directions: Heading east from the traffic light on Main Street, turn left on Mountain Road, right on Mountain Terrace, and right again to the end of the road to the trailhead. Limited parking is available here. The trail begins as a jeep road east to Bristol Reservoir. Bear left onto a woods road before the reservoir clearing and stay on the main path to the top of the ledges.

Trail: 2 miles round-trip from the end of Mountain Terrace.

Elevation: About a 400-foot elevation gain.

Degree of difficulty: Moderate.

ABBEY POND

[Fig. 32(8)] Abbey Pond is a secluded mountain pond ringed by sedge wetlands that makes a good destination for a rainy afternoon as well as a sunny day. The hike is short (3.8 miles round-trip) and easy enough to bring young children along, either in a backpack or on their own. The trail begins inauspiciously near an old gravel pit, but soon picks up a steep old woods road, climbs steadily alongside a small brook, then rounds off into well-developed second-growth hardwood forest with a rich understory of shrubs and wildflowers. The boulders along the margin of the pond were broken off the surrounding summits and left here by glacial ice.

Directions: From Bristol, take VT 116 south 8 miles to a gravel road on the left,

Cliff and Talus Formation

Talus is a collection of rock fragments, fist-sized or larger, that fall off and accumulate at the base of a cliff as it is attacked by frost action. Talus slopes typically remain unstable as long as the cliff keeps shedding boulders onto the slope below. By comparison with glacial till or outwash, a dry, shifting pile of rocks is a tough place for plant communities to invade, but they can do so in time. While stabilized talus slopes with well-established forest cover are abundant in Vermont, large, open talus slopes are uncommon. Bristol Cliffs and White Rocks are two of Vermont's premier examples of a cliff and open talus formation and associated vegetation.

marked by a USFS sign for the Abbey Pond Trail. From the south, the turnoff is 2.3 miles from the junction of VT 116 and VT 125 in East Middlebury. Turn onto the gravel road and continue 0.3 mile to a clearing, and park well off to the side of the road. The trail starts as a steep, washed-out road straight ahead.

Trail: 3.8 miles round-trip.

Elevation: 600 feet at the trailhead to 1,700 feet at the pond.

Degree of difficulty: Easy.

Surface and blaze: Old logging road grading into footpath. Blue blazes.

BIKE TOURS AROUND BRISTOL

Bristol is the home base of Vermont Bicycle Touring (Monkton Road, Bristol, VT, 05443, phone 802-453-4811). Both road and mountain cyclists will find Bristol to be a friendly way station, as it forms a nexus between the hard core hills like Appalachian and Lincoln gaps, the relatively easy riding of the Champlain Valley, and the dirt town and national forest roads around South Mountain and on into Lincoln and Ripton. Here are two good routes out of Bristol.

BRISTOL-MONKTON LOOP

[Fig. 32(1)] Twenty-four miles, mostly paved, this tour is an easy-to-moderate trip through open farmland, with sweeping views of the Adirondack and Green Mountains. From the traffic light in Bristol, take North Street, which eventually becomes Monkton Road. The access road to Winona Lake (*see* page 185) is about 4 miles on the right. In the village of Monkton Ridge, turn right on Starksboro Road, and continue straight at a crossroads onto States Prison Hollow Road, which includes a short (1.3 miles) unpaved section. Turn right at the stop sign on VT 116 to return to Bristol. This tour can be extended into a 30-mile loop by continuing north from Monkton Ridge into Hinesburg.

BRISTOL NOTCH LOOP

[Fig. 32(7)] Eighteen miles, mostly unpaved, this route goes through a cool wooded ravine and then through scenic hill country around Lincoln. Take South Street south from the traffic light in Bristol, down a steep hill and over a bridge. Stay on Lower

Notch Road on the left bank of the river, and then at 1.2 miles from the traffic light, bear left and uphill, along the base of Bristol Cliffs. Bear left on Notch Road and climb to the highest point of the road. At a stop sign, turn left onto Ripton Road, and where this turns right and becomes Lincoln-Ripton Road, continue straight and uphill on West Hill Road. At the parking area for Bristol Cliffs Wilderness, this turns right and becomes York Hill Road. At a stop sign after a bridge, turn left on VT 17 and back to Bristol. For a variation that avoids the ups and downs on West Hill Road, coast down the Lincoln-Ripton Road and pick up VT 17 in Lincoln village.

BRISTOL CLIFFS WILDERNESS

[Fig. 32(5)] Bristol Cliffs Wilderness is a 3,740-acre parcel of the Green Mountain National Forest that includes the 5-mile-long ridge of South Mountain and the steep cliffs on its west face. A parking area on one of Lincoln's back roads gives access to the gentle east slopes, but there are no formal trails here. Old logging road traces soon fade into the undergrowth, leaving you alone with your wits and compass.

For experienced hikers there is challenge and satisfaction in striking out east, over the hill, and coming out on the brow of Bristol Cliffs with its stands of red pine (*Pinus resinosa*) growing on bare rock, and sweeping views of the Champlain Valley and the Adirondacks. North and Gilmore ponds, secluded mountain ponds at elevations of over 2,000 feet on South Mountain, also make good targets for the orienteer.

A few sections of the national forest boundary extend to the Lower Notch Road that runs south out of Bristol near the base of the cliffs. From the road it is possible to pick your way up slope through rich hardwood forests to the base of the open talus slope under the cliffs. It is a place of abrupt changes in both the lay of the land and the plant communities on it, responding to the unusual microclimates associated with a cliff and talus formation.

The woods along the road are unusually rich, with a high diversity of trees, shrubs, and herbs, including spring wildflowers like wild ginger (*Asarum canadense*), hepatica (*Hepatica americana*), and large-flowered trillium (*Trillium grandiflorum*). These are growing in a loose, rocky soil with little or no accumulation of organic matter at the surface, indicating sweet (pH 6.5 to 7) soil conditions that allow for rapid decomposition of leaf litter.

Farther up slope, there are birches and hemlock, and even in midsummer you may feel a surprising cool breeze in your face as you climb. At the base of the open part of the talus slope, red spruce (*Picea rubens*) and lowbush blueberry (*Vaccinium* spp.) grow in a thick, cold, organic mat on the tops of big boulders that have tumbled from the cliff face above. One rule of cliff and talus formation is "the bigger they are the farther they go"—the momentum of the biggest boulders falling from the cliff usually carries them right to the base of the slope.

Plant communities here have to develop on bare rock, gradually building up organic soil from the remains of colonizing plants including lichens, mosses, and polypody fern (*Polypodium virginianum*), which forms a tangled mat of spreading rhizomes under its small, simple fronds. The rock itself breaks down very slowly and contributes little to the soil, especially during early stages of development. In some locations, Labrador tea (*Ledum groenlandicum*), a plant usually associated with arctic-alpine or northern bog environments, grows in full sun along the forest edge.

These cold environment plants all grow in a well-defined zone at the base of the open talus because of ice storage and cold air drainage there. Over the course of the winter, beds of ice form deep in the talus slope and may take most of the summer to melt. As long as the ice lasts, the air over the ice cools down and flows through the boulders to emerge at the bottom of the slope, creating a cool microclimate for plants like red spruce and Labrador tea—and the cool breeze you can feel as you approach from below. Mid-summer soil temperatures can be as low as 45 degrees Fahrenheit and the soil pH may be less than 4.0 among the roots of the spruce, cold and acid enough to slow nutrient and water uptake by the plants and bring decomposition to a near standstill.

The open talus is a desert of shifting boulders, unstable enough that visitors are well advised to stay off of it. The whole talus complex is about 500 feet high and 0.33-mile wide, divided by a strip of forest, and it is on the move. Expansion and contraction of the rocks and frost wedging cause the boulders to shift and occasionally tumble down slope. This continuous creep and tumble action, along with the big air spaces between the boulders, means that fine particles of rock or organic matter tend to sift downwards, so that permanent soil and plant cover can't form until the slope stabilizes. The odd pocket of soil may support a bit of struggling polypody fern or pale corydalis (*Corydalis sempervirens*), but lichens are the only plants that can survive on the dry rock faces.

A local name for the open talus is Rattlesnake Den. The warm, sun-drenched rocks are typical habitat for the Eastern timber rattlesnake (*Crotalus horridus*), now endangered in Vermont, and not seen at Bristol Cliffs since the 1800s, when snakes were killed by the hundreds in a single day. The caves and crevices are also good den sites for porcupine.

In part because of its status as a wilderness area, Bristol Cliffs Wilderness is difficult to access, but it provides a kind of wildness and seclusion that is rare so close to the Champlain Valley, and the cliffs are one of Vermont's finest natural areas, combining unusually rich forests with the specialized plant communities associated with the cliff and talus.

Directions: For off-trail hiking over South Mountain: From the traffic light in Bristol, take VT 116 west 1.6 miles, past Rocky Dale Gardens, and turn right on Lincoln Hill Road immediately after the New Haven River bridge. After about 1.9 miles, turn right over a green-painted steel bridge onto York Hill Road. The parking area is 1.8 miles farther, on the right, where the road takes a sharp left turn to become West Hill Road. A footpath beginning at the parking area will get you started, but before long you will be on your own.

Bristol Cliffs can be viewed and reached from Lower Notch Road. Take South Street south from the traffic light in Bristol, down a steep hill and over a bridge. Stay on Lower Notch Road on the left bank of the river, then at 1.2 miles from the traffic light bear left and uphill again. You will catch glimpses of the cliffs through the trees to your left. There is no formal parking or established trails, but some wooded sections along the road are part of the Green Mountain National Forest and can be used to gain access to the talus slopes at the base of the cliffs.

Activities: Off-trail hiking.

Closest town: Bristol, 3 miles north.

For more information: U.S. Forest Service Middlebury Ranger District; RD 4, Box 1260, Middlebury, VT 05753. Phone (802) 388-4362.

WINONA LAKE

[Fig. 32] The quartzite ridge that forms Bristol Cliffs takes a break where the New Haven River has sawed down through it, then continues north as the long, narrow ridge of Hogback Mountain. Winona Lake, tucked up under the west side of the mountain, is a small, warm water lake ringed by unusual bog and marsh communities. The lake is best explored in a canoe, which can be used to probe the shallow backwaters along the western and northern margins.

The bedrock under the small watershed that feeds the lake is mainly dolomite, a limy rock that makes for high pH water and associated plant communities. The wetlands around the lake, particularly the cedar-tamarack bog at the southern end, bleed organic acids into the water, staining it dark brown.

Early morning or twilight visits are almost sure to yield glimpses of beaver, and an osprey nesting platform on a small island in the lake has been home to a breeding pair for the last several years. Numerous other bird and mammal species are residents or frequent visitors. The lake is a superb warm-water fishery, featuring largemouth bass (*Micropterus salmoides*) and northern pike (*Esox lucius*) that especially take to the shallow, marshy waters at the northern end of the lake.

A state fish and wildlife boat ramp gives canoe and small boat access to the lake via the first few turns of Pond Brook, which flows north out of the lake and into Lewis Creek. A short walk along an old road (actually a low rock dam) north of the boat ramp will take you to a beaver dam a foot or two high that, nonetheless, has had a dramatic impact on the bog at the northern end of the lake.

Across the brook from the boat ramp are countless standing dead trees, mainly tamarack (*Larix laricina*) weathered to

WILD LEEK (Allium tricoccum) A leafless stem grows up to 18 inches tall and holds a cluster of white, starlike flowers that bloom in mid-summer.

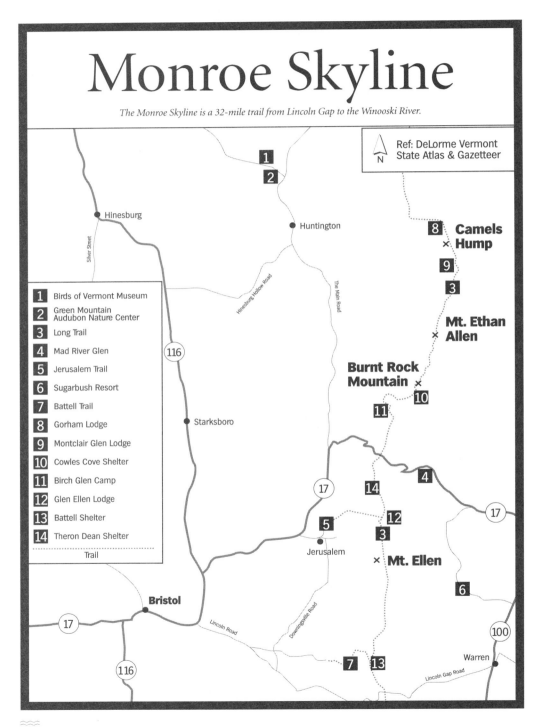

Monroe Skyline

The Monroe Skyline is a 32-mile trail from Lincoln Gap to the Winooski River.

Ref: DeLorme Vermont
State Atlas & Gazetteer

Hinesburg

Huntington

8 Camels
Hump

9

3

Mt. Ethan
Allen

Burnt Rock
Mountain

10

11

1	Birds of Vermont Museum
2	Green Mountain Audubon Nature Center
3	Long Trail
4	Mad River Glen
5	Jerusalem Trail
6	Sugarbush Resort
7	Battell Trail
8	Gorham Lodge
9	Montclair Glen Lodge
10	Cowles Cove Shelter
11	Birch Glen Camp
12	Glen Ellen Lodge
13	Battell Shelter
14	Theron Dean Shelter

Trail

Starksboro

116

Silver Street

Hinesburg Hollow Road

The Main Road

17

14

4

17

12

5

3

Jerusalem

Mt. Ellen

6

Bristol

17

Lincoln Road

Downingsville Road

7 **13**

Warren

100

Lincoln Gap Road

116

an old barn silver-gray, the broken-off branches providing convenient roosts for blackbirds (*Agelaius phoeniceus*) and tree swallows (*Tachycineta bicolor*). Tamaracks and other bog trees grow with their roots spreading out wide in the top few inches of bog peat, where oxygen can diffuse into the soggy mat from the air above. These trees were drowned when water levels rose after the beaver dam was built.

By mid-July, the two or three bends of Pond Brook between the boat ramp and the lake are lined with the blunt arrowhead leaves and purple flower spikes of pickerelweed (*Pontederia cordata*), which provides happy hunting and hiding places for northern pike (*Esox lucius*). The big white blossoms and split-round leaves of fragrant water lily (*Nymphaea odorata*) and 3-inch oval leaves of water shield (*Brasenia schreberi*) float on the dark water along the inside of the bends. Here and elsewhere along the lake margin, look for clumps of water willow (*Decodon verticillatus*), with clusters of bright magenta flowers at the base of paired whorled leaves on gracefully arching stems.

There are also several "islands," relatively high spots that support clumps of tamarack and red maple, along with—beware!—poison sumac (*Rhus vernix*), a close and more potent relative of poison ivy (*Rhus toxicodendron*) but also related to the common and nonpoisonous staghorn sumac (*Rhus typhina*). Like poison ivy, poison sumac produces clusters of white berries, which serve as winter food source for birds, and, like the other sumacs, the compound leaves turn scarlet in the autumn. It is usually found in wetlands that are weakly acid to neutral. These islands are often used by duck hunters to set up temporary blinds during the duck hunting season in October.

Directions: From the traffic light in Bristol, take North Street left off of Main Street. North Street becomes Monkton Road as it passes out into open farmland. At just under 4 miles from the light, look for a State Fish and Wildlife Access sign on the right and turn onto a gravel road that ends at a small boat ramp and canoe put-in.

Activities: Canoeing, fishing, bird and wildlife-watching.

Facilities: Small boat ramp.

Closest town: Bristol, 4 miles south.

For more information: Vermont Fish and Wildlife Department, Building 10 South, 103 South Main Street, Waterbury, VT O5671. Phone (802) 241-3700.

Monroe Skyline

[Fig. 33] The undulating ridge walk that Vermonters call the Monroe Skyline traverses some of the most spectacular scenery on the Long Trail. In its 32-mile stretch from Lincoln Gap to the Winooski River, the trail climbs to gorgeous vistas, drops into little vales, and traverses interesting rock outcrops in a kind of trail design that both writers and hikers have described as pure artistry.

In a 1919 letter published in The Burlington Free Press, one writer remarked, "There were ledges one-half mile long and as the trail wound round these all sorts of

DEER MOUSE
(Peromyscus
maniculatus)

fairy caverns came into view. It gave us a feeling that fairies, imps and gnomes scampered to cover just in time to hide from us."

The man responsible for the artistry was Professor Will S. Monroe, a New Jersey teacher who adopted Vermont as a second home just as the Long Trail was coming to life in the early 1900s. Beginning in 1916, Monroe cut the trail south across Camel's Hump and down toward Lincoln Gap. The path has stayed virtually the same ever since, and with good reason.

Among the highlights of this climb is Mount Abraham (4,006 feet) where hikers will find the third and smallest of Vermont's three alpine tundra areas. At just under 2 acres, plant diversity is limited, but look for mountain sandwort (*Arenaria groenlandica*) and alpine bilberry (*Vaccinium uliginosium*), among others.

As the trail continues north, hikers can see how ski areas and hiking trails coexist, an issue sometimes of great controversy in a state that depends heavily on alpine skiing as the backbone of its winter tourist economy. Sugarbush Resort dominates the eastern slopes of the hills from Lincoln Peak north to Mount Ellen, but ski trail crossings are kept to a minimum, and some hikers actually like the views the ski trails provide. Farther north on General Stark Mountain, the skier's cooperative Mad River Glen ski area provides an alternative to Sugarbush's size and glitz, with an antique, slow-moving single chair lift running right to the ridgetop as the crown of its three-lift system.

Directions: From Bristol to Lincoln Gap, go north on VT 116 from the center of Bristol village approximately 1.2 miles to a Y-junction in the road. Go right on Lincoln Road and continue approximately 5 miles to the top of Lincoln Gap and trailhead parking.

From Bristol to Appalachian Gap, go north on VT 116 to its junction with VT 17. Turn right onto VT 17 and go approximately 9.5 miles to the top of the gap and trailhead parking.

Trail: 11.1 miles, Lincoln Gap to Appalachian Gap one-way; 32 miles Lincoln Gap to the Winooski River one-way.

Elevation: 400 feet to 4,083 feet, with numerous ups and downs in between Lincoln Gap and the Winooski River.

Degree of difficulty: Strenuous.

Surface and blaze: Rocky ridge. White blazes.

For more information: Green Mountain Club, 4711 Waterbury–Stowe Road, Waterbury Center, VT 05677. Phone (802) 244-7037. Green Mountain National Forest, Rochester Ranger District, RR 2, Box 35, Rochester, VT 05767. Phone (802) 767-4261.

HIKING TRAIL ACCESS TO THE MONROE SKYLINE
BATTELL TRAIL

[Fig. 33(7)] Hikers enjoy this popular side trail to climb Mount Abraham, which is roughly 0.9 mile north of the Battell Trail's junction with the Long Trail. The trail and Battell Shelter were named for Col. Joseph Battell, who bought much of the ridgeline to protect it in the early 1900s. Mount Abraham (4,006 feet) was formerly known as Potato Hill, which may reflect the presence of hill farms that flourished in this area in the mid- to late 1800s. Potatoes were an especially important crop in Vermont after the Civil War, when the Green Mountain variety, which could be stored for up to 8 months, was developed. The lower portion of the trail climbs through a modern sugarbush.

Directions: From the center of Lincoln village, turn north onto Quaker Street, then take the first right onto Elder Hill Road, which is also Forest Road 350. Go 1.9 miles on this road to a left turn which leads to the trailhead in 0.1 mile.

Trail: 2 miles one-way.

Elevation: 1,470 feet to 3,200 feet.

Degree of difficulty: Strenuous.

Surface and blaze: Old carriage road grading into rocky foot path. Blue blazes.

For more information: Green Mountain Club, 4711 Waterbury–Stowe Road, Waterbury Center, VT 05677. Phone (802) 244-7037. Green Mountain National Forest, Rochester Ranger District, RR 2, Box 35, Rochester, VT 05767. Phone (802) 767-4261.

JERUSALEM TRAIL

[Fig. 33(5)] There's no easy way up Mount Ellen, but climbing the Jerusalem Trail is probably the easiest. The trail climbs through open hardwoods to its junction with the Long Trail. The Glen Ellen Shelter is just 0.1 mile north on the Long Trail, and Mount Ellen, with its good views to the west, is 1.8 miles south.

Directions: From the center of Bristol village, go north on VT 116 to its junction with VT 17. Turn right onto VT 17 and go approximately 3.5 miles to where VT 17 takes a sharp left. At this corner, turn right onto a gravel road, and take the first left onto Jerusalem Road. Go approximately 1 mile and turn left onto Jim Dwire Road. Follow this road 0.5 mile to the trailhead.

Trail: 2.5 miles one-way to Long Trail junction.

Elevation: 1,600 feet to 3,400 feet at junction with the Long Trail.

Degree of difficulty: Moderate.

Surface and blaze: Woods path with rocky sections. Blue blazes.

For more information: Green Mountain Club, 4711 Waterbury–Stowe Road, Waterbury Center, VT 05677. Phone (802) 244-7037. Green Mountain National Forest, Rochester Ranger District, RR 2, Box 35, Rochester, VT 05767. Phone (802) 767-4261.

SKI AREAS
SUGARBUSH RESORT

[Fig. 33(6)] One of Vermont's larger ski resorts, Sugarbush's 112 trails blanket the east side of the Lincoln range, including Lincoln Peak, Nancy Hanks Peak, and Mount Ellen. With the purchase of the resort by American Skiing Company in 1996, money has poured in to upgrade snowmaking and build a hotel and conference center to expand the year-round activities offered by the resort. If you're in the area at the end of the ski season, typically late April, it's worth it to check with the resort staff to find out when they're holding their annual pond skimming party. Pond skimming is the skier's equivalent of Evel Knievel's motorcycle stunts, except the skier tries to get up enough speed and lift to ski over the resort's snowmaking pond. Needless to say, most don't make it, though the event attracts ever-inventive Vermonters and zany equipment especially designed to meet the challenge.

Directions: From I-89, take Exit 10 for Waterbury. Immediately off the exit ramp, take U.S. 2 south for about 100 yards, and then turn left, or south toward Waterbury Village. Pass through the village, and on the eastern end, turn south on VT 100. Go approximately 12.5 miles south on VT 100 to the Sugarbush Access Road on the west side of the road. The resort is approximately 3 miles up the access road.

Activities: Downhill and cross-country skiing, snowboarding, snowshoeing, hiking, tennis, golf, mountain biking.

Facilities: 18 lifts, 112 trails, snowmaking, hotel and conference center, restaurants, retail and rental shop, child care, ski school, snowboard half-pipe, tennis courts.

Dates: Open year-round

Fees: There is a charge for trail and facility use.

Closest town: Warren, 4 miles.

For more information: Sugarbush Resort, Sugarbush Access Road, Warren, VT 05674. Phone (802) 583-2381.

MAD RIVER GLEN

[Fig. 33(4)] Mad River Glen is a ski area unlike any other: For starters, it's the only ski area in the United States owned by a skiers' cooperative, a group of fanatics who refused to let the quirky resort die when principal shareholder Betsy Pratt decided in December 1995 it was time to leave the business. People come to Mad River to experience skiing as it was when the sport first blossomed in the late 1940s. No high-speed quad chairlifts here. The main lift serving the mountain's summit is a single seater, a holdover from 1948, when the area first opened. And while the resort has installed snowmaking in recent years, for the most part, skiers ski natural snow, which makes the experience all the more challenging. After a day on the slopes, you'll understand why the bumper stickers say "Mad River Glen: Ski it if you can."

Directions: From I-89, take Exit 10 for Waterbury. Immediately off the exit ramp, take U.S. 2 south for about 100 yards, and then turn left, or south toward Waterbury Village. Pass through the village, and on the eastern end, turn south on VT 100. Go approximately 10 miles south on VT 100 to VT 17, just south of Waitsfield village. Turn west onto VT 17 and go approximately 4 miles to the ski area on the left.

Activities: Downhill skiing, hiking.

Red Spruce Decline

In late spring, hikers in the Green and other mountains throughout the northeastern region often notice that the needles of some red spruce (*Picea rubens*) trees are dying. They turn a distinctive red-orange color and eventually fall off, leaving bare twigs near the ends of the branches. This is a result of injury from cold stress during the previous winter.

In the northeastern mountains, red spruce appears to be living at the very edge of where it can live, since it is frequently injured by severe cold or other stresses that are common in the mountain environment. Mountain stands have also undergone a precipitous decline, with many of the bigger and older trees in many stands now dead and down. Early observations of spruce decline on the west slopes of Camel's Hump raised suspicions that the unusual mortality may be linked to acid precipitation.

At high elevations, forests spend more than 20 percent of the time bathed in clouds, which deposit fine droplets on the needles and other parts of the tree. When the clouds form in polluted air masses from the Midwest, sulfur and nitrogen oxides dissolve in the droplets to form acids that are considerably more concentrated than in acid rain. The pH in these dirty clouds can fall below 3.0.

Extensive research conducted by the University of Vermont and numerous other institutions has shown that prolonged exposure to acid cloud mist impairs the ability of the needles to survive cold stress, already a weakness in this species. The increased frequency and severity of winter injury is enough to push some trees over the edge. In some years, most recently 1984, 1989, and 1993, winter injury is so severe that it may kill off 100 percent of the youngest needles on some trees, putting a deep dent in the ability of the tree to feed itself by photosynthesis and its ability to get ready for the next winter. Repeated injury can put the tree into a death spiral, eventually weakening it enough so that it is vulnerable to attack by insects and fungi, which rapidly finish the job.

Recent evidence gives some hope that spruce populations are recovering from the severe decline of the 1960s and 1970s, perhaps because many of the vulnerable trees have already been killed off. But even among the survivors, at least a small amount of winter injury can be observed every spring.

Facilities: 4 lifts, 42 trails, snowmaking, ski school, child care, rental and retail shop, cafeteria.

Dates: Winter season, depending on snow.

Fees: There is a charge to use the facilities.

Closest town: Ira, 4 miles.

For more information: Mad River Glen, Waitsfield, VT 05673. Phone (802) 496-3551.

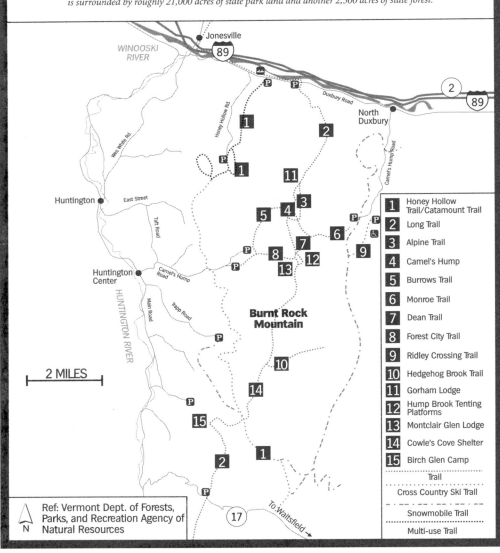

Camel's Hump State Park

Camel's Hump is the largest park in the state and one of the oldest pieces of public lands. The mountain is surrounded by roughly 21,000 acres of state park land and another 2,300 acres of state forest.

Jonesville

WINOOSKI RIVER

89

Duxbury Road

2 **89**

North Duxbury

Honey Hollow Rd

Wes White Rd

Camel's Hump Road

Huntington

East Street

Taft Road

1 Honey Hollow Trail/Catamount Trail
2 Long Trail
3 Alpine Trail
4 Camel's Hump
5 Burrows Trail
6 Monroe Trail
7 Dean Trail
8 Forest City Trail
9 Ridley Crossing Trail
10 Hedgehog Brook Trail
11 Gorham Lodge
12 Hump Brook Tenting Platforms
13 Montclair Glen Lodge
14 Cowle's Cove Shelter
15 Birch Glen Camp

Huntington Center

Camel's Hump Road

HUNTINGTON RIVER

Main Road

Tapp Road

Burnt Rock Mountain

2 MILES

Ref: Vermont Dept. of Forests, Parks, and Recreation Agency of Natural Resources

N

To Waitsfield →

17

········· Trail
··─··─· Cross Country Ski Trail
········· Snowmobile Trail
·········· Multi-use Trail

Camel's Hump State Park

[Fig. 34] With its distinctive double-humped profile, no other Vermont mountain is so easily recognized—or so often reproduced. Camel's Hump graces not only the state seal but has recently made the leap to Vermont's conservation license plate— with good reason. While at 4,083 feet the summit only ties for third highest peak, it is the state's highest undeveloped summit. Its flanks have been combed by scores of researchers and graduate students studying everything from small mammal popula- tions to soil formation. In fact, some of the most important studies in the nation detailing forest damage due to acid rain were conducted on Camel's Hump.

Surrounded by roughly 21,000 acres of state park land and another 2,300 acres of state forest, Camel's Hump is the largest park in the state and one of the oldest pieces of public lands. It was bequeathed to Vermont in 1911 by Col. Joseph Battell, a wealthy eccentric who made his money in publishing and who bought up a substantial portion of the Green Mountain ridgeline from Killington north simply because he didn't want to see the summits logged. (He gave much of his other land to Middlebury College.)

At first, the state managed the lands so that cutting was strictly limited. By 1969, the legislature created the park and designated lower elevation surroundings as a forest reserve where logging could take place. The mountain summit and adjoining 7,404 acres were protected as a natural area, with strict limitations on camping. Then and now, trail use is limited in the natural area to hikers, cross-country skiers, and snowshoers; at lower elevations, the state permits snowmobiling on specially main- tained trails.

The summit of Camel's Hump is made of 550 million-year-old, moderately meta- morphosed, grayish-green chlorite schist, called the Underhill formation. This rock type runs in a long band along the northern half of Vermont, and includes distinctive lenses of fine-grained quartz. The quartz bands highlight the schists and outline folds and crenulations in the rock, giving it an almost seersucker appearance. This long band of highly resistant rock, metamorphosed during the Taconic and Acadian orogenies, forms the summits of many of northern Vermont's higher mountain peaks.

But it is to the glaciers that Camel's Hump owes its distinctive two-humped shape. The summit is an extreme example of a roche moutonnée, literally "sheep rock," so named by geomorphologists because of a perceived similarity to sleeping sheep. As a glacier advances, it glides over ridgetops, smoothing them over. On the lee side, a steep slope forms as ice freezes into the hillside and plucks rocks away. Thus, on Camel's Hump, the northern flank of the mountain—the lower hump—is smoothed over, but the southern flank—the taller rock hump—forms a steep rock face.

The craggy summit cone is home to 10 acres of alpine vegetation—the second largest such patch in Vermont. In comparison, the largest patch on Mount Mansfield covers about 250 acres. Common plants include Bigelow sedge (*Carex bigelowii*), alpine bilberry (*Vaccinium uliginosum*), mountain sandwort (*Arenaria groenlandica*), crowberry (*Empetrum nigrum*), mountain cranberry (*Vaccinium vitis-idaea*), and Labrador tea (*Ledum groenlandicum*). These plants also owe their existence to the glacier, being the last remnants of the tundra vegetation that was widespread in Vermont immediately after the glacier. As the climate warmed, and trees moved in to colonize lower elevations, the only place where tundra vegetation was able to survive was on the few mountaintops where conditions were, and are, extreme enough to keep out competitors.

The harsh, high-elevation conditions don't just limit plant diversity—animal and bird species are limited, too. The few birds that do survive can be highly visible. Ravens (*Corvus corax*) wheel and make their funny "quork" call. In the subalpine fir thickets, white-throated sparrows (*Zonotrichia albicollis*) and dark-eyed juncos (*Junco hyemalis*) sing their delicate songs.

Red-backed voles (*Clethrionomys gapperi*), deer mice (*Peromyscus maniculatus*), and meadow voles (*Microtus pennsylvanicus*) burrow in the thin plant cover and overwinter under the snow. They feast on seeds and fruits, of which there can be a surprising abundance.

Though the alpine zone is what draws most hikers, the boreal and hardwood forests on the flanks of Camel's Hump have their own distinct and fascinating story to tell.

Logging, which was especially heavy in the late 1800s, changed the forests of Camel's Hump forever. The most valuable tree was red spruce (*Picea rubens*), which was used to make clapboards and shingles for Vermont's growing population. The Forest Mills Lumber Company, formed in 1859, with a sawmill at about 1,700 feet on the western side of the ridge, cut much of the valuable timber on the peak. Loggers initially selectively cut spruce where it intermingled with yellow birch and beeches, as was typical in forests that once ranged from about 1,800 feet to 3,500 feet. Logging essentially eliminated spruce from this forest type, because when the spruce was cut, the seed source was removed.

When spruce became important for paper pulp, the Forest Mills company, along with other companies established on the eastern side of the mountain, began to cut as high on the mountain as was physically possible. By 1882, loggers were cutting trees as small as 5 inches in diameter, and not just spruce. Pulpwood was so scarce in New England the scarcity spurred development of new paper-making technology. This new process allowed first the use of balsam fir and later hardwoods for pulp. Except for some remote pockets and the highest elevation forests (purchased by Battell in 1891), Camel's Hump was almost completed denuded by the end of the nineteenth century.

The cutting set the stage for a second catastrophe: a great fire that burned thousands of acres in 1903, sparing part of the western flanks of the mountain but burning almost everywhere else. Except where the state has subsequently planted or logged, many of the trees that now blanket the eastern flanks of Camel's Hump had their start in the aftermath of the fire.

Starting in 1913, the state planted large numbers of trees on the mountain's eastern flanks, partly to make up for all the damage from the fire and heavy logging, and partly as an experiment to see what would work. More than 300,000 Norway spruce (*Picea abies*), among other trees, were planted in groves that are still visible a short distance from the Monroe hiking trail today.

Where the Vermont Forestry Department didn't plant, nature took over. Most striking is a grove of heart-leafed paper birch (*Betula papyrifera* var. *cordifolia*) that covers much of the eastern slopes of the mountain starting at about 2,200 feet until it grades into high-elevation spruce and fir. Look for club moss (*Lycopodium lucidulum*), mountain wood fern (*Dryopteris campyloptera*), common wood sorrel (*Oxalis acetosella*), and large-leaved goldenrod (*Solidago macrophylla*) as dominant understory species in this zone, along with hobblebush (*Viburnum alnifolium*), a shrub with a name that is best understood after a long bushwhack.

Below the birch forest, and mixed in with it, maples and beeches dominate. Look carefully at the beech trees. While some have been severely damaged by a combination of an insect and a fungus (an affliction called beech scale-Nectria complex) others are scarred by more interesting inhabitants: black bears (*Ursus americanus*).

Look for a series of five dots each about 0.75 inch in diameter, wrapped around the tree as far up as just below the crown. The bears prefer the same trees, typically good nut producers, year after year. Each year adds more round dots to the canvas of the tree bark, with the oldest trees looking like a natural version of a Jackson Pollack painting.

Bears are not the only year-round inhabitants: The park is large enough to provide habitat for virtually every one of Vermont's larger mammal species. The ledges below the summit cone provide denning areas for bobcat (*Lynx rufus*), while the forests below provide browse for their favored prey, the snowshoe hare (*Lepus americanus*). Porcupine (*Erethizon dorsatum*) also find good den sites in the boulders under the ledges, and their presence makes this a good place to watch for fisher (*Martes pennanti*). Moose (*Alces alces*) winter in the high-elevation forests, browsing on striped maple (*Acer pensylvanicum*) buds and mountain ash (*Sorbus americana*) bark.

Directions: From I-89, take Exit 10 and go south on VT 100 to VT 2. Go east, or left, into Waterbury Village and take the first right on Winooski Street. Cross the Winooski River and then go right on River Road, a dirt road. Go 5.1 miles to Camel's Hump Road on the left, which follows Ridley Brook. Turn left here and climb 1.4 miles to a fork in the road, bear left and cross a bridge. Continue to climb another 2.4 miles to the eastern trailhead parking. For access from the western side, take I-89 to Exit 11. Go east on US 2 to Richmond village and take a right onto Bridge Street, crossing the Winooski River to Richmond's historic Round Church. Bear right at the church onto the Richmond-Huntington Road and follow it approximately 8 miles to Huntington Center. Turn left on Camel's Hump Road, and follow it 3.5 miles to the trailhead.

Activities: Hiking, snowshoeing, cross-country skiing, snowmobiling.

Facilities: Three lodges, 1 shelter, 2 tenting areas.

Dates: Open year-round, but trails above 2,500 feet are closed during mud season, typically early-Apr. to mid-Apr. through Memorial Day weekend.

Fees: A fee is charged for shelter and lodge use; camping elsewhere is free.

Closest town: Richmond.

For more information: Vermont Department of Forests, Parks, and Recreation, 111 West Street, Essex Junction, VT 05452. Phone (802) 879-6565 (winter). Green Mountain Club , 4711 Waterbury-Stowe Road, Waterbury Center, VT 05677. Phone (802) 244-7037.

HIKING TRAILS IN CAMEL'S HUMP STATE PARK

Although Camel's Hump is the centerpiece of the state park, the trail system includes a section of the Long Trail, as well as numerous side trails up smaller peaks in the park's southern end. Backcountry camping is restricted to lower elevations and away from trails. Above 2,500 feet, overnight camping is permitted only in the Green Mountain Club's shelters and lodges, and at Hump Brook and Honey Hollow tenting areas. Hikers should also take care when above treeline to stay on the rocks and avoid trampling rare alpine vegetation; the Green Mountain Club and the state of Vermont pay several ranger-naturalists to patrol the summit to aid hikers and keep them off fragile vegetation.

HEDGEHOG BROOK TRAIL

[Fig. 34(10)] This short access trail for the Long Trail is the easiest way to Burnt Rock Mountain in the southern end of Camel's Hump State Park. Burnt Rock is a bald summit with fabulous 360-degree views, and on its flanks, a geological oddity: a river-carved pothole etched into the side of a bedrock outcrop. The pothole was scoured by glacial meltwater that was either running under the glacier or plunging over openings in the ice to come into contact with the bedrock below.

Directions: From Waitsfield, go north 5 miles on VT 100 to the North Fayston Road. Turn west, or left on North Fayston Road and go approximately 4 miles to a

BEAVER
(Castor canadensis)
Beavers live in lakes and streams near trees that will be used for dams.

four-way intersection. Take the middle road, Big Basin Road, for 1 mile to the trailhead parking.

Trail: 2 miles one-way to Long Trail; Long Trail to summit of Burnt Rock Mountain, 0.6 mile.

Elevation: 1,400 feet to 3,150 feet.

Degree of difficulty: Moderate.

Surface and blaze: Woods path with steep rock scramble to reach Burnt Rock Mountain summit. Blue blazes; the Long Trail blazed in white.

FOREST CITY AND BURROWS TRAILS

[Fig. 34(8)] and [Fig. 34(5)] This pair of hiking trails can be combined for an enjoyable loop on the east side of the mountain; their trailheads are linked by a 0.8 mile connector trail from the Camel's Hump Road in Huntington. The Forest City Trail is named for a Civilian Conservation Corps camp that was located on this side of the mountain; some people say the name also comes from the Forest City Lumber Company, the early name for the company that logged much of the western side of the mountain in the late 1800s and early 1900s. As it travels up the southwest flank of the mountain, the Forest City Trail follows one of the company's old logging roads. It climbs to Montclair Glen, named by Professor Will Monroe, trail-builder extraordinaire, for his home in New Jersey. Monroe cut the Long Trail from Camel's Hump south to Middlebury Gap beginning in 1916. The Montclair Glen Lodge was built in 1948 by the Green Mountain Club and sleeps 10.

The Burrows Trail, the oldest trail on the mountain, travels up the northwest flank of the peak and traverses a University of Vermont research area where much of the early work on acid rain damage to forest ecosystems was conducted. The Burrows Trail also travels through some of the oldest spruce-fir forest on the mountain, one of the few mid- to high-elevation areas believed to have escaped the 1903 fire. Early visitors are reported to have ridden to just below the summit to the Green Mountain House, an overnight lodge built in 1859 that closed a decade later. The Camel's Hump Club, a Waterbury-based hiking group, maintained three huts near the old location of the Green Mountain House as hikers' shelters from 1912 to the early 1950s. A bare area at the junction of the Long and Burrows trails is still recognizable as the hut clearing.

Directions: Take I-89 to Exit 11. Go east on US 2 to Richmond village and take a right onto Bridge Street, crossing the Winooski River to Richmond's historic Round Church. Bear right at the church onto the Richmond-Huntington Road and follow it about 10 miles to Huntington Center. Turn left on Camel's Hump Road, and follow it 3.5 miles to the trailhead.

Trail: 7.6 miles as a loop. Forest City Trail, 2.2 miles, Burrows Trail, 2.4 miles, Long Trail link between the trails over the summit, 2.2 miles, connector trail linking Burrows and Forest City trails, 0.8 mile.

Elevation: 1,400 feet to 4,083 feet.

Bicknell's Thrush

Once thought to be a subspecies of the more common gray-cheeked thrush (*Catharus minimus*), Bicknell's thrush (*Catharus bicknellii*) was recognized as a species in its own right in 1995 by the American Ornithological Union. Look for these nondescript birds in the stunted spruce-fir forests above 3,000 feet, in the thick forest cover that effectively hides them and their nests. The bird is slightly smaller with a somewhat different song than its gray-cheeked relative, but the easiest way to distinguish it is timing: Gray-cheeked thrushes merely pass though Vermont on their way to northern breeding grounds, whereas Bicknell's thrushes nest here.

Although Bicknell's thrushes are not rare in Vermont, their designation as a distinct species makes them globally uncommon. The birds are known only from spruce-fir forests in northern New England and parts of Quebec and New Brunswick. Vermont is thought to have as much as 15 percent of the world's population. Much of the attention paid to the birds in recent years results from their choice of nesting habitat, which coincides precisely with high-elevation locations where Vermont's ski areas are trying to expand. Ski areas are paying for some of the research being done on the bird. Look for researchers atop Mount Mansfield, and in southern Vermont, on Stratton Mountain.

Degree of difficulty: Moderate to strenuous.
Surface and blaze: Well-worn footpath with rocky summit climb. Blue blazes.
MONROE AND DEAN TRAILS
[Fig. 34(6)] and [Fig. 34(7)] Named for Will S. Monroe, who cut the original path of the Long Trail from Camel's Hump south to Middlebury Gap, this trail was built in 1912 and is one of the most popular ways to the summit. The trail climbs through an extensive grove of paper birch (*Betula papyrifera* var. *cordifolia*) that dates from the 1903 fire.

The Monroe Trail is popular not only with hikers, but with birders. In its low-elevation hardwood forests, birders have counted 21 species of breeding birds, including barred owls (*Strix varia*), yellow-bellied sapsuckers (*Sphyrapicus varius*), wood and hermit thrushes and veerys (*Hylocichla mustelina, Catharus guttatus* and *C. fuscescens*), Eastern wood pewee (*Contopus virens*), white-breasted nuthatches (*Sitta carolinensis*), and a number of warblers, such as black-and-white warblers (*Dendroica striata*), black-throated green and black-throated blue warblers (*Dendroica caerulescens* and *D. virens*), and Blackburnian warblers (*Dendroica fusca*).

A short trail, the Dean Trail, links the Monroe Trail with the Long Trail at Wind Gap, a saddle below the steep southern cliffs of the peak, near Montclair Glen Lodge. The Long Trail climbs from Wind Gap to the summit via a grueling but spectacular route, with good views interspersed with woods walking. About 0.75 mile up the Dean Trail toward Wind Gap, a beaver pond offers breathtaking views of the summit and a potential terminus of a hike for children who aren't old enough to make the top. The pond also offers good habitat for olive-sided flycatchers (*Contopus borealis*), ruby-crowned kinglets (*Regulus calendula*), and mourning warblers (*Oporornis philadelphia*).

From its junction with the Dean Trail, the Monroe Trail climbs through a few switchbacks in a spruce-fir forest, and then back into a high-elevation band of paper birch (*Betula papyrifera*). It ends by climbing through stunted balsam firs (*Abies balsamea*), ideal habitat for the globally rare Bicknell's thrush (*Catharus bicknelli*), until it reaches the rocky summit cone.

Directions: From I-89, take Exit 10 and go south on VT 100 to VT 2. Go east, or left, into Waterbury Village and take the first right on Winooski Street. Cross the Winooski River and then go right on River Road, a dirt road. Go 5.1 miles to Camel's Hump Road on the left, which follows Ridley Brook. Turn left here and climb 1.4 miles to a fork in the road, bear left and cross a bridge. Continue to climb another 2.4 miles to trailhead parking.

Trail: 6.1 miles as a loop. Monroe Trail, 3.1 miles; Dean Trail, 1 mile; Long Trail link between the trails over the summit, 2 miles.

Elevation: 1,400 feet to 4,083 feet.

Degree of difficulty: Moderate.

Surface and blaze: Well-worn footpath with rocky summit climb. Blue blazes.

LONG AND ALPINE TRAILS

[Fig. 34(2)] and [Fig. 34(3)] To its aficionados, the southbound section of the Long Trail over Bamforth Ridge is simply the finest way up the finest mountain in Vermont. The trail climbs from the Winooski River, the lowest point on the Long Trail, to the summit of Camel's Hump, one of the highest, making this the largest vertical climb on the Long Trail, over 3,600 feet in all. Along the way it takes in a wide range of plant communities and a gradually expanding view of Vermont and, ultimately, parts of New York and New Hampshire.

Still known to many as the Bamforth Ridge Trail, the Long Trail was recently rerouted onto this long and rough but spectacular ridge walk. The Green Mountain Club's Gorham Lodge, 0.7 mile north of the summit, provides overnight accommodations (there is a fee).

The trail begins easily in a glade of sugar maple (*Acer saccharum*), with an almost

GREAT HORNED OWL
(*Bubo virginianus*)
This owl, growing to two feet in height, will prey on medium sized mammals or birds, including waterfowl, grouse, skunks and porcupines.

Airplane Crash

On a moonless night in October, 1944, a B-24J Liberator bomber from Westover Air Force Base in Massachusetts on a routine training mission crashed into the eastern side of Camel's Hump. The collision killed nine crew members and left one survivor, who spent two nights on the mountain before rescuers could get him down. PFC James W. Wilson, then a 19-year-old Army Air Corps gunner from Florida, lost both hands and feet to frostbite. He survived and later established a successful law practice in Denver, Colorado.

No one knows why the plane was traveling at 4,000 feet instead of the standard 8,000 feet—some speculate the crew was just trying to stay warm in the cool of the late fall. There had been an early snowfall. Whatever the cause, the plane struck just 100 feet below the summit cone, cartwheeled south, and scattered men and 36,000 pounds of debris all over the snow-covered peak.

Rescuers carried out the bodies of the men who were killed. Souvenir hunters and scrap metal dealers have mostly removed the debris, but more than 50 years after the crash, an untarnished aluminum wing section on the Alpine Trail remains as a telling memorial. A plaque commemorating the lost airmen was dedicated at the base of the Monroe hiking trail 45 years after the crash, on October 16, 1989.

continuous groundcover of silvery spleenwort (*Athyrium thelypteroides*) mixed with numerous other ferns and herbs of rich forest soils, such as maidenhair fern (*Adiantum pedatum*) and blue cohosh (*Caulophyllum thalictroides*).

After a mile or so the trail climbs sharply to the rocky ridge crest, where it winds wildly around and over a series of open rock knobs. This makes for a gradually unfolding view of the landscape, beginning with a little window on the Winooski Valley and gradually building to the grand summit view of the entire stretch of the Green Mountains from Jay Peak to Killington, the Adirondacks looming over Lake Champlain and its surrounding lowlands, and the distant White Mountains. On the lower reaches, Mount Mansfield remains mostly hidden behind the bulk of Bolton Mountain, but finally emerges to dominate the view to the north.

The thin soils of the ridgetop, combined with exposure to fierce winds out of the north and west, bring boreal forest communities down as low as 2,000 feet. On convex sections there are large areas of bare rock, scraped clean by glacial ice, and thin organic soils where coniferous species dominate: hemlock (*Tsuga canadensis*) at the lowest elevations, soon giving way to red spruce (*Picea rubens*) and balsam fir (*Abies balsamea*) higher up. Lowbush blueberries (*Vaccinium* spp.) are abundant on the sunnier stretches, and pockets in the rock support microwetlands, dominated by sedges (*Scirpus* spp.). Look for glacial striations on the ledges, particularly on steep faces where they haven't been erased by weathering.

In the more protected concave reaches, the ice left a veneer of till, which supports hardwood forests dominated by white and yellow birches, with common ferns and wildflowers such as mountain wood fern (*Dryopteris campyloptera*), clintonia (*Clintonia borealis*), and Canada mayflower (*Maianthemum canadense*) in the understory. Above Gorham Lodge, the trail climbs rapidly through moist fir forests that diminish in stature to subalpine scrub just below the rocky alpine zone around the summit.

The Alpine Trail [Fig. 34(3)] leaves the Long Trail below Gorham Lodge and makes a long climbing traverse around the east slope of the mountain, crossing the Monroe Trail before making a final steep run for the summit. In the spruce, fir, and birch forests above the Monroe Trail, it passes by a wing section of the B-24J bomber that crashed on the upper slopes of the mountain in 1944. While the Alpine Trail can serve as a foul-weather bypass around the summit when the wind is out of the west, the final section is steep and rugged, so it doesn't necessarily save much in the way of effort.

For a great traverse, drop a car or mountain bike at the Monroe trailhead, then hike the Long, Dean, and Monroe trails, a total of 9.2 miles, many of them fairly rugged. For cyclists, the ride back involves a thrilling descent of Camel's Hump Road, then a nice 2.9-mile ramble along the banks and floodplain of the Winooski River.

Directions: From I-89, take Exit 10 and go south on VT 100 to VT 2. Go east, or left, into Waterbury Village and take a right on Winooski Street. Cross the Winooski River and then go right on River Road, a dirt road. Go approximately 7.5 miles to the trailhead on the left, or south side of the road.

Trail: Long Trail from Winooski River to summit, 5.2 miles one-way. Alpine Trail, 1.7 miles one-way.

Elevation: 400 feet to 4,083 feet.

Degree of difficulty: Strenuous.

Surface and blaze: Mostly rocky footpath and open ledge; can be quite slippery when wet. White or blue blazes.

QUEEN ANNE'S LACE
(Daucus carota)
A very common non-native wildflower found across North America from Alaska to Mexico. Growing to 5 feet tall, the flowers are creamy white with a single dark flower in the center.

CROSS-COUNTRY SKIING IN CAMEL'S HUMP STATE PARK
HONEY HOLLOW TRAIL

[Fig. 34(1)] This is a popular but challenging leg of the Catamount Ski Trail, the state's end-to-end cross-country ski trail (*see* page 304). It begins at the Camel's Hump Nordic Ski Center, which is now being run by a cooperative of Vermonters, and ends in Jonesville by the Winooski River, almost 1,000 feet lower than the starting point. The descent from the height of land covers 1,500 vertical feet in a mixture of exciting steep shots and easy double-pole road grades, with a short uphill climb in the middle. You will need to pay a trail fee and obtain a map at the touring center. Although it's possible to ski it round-trip, the best way to enjoy the trail is to spot a car at the trailhead on River Road in Jonesville where the ski trip ends; this maximizes the downhill part of the excursion.

A section of trail crosses through recently logged areas and its exact location can shift yearly depending upon the logging activity in the area. At its highest point on the ridge, look along the trail for moose (*Alces alces*) sign. Moose like to scrape the bark off mountain ash (*Sorbus americana*) in long strips with their lower incisors (they have no upper incisors), leaving 2-foot long, 0.5-inch wide scars on the tree's bark.

Directions: To the Camel's Hump Nordic Ski Center trailhead from Huntington Village, go south on Main Street to where it turns a sharp right uphill. Leave Main Street here and go straight on East Street. Follow East Street approximately 2 miles to Handy Road, turn left on Handy Road and look for trail signs and parking for Camel's Hump Nordic Ski Center. From Richmond Village to the trail junction at the end of the ski, go east on VT 2 approximately 4 miles to the green metal bridge over the Winooski River. Cross the bridge and take your first left onto River Road. The end of the trail meets River Road in Jonesville, approximately 2.2 miles from the bridge over the Winooski.

COMMON
JUNIPER
(Juniperus communis)
Also known as dwarf juniper, the common juniper produces berries that are used as flavoring in gin.

Trail: 6.9 miles one-way from the Camel's Hump Nordic Ski Center to River Road in Jonesville.

Elevation: Approximately 1,500 feet elevation change.

Degree of difficulty: Strenuous.

Surface and blaze: Ungroomed backcountry ski trail. Blue plastic diamonds bearing Catamount Trail symbol.

RIDLEY CROSSING TRAIL

[Fig. 34(9)] This new ski trail winds through the low-elevation hardwood forests at the base of Camel's Hump, with glimpses of the summit and ledgy eastern slopes of the mountain. A short spur trail links Ridley Crossing with the Monroe Trail, which is used by snowshoers and by expert cross-country skiers for winter ascents of Camel's Hump.

Directions: From I-89, take Exit 10 and go south on VT 100 to VT 2. Go east, or left, into Waterbury Village and take the first right on Winooski Street. Cross the Winooski River and then go right on River Road, a dirt road. Go 5.1 miles to Camel's Hump Road on the left, which follows Ridley Brook. Turn left here and climb 1.4 miles to a fork in the road, bear right and cross a bridge. Continue to climb another 2.4 miles to trailhead parking.

Trail: 1 mile one-way.

Elevation: 200-foot elevation gain.

Degree of difficulty: Easy.

Surface and blaze: Ungroomed snow surface. Plastic trail markers.

MOUNTAIN BIKING AND HORSEBACK RIDING IN HONEY HOLLOW

[Fig. 34] The main Honey Hollow logging access road and some side roads are open to mountain bikes and horses on a trial basis. Together with Honey Hollow Road (Richmond Town Highway 12), a dirt road up the

BEE BALM
(*Monarda didyma*)

west side of Preston Brook, the open trails form a figure 8 with a 5.2-mile lower loop and a 1.9-mile upper loop, with 0.4 miles of paved road between Honey Hollow Road and the trailhead. This network forms the Honey Hollow Multi-Use Trail. Some of the woods road sections tend to be muddy and may be closed in the spring and during and after wet periods. While the area is logged, the state manages it with a light touch so cutting is selective or in small patches. This kind of management makes especially good habitat for white-tailed deer (*Odocoileus virginianus*) and a variety of forest edge and brush-loving songbirds such as chestnut-sided warblers (*Dendroica pensylvanica*) and indigo buntings (*Passerina cyanea*).

Directions: From Richmond Village, go east on VT 2 approximately 4 miles to the green metal bridge over the Winooski River. Cross the bridge and take your first left onto River Road. Honey Hollow Road (Town Highway 12) is at about 1.8 miles from the turnoff, and the parking area and main trail access is at 2.2 miles.

Trail: 8-mile loop.

Elevation: 400 to 1,500 feet.

Degree of difficulty: Moderate.

Surface and blaze: Old road. Sections open to bikes and horses are blazed with orange plastic diamonds.

Green Mountain Audubon Nature Center

[Fig. 33(2)] Molded into a terraced hillside and bounded by the Huntington River, the Green Mountain Audubon Nature Center is wonderful for anyone wishing to visit a sampling of Vermont's forest types in a relatively small area. The 230-acre preserve contains a mature hemlock (*Tsuga canadensis*) forest, a grove of Eastern white pines (*Pinus strobus*) overlooking a beaver pond, and a working sugarbush with more than 800 taps, where every spring the center collects sap and makes maple syrup. In what has become a rite of spring for many area residents, the center hosts sugar-on-snow parties each weekend during the sap run, complete with pickles, doughnuts, and demonstrations of contemporary and Native Americans techniques for syrup-making.

Part of the reason for the area's diversity is the deposits that underlie the nature center. The hillside is a kame terrace, deposited during glacial retreat by a meltwater stream running in a pocket between the glacier ice and the bedrock of the ridge. Because the sands and gravels are water-borne, they are sorted by size and weight. Running water can carry fine particles much farther than it can carry heavier stones or gravel, so the largest stones are always closest to the water source. In the case of a kame terrace, this sorting is destroyed to some extent when the glacier melts, essentially removing one side support for the terrace.

The center also contains river terraces associated with the Huntington River, which is gradually cutting down through the landscape, leaving behind flat-topped terraces that look like giant stairsteps to the riverbed.

The diversity of deposits and associated moisture regimes makes for the diversity of forests. Look for alder (*Alnus incana*) along small drainages, with northern hardwood species of sugar maple (*Acer saccharum*), American beech (*Fagus grandifolia*), and yellow birch (*Betula alleghaniensis*) in the sugarbush.

Beaver have also changed the nature center: A beaver pond full of dead trees offers excellent habitat for cavity-nesting birds such as wood ducks (*Aix sponsa*) and tree swallows (*Tachycineta bicolor*). Kingfishers (*Ceryle alcyon*) work the pond, and spring peepers (*Hyla crucifer*) make the area deafening in the spring.

Directions: From the stoplight in the center of Richmond village, turn south onto Bridge Street and cross the Winooski River. At the Round Church, bear right on the Richmond-Huntington Road and go 5.3 miles. Look for signs and parking on the right; the Nature Center office and additional parking are on Sherman Hollow Road, which is the next right after the lower parking area.

Activities: Hiking, bird-watching, interpretative programs, workshops.

Facilities: Visitor center, shop, nature trails, restrooms.

Dates: Open year-round.

Fees: A fee is charged for special activities and workshops; trail use is free.

Closest town: Huntington, 2 miles south.

For more information: Green Mountain Audubon Society Nature Center, 255 Sherman Hollow Road, Huntington, VT 05462. Phone (802) 434-3068.

Birds of Vermont Museum

[Fig. 33(1)] Since the late 1970s, self-taught naturalist Bob Spear has devoted his life's work to carving the 268 species of birds native to Vermont. The carvings are truly extraordinary: some have taken more than 500 hours, and with good reason. Each individual feather, right down to the barbs, has been carved into basswood that Spear prefers to use. Though Spear's focus is on Vermont, he's also made life-sized carvings of 16 extinct, or nearly extinct, birds of North America, several threatened tropical species, and the Jurassic dinosaur-bird Archaeopteryx lunching on a small reptile. The two-story antique barn is a perfect setting for the collection, augmented by a huge picture window where visitors can watch (and hear) birds in nearby fields and at birdfeeders that are part of the museum's 33 acres. Spear's workshop, and Spear himself, are also part of the visit.

Directions: From the stoplight in the center of Richmond village, turn south onto Bridge Street and cross the Winooski River. At the Round Church, bear right on the Richmond-Huntington Road and go 5.3 miles. Turn right onto Sherman Hollow Road and pass the Green Mountain Audubon Nature Center headquarters on your left. The museum is on the right 0.5 mile after the nature center office.

Activities: Hiking, bird-watching, interpretative programs, workshops.

Facilities: Visitor center, shop, restrooms.

Dates: Open mid-May through end of Oct.

Fees: A fee is charged for admission.

Closest town: Huntington, 2.5 miles south.

For more information: Birds of Vermont Museum, 900 Sherman Hollow Road, Huntington, VT 05462. Phone (802) 434-2167.

GREAT BLUE HERON
(Ardea herodias)
Often spotted standing or stalking in water, this heron catches fish by using its bill like forceps. It grows to 4 feet tall and has a wingspan of 6 feet.

Northern Green Mtns.

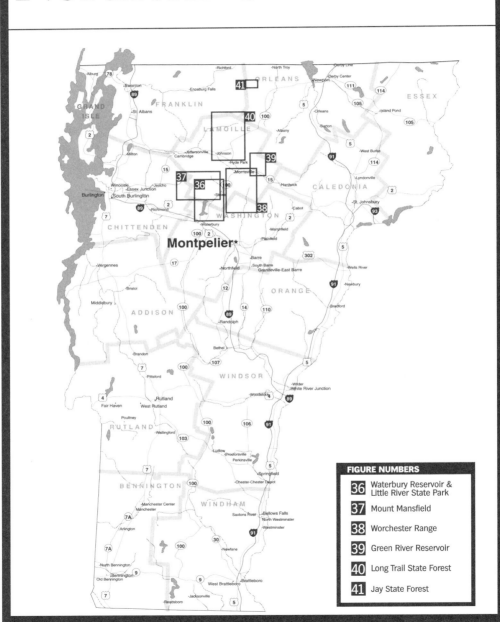

FIGURE NUMBERS

36	Waterbury Reservoir & Little River State Park
37	Mount Mansfield
38	Worchester Range
39	Green River Reservoir
40	Long Trail State Forest
41	Jay State Forest

Northern Green Mountains

Northward of Granville, the Green Mountains do not form the true divide between the Lake Champlain and Connecticut River basins. Two rivers—the Winooski and the Lamoille—collect water and sediment flowing from the piedmont, east slope, and central valleys of the Greens. They cut northwest across the mountains in deep valleys with well-developed floodplains, emptying water and ground-up mountain into Lake Champlain. A third, the Missisquoi, also takes piedmont and east slope water and makes a loop through Quebec, around the northern end of the range.

The northward-climbing ridge of Mount Mansfield fills much of the space between the water gaps of the Winooski and the Lamoille, and was for a brief spell a great island mountain surrounded by the waters of Lake Vermont and the waning ice of the Laurentide ice sheet. These and higher level ice-dammed lakes have left their

[*Above:* Debris flow at Smugglers Notch]

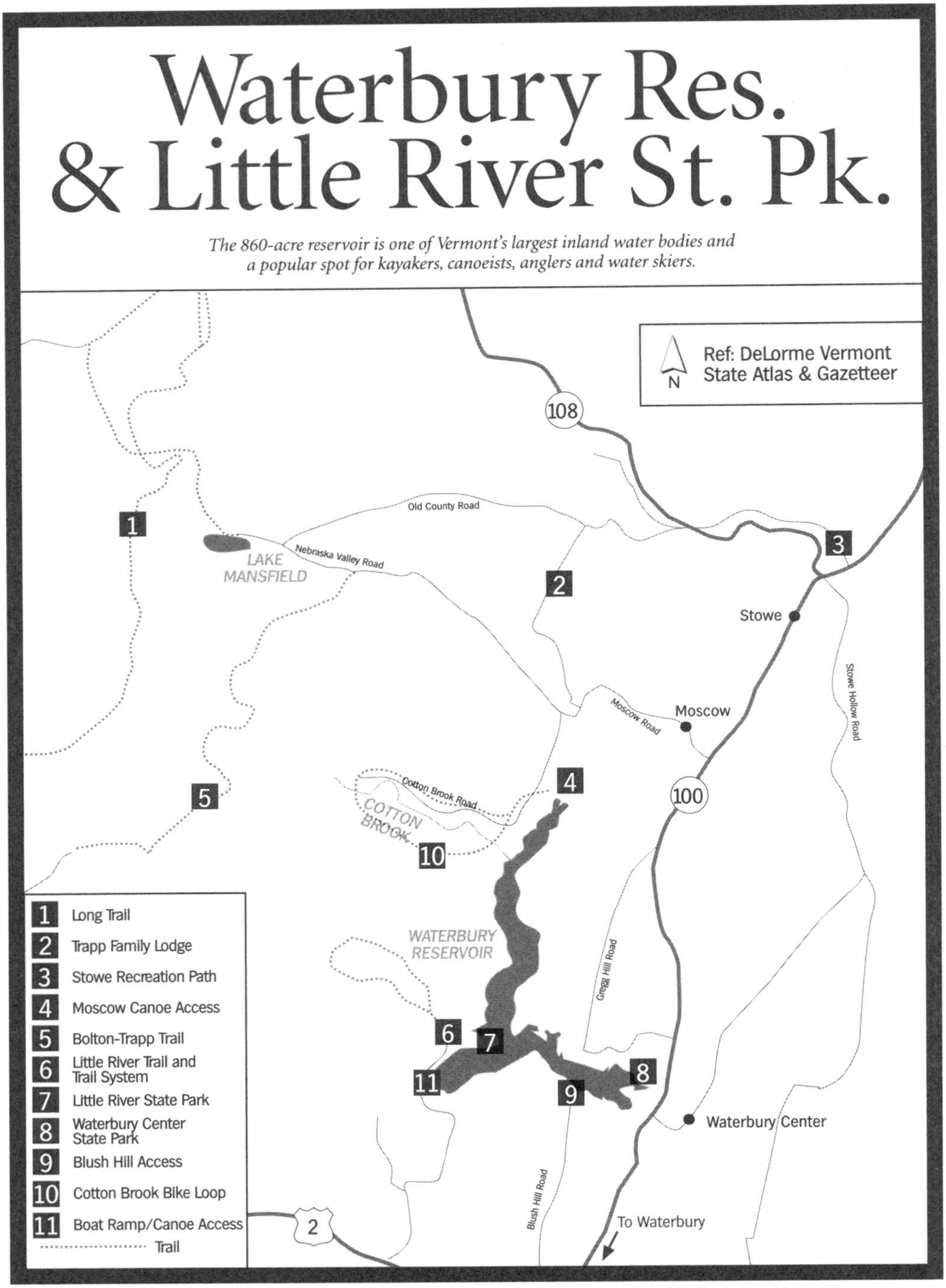

Waterbury Res. & Little River St. Pk.

The 860-acre reservoir is one of Vermont's largest inland water bodies and a popular spot for kayakers, canoeists, anglers and water skiers.

Ref: DeLorme Vermont State Atlas & Gazetteer

108

Old County Road

1

Nebraska Valley Road

LAKE MANSFIELD

3

2

Stowe

Moscow Road

Moscow

Stowe Hollow Road

5

Cotton Brook Road

COTTON BROOK

4

100

10

WATERBURY RESERVOIR

Gregg Hill Road

6 **7**

8

11

9

Waterbury Center

Blush Hill Road

2

To Waterbury

1	Long Trail
2	Trapp Family Lodge
3	Stowe Recreation Path
4	Moscow Canoe Access
5	Bolton-Trapp Trail
6	Little River Trail and Trail System
7	Little River State Park
8	Waterbury Center State Park
9	Blush Hill Access
10	Cotton Brook Bike Loop
11	Boat Ramp/Canoe Access
....	Trail

mark in the form of raised deltas and beaches far from and well above present-day shores. Oversized gorges like Devil's Gulch mark places where, for a time, the backed-up waters of the lakes spilled over the hills.

Northward from the Lamoille, the mountains fragment into water- and ice-worn humps of increasingly boreal character. The roads follow the streams and, no longer confined by the great north-south ridges, seek low divides between the streams and divide the land up into a quilt of irregular polygons. Ultramafic serpentine rock forms slivers and fingers along the eastern side of the range, the source of the asbestos mined on Belvidere Mountain, its deep-crust chemistry a driving force in the assembly of a unique flora and the evolution of an endemic species of maidenhair fern (*see* page 245).

Waterbury Reservoir and Little River State Park

[Fig. 36] Nestled against the lower flanks of Bolton and Ricker mountains, Waterbury Reservoir is one of only a few water bodies in the state with a virtually undeveloped, heavily wooded shoreline. Its long, narrow arms give it a wild feel that belies its location, close to Interstate 89 and the resort town of Stowe.

At 860 acres, the reservoir is one of Vermont's largest inland water bodies, and it is a popular spot for kayakers and canoeists, anglers and water skiers, all of whom do a delicate dance around one another in order to share the water. The state has helped with this balancing act by designating the northern and eastern arms of the reservoir as no-wake, 5-mph zones, which effectively limits these areas to canoeists and anglers trolling for the lake's well-known fishery of smallmouth bass (*Micropterus dolomieui*) and brown trout (*Salmo trutta*). Water skiers generally stay in the western part of the lake where a slalom course is set up every summer.

From the quiet, canoes-only put-in on the northern arm, look for yellowthroats (*Geothlypis trichas*) flitting in the alder (*Alnus incana*) and spotted sandpipers (*Actitis macularia*) running and bobbing along the margins of the shore. There are fewer birds here than you might expect, however, given the reservoir's undeveloped nature. For some birds like common loons (*Gavia immer*), the reservoir is too busy with boat traffic. Another deterrent is the seasonal water level fluctuation. Over the fall and winter, the reservoir is dropped to about a third of its surface area to store snow melt waters in the spring.

Along the southern arm and at the entrance to the eastern arm, the young lake has rapidly eroded steep bluffs in lake bottom and deltaic sediments deposited when a much deeper, ice-dammed lake filled the Lamoille Valley. Nearest the southern end, the sediments are clays with varves, distinct bands of lighter or darker gray that record seasonal pulses of sediment associated with summer melting of the retreating

The 1927 Flood

The dam at Waterbury Reservoir was built in response to Vermont's single largest natural disaster: the 1927 Flood. On November 2, 3, and 4, 1927, more than 8 inches of rain fell on ground already saturated by a wetter-than-normal autumn. Virtually every one of the state's rivers spilled over its banks in the early November storm. The Winooski, the state's largest river, flooded the second story of downtown buildings in the capital city, Montpelier. Not far from where Waterbury Reservoir is now located, floodwaters carried away barns and farmhouses.

All told, 84 people died in the flood, and 55 of them drowned in the Winooski or its tributaries. Farmers were among the most affected, because the biggest and best farms were typically along the fertile river valleys. Roughly 690 farms lost 187 houses, 200 barns, and 257 other structures. Almost 2,000 cows drowned in the floodwaters, and an estimated 7,000 acres of farmland either suffered severe erosion or were covered by flood debris.

A second flood in 1936 spurred federal action. The U.S. Army Corps of Engineers built a series of flood control structures, including Waterbury Reservoir, designed to slow floodwaters and prevent future disasters. Construction of the earthen-fill dam, Vermont's largest such structure, required the efforts of more than 2,000 men from the Civilian Conservation Corps, who completed the dam in 1938. Little River State Park now occupies the grounds of the old CCC headquarters.

ice. Above these are thick sequences of silts and fine sands, likely formed as streams rapidly built deltas around the shores of the glacial lake. Some beaches under the bluffs are littered with curious concretions formed by natural cementation in localized bands of sediment, and range in shape from broad, thin plates to grapelike clusters. They were eroded out of the bluffs above and rinsed by wave action along the water line.

Because Waterbury Reservoir is in the 38,600-acre Mount Mansfield State Forest, there are ample opportunities for mountain biking, backcountry skiing, and bushwhacking in the wooded hills north and west of the reservoir, with access off of Moscow Road in Stowe. The state logs in this area, so be on the alert for logging trucks, but for the most part, expect a scenic trip through second-growth maple-beech-birch forests above the reservoir, and hemlock forests near the water's edge and in ravines and cool, low spots.

LITTLE RIVER STATE PARK

[Fig. 36(7)] One of Vermont's more popular campgrounds, Little River State Park offers 81 sites and 20 lean-tos, along with access to Waterbury Reservoir and to hiking trails on the southern fringe of the Mount Mansfield State Forest. But trails around the campground are also a fascinating and prime example of Vermont's abandoned landscape, or places where small farming communities once thrived but were later left in the westward migration of the mid- to late-1800s.

The campground has maps and a self-guided history trail where visitors can see old cellar holes, family cemeteries, and abandoned orchards. The flanks of Ricker Mountain, where Little River State Park is now located, were first settled in 1790, with the peak population in the mid-1800s, when the railroad first passed through nearby Waterbury.

Nearly 50 families homesteaded here, raising sheep and cows, making maple syrup, and tending apple orchards. Three hikes of varying difficulties and lengths travel past many family homesteads, but it can be fun to do your own sleuthing too. If the thick mantle of green hides cellar holes and tombstones, look for vegetative clues of past human habitation, especially apple trees, or elderberries (*Sambucus canadensis*), favored by homesteaders for their juice, which could be made into a tart jelly with a distinctive taste.

Directions: From the junction of VT 100 and U.S. 2 in Waterbury, head west on U.S. 2 for 1.5 miles, then turn right on Little River Road and go 3.5 miles north to the park.

Activities: Camping, hiking, fishing, swimming, mountain biking.

Facilities: 81 campsites, 20 lean-tos, restrooms, showers, swimming beach, boat launch, softball field, hiking trails.

Dates: Open mid-May to mid-Oct.

Fees: There is a fee for day use and camping.

For more information: Little River State Park, RD 1 Box 150, Waterbury, Vermont 05676. Phone (802) 244-7103 (summer).Vermont Department of Forests, Parks, and Recreation, District 4, 324 North Main Street, Barre, VT 05641. Phone (802) 476-0170 (winter).

LITTLE RIVER TRAIL SYSTEM

[Fig. 36(6)] An 8.2-mile multi-use trail network follows old farm roads along Stevenson Brook above Little River State Park, exploring the old cellar holes, stone walls, and cemeteries of the Ricker Mountain settlement. The 3-mile Woodward Hill Trail links the campground area to the old CCC camp below the dam. The multi-use trails in Little River State Park are open to horses but not mountain bikes, while some trails are for foot travel only. A detailed map and pamphlets for self-guided nature (0.5 mile, easy) and history (about 3.5 miles, moderate) hikes are available at the state park office.

Trail: Loops of 0.5 to about 5 miles.

Elevation: 500 to 1,800 feet.

Degree of difficulty: Easy to moderate.

Surface and blaze: Old road and footpath, orange diamonds and blue blazes.

WATERBURY CENTER STATE PARK

[Fig. 36(8)] A day-use access area, Waterbury Center State Park is located off of VT 100 just before the village of Waterbury Center.

Directions: From Interstate 89 Exit 10, head north on VT 100 for approximately 3 miles and look for Old River Road on your left, or west side. The access area is at the end of this road, approximately 0.4 mile from VT 100.

Activities: Picnicking, boating, swimming, fishing, water skiing, bird-watching.

Facilities: Day-use area with canoe and kayak rentals, swimming beach, picnic area, boat access, restrooms.

Dates: Open year-round, with rental equipment available May-Oct.

Fees: There is a summer day-use fee.

For more information: Waterbury Center State Park, RD 1 Box 177, Waterbury Center, VT 05677. Phone (802) 244-1226 (summer).Vermont Department of Forests, Parks, and Recreation, District 4, 324 North Main Street, Barre, VT 05641. Phone (802) 476-0170 (winter).

BLUSH HILL ACCESS

[Fig. 36(9)] This is a gravel boat ramp on Waterbury Reservoir's eastern arm that is popular with anglers and water skiers.

Directions: From the junction of VT 100 and I-89, go north on VT 100 past the northbound exit ramp and take an immediate left onto Blush Hill Road, which climbs steeply onto a ridgeline and parallels VT 100. Travel 3 miles, remaining on the main road until you come to the end of the road and the access.

MOSCOW CANOE ACCESS

[Fig. 36(4)] Boat access on the northern tip of the reservoir is limited to canoes and kayaks. The parking area is also used by mountain bikers in the summer and cross-country skiers and snowmobilers in the winter for access to the Little River Trail.

Directions: From the junction of VT 100 and I-89, travel 7 miles north on VT 100 to Moscow Road on the left. Turn onto Moscow Road and go approximately 2.2 miles. The road will make a hard left, then a hard right. Where the road makes a hard right, go straight on an unpaved road for approximately 1.2 miles; the access is on your left.

LITTLE RIVER TRAIL

[Fig. 36(6)] The Little River Trail traverses the headwaters of Cotton Brook on the wild western side of Waterbury Reservoir, connecting the Moscow canoe access to Little River State Park and a parking area below the reservoir dam. It starts out as a gated logging access road (used as such only occasionally, often in winter), and after 7.6 miles it connects to the multi-use trail network above Little River State Park, which makes various mountain bike, hiking, and cross-country ski loops possible. Side trails connect it to the Bolton-Trapp backcountry ski trail on Bolton Mountain. The trail is shared by snowmobiles in winter and may be plowed for logging, so it's best to check for conditions.

The 11-mile mountain bike loop begins at the Moscow end of the trail and climbs 800 feet on the road over 6.7 miles, then descends a steep, winding old woods road back to the main road about 1.0 miles from the gate. The latter section may be closed in spring or during wet periods to prevent damage to the trail. It is flagged with white diamonds with the silhouette of a cyclist.

Skiers can make a loop out of the Little River Trail by skiing on Waterbury Reservoir. In winter, a heavy blanket of snow muffles the sounds of busy VT 100 and freezes Waterbury Reservoir into an Antarctic landscape. It can be especially spooky on colder days when the ice pops and booms.

Trail: 13.6 miles one-way from Moscow to Little River State Park. 11-mile mountain bike loop.

Elevation: 700 to 1,500 feet.

Degree of difficulty: Moderate.

Surface and blaze: Paved and dirt road, old woods road. Orange diamonds and blue paint blazes.

BOLTON-TRAPP TRAIL

[Fig. 36(5)] As the name implies, this classic backcountry ski trail runs from Bolton Valley Ski Resort off of Interstate 89, at the base of Bolton Mountain, 12 miles north to the Trapp Family Lodge (of *Sound of Music* fame) on the fringes of Stowe Village. Steep side trails that connect with the Little River Trail provide fun descents for telemarkers and make several loop variations possible for those who don't want to ski the whole length or make the long drive around for car drop-off and pick-up.

The most important thing to remember with this tour is to pick the best possible weather and snow conditions you possibly can: The trail is narrow, steep in places, and remote. Route finding can be a challenge even in good weather, depending upon how much frost and snow cover the trees and associated markers. The tour is part of the Catamount Trail, Vermont's 300-mile-long end-to-end ski trail, and is marked with blue diamond-shaped plastic trail markers.

Most skiers begin in Bolton and end at Trapp's. Stop at the Bolton Cross-Country Center to pay a trail fee and be sent off through the maze on the right touring center trail. From Bolton, the trail climbs steeply, in places traveling through a series of switchbacks. At the top of the touring center trail system, the backcountry Cotton Brook Trail drops off to the right, and the main trail climbs through a small birch glade that is open enough for telemark skiing. After about 2.8 miles, the trail goes downhill for a short while, heads east on the flanks of Bolton Mountain, and then north again and down. Eight miles from Bolton, the trail crosses the Nebraska Valley Road, where it's possible to leave a car if you want a shorter ski or don't want to climb the last (ouch!) 3.5 miles to Trapp's.

BROWNHEADED COWBIRD
(Molothrus ater)
The cowbird lays its eggs in the nests of other birds that feed the newly hatched intruder until it can fly.

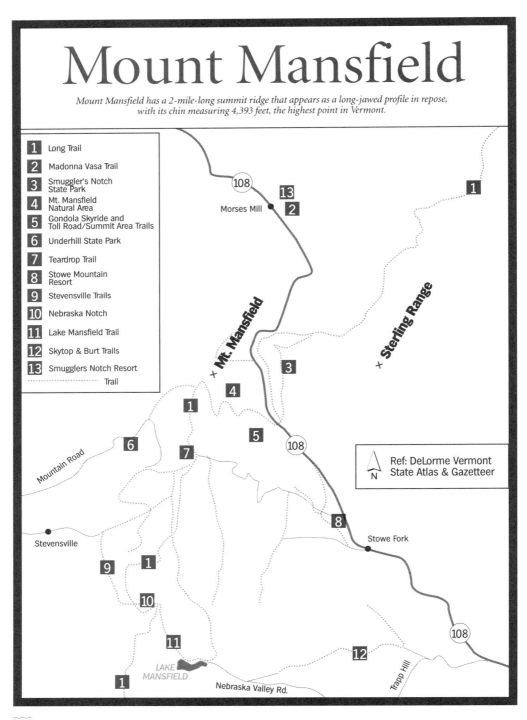

Mount Mansfield

Mount Mansfield has a 2-mile-long summit ridge that appears as a long-jawed profile in repose, with its chin measuring 4,393 feet, the highest point in Vermont.

1 Long Trail
2 Madonna Vasa Trail
3 Smuggler's Notch State Park
4 Mt. Mansfield Natural Area
5 Gondola Skyride and Toll Road/Summit Area Trails
6 Underhill State Park
7 Teardrop Trail
8 Stowe Mountain Resort
9 Stevensville Trails
10 Nebraska Notch
11 Lake Mansfield Trail
12 Skytop & Burt Trails
13 Smugglers Notch Resort
.... Trail

Morses Mill

Mt. Mansfield

Sterling Range

Mountain Road

Stevensville

Stowe Fork

Ref: DeLorme Vermont State Atlas & Gazetteer
N

LAKE MANSFIELD

Nebraska Valley Rd.

Trapp Hill

Detailed maps of this and other backcountry trails are available at touring centers and ski shops in the area.

Directions: For the trailhead at Bolton Valley: from the junction of VT 100 and U.S. 2 in Waterbury, head west on U.S. 2 approximately 7 miles. Bolton Valley Access Road is on the right. Climb 5 miles to the ski area. For the trail crossing on Nebraska Valley Road: from the junction of VT 100 and U.S. 2, head north on VT 100 for 7 miles to Moscow Road on the left. Turn left onto Moscow Road and go approximately 2.2 miles. The road will make a hard left, then a hard right; follow the road as it makes this right (straight ahead is the Moscow canoe access and Cotton Brook Road). This is Nebraska Valley Road. Continue for about 4 miles and look for a small plowed parking area on the left. The Trapp Family Lodge is located on the outskirts of Stowe. From the center of Stowe Village, go west on VT 108 for 2 miles and look for Luce Hill Road on the left. Climb Luce Hill Road for 1.5 miles to Trapp Hill Road on left. Take Trapp Hill Road 1.2 miles to the center.

Activities: Snowshoeing, backcountry skiing.

Facilities: Bolton Valley and the Trapp Family Lodge have ski shops with restaurants, restrooms, and waxing rooms.

Fees: There is a fee for groomed trail access to the backcountry trail.

Trail: 11.8 miles one-way from Bolton to Trapp's; 12- to 15-mile loops from Bolton Valley or Nebraska Valley Road.

Elevation: 1,300 foot elevation gain.

Degree of difficulty: Strenuous, strong intermediate to expert skiers.

For more information: Catamount Trail Association, PO Box 1235, Burlington, VT 05402. Phone (802) 864-5794.

Mount Mansfield

[Fig. 37] Seen from the fields and hilltops of the Champlain Valley or the Stowe area, Mount Mansfield's 2-mile-long summit ridge appears as a long-jawed profile in repose. The high points are named accordingly, from the Forehead and Nose at the southern end to the Chin, at 4,393 feet the highest point in Vermont, and the Adam's Apple to the north. Measured in feet above sea level, Vermont's highest peak does not compare to the summits of the White Mountains to the east or the Adirondack High Peaks to the west, but on a clear day it offers expansive views of both of these ranges and all the territory in between, including the great blue swath of Lake Champlain and the patchwork of pastures and plowed fields around it.

The summit ridge of Mount Mansfield is a University of Vermont Natural Area, and the 7-mile-long oblong footprint of the mountain includes lands in Vermont's largest state forest and two state parks. With one of Vermont's premier ski areas on its western flank, access by road at one end of the ridge and by gondola at the other in summer

Red Squirrels

Just about anywhere in North America there are extensive coniferous forests, there are also red squirrels (*Tamiasciurus hudsonicus*) or a closely related species. Although they will eat a variety of other plant and animal foods, red squirrels' major food is always the seeds of spruce, fir, and other cone-bearing trees. They collect cones, usually while they are still green, by nipping the twig at their base and letting them fall to the ground. They will gather, store, and feed on cones at a favored spot, resulting in a pile of scales called a midden. In Vermont, middens tend to be small and located on stumps or logs, but in some areas the midden piles are used for many years and can be three to four feet deep, usually around the base of a tree. Because conifer seeds are winged and wind dispersed, and the squirrels are so efficient at destroying the seeds, they are seed predators rather than dispersers. The resulting selective pressure may have driven the development of the thick-scaled, barbed cones of some pine species, including the five-pound cones of the Coulter pine of California.

and early autumn, and a collection of transmission towers clustered around the Nose (known to some as "the Nose Hairs"), this mountain is not wilderness. But it is laced by an extensive system of trails that can lead the inquisitive hiker off the well-beaten Long Trail to a measure of wildness and privacy on all but the busiest summer days.

STOWE MOUNTAIN RESORT

[Fig. 37(8)] Stowe Mountain Resort's downhill ski area covers the east side of the mountain and the south side of Spruce Peak in the Sterling Range. Some of the ski trails at Stowe date back to the early days of skiing in Vermont, when the Civilian Conservation Corps was engaged in cutting trails for city dwellers that came up on the ski trains. While some of these have been widened and are regularly groomed to modern standards, a few remain as the backcountry backbone of the resort's fine cross-country ski area, which also has an extensive groomed trail system for both skate and classical skiers. In summer, two ski lifts are used for mountain bike access to selected trails, and there is an in-line skate/skateboard park and alpine slide. The resort also offers summer and autumn visitors easy access to Mansfield's summit ridge via a toll road and its eight-passenger gondola.

Activities: Downhill and cross-country skiing, hiking, mountain biking, sightseeing.

Facilities: Full service resort with a variety of accommodations and activity centers.

Dates: Year-round.

Fees: There are fees for use of the resort's facilities.

Closest town: Stowe, 6 miles.

For more information: Stowe Mountain Resort, 5781 Mountain Road, Stowe, VT, 05672. Phone (802) 253-3000.

THE TOLL ROAD

[Fig. 37(5)] For better and for worse, the summit ridge of Mount Mansfield is accessible by driving up the Stowe Mountain Resort's 4.5-mile-long Toll Road. On the better side, it allows people who cannot or choose not to ascend the mountain by more arduous paths to enjoy the view and experience first-hand the natural history of the mountain summit. On the other hand, those people can add up quickly on a fair summer day and, together with those who take the various other routes up the mountain, make this one of the Northeast's busiest summits. The road also gives vehicle access to the television and radio transmission towers clustered on and around the Nose, the mountain's secondary summit.

In a story that is familiar to visitors to other northeastern summits, like Mount Washington in New Hampshire, the Toll Road was built around 1870 to give horse-and-carriage access to a hotel near the site of the present Green Mountain Club information center and summit parking area. The summit hotel was built in 1859, and hosted many a party until it was razed in 1964, as much a victim of changing preference as old age.

In summer, the Toll Road is open to hikers but not cyclists. In winter it is used as a downhill ski trail, and cross-country skiers often ride the lift up and ski down, but skiing up the road is discouraged. It is also the downhill leg of America's oldest downhill/cross-country combined race, the Stowe Derby, which runs from near the top of the mountain 10 miles (16 km) into the town of Stowe. It began in 1945 as a personal challenge between two transplanted Europeans, Sepp Ruschp (founder of the ski area) and Erling Strom; Ruschp won. After 9 years of fun, there was an 18-year hiatus, but the race now hosts up to 1,000 skiers of all ages, with a 6-km short course for younger skiers.

Directions: From Stowe, take VT 108 north (the Mountain Road) 6 miles to the Toll House Area parking lot just below the Inn at the Mountain on the left-hand-side of the road. The Toll Road starts at the tollhouse on the far side of the parking lot.

Activities: Easy to strenuous hiking, skiing, scenic driving.

Facilities: Green Mountain Club information center and restrooms.

Dates: Mid-May through mid-Oct.

Fees: There is a fee for car, driver, and passengers.

Closest town: Stowe, 6 miles.

For more information: Stowe Mountain Resort, 5781 Mountain Road, Stowe, VT, 05672. Phone (802) 253-3000. For information on the Stowe Derby, contact the Mount Mansfield Ski Club, 403 Spruce Peak, Stowe, VT 05672. Phone (802) 253-7704.

THE GONDOLA

[Fig. 37(5)] The other way up the mountain by mechanized means is Stowe Mountain Resort's gondola ski lift, which is also used by sightseers in summer and winter. Unlike the Toll Road, it stops short of the summit ridge, leaving visitors to either enjoy views to the south and east only, or pick their way up the strenuous Cliff

Trail to make the final 500-foot elevation gain to the Long Trail at the Lower Lip.

Directions: From Stowe, take VT 108 north (the Mountain Road) 7.5 miles and turn left into the ski area parking lot.

Activities: Sight-seeing, hiking, skiing, snowshoeing.

Facilities: Snack bar and restrooms at base and summit; restaurant at summit.

Dates: Mid-June through mid-Oct., winter ski season.

Fees: There is a fee.

Closest town: Stowe, 6 miles.

For more information: Stowe Mountain Resort, 5781 Mountain Road, Stowe, VT, 05672. Phone (802) 253-3000.

MOUNT MANSFIELD NATURAL AREA

[Fig. 37(4)] W.H.H. Bingham, the developer of the Toll Road and summit hotel, deeded 400 acres along the summit ridge of Mount Mansfield to the University of Vermont in 1859. In the 1950s and 1960s the university allowed construction of the radio and television transmission towers along the southern end of the ridge, but otherwise the area is preserved as a natural area for scientific study and recreation. Adjacent lands on both sides of the ridge are in Mount Mansfield State Forest.

The very crest of the ridge is mostly bare rock for long stretches, in places kept open by relentless winds that scour away nascent soils and winter snows alike, in others probably opened up by over a century of booted foot traffic. The rock is light gray-green quartz-muscovite-chlorite schist, with lumpy lenses of white quartz that congealed out of the half-melted rock during the Acadian orogeny 350 million years ago. The folded or wrinkled appearance of the rock also attests to the intense temperature and pressure of mountain building, which hardened the rock to make the erosion-resistant summits of this and other Green Mountain peaks. In places, glacial scouring has smoothed the rock and scored it with striae—grooves or scratches in the rock that run parallel to the direction of ice flow.

Off the trail, in every crevice and pocket that offers a hope of shelter from the wind, grow some of the toughest plants on earth, residents of alpine tundra communities like those that grow on high mountain summits all over the world. Inuit people from Alaska to Greenland, Scandinavian Sami, and peoples of northern Siberia would all recognize the alpine bilberry (*Vaccinium uliginosum*), mountain cranberry (*V. vitis-idaea*), dwarf willows (*Salix* spp.), sedges (*Carex* spp.), and other plants that grow in mats and pockets on the windswept ridgeline. These are not just similar but in many cases the same species that grow in the arctic tundra, more than a thousand miles to the north. Ten thousand years ago, in the cold climate near the retreating ice sheet, these were among the dominant plants over all of Vermont, and they have persisted since that time as alpine islands in a sea of lowland vegetation.

In all tundra environments, low temperatures and wind set stringent limits on plant growth and decay, resulting in low-profile, tangled mats of slow-growing shrubs rooted in a few precious inches of black organic soil. Like the deeper organic soils found in northern bogs, which support some of the same plant species, these soils are quite acid, with poor nutrient availability. Plants up here can escape frost for only two or three months of the year, and even during the growing season, air and soil temperatures are often low enough to hold photosynthesis, nutrient absorption, and other metabolic processes to a grindingly slow rate. In winter anything exposed above the snow is subject to attack by abrasive, wind-borne ice crystals. Rocks that offer a local pocket of shelter from the wind may allow establishment of black spruce (*Picea mariana*) or balsam fir (*Abies balsamea*), which are pruned promptly anytime they send a shoot up into the wind. They grow along the ground in a straggling growth form called krummholz, the story of their struggle written in their twisted stems.

Small examples of other tundra community types grow in local habitat pockets along the ridgeline. Pockets of sandy soil, often deposited by water flowing along the trail, are good places to look for colonies of alpine sandwort (*Arenaria groenlandica*), with soft green leaves and white, five-petaled flowers that look surprisingly tender for the harsh alpine environment. It gets away with this because it is an annual plant that overwinters only as seed, so that the growing parts of the plant do not harden for winter. More protected pockets may support low-growing shrubs such as Labrador tea (*Ledum groenlandicum*) or dwarf birches (*Betula glandulosa*). Pockets in the bedrock that hold water near the surface are occupied by small alpine bogs, where growth is limited by acid, oxygen- and nutrient-poor soil conditions. Only specially adapted plants such as peat mosses (*Sphagnum* spp.), cottongrass (*Eriophorum* spp.), and pale laurel (*Kalmia polifolia*) can grow here.

You don't have to drop far off the summit ridge to get into stunted forests of balsam fir and scattered red spruce (*Picea rubens*). Here the pruning action of the wind is not as intense as on the ridgetop, but plant growth is still slow in the thin soil and low temperatures. These subalpine spruce-fir forests are the home of Bicknell's thrushes (*Catharus bicknellii*), whose choked-off songs, along with the ethereal whisper of the blackpoll warbler (*Dendroica striata*), the sewing-machine chipping of dark-eyed juncos (*Junco hyemalis*), and the cheerful singsong of the white-throated sparrow (*Zonotrichia albicollis*), are key sounds in early summer. Dense conifers are also preferred cover for snowshoe hare (*Lepus americanus*), which are hunted by bobcat (*Lynx rufa*); the tracks of both are abundant in winter snows. In taller spruce forests farther below the tree line, red squirrels (*Tamiasciurus hudsonicus*) feed primarily on spruce and fir seeds and aggressively defend territories with vigorous chattering, posturing, and the occasional high-speed acrobatic chase. They are favored prey for larger owls and the state endangered pine marten (*Martes americana*), which is no longer found on Mount Mansfield but may yet return.

SUMMIT AREA TRAILS

[Fig. 37(5)] The summit ridge of Mount Mansfield has a network of trails of varying difficulty, which can be threaded together to make loop hikes ranging from an easy hour to an all-day adventure. Because of the tremendous amount of foot traffic along these trails, hikers should keep their feet on the path and especially avoid stepping on any vegetation. In summer, a crew of Green Mountain Club ranger-naturalists patrols the ridge, reminding visitors to stay on trails and answering questions about the mountain and its trails.

The Long Trail is the main highway and takes an exposed line on the ridge crest over most of its 2-mile length between the Forehead and the Chin. From the open ground of the Forehead, the trail rolls along the ridgetop, dipping into subalpine forest on either side of the Nose, then continuing for an easy mile over mostly open ledge before the final, somewhat steeper climb to the Chin. About 0.3 mile north of the Nose, look for the Drift Rock, a chunk of schist some 12 feet long and 8 feet high that was left on the ridgetop by ice that once covered the summit. While Drift Rock rests on bare rock, nearby are good examples of the heath mat and krummholz communities that characterize the ridgetop.

The Cliff Trail (1.1 miles, very strenuous) and Canyon Trail (1.8 miles, very strenuous) roughly parallel the Long Trail between the Nose and Lower Lip, to the east and west, respectively, and may offer more shelter from wind and rain but are also considerably more rugged, passing over and in some cases through jumbles of boulders. These trails are best enjoyed by experienced hikers with light packs on a fair day. Wind and rain or a heavy pack make them extremely challenging. Other important links are the Amherst (0.3 mile, easy), Lakeview (0.8 mile, moderate), Forehead Bypass (1.2 miles, strenuous), and Subway (0.3 mile, very strenuous) trails.

Trail: Network totaling about 10 miles, loops ranging from 0.75 mile to 5 miles from the top of the Toll Road or gondola.

Elevation: 3,500 feet to 4,393 feet.

Degree of difficulty: Easy to very strenuous, depending on route and weather.

Surface and blaze: Mostly ledge and boulders. White or blue blazes.

SMUGGLERS NOTCH STATE PARK

[Fig. 37(3)] Early in the morning on July 13, 1983, a jogger running on VT 108 near the head of Smuggler's Notch heard what he described as a sonic boom. Startled, he looked up to see boulders tumbling across the road. An overhanging 11,500-ton block of rock had broken off of the notch walls nearly 1,500 feet above the road, fallen 50 feet, and shattered against solid ledge. The fragments slid and tumbled down the steep slopes above the road, flattening a forest of yellow birch that lay in their path. The slide stopped just short of the road, but a few vanguard boulders dodged the last few trees and left craters in the road surface. One fragment of the boulder that stopped partway down the slide is clearly visible in the drive up to the notch from Stowe—a massive chunk of unweathered light gray rock with a bold white stripe across the middle. Another school bus–sized fragment from the same event rests only 10 yards off VT 108 at the height of land, marking the toe of the slide.

This rock fall and debris slide is one example of a kind of event geologists call mass wasting: the downslope movement of unconsolidated material under the direct influence of gravity. The 1983 event was not the last such event in Smugglers Notch. In May 1986, heavy spring rains loosened soil and rock on steep slopes all around Smuggler's Notch, resulting in at least eight debris flows, including one that buried a section of VT 108 south of the notch. This last flow is now a lightly vegetated lobe of sand, gravel, and boulders at the bottom of a bouldery gully, right by the roadside. In a debris flow, unconsolidated sediments such as glacial till are lubricated by water, so that they flow downhill in a loose slurry of sediment and water, often carrying large boulders.

Numerous other mass wasting events have been reported in the Smugglers Notch area over the last century and a half, and many more must have occurred in the 10,000 years since retreat of the ice. In its passage through Smugglers Notch, VT 108 winds around several other enormous boulders so tightly as to prohibit passage by buses and large campers, and forested talus slopes extend up the sides of the notch to the base of the cliffs on both sides.

Even-Aged Birch

Fifteen years after the big event, the lower half of the debris slide in Smugglers Notch is already covered by a dense stand of white and yellow birch saplings, which have taken over where earlier invaders like purple-flowering raspberry (*Rubus odorata*) have left off. As the canopy closes and they begin to compete for light, these young trees will gradually thin out to become a forest of trees that are all about the same age, or "even-aged." Across the way, on the Long Trail up to Sterling Pond, there is an older even-aged birch stand that probably dates to the 1938 hurricane, which devastated mountain forests throughout northern New England. Birches produce many light, wind-dispersed seeds that travel far but germinate and establish well only on disturbed soil in full sun. Only over a longer period will shade-tolerant trees like spruce, beech, and maple begin to take over—unless another big rock comes down.

This kind of unruly behavior is typical of mountain landscapes that have been steepened by the scouring and plucking action of glacial ice. Notches like Smugglers are created by glaciers flowing over low points in a mountain ridge like water spilling over the lip of a pitcher. The ice concentrates its erosive power on these low points, deepening them to form steep-walled notches. The final cutting of Smugglers Notch was likely done by torrents of water flowing out of a high level, ice-dammed lake during glacial retreat. Water is still at work in the notch, but now as an agent in frost-wedging. Repeated freezing of water in cracks in the rock, and heating and cooling that causes the rock to expand and contract, gradually loosens sections of the rock face until they are ready for gravity to take them on the next stage of their journey.

Precisely because it was not the easiest way across the mountains, legend has it that the notch was used by smugglers carrying goods to and from market in Montreal during the trade embargo against Britain in the early nineteenth century, and whiskey during Prohibition. The boulder caves near the parking area are rumored to have been used for shelter or as places to stash contraband. Today the caves invite inquisitive tourists, who have worn paths in the thin soils between and over the boulders nearest the road, while the cliffs above attract rock climbers in summer and ice climbers in winter. Some of the ledges host populations of rare, arctic-alpine plant species, some of which are further threatened by unwitting hikers and climbers. Another state endangered species, the peregrine falcon (*Falco peregrinus*), nests high on the cliffs.

VT 108 between Stowe and Smugglers Notch ski areas is not plowed in winter, when it is shared by snowmobilers, cross-country skiers, and backwoods alpine skiers who use it to return to the ski areas after off-piste runs. The state park includes a campground, and the state also runs a ski dorm, both on the Stowe side of the notch.

Directions: Take VT 108 north from Stowe. The campground and ski dorm are about 7.5 miles on the east side of the road, and Smuggler's Notch is about 9 miles. VT 108 continues another 9 miles to Jeffersonville and VT 15.

Activities: Hiking, biking, bird-watching, rock and ice climbing, cross-country and backcountry skiing, camping.

Facilities: 21 campsites, 14 lean-tos, restrooms, showers, hostel-style State Ski Dorm open to high school and college undergraduates, and others as space is available, outhouses at Smugglers Notch parking area.

Dates: VT 108 is open to vehicles from around May 1 to Nov. 1, not suitable for campers and trailers. The campground is open mid-May through mid-Oct., and the Ski Dorm is open June 15 through Oct. 15 and Nov. 15 through Apr. 30.

Fees: There are fees for camping and bunks in the State Ski Dorm.

Closest town: Stowe, 8 miles.

For more information: Smugglers Notch State Park, Box 7248, Mountain Road, Stowe, VT 05672. Phone (802) 253-4014 (summer). Vermont Department of Forests, Parks, and Recreation, 324 North Main Street, Barre, VT 05461-4109. Phone: (802) 476-0170 (winter). Vermont State Ski Dorm, Stowe, VT 05672. Phone (802) 253-4010.

TRAILS ON MOUNT MANSFIELD

Day hike loops on the east side of Mount Mansfield can be constructed from any pair of three trails, all accessible from VT 108 between Stowe and Jeffersonville.

The Long Trail southbound from VT 108 ascends 1.7 miles (moderate) through beech-birch-maple forests to Taft Lodge, a cabin (caretaker and fees in summer) rebuilt by the Green Mountain Club in 1996, then continues 0.6 mile (strenuous) to the summit of the Chin to join the network of trails on the summit ridge. The Profanity Trail (0.5 mile, strenuous) from Taft Lodge provides a steep, foul weather summit bypass, joining the ridgetop a short distance south of the Chin.

The Haselton Trail (2.1 miles, moderate to strenuous) originates near the base of the gondola, ascends across several ski trails, then climbs the Nose Dive ski trail to join the Toll Road near the Nose.

The Hell Brook Trail (1.5 miles, very strenuous) is the shortest trail to Vermont's highest point, making it one of Vermont's toughest trails—steep enough that it is really better to ascend rather than descend. It passes through midelevation forests of red spruce and yellow birch that were never logged. While the trees are not all that big, they grow slowly on these steep slopes, and many are probably over 200 years old. The trail leaves VT 108 0.5 mile south of Smuggler's Notch and follows Hell Brook straight up the steep slopes just south of the big, west-facing walls and ledges of Smuggler's Notch to gain the summit ridge at the Adams Apple. The Hell Brook Cutoff (0.7 mile, moderate) connects it to Taft Lodge on the Long Trail.

FISHER
(Martes pennanti)
A boreal species, the shy fisher is an adept climber and swimmer that eats porcupines and snowshoe hares.

Trail: Loops up to 6 miles.

Elevation: 1,600 to 4,393 feet.

Degree of difficulty: Moderate to very strenuous.

Surface and blaze: Well-worn rocky footpath, with open ledge near summits. Blue or white blazes.

STERLING RANGE

[Fig. 37] The Sterling Range forms the east side of Smuggler's Notch and offers views of the notch, including the big rock slide, and Mount Mansfield. By walking a 1.5-mile section of VT 108, the two trails on the west side of the range can be linked together to make a day or overnight loop.

The Long Trail northbound leaves VT 108 near the head of the notch, and ascends 1.4 miles (moderate) through even-aged stands of yellow and paper birch, probably dating to the 1938 hurricane, to Sterling Pond, which has Green Mountain Club shelters near its north and east sides. The Long Trail continues over Madonna Peak (3,668 feet, 2.6 miles from VT 108), where it encounters a chair lift at the top of Smuggler's Notch ski area and passes two more shelters to Whiteface Mountain (3,715 feet, 4.9 miles) before descending to VT 15 in Morristown. Whiteface Mountain can also be climbed as an 8.7-mile loop from back roads in Morristown.

The 3.7-mile (strenuous) Elephant's Head Trail leaves from a picnic area on the east side of the highway, climbs through birch forest, and crosses the path of the 1986 debris flow twice before reaching a 0.1-mile spur trail to the top of its namesake, a dome-browed cliff on the east side of the notch. It joins the Long Trail at Sterling Pond Shelter.

Trail: 5.1-mile loop, with side trips of up to 7 miles (round-trip)

Elevation: 1,600 to 3,000 feet (Sterling Pond) or 3,715 feet (Whiteface Mountain).

Degree of difficulty: Moderate to strenuous.

Surface and blaze: Well-worn rocky footpath. Blue or white blazes.

SMUGGLERS NOTCH RESORT

[Fig. 37(13)] On the other side of its namesake from the state park, on the west slopes of the Sterling Range, Smuggler's Notch ski area is smaller than it's over-the-hill neighbor, Stowe, but is widely recognized as an excellent family ski area with good instructional programs. In summer, the resort sponsors a wide variety of family-oriented outdoor activities on the mountain and in the region, including hiking, mountain biking, canoeing and kayaking.

Directions: From the junction of VT 15 and VT 108 in Jeffersonville, take VT 108 south about 5 miles and turn left into the resort's main parking area.

Activities: Downhill skiing, hiking, mountain biking, canoeing and kayaking nearby, numerous family activities.

Facilities: Full service resort with lodging, ski lifts, equipment rentals, activity centers.

Dates: Year-round.

Fees: There are fees for use of the resort's facilities.

Closest town: Jeffersonville, 5 miles.

For more information: Smugglers Notch, 4323 VT Route 108 South, Smugglers Notch, VT. Phone (800) 451-8752.

UNDERHILL STATE PARK

[Fig. 37(6)] The east and west slopes of Mount Mansfield were once both part of the town of Mansfield, but in a town with a high mountain running right down its middle, just deciding where to hold the town meeting must have been an interesting proposition. Eventually the town was split, one piece joining Stowe and the other Underhill. The latter is now the quiet side of Mount Mansfield. The Stowe side swarms with skiers or sightseers riding the lifts or shifting gears up and down the Toll Road and Smuggler's Notch, but the Underhill side usually hosts hikers who are determined to reach the summit under their own power, and are willing to spend at least the better part of a day doing so.

A 4-mile road out of the village of Underhill Center leads to the park. A gate just past the park's main campground and headquarters ensures that the last few miles of the road are the province of hikers. In winter the road is not plowed past the last residence, about 2 miles below the summer parking area, so that skiers and winter hikers have an even bigger piece all to themselves. Within the park the road is called the CCC Road, a nod to the depression-era Civilian Conservation Corps that up-graded the road from the rough track that once supplied the nineteenth century Halfway House, the first hotel on the mountain. Over the last mile beyond the Halfway House site, the road peters out into a footpath.

Directions: From Jericho, take VT 15 east 4 miles, and, where the road curves left in Underhill Flats, bear right onto River Road. Follow this 2.8 miles to a stop sign in Underhill Center, and continue straight ahead 1 mile on Pleasant Valley Road to the second right, Mountain Road, which reaches the park entrance in 2.7 miles. In winter, the road is plowed to about 1.5 miles below the park entrance.

Activities: Hiking, snowshoeing, cross-country and backcountry skiing, camping.

Facilities: 11 campsites and 6 lean-tos (short walk in from parking area, RVs not recommended), separate camping area with 9 lean-tos for organized groups, information center and restrooms in summer.

Dates: Campground, mid-May through mid-Oct.

Fees: There are fees for camping and day use in summer.

Closest town: Underhill Center, 5 miles.

For more information: Underhill State Park, PO Box 249, Underhill Center, Vermont 05490. Phone (802) 899-3022 (summer), Vermont Department of Forests, Parks, and Recreation, 111 West Street, Essex Junction, VT 05452-4695. Phone (802) 879-6565 (winter).

TRAILS IN UNDERHILL STATE PARK

The final southward traverse of the CCC Road links together four strenuous trails that ascend the west slopes of Mount Mansfield, which can be joined with the summit ridge trails to make fine day or overnight loops. From north to south these are the Sunset Ridge (2.1 miles plus 1.0 mile of CCC Road), Laura Cowles (1.4 miles plus 1.0 mile), Halfway House (1.1 miles plus 1.2 miles), and Maple Ridge (1.3 miles plus 2.1 miles) trails. All four trails join the summit ridge trail system at various points between the Forehead and the Chin.

For a glorious 10-mile day hike, you can link the Sunset Ridge and Maple Ridge trails, which follow exposed, rocky ridges with continuous views, with a hike along the entire summit ridge from the Chin to the Forehead. The Sunset Ridge and Laura Cowles trails combine to make a 6-mile loop to the Chin.

While all trails to the summit ridge are strenuous, the easy 3.6-mile round-trip hike to Cantilever Rock makes a fine half-day hike suitable for children. It is reached by a short (0.1 mile, easy) spur trail off of the Sunset Ridge Trail. Cantilever Rock is a striking, 40-foot finger of rock jutting horizontally out from a steep cliff some 60 feet above the rocks below. It was split from the ledge by frost wedging, but instead of falling off, it swung away from the ledge, with 10 feet of its base held in a pinch grip by the solid rock above and below.

Trail: Loops of up to 10 miles.

Elevation: 1,800 feet (Underhill State Park trail parking) to 4,393 feet.

Degree of difficulty: Easy to strenuous.

Surface and blaze: Well-worn rocky footpath, steep open ledge. Blue or white blazes.

HOBBLEBUSH
(Viburnum alnifolium)
This plant has white flower clusters and dark purple berries. The flower buds provide winter browse for deer.

▨ NEBRASKA NOTCH

[Fig. 37(10)] While Smuggler's Notch and Underhill State Park offer the best and easiest access to the upper slopes of Mount Mansfield, busy trails and road and ski lift access give them a decidedly nonwilderness flavor. Nebraska Notch, a deep, ice-carved gouge that defines the southern end of the mountain, provides relatively quiet access to the Long Trail south of the Forehead and is a good day hike destination in its own right. There is trail access from the east or Stowe side, and the west or Underhill side. Nebraska Notch is in Mount Mansfield State Forest. Two Green Mountain Club cabins and a tenting area along the Long Trail provide overnight facilities.

At around 1,800 feet in elevation, the notch is still within the hardwood forest zone, so the trails on both sides ascend through forest of beech, birch, maple, and hemlock. In some areas, the soil is rich enough to support a better-than-average variety of wildflowers. Nebraska Notch hosts a population of beaver, which have dammed the headwaters of streams that flow both east and west of the divide, creating a lovely pair of mountain ponds. In the spring of 1995, a beaver dam on the east side burst and the ensuing flood washed out sections of the Lake Mansfield Trail down to bedrock, in places leaving a tangled mat of bare tree roots. The beaver have not yet reoccupied the site, so it is now a beaver meadow, supporting a dense growth of sedges and wildflowers.

The very head of the notch is filled in by a jumble of boulders that have fallen from the ledges above, forming a small labyrinth of caves and crevices, some with perennial ice. These provide good habitat for porcupine (*Erethizon dorsatum*), which den in the caves and feed on the bark and twigs of trees. Look for patches of bark gnawed away at the base of the trees, with fine parallel grooves left by the porcupine's sharp incisors. The same animals have artfully rounded the corners of the tables and other woodwork at Taylor Lodge, the Green Mountain Club shelter in the notch, to the point where the club has fenced off the porch with wire mesh to prevent further damage. The main predator of the porcupine is the fisher (*Martes pennanti*), a 3-foot-long weasel that willingly takes a few quills under its skin in exchange for a big meal. Seeing a fisher takes equal parts luck and stealth, but watching one flow through the forest is unforgettable, and Nebraska Notch is as good a place as any to do so.

Directions: From Stowe, take VT 100 south about 2.5 miles and turn right on Moscow Road toward the village of Moscow; the turn off is about 7 miles from the junction of U.S. 2 and VT 100 in Waterbury. At about 2 miles, the road curves left, then sharply right to become the unpaved Nebraska Valley Road. After another 4 miles the road ends at the Lake Mansfield Trout Club, a private club that provides parking for hikers in a small lot to the right. The area around the lake is private property. To get to the Stevensville Trails (*see* page 228) from Jericho, take VT 15 east 4 miles and where the road curves left in Underhill Flats bear right onto River Road. Follow this 2.8 miles to a stop sign in Underhill Center; continue straight ahead about 0.2 mile and turn right on Stevensville Road. Park at the end of the road, 2.5 miles from the turnoff, or in a winter parking area by Maple Leaf Farm.

Activities: Day and overnight hiking, backcountry skiing.

Facilities: No public facilities at the trailheads; 2 shelters and a tenting area on the Long Trail.

Dates: Open year-round.

Fees: There is a fee for overnight camping or lodging at Green Mountain Club facilities in summer.

Closest town: Stowe, 8.5 miles; Underhill Center, 2.7 miles.

For more information: Vermont Department of Forests, Parks, and Recreation, 324 North Main Street, Barre, VT 05461-4109. Phone (802) 476-0170. Green Mountain Club, Route 100, Waterbury Center, VT 05677. Phone (802) 244-7037.

AMERICAN GOLDFINCH
(*Carduelis tristis*)

LAKE MANSFIELD TRAIL

[Fig. 37(11)] This trail follows the base of the forested slopes above Lake Mansfield, then traverses steep south-facing slopes above one of the small streams that feed the lake. Groundwater seepage along the trail supports dense stands of pale touch-me-not (*Impatiens pallida*), an annual plant with dangling yellow flowers that is found on moist or perennially disturbed soils. A short way above a small gorge and waterfall, the trail ascends through an area of forest that was scoured, in places right down to bedrock, by a flood resulting from a beaver dam failure in 1994. The trail crosses the stream just below a beaver meadow before the final traverse to Taylor Lodge, on the Long Trail. The lodge sits on a ledge with views over the Nebraska Valley.

The Clara Bow Trail provides a strenuous, 0.4-mile alternate route from Taylor Lodge to the Long Trail. It stays close to the floor of the notch and passes over and under the mossy boulders that have collected there, and makes a passage by a ladder made of birch poles through a large boulder cave. Nearest the lodge, the trail passes through a dense growth of wood nettle (*Laportea canadensis*) which has stinging hairs like other nettles, making long pants desirable attire (although the effects rarely last more than half an hour).

Trail: 1.6 miles one-way.

Elevation: 1,400 to 1,850 feet.

Degree of difficulty: Easy.

Surface and blaze: Woods road grading into narrow footpath. Blue blazes.

A dragonfly nymph on a cattail.

STEVENSVILLE TRAILS

[Fig. 37(9)] This group of three main trails can be tied together by a 4-mile stretch of the Long Trail, the Maple Ridge Trail, and other connecting links to make day or overnight loops on the relatively quiet south end of Mount Mansfield.

The Nebraska Notch Trail (1.5 miles, easy) takes a long, gradual approach to its namesake, through hardwood forests, joining the Long Trail near the beaver pond on the west side of the notch, 0.7 mile from Taylor Lodge. It makes a good, moderate backcountry ski tour in winter.

The Butler Lodge Trail (1.9 miles, moderate) ascends the valley of Stevensville Brook to Butler Lodge, a picturesque cabin of spruce logs weathered silver-gray, 0.1 mile off the Long Trail south of the Forehead. The lodge has sweeping views of the central Green Mountains, the northern Champlain Valley, and the Adirondacks.

The Frost Trail (1.2 miles, moderate) ascends the lower stretch of Maple Ridge, and joins the Maple Ridge Trail near the end of the CCC Road (*see* page 224); the total distance from Stevensville to the Forehead is 2.5 miles (strenuous).

The Rock Garden (0.6 mile, moderate) and Wampahoofus (0.8 mile, very strenuous) trails link Butler Lodge to the Maple Ridge Trail. The Forehead Bypass (1.2 miles, strenuous) provides a foul weather route around the exposed ledges of the Forehead, joining the Long Trail near the Nose.

Trail: 4.5- to 8-mile day or overnight loops.

Elevation: 1,400 to 3,940 feet.

Degree of difficulty: Moderate to strenuous.

Surface and blaze: Well-worn rocky footpath, steep open ledge. Blue or white blazes.

BACKCOUNTRY SKI TRAILS AROUND MOUNT MANSFIELD

Many of Vermont's best backcountry ski runs are guarded secrets—off-piste passages through powder-filled glades tracked only by skiers bold enough to dive into the woods on their own. Around Mount Mansfield, however, there is an extensive and delightful system of backcountry trails, ranging in difficulty from moderate tours to steep climbs and descents, that are fair game for anyone with a map, appropriate skills and equipment, and a nose for good snow. The Civilian Conservation Corps cut many of the trails during the Great Depression, in the days when real skiing meant climbing the mountain on your own and ski lifts were just for practice. These trails have been either maintained informally over the years or recently reopened.

The trails are centered around the Mount Mansfield Ski Touring Center, with links to the Trapp Family Lodge trail system. Although there are some free access points to the trail system, these two touring centers provide access for day loops, and their trail fees contribute to maintenance of the backcountry trails as well as the groomed trails used to get to them. Other Stowe cross-country ski areas are also linked in a larger network, through which the Catamount ski trail (*see* page 304) passes on its way from Massachusetts to Quebec.

While many of the backcountry trails can be negotiated and even enjoyed on old-style touring equipment, it's more fun with modern backcountry ski equipment, including climbing skins. Snow conditions are highly variable, and crusty or deep, wet snow can turn an easy tour into a long grind or a mellow downhill into a danger-ous survival experience. Snow reports are available from the touring centers or the Green Mountain Club.

For more information: Mount Mansfield Ski Touring Center, 5781 Mountain Road, Stowe, VT 05672. Phone (802) 253-7311. Trapp Family Lodge Cross-Country Center, 42 Trapp Hill Road, Stowe, VT 05672. Phone (802) 253-5720. Green Moun-tain Club, RR 1 Box 650, Waterbury Center, VT 05677. Phone (802) 244-7037.

THE TEARDROP TRAIL

[Fig. 37(7)] One of the early ski trails on Mount Mansfield, the Teardrop (strenuous), starts below the Forehead of Mount Mansfield, somewhere near where the eye of the profile would be. It runs down the west slopes of Mansfield like the track of a tear down a weather-beaten old man's face, cutting first across the slope, then straight down, then across again, reaching the end of the CCC Road after about a mile and 1,100 vertical feet. The trail jogs left on the road and drops off again, to join an old logging road that runs out to Mountain Road in Underhill below the state park entrance.

Two other trails of yore, Nose Dive and Chin Clip, also take their names from their points of origin on the ridge, but have been widened out as modern downhill ski trails on the Stowe side of Mount Mansfield. The Teardrop and its backcountry cousin, the Bruce Trail, bear little resemblance to these tamed runs. They are narrow and given to sudden twists and drop-offs that demand agile footwork, especially in less-than-ideal snow conditions. To make first tracks on these trails is the dream of many a Vermont backcountry skier, but it is a privilege reserved for weekday skiers and early birds, since both of these trails, along with many more obscure chutes and glades on the mountain, are accessible from the tops of the lifts.

Thrill-seekers often climb and descend the Teardrop from the CCC Road or descend and climb back out to the downhill ski area. More contemplative skiers can descend from the Nose, make the long traverse across the little-used WB Trail, and return to Stowe via the Underhill or Overland trails, which provide more forgiving but still satisfying runs down the east side of the ridge. Good map skills are required to find the trail from above; the upper end of the trail is unmarked, but leaves the Long Trail near the low point in the saddle between the Nose and the Forehead. The WB Trail begins on the section of Teardrop below the CCC Road, and is thinly blazed with red plastic rectangles, but is otherwise unmarked.

Trail: 12-mile loop (via WB and Overland trails).

Elevation: 1,100 to 4,000 feet.

Degree of difficulty: Strenuous.

Surface and blaze: Ungroomed narrow ski trails. Red plastic rectangles mark the Overland and WB trails.

SKYTOP AND BURT TRAILS

[Fig. 37(12)] Skytop is an excellent tour for intermediate skiers with a strong snowplow or experts capable of cutting turns in deep snow. For either group it is best done by ascending the west end of the ridge from the high pastures near the Trapp Family Lodge trailside cabin, which makes a good rest stop, especially on cold days. The trail zigzags up to the ridge crest, then rolls along the ridge for 1.5 miles before descending abruptly to Dewey Saddle. The ridgetop provides peek-a-boo views through gnarled old yellow birches, then spruce and fir, but there is always the feeling of being on top of something, with light shining freely through the trees.

These high ridges are favorite wintering grounds for moose (*Alces alces*), which shelter in the spruce and fir and fan out to feed on hardwood bark and buds, particularly of mountain ash (*Sorbus americana*). Look for trees with large patches of bark stripped off, well above ground level, in long parallel grooves, the marks of the moose's lower incisors as it rakes upwards.

The short (50 yards) but very steep descent to Dewey Saddle, just below the Lightning Knoll viewpoint, is best walked by all but the most experienced skiers. In the saddle there is an overhanging ledge, often decorated by a curtain of blue- and yellow-stained ice, which provides some shelter from the wind. Descent to the Mount Mansfield Touring Center trail system is via the Burt Trail, which zigzags down a north-facing slope, also good moose habitat. Experienced skiers may find it fun to cut the corners.

Trail: 13-mile loop from Mount Mansfield Touring Center.

Elevation: 1,000 to 2,800 feet.

Degree of difficulty: Moderate to strenuous.

Surface and blaze: Ungroomed narrow ski trails. Red plastic rectangles.

THE MADONNA VASA TRAIL

[Fig. 37(2)] For those more interested in touring than turning, the Madonna Vasa Trail skirts the north and west slopes of Mount Mansfield, from Smuggler's Notch ski area to Mountain Road in Underhill. While more of a classic long-distance touring trail than others in the system, it has plenty of ups and downs to keep you on your toes. Long distance skiers can close the loop by using the CCC Road to pick up other trails in the backcountry system, but most will probably want to drop a car at the end of the trail.

Trail: 16 miles one-way.

Elevation: 1,200 to 1,500 feet.

Degree of difficulty: Moderate.

Surface and blaze: Ungroomed narrow ski trail. Red plastic rectangles.

BICYCLE TOURING IN THE STOWE AREA

Cycling in the Stowe area begins with an easy ride on the Stowe Recreation Path with its glorious views of Mount Mansfield. From there it spreads out into the countryside with something for every rider from paved road tourists to single-track-minded mountain bikers, including lift-served descents of some of Mount Mansfield's ski trails.

For more information: Mountain Bike Shop, Mountain Road, Stowe VT 05672. Phone (802) 253-7919. Mount Mansfield Mountain Bike Center, 5781 Mountain Road, Stowe, VT, 05672. Phone (800) 253-4754.

THE STOWE RECREATION PATH

[Fig. 36(3)] The 5.3-mile Stowe Recreation Path, completed in 1989, winds back and forth across the West Branch, a small river that drains the west face of Mount Mansfield. The river provides excellent examples of meandering in a young stream, with well-developed cut banks, where the river erodes at the outside of each bend, and point bars, where the river deposits sediment at the inside of each bend. The point bars are colonized by willows, which tend to slow the river's floodwaters and collect more sediment, gradually building a floodplain. This young river is working mainly with coarse sand, gravel, and cobbles, but the processes are the same as on bigger, more mature rivers like the Winooski or even the Mississippi, which carry finer sediments. The broad floodplain has excellent views of Mount Mansfield, with field and forest in the foreground.

In summer, cyclists, in-line skaters, runners, and walkers share the path. Runners and walkers use it in winter, and it is not groomed for skiing but provides good cross-country skiing in soft snow conditions.

Directions: Recreation Path parking and access: behind the town hall in Stowe Village; there are other access points along VT 108 north.

Activities: Bicycling, in-line skating, running, walking, cross-country skiing.

Facilities: Outhouses at access points.

Dates: Open year-round.

Fees: None.

Closest town: Stowe.

For more information: Stowe Area Association, Main Street, Stowe, VT 05672. Phone (802) 253-7321 or (800) 247-8693.

Worcester Range

Most of the Worcester Range is protected by the 13,400-acre Putnam State Forest, with the northern most peak of Mount Elmore in its own state park.

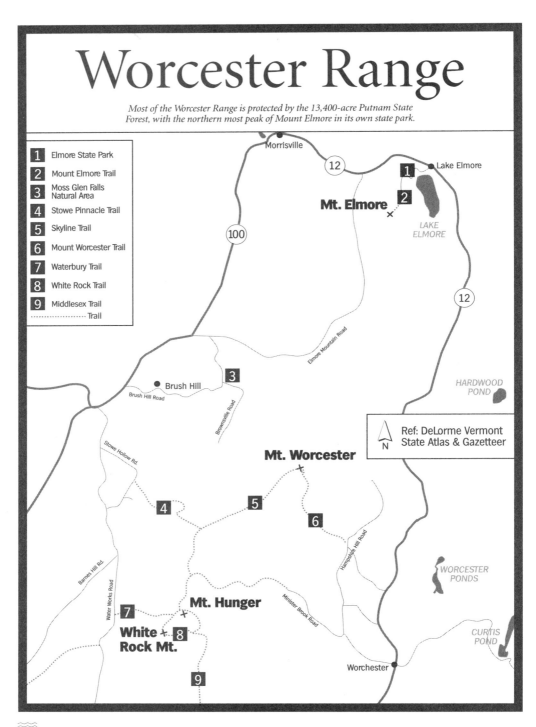

1 Elmore State Park

2 Mount Elmore Trail

3 Moss Glen Falls Natural Area

4 Stowe Pinnacle Trail

5 Skyline Trail

6 Mount Worcester Trail

7 Waterbury Trail

8 White Rock Trail

9 Middlesex Trail

.... Trail

Morrisville

12

1 Lake Elmore

2

Mt. Elmore

LAKE ELMORE

100

12

Elmore Mountain Road

Brush Hill

3

Brush Hill Road

HARDWOOD POND

Brownsville Road

Ref: DeLorme Vermont State Atlas & Gazetteer

N

Stowe Hollow Rd.

Mt. Worcester

4

5

6

Hampshire Hill Road

WORCESTER PONDS

Barnes Hill Rd.

Water Works Road

Mt. Hunger

7

Minister Brook Road

White Rock Mt.

8

CURTIS POND

9

Worcester

The Worcester Range

Red trillium has a stalkless flower above its three whorled leaves.

[Fig. 38] With its rocky summits and panoramic views, the Worcester Range is a hiker's delight. Several of the summit trails are short enough to enable school-age children to reach the top under their own steam. Most of the range is protected by the 13,400-acre Putnam State Forest, with the northernmost peak of Mount Elmore in its own small state park. The state has granted protection to all the land in Putnam State Forest above 2,500 feet in elevation—4,032 acres in total—as part of a state natural area because of the large continuous forests of red spruce and balsam fir here. The open summits of Stowe Pinnacle, and Hunger, Worcester, and Elmore mountains show good examples of the area's major bedrock type, an Ordovician-age chlorite schist that was cooked and compressed beginning with the Taconic orogeny some 445 million years ago. The rock type does include areas where granular white quartz dominates, giving the open summits their milky white appearance and in some areas concentrating in spectacular, thick white veins.

Vermont woodland spring wildflowers dot the lower elevation hardwood forests, with patches of bloodroot (*Sanguinaria canadensis*) and spring beauty (*Claytonia virginica*). Red trillium (*Trillium erectum*), Canada mayflower (*Maianthemum canadense*), and large stretches of mountain wood fern (*Dryopteris campyloptera*) are common along some trails, with scattered occurrences of blue cohosh (*Caulophyllum thalictroides*), wild ginger (*Asarum canadense*), and Canada violet (*Viola canadensis*). In the higher elevation spruce-fir forest, look for starflower (*Trientalis borealis*), blue-bead lily (*Clintonia borealis*), and wood sorrel (*Oxalis acetosella*).

Putnam State Forest is a particularly good place to see warblers just before the trees leaf out in early May. Look for magnolia warblers (*Dendroica magnolia*) around 2,500 feet where the hardwoods mix with evergreens, and chestnut-sided warblers (*Dendroica pensylvanica*) near the trailheads.

The musical song of winter wrens (*Troglodytes troglodytes*) is readily heard in midelevation, moist streamside hemlock forests, and the songs of black-throated blue and black-throated green warblers (*Dendroica caerulescens* and *D. virens*) mark the transition from low-elevation hardwood forests to high-elevation evergreen forests, where dark-eyed juncos (*Junco hyemalis*) then dominate. The easy-to-identify calls of red-eyed vireos (*Vireo olivaceus*) and ovenbirds (*Seiurus aurocapillus*) are common well into the warm midsummer days after most of the rest of Vermont's breeding birds have quieted down and set about raising their nestlings.

Directions: Access via a number of hiking trailheads, including Hunger and Worcester mountains and Stowe Pinnacle.

Activities: Hiking, bird-watching, cross-country skiing, snowshoeing.

Facilities: Hiking trails.

Dates: Open year-round, but the state discourages hikers from using higher elevation trails during mud season, typically early Apr. to mid-May.

Fees: None.

Closest town: Waterbury, 4 miles.

For more information: Vermont Department of Forests, Parks, and Recreation, District 4, 324 North Main Street, Barre, VT 05641. Phone (802) 476-0170.

MOUNT HUNGER
WATERBURY TRAIL

[Fig. 38(7)] This is the most popular way to reach the summit because of its relatively steady climb, a lovely waterfall about halfway to the summit, and extensive blueberry patches at the top.

Directions: From the junction of VT 100 and Interstate 89, go north on VT 100 approximately 1.2 miles to Guptil Road on the right, just after the Ben & Jerry's ice cream factory. Turn right and go approximately 1.8 miles into the small village of Waterbury Center. Turn right on Maple Street, and climb the hill for 0.8 mile, staying on the main road and avoiding two left-hand, dead-end roads. The road will turn into Loomis Hill Road. Follow Loomis Hill to a T junction and turn left onto Sweet Road. The trailhead, with two parking lots, is on the right about 1 mile after the road junction.

Trail: 1.9 miles one-way.

Elevation: About a 2,300-foot elevation gain.

Degree of difficulty: Easy to moderate, with a short steep climb near the summit.

Surface and blaze: Well-worn footpath with rocky sections. Blue blazes.

MIDDLESEX TRAIL

[Fig. 38(9)] This less-traveled trail is a longer way to reach Mount Hunger but popular with hikers who are starting their trek south or east of Waterbury. A grove of sizable paper birches below the summit offers excellent backcountry skiing possibilities for those who don't mind executing turns in tight places. This is also a popular snowshoeing area because of its relatively steady climb through a fine maple-beech-birch forest. The trail follows an old carriage road built in the late 1800s to take guests from a Montpelier hotel to the summit. Making the summit can be difficult in the winter, however, because a series of slabs below the peak make it hard to climb to the top if it's at all icy.

Directions: From Montpelier center at the junction of State Street and Main, turn left on Main Street for about 0.3 mile. At the intersection, turn left on Spring Street and take an immediate right onto Elm Street. This becomes VT 12. Follow VT 12 about 4.8 miles, past the Wrightsville Dam and look for Shady Rill Road on the left. Turn left onto Shady Rill Road and go 2.2 miles. Turn right onto Worcester Road. After about 0.5 mile, bear left at a fork onto Bear Swamp Road, and then almost immediately, bear left again and go approximately 2 miles to the trailhead.

Trail: 2.8 miles one-way.

Elevation: 1,900-foot elevation gain.

Degree of difficulty: Moderate.

Surface and blaze: Wide footpath with rocky sections and steep slabs near the summit. Blue blazes.

MAIDENHAIR FERN
(Adiantum pedatum)
Identified by its fan-shaped whorls of leaflets growing off of black, wiry stalks, this fern is found in rich woods.

WHITE ROCK TRAIL

[Fig. 38(8)] At the southern end of the Worcester Range, White Rock Mountain with its good views and remote, rocky trail, is best visited as a part of a loop from the Mount Hunger summit.

The White Rock Trail leaves the Middlesex Trail after 1.6 miles, and climbs 0.9 mile to the summit of White Rock. The trail then travels another 0.8 mile to a junction with the Waterbury Trail. From this junction, it is 0.2 mile to the summit of Mount Hunger.

Directions: Accessed from either the Middlesex Trail or the Waterbury Trail.

Elevation: 800-foot elevation gain from the Middlesex Trail to White Rock summit.

Degree of difficulty: Moderate.

Surface and blaze: Rugged footpath with scrambles over rock; trail finding can be a challenge. Blue blazes.

SKYLINE TRAIL

[Fig. 38(5)] This newly cut trail links Mount Hunger to the summit of Mount Worcester with eventual plans to connect the trail to Mount Elmore.

Directions: Easiest access from the south via the Waterbury or Middlesex trails on Mount Hunger, or from the north via Stowe Pinnacle or Worcester Mountain trails.

Trail: 4.5 miles from Mount Hunger to Mount Worcester summit.

Elevation: About 200 feet of absolute elevation change between Mount Hunger and Mount Worcester.

Degree of difficulty: Moderate.

Surface and blaze: Narrow, newly cut footpath along wooded ridgetop. Blue blazes.

STOWE PINNACLE TRAIL

[Fig. 38(4)] The proximity of Stowe Village combined with the short hike and expansive views make this one of the more heavily traveled hikes in the region. Since there are several viewpoints and possible turn-around spots below the actual summit, the trail is a good choice as a first hike for children.

Directions: From the junction of VT 100 and VT 108 in Stowe Village, go north on VT 100 and take the second left onto School Street. Follow School Street past Tabor Hill Road and bear right onto Stowe Hollow Road, which will turn into Upper Hollow Road. Pass Pinnacle Road on the left and look for the trailhead parking lot 0.1 mile beyond on the left.

Trail: 1.6 miles one-way.

Elevation: About 1,500 feet.

Degree of difficulty: Easy to moderate.

Surface and blaze: Well-worn footpath with rocky sections and a steep scramble near the top. Blue blazes.

WORCESTER MOUNTAIN TRAIL

[Fig. 38(6)] This out-of-the-way peak near the northern end of the Worcester Range offers good views and blueberries from its open summit. A spectacular quartz vein splits the bedrock just below the top.

Directions: From the center of Worcester village, at the intersection of VT 12 with Minister Brook Road and Calais Road, turn west onto Minister Brook Road and go 1.5 miles to an intersection with Hampshire Hill Road and turn north or right onto Hampshire Hill. Go 2.5 miles to Mountain Road. Turn left onto Mountain Road; trailhead is 0.1 mile ahead.

Trail: 2.4 miles one-way.

Elevation: About 2,000 feet.

Degree of difficulty: Moderate.

Surface and blaze: Abandoned logging road eventually narrowing to footpath with rocky sections. Blue blazes.

MOSS GLEN FALLS NATURAL AREA

[Fig. 38(3)] This 80-acre preserve in the Putnam State Forest is home to one of the state's highest waterfalls, dropping more than 100 feet in a narrow chute. The cool, northwest-facing dark ravine is hemlock (*Tsuga canadensis*) forest, with limited plant diversity but a fine, wild feel to the place. Look for the tiny white flowers of water pennywort (*Hydrocotyle americana*) and the trumpet-shaped purple flowers of mad-dog skullcap (*Scutellaria lateriflora*) in the low wet areas near the stream, both good examples of plants typical of stream and wetland edges. In the wet area near the trailhead, listen for yellow warblers (*Dendroica petechia*) and song sparrows (*Melospiza melodia*) as they fly around the alder (*Alnus incana*) thickets.

Directions: In Stowe from the junction of VT 100 and VT 108 go north on VT 100 approximately 3 miles and turn right on Randolph Road. Take the first right

onto Moss Glen Falls Road and follow this for 0.5 mile
to the obvious parking area and trailhead.

Trail: 0.5 mile one-way.

Elevation: About 150 feet.

Degree of difficulty: Easy.

Surface and blaze: Well-worn footpath, with some
stone steps. No blazes.

RED-SPOTTED NEWT
(Notophthalmus viridescens
viridescens)

ELMORE STATE PARK

[Fig. 38(1)] This remote park was a gift to the
people of the state by residents of the little village of
Elmore, who deeded 30 acres along the lake shore to the state in 1936. Like a number
of other state facilities, Elmore also owes its existence to the Civilian Conservation
Corps, which built the park's bathhouse, fire tower, and caretaker's cabin in the
1940s. Since then, the park has grown to 700 acres.

Anglers can ply shallow Lake Elmore for warm-water fish species, including
largemouth and smallmouth bass, and bullhead. Northern pike are the lake's most
popular sport fish.

Mount Elmore's biggest attraction is its summit fire tower, which offers spectacular views of the southern Worcester Range, Mount Mansfield, and the distant peaks
of New Hampshire's White Mountains. To the northwest is Belvidere Mountain with
huge piles of asbestos mine tailings, home to what was once one of the largest
asbestos mines in the country. The fire tower offers fine views of more than just
mountains: It also lures birders in the spring and fall who use it as an outlook for
migrating hawks.

Directions: From the center of Morrisville, take VT 12 south approximately 5
miles to Elmore State Park on the west side of the road.

Activities: Camping, swimming, picnicking, hiking, bird-watching.

Facilities: 45 campsites, 15 lean-tos, picnic shelter, playground, concession stand,
restrooms, showers, boat rentals, nature trail.

Dates: State park open mid-May to mid-Oct. Hiking trails open year-round, but
the state discourages hikers from using higher elevation trails during mud season,
typically early Apr. to mid-May.

Fees: There is a fee when the park is open.

Closest town: Morrisville, 4 miles.

For more information: Elmore State Park, 856 VT Route 12, Lake Elmore, 05657.
Phone (802) 888-2982 (summer). Vermont Department of Forests, Parks, and Recreation,
District 4, 324 North Main Street, Barre, VT 05641. Phone (802) 479-3241 (winter).

MOUNT ELMORE TRAIL

[Fig. 38(2)] As the northernmost peak in the Worcester Range, Elmore offers fine
views from its fire tower. It holds the additional attraction of Balanced Rock, a glacial

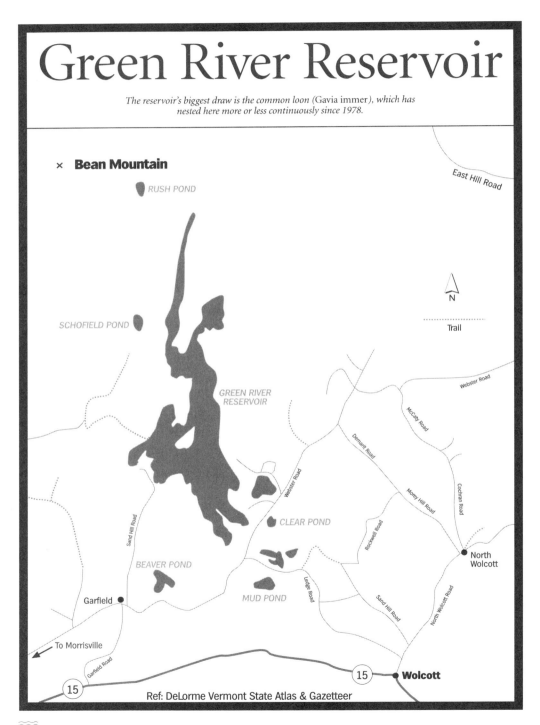

Green River Reservoir

The reservoir's biggest draw is the common loon (Gavia immer), which has nested here more or less continuously since 1978.

× **Bean Mountain**

RUSH POND

SCHOFIELD POND

N

Trail

GREEN RIVER RESERVOIR

East Hill Road

Webster Road

McCaty Road

Demark Road

Webster Road

Morey Hill Road

Cochran Road

CLEAR POND

Sand Hill Road

Rockwell Road

● North Wolcott

BEAVER POND

Ledge Road

Sand Hill Road

North Wolcott Road

Garfield ●

MUD POND

To Morrisville ←

Garfield Road

15

15

● **Wolcott**

Ref: DeLorme Vermont State Atlas & Gazetteer

erratic perched at a precarious but immovable angle not far from the summit. Beavers (*Castor canadensis*) have created a small pond near the trailhead where red-spotted newts (*Notophthalmus viridescens*) can be seen floating lazily in the pond's warm shallows.

Directions: The trailhead is 0.8 mile by road from the state park entrance gate.

Trail: 2.1 miles one-way to summit; Balanced Rock Trail 0.5 mile one-way from junction with trail just below the summit.

Elevation: 1,450-foot elevation gain.

Degree of difficulty: Moderate.

Surface and blaze: Well-worn footpath with rocky sections and a steep scramble near the summit. Blue blazes.

Green River Reservoir

[Fig. 39] Nesting loons, tiny islands with inviting rock slabs at just the right angle for sunbathing, and cool, clean water for swimming make this 554-acre reservoir a favorite among canoeists. The fact that nesting loons return to the reservoir year after year says something about its wilderness character. Its long arms make it easy to get away from other boaters, and are worth exploring for their own sake.

For decades Morrisville Water and Light, the local utility that owned the reservoir and the surrounding 1,600 acres, prohibited motorboats while allowing people to canoe and camp on the reservoir without any regulation whatsoever. As a result, it was often crowded on hot weekends or holidays and there was no guarantee of getting a place to put up your tent. Locals would sometimes reserve the best camp-sites by erecting a tent on a favorite spot a day or two before they intended to camp!

In 1998, Morrisville voters endorsed a plan to sell the utility's lands around the reservoir to the state. While the state does not plan extensive development, some regulation of camping is likely in order to reduce impact.

Two bedrock types, both Ordovician in age, characterize the reservoir. Rocks on the western shore are an assemblage dominated by greenstones and amphibolites. The rest of the reservoir is underlain by the same green-tinged chlorite schist with granular quartz bands that make up the Worcester Range. Several large outcrops mark the perimeter of the reservoir—some colonized by thick carpets of rock polypody (*Polypodium virginianum*).

The reservoir's northern arm, the narrowest, is blocked at the end by a beaver dam. Here you can see tamaracks (*Larix laricina*) and black spruce (*Picea mariana*) along with mountain holly (*Nemopanthus mucronata*) as the dominant tall shrub. In the ground layer, look for goldthread (*Coptis groenlandica*), blue-bead lily (*Clintonia borealis*), and three-seeded sedge (*Carex trisperma*).

Elsewhere the shoreline is edged by a mixed northern hardwood forest of sugar maple (*Acer saccharum*) and red maple (*Acer rubrum*), yellow birch (*Betula alleghaniensis*)

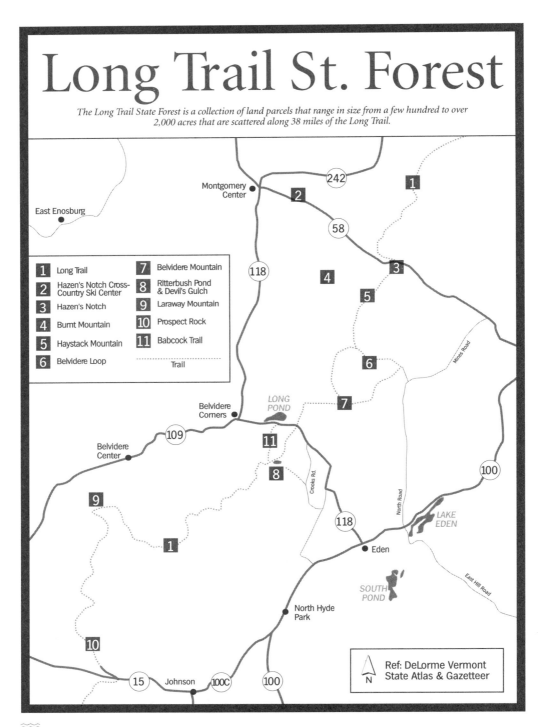

Long Trail St. Forest

The Long Trail State Forest is a collection of land parcels that range in size from a few hundred to over 2,000 acres that are scattered along 38 miles of the Long Trail.

East Enosburg

Montgomery Center

242

2

58

118

1	Long Trail	7	Belvidere Mountain
2	Hazen's Notch Cross-Country Ski Center	8	Ritterbush Pond & Devil's Gulch
3	Hazen's Notch	9	Laraway Mountain
4	Burnt Mountain	10	Prospect Rock
5	Haystack Mountain	11	Babcock Trail
6	Belvidere Loop		Trail

4

3

5

6

7

LONG POND

Belvidere Corners

109

Belvidere Center

11

8

Crooks Rd.

100

9

118

North Road

LAKE EDEN

1

Eden

10

15

Johnson

100C

100

North Hyde Park

SOUTH POND

Mines Road

East Hill Road

Ref: DeLorme Vermont State Atlas & Gazetteer
N

and white birch (*Betula papyrifera*), with hobblebush (*Viburnum alnifolium*) as the dominant understory shrub. The combination makes for spectacular viewing in the fall, when the low hillsides that wrap around the reservoir seem aflame with color. Hemlock (*Tsuga canadensis*) and balsam fir (*Abies balsamea*) add tinges of deep green to the landscape where they occupy small seeps and drainages.

Most people come to Green River Reservoir for the canoeing, but the reservoir does support a modest warm-water fishery with smallmouth bass (*Micropterus dolomieui*), bullhead (*Ictalurus nebulosus*), yellow perch (*Perca flavescens*), and chain pickerel (*Esox niger*).

The reservoir's biggest draw is the common loon (*Gavia immer*), which has nested here more or less continuously since 1978. According to the state's Nongame and Natural Heritage Program, out of the 27 Vermont lakes and ponds where loons are known to nest, Green River Reservoir is far and away the most productive. In the period from 1978 to 1997, loons here successfully fledged 27 chicks.

Other dominant wildlife include beaver (*Castor canadensis*), river otter (*Lutra canadensis*), and nesting wood ducks (*Aix sponsa*). It's not uncommon in the spring or early summer to scare up a moose (*Alces alces*) feeding on tender green lakeside plants.

Directions: From the center of Morrisville at the junction of VT 100 and VT 15A, go east on VT 15A about 2.2 miles to where it joins VT 15. Continue east on VT 15 and take your next, almost immediate, left north onto Garfield Road, which begins paved but turns to dirt in about 2.5 miles. Go 3.1 miles to a Y junction and go right, then take your first left onto Green River Dam Road. Stay on the main road, bearing left at about 1 mile when the main road meets a smaller road. Look for parking on the roadside about 0.2 mile after this road junction. The road is dirt and heavily rutted.

Activities: Canoeing, camping, bird-watching, fishing, cross-country skiing, snowshoeing.

Facilities: Carry-in canoe access.

Dates: Open year-round.

Fees: None.

Closest town: Morrisville, 8 miles.

For more information: Vermont Department of Forests, Parks, and Recreation, 324 North Main Street, Barre, VT 05461-4109. Phone (802) 476-0170.

Long Trail State Forest

[Fig. 40] The Long Trail State Forest is a collection of land parcels ranging in size from a few hundred to over 2,000 acres, scattered along 38 miles of the Long Trail, from the Lamoille River north to Jay Pass. Some sections of the Long Trail in this region are on private property but are open to public use in the trail corridor.

Geologically, this is the widest section of the Green Mountains, but repeated

Loons in Vermont

In spite of Vermont's rural character, common loons (*Gavia immer*) have had a hard time thriving in the Green Mountain state. The birds' historic breeding range once extended south to Connecticut and northeastern Pennsylvania, but lakeshore development coupled with the birds' well-known aversion to human disturbance has all but eliminated breeding pairs in southern New England.

Early records on loons in Vermont are scarce, making it difficult to estimate historic population numbers, although Zadock Thompson, a nineteenth-century Vermont naturalist, does describe the birds as being "not uncommon" on the state's lakes and ponds.

Biologists estimate the state's current population at about 125 loons, which includes both nesting pairs and immature birds. Loons overwinter along the East Coast and return to Vermont just after ice-out in mid-April or early May.

Typically, about 25 pairs will nest on about 27 lakes, ponds, and reservoirs, with roughly two dozen chicks surviving to the fall.

Loons favor undisturbed islands or marshy shorelines for nest sites because these offer the best predator protection for a bird that is ungainly on land. Their ungainliness also explains why water level fluctuations are problematic. Nests are usually on the water's edge, which limits the distance the loon has to travel on land. But if the water level drops, as often happens in a reservoir used for power generation, the loon has to spend more time on land, making it vulnerable to predators. Sudden water level increases pose a different problem: They simply flood the loons' nests.

Vermont has attempted to boost its loon population by providing floating artificial nesting platforms in some water bodies. The state also marks the perimeter of loon nesting areas to keep boaters a safe distance away. Disturbing nesting loons can result in a $300 fine. State officials say canoes often pose more problems than motorboats, because canoeists incorrectly believe their silent craft won't bother the birds.

waves of glaciation have worn most of the once-mighty summits down to wooded hills. The few that stand above 3,000 feet have sweeping views unimpeded by neighboring summits. Scattered outcrops of rare ultramafic rocks, ranging from serpentine and dunite ledges hidden in the deep woods to the huge asbestos deposit on the south and east flanks of Belvidere Mountain, entice geologists and botanists alike.

Directions: Access by various roads and trails.

Activities: Hiking, cross-country skiing.

Facilities: Green Mountain Club shelters on the Long Trail.

Dates: Year-round.

Fees: None.

For more information: Green Mountain Club, RR 1 Box 650, Waterbury Center, VT 05677. Phone (802) 244-7037.

PROSPECT ROCK

[Fig. 40(10)] The short, steep climb to Prospect Rock on the Long Trail gives views of the Sterling Range and the winding Lamoille River. Like the Winooski, the Lamoille originates in the hills of the Vermont piedmont to the east, and cuts across the Green Mountains to empty into Lake Champlain. Between Johnson and Jeffersonville it meanders through a broad, agricultural floodplain. A keen eye may be able to pick out abandoned loops of the river in the form of curved oxbow ponds or wetland dimples in the cornfields.

Directions: Take VT 15 west from Johnson 1.5 miles. Immediately before the bridge over the Lamoille River, turn right onto Hogback Road. There is a small parking area on the left, 2.2 miles from VT 15. The trail begins on the right side of Hogback Road, 0.1 mile past the parking area.

Trail: 1 mile one-way.
Elevation: 510 to 1,040 feet.
Degree of difficulty: Easy.
Surface and blaze: Rocky footpath. White blazes.

Indian Poke

The branching clusters of star-shaped, leaf-green flowers of Indian poke (or false hellebore, *Veratrum viride*) are not much of a temptation for bees, but they have a faint, bad odor that attracts their real pollinators—flies. The big, ribbed leaves and especially the roots are loaded with poisonous alkaloids. Native Americans used extracts to treat stomach pain and sore muscles, and related species were used by Europeans for a variety of afflictions—carefully, one hopes, for too much can cause vomiting, convulsions, and heart failure.

LARAWAY MOUNTAIN

[Fig. 40(9)] The ledgy slopes of Laraway Mountain rise steeply above the floodplain of the north branch of the Lamoille River in Waterville and Belvidere. The Long Trail passes under the steep east-facing ledges and ascends to Laraway Lookout, where there are views of the Lamoille Valley and an unusual perspective on Mount Mansfield. It can be climbed one-way via the Long Trail or done as loop using the Davis Neighborhood Trail and an unimproved road from Codding Hollow back to Davis Neighborhood. The Green Mountain Club's Corliss Camp, a small cabin, is at the junction of the Long and Davis Neighborhood trails.

Directions: For the Long Trail, from Waterville, go north on VT 109 approximately 1.8 miles to Codding Hollow Road. Turn right, or east, on Codding Hollow, and bear left at a fork after a covered bridge. Park in a clearing about 2.5 miles from VT 109. For the Davis Neighborhood Trail, from Johnson, take VT 15 west 1.2 miles to Foot Road. Turn right, or north, on Foot Road and cross two intersecting roads to roadside parking at the trailhead, 4 miles from VT 15.

Trail: 1.8 miles one-way, or 8.2-mile loop.

Elevation: 1,200 to 2,790 feet.

Degree of difficulty: Moderate.

Surface and blaze: Unimproved road, rocky footpath, and some open ledge. Blue blazes on side trails, white blazes on Long Trail.

RITTERBUSH POND AND DEVIL'S GULCH

[Fig. 40(8)] This moderate hike on the Long Trail takes in local views from Ritterbush Lookout, skirts the pond, then traverses the bouldery floor of Devil's Gulch, a small, partially collapsed notch and gorge.

The 70-foot-high walls were carved by glacier ice, but a few pothole fragments among the boulders at the bottom indicate that glacial meltwater may also have done some work here. During glacial retreat, an arm of the ice-dammed lake that flooded the Lamoille River valley extended as far as Ritterbush Pond, and Devil's Gulch may have served as a temporary outlet. Frost action has broken up the walls of the gorge, creating the disarray of boulders at the bottom—a natural playground for children and adults alike, and a moist, shady habitat for lichens, mosses, and ferns.

The trail passes under an impressive 25-foot slab, topped by a mat of rock polypody (*Polypodium virginianum*) and rock tripe (*Umbilicaria* spp.), a black foliose lichen. Ice stored under the boulders feeds cold water springs and creates cold air pockets in early summer. Scattered red spruce (*Picea rubens*) trees grow on the high cliffs on the north wall, while mountain wood fern (*Dryopteris campyloptera*) and wood nettle (*Laportea canadensis*) grow on and among the boulders.

In the area around Ritterbush Pond, the trail traverses the Babcock Nature Preserve, a 100-acre natural area administered by Johnson State College. The preserve is the northernmost known breeding location of the Louisiana waterthrush (*Seiurus motacilla*). Ritterbush Camp, a Green Mountain Club Shelter on this section of the Long Trail, was removed in 1998 and is due to be replaced by a new shelter or tent platforms. As it approaches Devil's Gulch, the Long Trail crosses several seeps that support large patches of Indian poke (*Veratrum viride*). This hike can be done as a loop by taking the Babcock Trail past Big Muddy Pond and walking a 0.5-mile section of VT 118.

Directions: From Eden at the junction of VT 100 and VT 118, take VT 118 north 4.9 miles to where the Long Trail crosses VT 118. Park on the shoulder or a small parking lot on the north side of the road.

Trail: 5-mile loop.

Elevation: 1,280 to 1,660 feet.

Degree of difficulty: Moderate.

Surface and blaze: Rocky footpath with ledge, over and under boulders in Devil's Gulch. White blazes.

Green Mountain Maidenhair Fern

The graceful fan-shaped fronds of the common maidenhair fern (*Adiantum pedatum*) are familiar to backwoods botanists throughout the eastern United States. But the maidenhairs growing in the woods near the old asbestos mine on Belvidere Mountain, and on scattered dunite outcrops in the region around it, have a stiffer look, with less of an arch at the base of the fan, and fewer, stiffer side branches. Once considered a serpentine-adapted variety of the common maidenhair, the Green Mountain Maidenhair (*Adiantum viridimontanum*) has recently been given full species status as a result of research by Cathy Paris, a botanist at the University of Vermont's Pringle Herbarium. She found that the new, endemic species evolved recently by allopolyploidy, a kind of overnight speciation that is common in ferns. It involves hybridization between two parent species and a doubling of chromosome number in a single step, resulting in the reproductive isolation that defines different species.

BELVIDERE MOUNTAIN

[Fig. 40(7)] For much of its 75-year history, the open-pit asbestos mine on Belvidere Mountain was not much of a money-maker, in part because of the public health bill that came due in the 1970s, after over 50 years of research documenting the ill effects of asbestos. Workers stopped digging in 1975, but the mine remains a deep wound in the earth's crust, guaranteed to offend most environmentally minded people.

But whether they are viewed from a distant Green Mountain summit, from the road leading past the mines, or from Belvidere's summit, the great gash in the side of the mountain, and the impossibly huge, barren piles of tailings that have accumulated around its base constantly draw the eye, for they give us a glimpse inside the earth. And Belvidere Mountain is an interesting piece of earth, for you don't find asbestos just anywhere.

On the geologic map of Vermont, the strips of gray, green, and brown that indicate the schists and phyllites of the eastern side of the Green Mountains are flecked with blobs of scarlet and orange, mainly on the east side of the range, including one centered on the east slopes of Belvidere Mountain. These indicate bodies of rock that originated as slivers of oceanic crust that were carried up onto the edge of the continent during the Taconic orogeny, around 450 million years ago, when an offshore volcanic island-arc drifted in from the Proto-Atlantic ocean and collided with the continent. While most of the oceanic crust between the islands and continent was destroyed by subduction, as the continental edge rode over the descending oceanic plate it scraped off most of the sediments that had accumulated over the oceanic crust during its lifetime of 100 to 200 million years. These formed a messy wedge of folded and faulted rocks on the continental edge, and the scraping off process also picked up fragments of oceanic crust and mixed them into the wedge.

Oceanic crust is low in silica and composed of a characteristic suite of rocks and minerals which are collectively called ophiolites, and are described as ultramafic, meaning extremely low in silica and rich in magnesium, iron, and other metals. Because of their unique origin, ophiolites in continental crust are rare, and they always occur in bands of rock in mountain ranges, indicating a suture zone where rocks were carried to a continental edge and plastered on by plate tectonic processes. Ophiolite rocks are found in chunks and slivers in a 10-mile-wide serpentine belt that extends along the east slopes and foothills of the Appalachians from Alabama to Newfoundland.

Vermont's talc and asbestos mines are located in bodies of ultramafic rock. The mineral asbestos is a fibrous form of serpentine, a group of minerals created by alteration of peridotite, the main rock type in the deepest layers of oceanic crust, which is essentially identical in chemical composition with the molten rock of the earth's mantle. The dark, gray-green rock formed of serpentine minerals is called serpentinite, while talc forms white to green soapstone, both common rock types in Vermont ophiolites. A third common type, dunite, consists almost entirely of olivine.

Soils formed from ophiolite rocks are low in most important plant nutrients and may have high or even toxic concentrations of metals such as nickel, cobalt, and chromium, which weather out of the ultramafic rock. More extensive and ecologically older ophiolite areas than those in Vermont usually support a unique flora that can tolerate the infertile soil conditions. Vermont's serpentine flora does not, for the most part, include any unique species, but is comprised of an odd assemblage of ferns, grasses, sandworts, and other species, some of which are quite rare in the state.

COYOTE
(Canis latrans)
Easily adapting to the presence of man, the coyote often preys on rodents, small animals, and livestock. It is a member of the dog family and has been known to mate with domestic dogs.

On the lower slopes of Belvidere Mountain, near the asbestos mine, a botanist from the University of Vermont recently discovered a new species of maidenhair fern (*Adiantum viridimontanum*), which grows only in serpentine soils.

BELVIDERE LOOP

[Fig. 40(6)] The Long Trail passes over Belvidere Saddle, a short distance below the summit, but the mountain can be climbed as a loop via the Forester's, Long, and Frank Post trails. The drive to the trailhead from Eden Mills goes right by the asbestos mine with its barren piles of tailings. The Forester's Trail ascends through mixed hardwoods grading into spruce fir at higher elevations. The summit ledges are partly covered by stunted spruce-fir forest, but there is a fire tower with 360-degree views of the Green, White, and Adirondack mountains—and a bird's eye view of the mine tailings. As you hike, look for off-white layers in ledges and rock fragments in the trail, and check them for a soapy feel. These are deposits of talc, and the greasy feel comes from the soft, parallel layers of this platy mineral.

The Long Trail follows Belvidere's north ridge down to a saddle, where the Frank Post Trail comes in from the west. On July 15, 1997, a series of intense wee-hours thunderstorms drenched northeastern Vermont in several inches of rain, resulting in severe flooding that washed out roads and bridges throughout the region. The same rains also washed out a beaver dam above Tillotson Camp on the Frank Post Trail, resulting in a flash flood that scoured the bed of the small mountain brook along the trail to a width of 10 feet or more, washing away all soil and plant cover down to coarse rock and open ledge. The drained beaver pond is now becoming a beaver meadow populated by sedges and wildflowers, but the beaver may someday return and repair the dam.

Directions: From VT 100 in Eden Mills, take Asbestos Mine Road north 5.2 miles and turn left on Tillotson Road; the Frank Post Trail begins at the end of the road, and the Forester's Trail forks right off of it after 0.6 mile.

Trail: 7.7-mile loop.

Elevation: 1,700 to 3,360 feet.

Degree of difficulty: Moderate.

Surface and blaze: Rocky footpath, some muddy sections. Blue or white blazes.

HAZEN'S NOTCH

[Fig. 40(3)] The steep walls of Hazen's Notch, dominated by the south-facing cliffs of Sugarloaf Mountain, were carved by ice flowing across the spine of the Green Mountains. A 10-mile dirt road, VT 58, passes through the notch, and over its eastern half follows the route of the Bayley-Hazen Military Road, built in 1779. The Long Trail passes over the 1,780-foot height of land, and the Hazen's Notch Association maintains hiking and cross-country ski trails on and around Burnt Mountain, west of the notch. The state lands in the notch include a 200-acre natural area.

Directions: From Lowell on VT 100, take VT 58 west 5.5 miles, or from

Montgomery Center take VT 58 east 5.5 miles.

Activities: Hiking, snowshoeing, cross-country skiing.

Facilities: None.

Dates: Seasonal. VT 58 through the notch is not plowed.

Fees: None.

Closest town: Lowell, 5.5 miles.

For more information: Green Mountain Club, 4711 Waterbury–Stowe Road, Waterbury Center, VT 05677. Phone (802) 244-7037. Hazen's Notch Association, Route 242, Box 1010, Montgomery Center, VT 05471. Phone (802) 326-4789.

HAYSTACK MOUNTAIN

[Fig. 40(5)] Haystack Mountain forms the southern wall of Hazen's Notch, and the steep climb up the Long Trail rewards hikers with views from the summit knob. Although they are hard to reach, the north-facing dunite ledges near the summit support a well-developed serpentine community that includes arctic-alpine plants such as black crowberry (*Empetrum nigrum*) and more ubiquitous cliff and ledge species like harebell (*Campanula rotundifolia*). The ledges can be glimpsed from the summit viewpoint, where stunted black spruce (*Picea mariana*) grow along the brow of the cliff. The ledges support the only known U.S. population of marcescent sandwort (*Arenaria marcescens*), which grows more abundantly on serpentine ledges in Quebec and Newfoundland.

Directions: From Lowell on VT 100, take VT 58 west 5.5 miles, or from Montgomery Center take VT 58 east 5.5 miles to the height of land. Park along the road.

Trail: 2 miles one-way.

Elevation: 1,780 to 3,180 feet.

Degree of difficulty: Strenuous.

Surface and blaze: Rocky footpath. White blazes.

BURNT MOUNTAIN

[Fig. 40(4)] In spite of its small size, the two viewpoints on Burnt Mountain offer dramatic views of Hazen's Notch and Jay Peak and other northern summits. The Burnt Mountain Trail is part of a network of hiking and ski trails maintained by the nonprofit Hazen's Notch Association, which also runs educational programs for area schoolchildren. The old apple orchards at the start of the trail have recently been cleared out as part of an ambitious effort to restore a turn-of-the-century Vermont hill-country farm. On the summit ridge, the trail passes through a glade of heart-leaved paper birch (*Betula papyrifera* var. *cordifolia*), before descending to the southern viewpoint.

Directions: From Montgomery Center at the junction of VT 118 and VT 58, take VT 58 east 2.1 miles, turn right on Rossier Road, and follow it to the parking area at its end.

Trail: 2.2 miles one-way.

The Bayley-Hazen Military Road

In the summer of 1776, 110 men under the command of General Jacob Bayley, working for $10 a month, food, and a half-a-pint of rum a day, cut 14 miles of road through the virgin hardwood forests of the northern Green Mountain foothills in eastern Vermont. This first section of the Bayley-Hazen Military Road began at Wells River along the Connecticut River and aimed straight over hill and dale for Montreal. It was built to serve as a strategic Lake Champlain bypass for a possible invasion and annexation of Canada as a 14th colony. Work was not resumed until 1779, when the local militia under Colonel Moses Hazen pushed the road another 40 miles to the height of land in Hazen's Notch, where a small stone memorial marks its end. By that time British fortunes in the war had been reversed, leaving the last 60 miles of the road—and the invasion of Canada—unfinished. But the road soon took up its secondary role as an economic highway, only to be forgotten again in the age of coal and steam. Today, much of the road still serves as everything from farm and forest roads to sections of state highway, including the southeastern half of VT 58 through Hazen's Notch. The Catamount Trail, Vermont's end-to-end ski trail (*see* page 304), follows the old military road corridor over the Lowell Mountains between Albany and Lowell, then passes through Hazen's Notch on its way to the Canadian border.

Elevation: 1,500 to 2,626 feet.

Degree of difficulty: Moderate.

Surface and blaze: Old road, forest floor, and rock. Blue plastic diamond trail markers or blue blazes.

HAZEN'S NOTCH CROSS-COUNTRY SKI CENTER

[Fig. 40(2)] This small cross-country area has 30 miles (50 kilometers) of trails of which 19 miles (30 km) are groomed. The area is known for its deep, reliable snow-pack. The Catamount Trail (*see* page 304), Vermont's end-to-end ski trail, passes through Hazen's Notch and down to the Hazen's Notch Cross-Country Ski Center.

Directions: From Montgomery Center, go east on VT 58 approximately 2 miles to the center on the north, or left-hand side of the road.

Activities: Hiking, cross-country skiing, snowshoeing.

Facilities: Hiking and ski trails, bed-and-breakfast lodging, small shop, and information center.

Dates: Hiking trails open year-round.

Fees: There is a trail fee.

Closest town: Montgomery Center, 2 miles.

For more information: Hazen's Notch Cross-Country Ski Center, RR 1 Box 730, Montgomery Center, VT 05471. Phone (802) 326-4708.

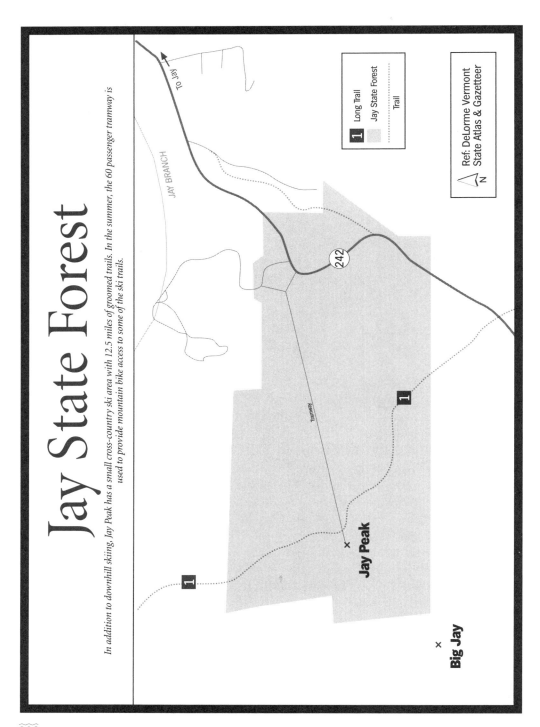

Jay State Forest

In addition to downhill skiing, Jay Peak has a small cross-country ski area with 12.5 miles of groomed trails. In the summer, the 60 passenger tramway is used to provide mountain bike access to some of the ski trails.

TO JAY

JAY BRANCH

242

Tramway

× **Jay Peak**

× **Big Jay**

	Long Trail
	Jay State Forest
⋯⋯	Trail

Ref: DeLorme Vermont
State Atlas & Gazetteer

N

Jay State Forest

[Fig. 41] Much of the 3,000-acre Jay State Forest is taken up by Jay Peak ski area, which has a 60-passenger skiing and sight-seeing tramway that extends right to the windswept summit of 3,861-foot Jay Peak, the highest Green Mountain peak north of Mount Mansfield. The Long Trail ascends Jay Peak from the south, then wanders north over its last 10 miles to Journey's End at the Canadian border. On a clear day, the 360-degree view from this isolated summit is spectacular. It takes in the White, Green, and Adirondack mountains and parts of Canada and Lake Memphremagog.

In addition to downhill skiing, Jay Peak has a small cross-country ski area with 12.5 miles of groomed trails. In summer the tramway is used to provide mountain bike access to some of the ski trails.

Directions: From Jay Village, go west 3.7 miles on VT 242 to Jay Peak Ski Area.

Activities: Sight-seeing on a tramway, hiking, mountain biking, cross-country and downhill skiing.

Facilities: Restrooms at base and summit.

Dates: Open late June through Labor Day, weekends through mid-Oct.; open for the winter ski season.

Fees: There is a fee for the tramway and ski trail use.

Closest town: Jay, 3.7 miles.

For more information: Vermont Department of Forests, Parks, and Recreation, 324 North Main Street, Barre, VT 05461-4109. Phone (802) 476-0170. Jay Peak, Route 242, Jay, VT 05859. Phone (802) 988-2611.

⬛ THE LONG TRAIL TO JAY PEAK

[Fig. 41(1)] Beginning in mixed forests in Jay Notch, this moderate hike ends with a scramble up the exposed, windswept south ridge of Jay Peak. While construction of the tramway and ski trails inflicted major disturbance on the summit area, there are scattered pockets of spruce and fir krummholz. In mid to late summer, scattered clumps of lowbush blueberry on the ledges provide a welcome distraction.

Directions: From Jay, go west on VT 242 approximately 5.1 miles to the trailhead. Parking is at the height of land just south of the trailhead.

Trail: 1.7 miles one-way.

Elevation: 2,180 to 3,861 feet.

Degree of difficulty: Moderate.

Surface and blaze: Rocky footpath and ledge. White blazes.

Piedmont & N.E. Kingdom

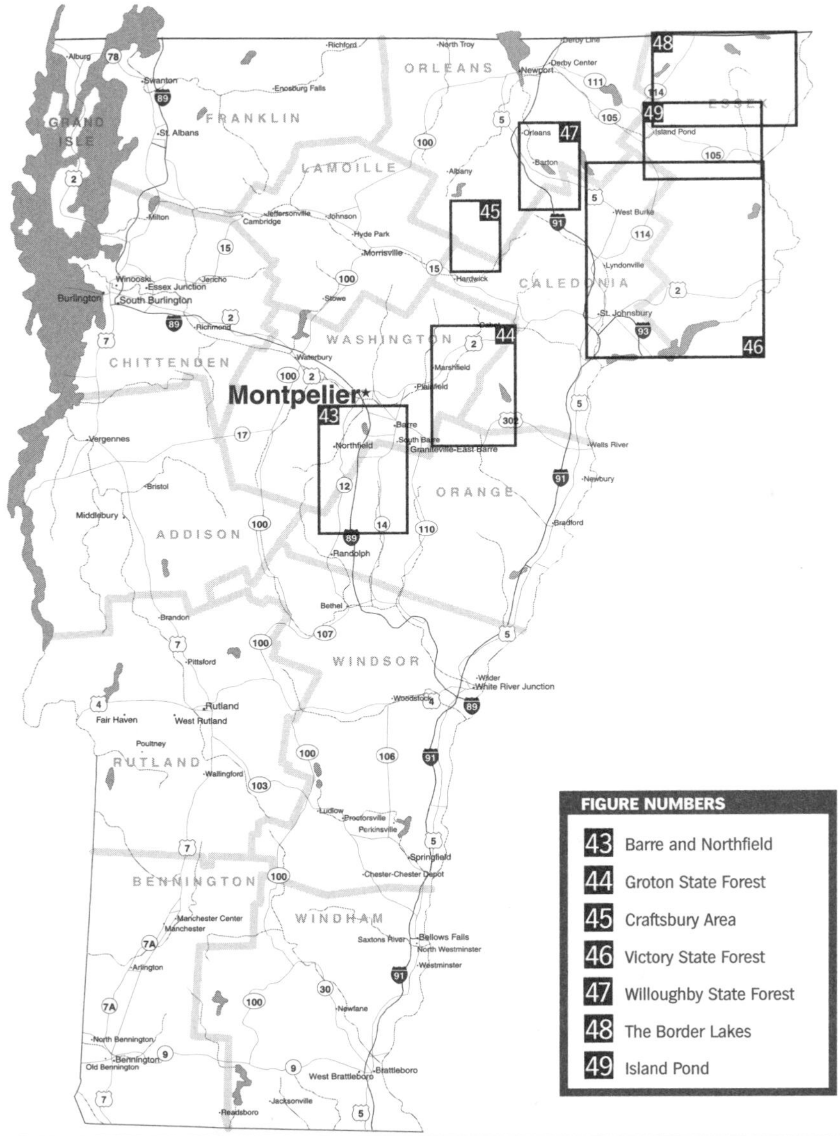

FIGURE NUMBERS

43 Barre and Northfield
44 Groton State Forest
45 Craftsbury Area
46 Victory State Forest
47 Willoughby State Forest
48 The Border Lakes
49 Island Pond

Northern Piedmont and Northeast Kingdom

E ast of the Green Mountains, Vermont's landscape falls away to rolling piedmont hills, incised by streams flowing west to Lake Champlain via the Winooski, Lamoille, and Missisquoi rivers or southeastward into the Connecticut River.

North of Ascutney, the bedrock of eastern Vermont is a broad mass of schists and
phyllites superficially similar to those of the Green Mountains, but in this case
derived primarily from sediments of volcanic origin that settled on the ocean floor
between the mainland and a line of volcanic islands. In the Taconic orogeny, these
islands collided with the continent, and their remains are now compressed into a
band of metamorphic rocks that are found mainly in western New Hampshire, but
with some sections in Vermont along the Connecticut River.

The metamorphic rocks are punctuated by large plutons of granitic rock of varied

[*Above:* A view of Groton Pond from Owl's Head in Groton State Forest]

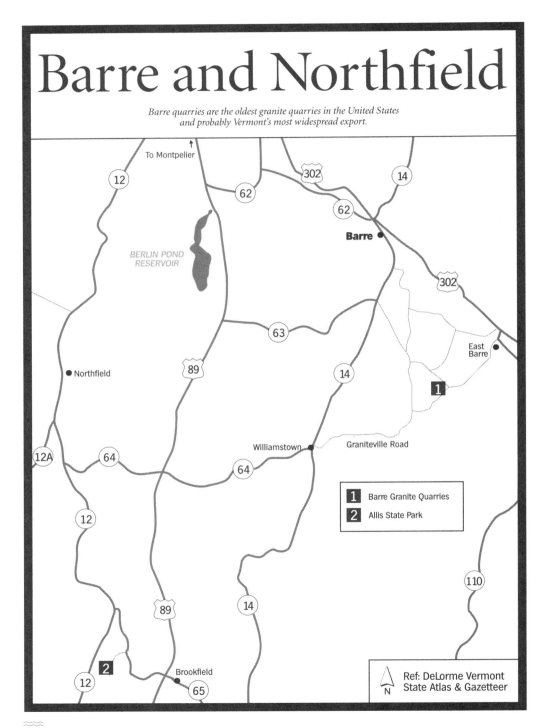

Barre and Northfield

*Barre quarries are the oldest granite quarries in the United States
and probably Vermont's most widespread export.*

To Montpelier

12

62

302

14

62

Barre

BERLIN POND
RESERVOIR

302

63

89

• Northfield

14

East
Barre

1

12A

64

64

Williamstown

Graniteville Road

12

| 1 | Barre Granite Quarries |
| 2 | Allis State Park |

110

89

14

2

12

Brookfield

65

N Ref: DeLorme Vermont
State Atlas & Gazetteer

mineral composition. Where the composition and grain size of the granite make it more resistant than the surrounding rock, it tends to stand high, as in the relatively big hills in and around Groton State Forest. But granitic rock with a higher proportion of soft minerals and bigger grains tends to erode more easily, and can form lowlands such as the swampy Nulhegan Basin east of Island Pond.

In the piedmont south of Saint Johnsbury, second-growth hardwood forest has reclaimed much of the landscape, whether it was cleared for farming or stumped off for timber. Spruce-fir forest is found only on the higher hilltops. Farms still occupy the fertile river bottoms or cling stubbornly to expanses of hillside. The steepest and rockiest slopes escaped the plow but were not spared the ax.

In the days before interstate highways, the region north and northeast of Saint Johnsbury was dubbed the Northeast Kingdom by Governor George Aiken, in recognition of its profound isolation; one town in the region did not have electricity until 1963. Here the conifers creep down off the hilltops and begin to occupy the slopes and the poorer valley soils, and were probably more dominant before logging. Among these is white spruce (*Picea glauca*), which is found from here north and westwards across Canada and into Alaska, but is generally absent from the rest of Vermont. In the highlands of the far northeastern corner of the region, spruce-fir is the dominant forest type, a southern finger of the vast boreal forest of Canada.

With the boreal forest comes a distinctive suite of animals that are adapted to its rigors and rewards. Red squirrel (*Tamiasciurus hudsonicus*), snowshoe hare (*Lepus americana*), porcupine (*Erethizon dorsatum*), fisher (*Martes pennanti*), and bobcat (*Lynx rufus*) are common mammals. The bird list includes uncommon or rare species such as the black-backed woodpecker (*Picoides arcticus*), gray jay (*Perisoreus canadensis*), boreal chickadee (*Parus hudsonicus*), rusty blackbird (*Euphagus carolinus*), and the state-endangered spruce grouse (*Dendragapus canadensis*). The Northeast Kingdom was the last stronghold in the state for extirpated species such as the pine marten (*Martes americana*, recently reintroduced), timber wolf (*Canis lupus*), lynx (*Lynx canadensis*), and catamount (the local name for mountain lion, *Felis concolor*). It was also the first beachhead for the re-establishment of such prodigal species as beaver (*Castor canadensis*), loon (*Gavia immer*), and moose (*Alces alces*), which may yet be rejoined by the missing predators.

Barre and Northfield

▒ BARRE GRANITE QUARRIES

[Fig. 43(1)] Though maple syrup is surely Vermont's most famous export, Barre's fine-grained granite, used across the nation for tombstones, is probably its most widespread. Vermonters first began carving into Barre Granite just after the War of

1812, making the Barre quarries the oldest granite quarries in the United States. One quarry, the Rock of Ages pit, is also the largest such quarry in the world, covering 50 acres and dipping about 475 feet into the ground. Barre Granite has been carved into memorial monuments of all kinds, including a full-sized replica of a Mercedes-Benz sedan and a giant version of the rock group the Rolling Stones' trademark lips and tongue—the latter for a cemetery in Massachusetts.

The rock from which all this is derived is part of the 350-million-year-old New Hampshire series, which formed during the final stages of the closing of Iapetus. When this progenitor of the Atlantic slammed shut, welding a piece of the European plate to what we now know as Vermont, the collision was accompanied by melting of rocks to form huge pools of magma deep in the crust. These plutons, as geologists call them, cooled slowly and uniformly. The crystals that formed in the Barre Granite as the molten rock cooled are correspondingly large, as is the pluton itself. Geologists believe the deposit from which Barre Granite is quarried is 4 miles long, 10 miles wide, and 10 miles deep. At the present rate of excavation of about 3 million cubic feet each year, the deposit should last an estimated 1,000 years.

But what makes this salt-and-pepper rock so valuable is its uniquely uniform nature: It's virtually impossible to tell the difference between rocks taken from different parts of the quarry. That, combined with the rock's ability to take a high polish, is what has made Barre Granite so desirable as monument stone. Some of the best examples of this stone can be seen right in Barre's own Hope Cemetery, where the stone wrought by generations of stone cutters marks the graves of family and friends.

A trip to the Barre Granite quarries also offers a chance to see the largest derricks in the world, capable of lifting 250-ton blocks of granite from the very bottom of the quarry. To do this, the derricks are 250 feet tall with guy wires anchored 1 mile or more away.

Directions: From Exit 7 on I-89, follow the exit ramp directly onto VT 62 and head east to Barre, about 5 miles. Turn right onto US 302/VT 14, and go 0.5 mile to where VT 14 goes right. Look for Quarry Hill Road in about 1 mile and turn left. Go 2.5 miles to Graniteville Road and turn left, follow the signs for the quarry and the visitor center. For Hope Cemetery, from the junction of VT 62 and US 302/VT 14 in Barre, go north on VT 14, which is Maple Avenue, for approximately 3 miles. Look for signs for the cemetery on the left.

Activities: Self-guided and guided tours, photography.

Facilities: Visitor center, restrooms, gift shop, snack bar.

Dates: Open May through Oct.

Fees: There is a fee for the quarry tour.

Closest town: Barre, 5 miles.

For more information: Rock of Ages, PO Box 482, Barre, VT 05641. Phone (802) 476-3119.

ALLIS STATE PARK

[Fig. 43(2)] The Allis family first came to Vermont in the late 1700s and cleared the land around Bear Mountain for farming. In 1910, an Allis descendant named Wallace bought the land to farm and use as a summer home. In 1931, Allis gave his Bear Mountain Farm to the state for use as a state park for "quiet contemplative recreation."

Coming into state hands as it did during the height of the depression, the park was an ideal project for the Civilian Conservation Corps, or the CCC. The CCC provided employment for young men aged 17 to 25 building fire roads, picnic areas, campgrounds, ski trails, and nature trails; in Allis State Park, the CCC built a fire tower, the picnic area, and the campground.

The fire tower offers spectacular views of the central Green Mountains, including Mount Mansfield, Camel's Hump, the Lincoln range, Killington, and the White Mountains to the east. A small limestone outcrop along the nature trail is punctuated by a small solution

PILEATED WOODPECKER (Dryocopus pileatus)

cave, formed by slightly acidic groundwater dissolving the limestone, thought to once have been a bear's den. Even without the outcrop as a clue, observant hikers can tell the area is underlain by nutrient-rich soil. The most obvious evidence is a few butternut trees (*Juglans cinerea*) and a patch of maidenhair fern (*Adiantum pedatum*), both easily seen from the nature trail.

Directions: From Brookfield Village, go west on VT 65 through town and under the Interstate. Continuing on VT 65, go approximately 2 miles to the park entrance on the left, or west side of the road.

Activities: Camping, picnicking, hiking.

Facilities: 18 tent sites, 8 lean-tos, restroom, showers, playground, picnic area, nature trail.

Dates: Open Mid-May to Sept.

Fees: There is a fee for day-use and camping.

Closest town: Brookfield, 2 miles.

For more information: Vermont Department of Forests, Parks and Recreation, RR 1, Box 33, North Springfield, VT 05150. Phone (802) 886-2215 (winter), (802) 885-8855 (summer).

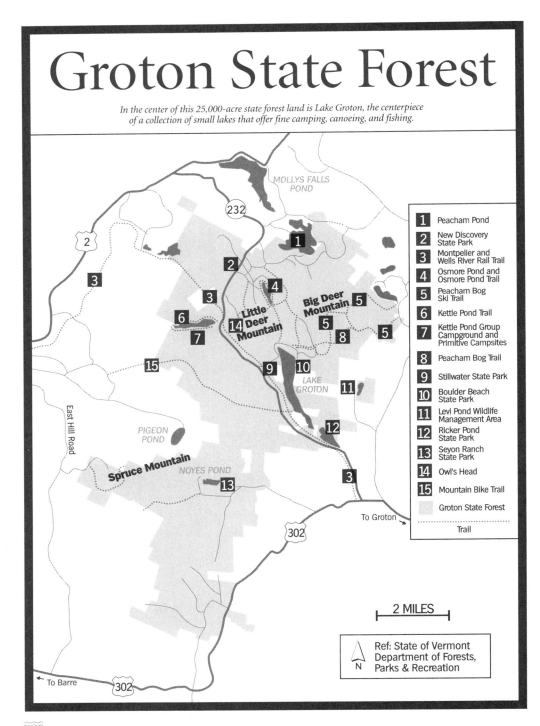

Groton State Forest

In the center of this 25,000-acre state forest land is Lake Groton, the centerpiece of a collection of small lakes that offer fine camping, canoeing, and fishing.

MOLLYS FALLS POND

232

2

3

3

1

2

4

Little Deer Mountain

14

Big Deer Mountain

5

6

7

15

9

10

LAKE GROTON

5

5

8

11

East Hill Road

PIGEON POND

12

Spruce Mountain

NOYES POND

13

3

To Groton

302

To Barre

302

1	Peacham Pond
2	New Discovery State Park
3	Montpelier and Wells River Rail Trail
4	Osmore Pond and Osmore Pond Trail
5	Peacham Bog Ski Trail
6	Kettle Pond Trail
7	Kettle Pond Group Campground and Primitive Campsites
8	Peacham Bog Trail
9	Stillwater State Park
10	Boulder Beach State Park
11	Levi Pond Wildlife Management Area
12	Ricker Pond State Park
13	Seyon Ranch State Park
14	Owl's Head
15	Mountain Bike Trail
	Groton State Forest
	Trail

2 MILES

Ref: State of Vermont Department of Forests, Parks & Recreation

N

Groton State Forest

[Fig. 44] Groton State Forest occupies a 25,000-acre patch of rumpled high ground in the low rolling foothills east of the Green Mountains. It is high ground because it is underlain almost entirely by an enormous lump of hard granite: the Knox Mountain pluton of the New Hampshire plutonic series. It was formed during the Acadian orogeny, about 350 million years ago, by melting of pre-existing rocks to form a bubble of magma deep in the Earth's crust. A small arm of this pluton is the source of the famous Barre Granite.

Although it doesn't stand as high as the Green Mountains, this tough body of rock forms summits up to 3,300 feet high in the southern section of the forest, and these lack the long, stretched-out ridge structure of the Green Mountains. Two-mile-long Lake Groton is the centerpiece of a collection of small lakes that offer fine camping, canoeing, and fishing. North of the lake is a range of rock knobs with steep, ice-plucked south faces and dark, evergreen crowns of spruce-fir forest that are linked to the forest's campgrounds by a network of trails. The surrounding northern hardwood forests have plenty of healthy red spruce mixed in.

The first English settlers with their axes and plows found their way into the Groton area right after the Revolution. These rocky hills did not lend themselves even to hard-scrabble hill farms, so the economy from the beginning was largely based on wood. It began with a trickle of potash, charcoal, and what little lumber could find its way down the hard road to the Connecticut River. But by 1873, the Montpelier and Wells River Railroad slashed diagonally across Groton and the present state forest lands, providing an outlet for a tidal wave of timber and an inlet for the region's first flatlanders—summer tourists up from Boston and New York to swat blackflies with the locals.

At the turn of the century, logging camps and sawmills were scattered over the granite hills, some now the site of the forest's five state parks. Fueled in part by logging slash, and sparked by cinders from the wood-burning engines on the railway, severe fires in 1876, 1883, and 1908 burned over thousands of acres of uncut forest, much of it dominated by spruce, fir, and pine. The 1883 fire consumed most of a logging settlement, and the residents spent the night on logs in the lake to escape the flames. Birch, beech, and maple were quick to take advantage of the openings, and they dominate most of the area today, producing forest products at a considerably more conservative pace than at the turn of the century. The railway line, abandoned in 1956, is now a 15-mile backwoods rails-to-trails mountain bike path and snowmobile/ski trail.

A history guide, available at area state parks, offers more detail on the rich history of the area.

▓ SEYON RANCH STATE PARK

[Fig. 44(13)] Noyes Pond in Seyon Ranch State Park is a 39-acre lake in the bottom of a broad valley on the west side of the state forest, well away from the busy

AMERICAN BEECH
(Fagus grandifolia)
This beech is identified by thin gray bark and papery leaves that may stay on all winter to twist and rustle in the wind.

larger lakes and ponds. The fishing regulations are for purists: fly-fishing only, with barbless hooks, from boats only, and the boats must be rented from the park. Even privately owned canoes are not allowed on the pond. This kind of privacy not only makes for good fly-fishing, but also it ups the odds of seeing moose (*Alces alces*) and other wildlife in the area around the pond.

The ranch is a rustic 15-bed lodge with private and semiprivate rooms, serving three meals a day. Small groups may reserve up to three nights with advance payments, while individuals are accepted no sooner than two weeks before arrival on a space-available basis.

Directions: From Groton, go 3 miles west on US 302, then turn right on Seyon Pond Road.

Activities: Fly-fishing, canoeing, hiking, wildlife-watching.

Facilities: Lodge with dining room, boat rentals.

Dates: Open mid-Apr. to late-Oct.

Fees: There are fees for lodging.

Closest town: Groton, 6 miles.

For more information: Seyon Ranch State Park, Groton, VT 05046. Phone (802) 584-3829 (summer). Vermont Department of Forests, Parks, and Recreation, 324 North Main Street, Barre, VT 05461-4109. Phone (802) 476-0170 (winter).

RICKER POND STATE PARK

[Fig. 44(12)] Ricker Pond State Park is just south of Lake Groton. The small pond was the site of Captain Edmund Morse's sawmill and gristmill, the first mill in the area, built in 1790. A small beaver pond and wetland divide the campground and are good places to watch beaver at work and swat mosquitoes after an evening meal. The Montpelier and Wells River Rail Trail passes nearby, making this a good jumping-off point for a bike ride.

Directions: On US 302 about 1.5 miles west of Groton, turn left on VT 232. The campground turnoff is on the right, about 2.5 miles from the junction.

Facilities: Campground with tent sites and lean-tos, swimming beach, sanitary station, boat ramp.

Dates: Open mid-May to Labor Day.

Fees: There is a fee for camping.

Closest town: Groton, 4 miles.

For more information: Ricker Pond State Park, Groton, VT 05046. Phone (802) 584-3821 (summer). Vermont Department of Forests, Parks, and Recreation, 324 North Main Street, Barre, VT 05461-4109. Phone (802) 476-0170 (winter).

STILLWATER AND BOULDER BEACH STATE PARKS

Stillwater State Park [Fig. 44(9)], near the north end of Lake Groton, is the area's largest campground. The lake is shared by private summer residences along some sections of the shoreline. Big Deer Campground, in the woods north of the lake, takes the overflow from Stillwater as needed. The campground areas are not usually open for day use, but Boulder Beach State Park [Fig. 44(10)], just down the road, is a day-use area with a broad beach and other amenities. Living up to its name, the sandy beach has scattered boulders half buried in the sand that are fun for kids.

The nearby Groton Nature Center has a 0.6-mile nature trail and interpretive programs during the summer months. The center has displays on local geology, flora and fauna, and a unique floor made of samples of Vermont limestone, granite, and other rock types. The center is the starting point for the trail to Peacham Bog and one of the approaches to Big Deer Mountain.

Directions: On US 302 about 1.5 miles west of Groton, turn left on VT 232. Turn right about 5 miles from the junction.

Facilities: Campground with tent sites and lean-tos, swimming beach, sanitary station, boat ramp and dock, playground, interpretive center. At Boulder Beach: picnic area, picnic shelter, swimming beach, canoe put-in, snack bar, restrooms.

Dates: Open mid May to mid-Oct.; Boulder Beach closes but remains accessible after Labor Day.

Fees: There is a fee for camping.

Closest town: Groton, 6 miles.

For more information: Stillwater State Park, Groton, VT 05046. Phone (802) 584-3822 (summer), (802) 476-0170 (winter). Boulder Beach State Park, RR 2 Box 232, Groton, VT 05046. Phone (802) 584-3823 (summer). Vermont Department of Forests, Parks, and Recreation, 324 North Main Street, Barre, VT 05461-4109. Phone (802) 476-0170 (winter).

PEACHAM BOG TRAIL

[Fig. 44(8)] Perched on a broad, bouldery outwash flat above Coldwater Brook, 200-acre Peacham Bog's center is slightly raised above its margins. While raised or domed bogs are more common in Maine and the Adirondacks, this is one of only a few examples in Vermont.

Bogs are formed by the deep accumulation of undecomposed peat, mainly mats of sphagnum mosses. Where the climate is moist enough to keep the peat wet and cold enough to keep decomposition rates to a minimum, peat can accumulate above the soil water table. In raised bogs, rainfall provides the only water entering the peat, and the bog is termed ombrotrophic, or rain-fed. Rain bears little in the way of dissolved nutrients, resulting in extremely poor nutrient status.

Ombrotrophic bogs, including Peacham Bog, have a characteristic suite of plants that, while low in diversity, is uniquely adapted to the acid and nutrient-poor soil conditions. Large areas are dominated by low shrubs such as leatherleaf (*Chamaedaphne calyculata*), Labrador tea (*Ledum groenlandicum*), and rhodora (*Rhododendron canadense*), a deciduous azalea with showy pink flowers in early summer. Various kinds of sedges, including cottongrasses (*Eriophorum* spp.) with their conspicuous cottony white or rust-colored seed heads, may form mats or tussocks. Stunted black spruce (*Picea mariana*), often with a lollipop growth form, forms small groves in the center, and taller black spruce and tamarack (*Larix laricina*) trees grow around the margins. The insectivorous northern pitcher plant (*Sarracenia purpurea*) and sundew (*Drosera rotundifolia*) obtain some nutrients, notably nitrogen, by capturing and digesting small insects.

After cutting through a recently logged area, the trail makes a bouldery march through hardwood forests, then passes through a wet spruce-fir forest with a nice diversity of boreal ground cover, including bunchberry (*Cornus canadensis*), goldthread (*Coptis trifolia*), twinflower (*Linnaea borealis*), dewberry (*Dalibarda repens*), and creeping snowberry (*Gaultheria hispidula*). A boardwalk makes a loop through the bog, sampling the spruce and tamarack communities near the edge and the more open ground near the center.

Directions: The trail begins at the eastern end of the Groton Nature Center parking lot, between Stillwater and Boulder Beach State Parks.

Trail: 2.5 miles one-way.

Elevation: Around 1,500 feet.

Degree of difficulty: Moderate.

Surface and blaze: Old road and squishy peat. Blue blazes.

PEACHAM BOG SKI TRAIL

[Fig. 44(5)] When snow comes to Groton, the railroad bed and unplowed jeep roads make for good beginner to intermediate cross-country skiing, but they see a fair bit of snowmobile traffic on weekends. Many of the hiking trails are quite rocky and are worth skiing only in deep snow. But the Vermont Department of Forests, Parks, and Recreation is developing new cross-country ski trails in the area around Peacham Bog. The main trail runs from the nature center, where there is winter parking, across Peacham Bog to Martin's Pond at the eastern edge of the forest. It takes a solid foot or more of snow to get across the bog without hitting wet spots that can instantly ice up a pair of skis, but bogs like Peacham have an especially high lonesome feel in winter.

Trail: Nature Center to Martins Pond, about 5 miles one-way. Alternate route from Peacham Bog to Green Bay Road in Peacham, about 2.5 miles one-way.

Elevation: 1,100 to 1,700 feet.

Degree of difficulty: Moderate.

Surface and blaze: Blazed with blue plastic diamonds.

KETTLE POND GROUP CAMPGROUND AND PRIMITIVE CAMPSITES

[Fig. 44(7)] Kettle Pond is a campground designated specifically for large group use, but there are also several remote campsites, some with lean-tos, dispersed along the shores of the pond and accessible by canoe or trail.

When the group camping area isn't too busy, the small pond makes for good quiet water canoeing, and the trail that wends among the boulders around the pond makes a nice short day hike. The pond is one of three in the Groton area that supports breeding common loons (*Gavia immer*). Portions of the pond and the trail may be closed during the breeding season. Highbush blueberries (*Vaccinium corymbosum*) and huckleberries (*Gaylussacia baccata*) along some sections of the shoreline ripen in late July. While picking, look for scattered rhododendrons (*Rhododendron maximum*), which are just barely hanging on in the shade of the surrounding trees.

The group campground has 27 lean-tos in five separate clusters. These may be used by multifamily groups as well as organizations. The remote campsites are open to individuals by reservation through Stillwater State Park.

Directions: On US 302 about 1.5 miles west of Groton, turn on VT 232, heading north. Turn left about 6.5 miles from the junction. When the group camping area is closed, you can park on VT 232 just north of the entrance and walk or canoe-carry in about 0.3 mile.

Facilities: Group campground, pit toilets, and remote campsites.

Dates: Open mid-May to Oct.

Fees: There is a fee for camping, payable at Stillwater State Park.

Closest town: Groton, 7.5 miles.

For more information: Kettle Pond Group Campground, Marshfield, VT 05658. Phone (802) 584-3820 (summer). Vermont Department of Forests, Parks, and Recreation, 324 North Main Street, Barre, VT 05461-4109. Phone (802) 476-0170 (winter).

KETTLE POND TRAIL

[Fig. 44(6)] This trail stays close to the shore of Kettle Pond and passes over and among big boulders along the south shore. It gives access to some of the lean-to campsites and blueberry picking spots around the pond.

Directions: The trail begins at a parking area on VT 232 just north of the turnoff to the Kettle Pond Group Campground.

Trail: 3-mile loop.

Elevation: Around 1,450 feet.

Degree of difficulty: Easy.

Surface and blaze: Rocky footpath, some wet spots. Blue blazes.

NEW DISCOVERY STATE PARK AND OSMORE POND

[Fig. 44(2), Fig. 44(4)] This woodland campground may be a little quieter than the lakeshore campgrounds during the busy midsummer period. About 0.5 mile down the road there is a picnic area on the northwestern shore of Osmore Pond.

Like Kettle Pond, Osmore is a small mountain pond not far from busy Lake Groton as the crow flies, but a world away in character. There is a picnic area with a shelter on the northwestern shore, but the rocky shoreline is otherwise undeveloped and surrounded by maturing mixed hardwood and conifer forest.

By late summer the shrubs around the shore bear fruit, including blueberries (*Vaccinium* spp.) and raspberries (*Rubus* spp.), as well as viburnums and other species favored more by birds than humans. Although loons (*Gavia immer*) have not nested here in recent years, they often fly in from other ponds in the area.

There are three lean-tos on the eastern shore, accessible either by canoe or the trail that circles the lake. There is another lean-to on the Big Deer Mountain Trail east of the pond.

Directions: On US 302 about 2 miles west of Groton, turn on VT 232, heading north. Turn right about 8 miles from the junction. Continue past the campground to get to the Osmore Pond picnic area and canoe put-in.

Facilities: Campground with tent sites and lean-tos, play area, picnic area, remote campsites.

Dates: Open mid-May through Labor Day.

Fees: There is a fee for day use and for camping at the developed campground and remote sites.

Closest town: Groton, 9 miles.

For more information: New Discovery State Park, Marshfield, VT 05658. Phone (802) 584-3820 (summer). Vermont Department of Forests, Parks, and Recreation, 324 North Main Street, Barre, VT 05461-4109. Phone (802) 476-0170 (winter).

OSMORE POND TRAIL

[Fig. 44(4)] This trail circles the pond with access to lean-tos and campsites around the pond, and provides a jumping-off point for a day hike up Big Deer and Little Deer mountains.

Directions: The trail begins at the Osmore Pond picnic shelter.

Trail: 2-mile loop.

Elevation: Around 1,460 feet.

Degree of difficulty: Easy.

Surface and blaze: Rocky footpath, some wet spots. Blue blazes.

PEACHAM POND

[Fig. 44(1)] Not far from New Discovery State Park, Peacham Pond is a fine pond for canoeing. There is scattered, modest development on the east and west shores, but the south shore is Groton State Forest land and the northern bay is bordered by marshes that are frequented by a variety of birds and other wildlife. The shallow water flora includes quillwort (*Isoetes echinospora*), water horsetail (*Equisteum fluviatile*), burreed (*Sparganium angustifolium*), pondweeds (*Potamogeton* spp.), and fragrant and yellow water lilies (*Nymphaea odorata* and *Nuphar variegatum*).

The pond is an important breeding and feeding area for loons (*Gavia immer*). Two pairs of loons nest on the more secluded stretches of shoreline, and up to 14 nonbreeding loons have been observed on the pond in late summer.

Directions: From the junction of VT 232 and VT 2 in Marshfield, take VT 232 south about 3 miles and turn left on a dirt road; this turnoff is about 1 mile north of the entrance to New Discovery State Park on VT 232. Bear right at a fork with a stone marker for Peacham Pond, and continue about 0.6 mile to the public access.

Activities: Canoeing, fishing, bird- and wildlife-watching.

Facilities: Boat ramp.

Dates: Open year-round.

Fees: None.

Closest town: Marshfield, 5 miles.

For more information: Vermont Department of Fish and Wildlife, 324 North Main Street, Barre, VT 05641. Phone (802) 479-3241.

PIPSSISEWA
(Chimaphila umbellata)
The Cree Indians named this plant "pipsisikwev," meaning "it breaks into small pieces" because of their belief in its ability to break down kidney stones and gallstones.

GROTON SUMMITS

Groton State Forest has miles of hiking trails that link the campgrounds, ponds, and summits. While the summits are modest in size, they offer up views that range from intimate glimpses of local hills and ponds to grand views of the Green and White mountains. A map of the trail system is available at the state park entrance stations.

OWLS HEAD

[Fig. 44(14)] The CCC-built stone shelter on the ice-scoured granite summit of

Owl's Head is the state forest's emblem. The summit rock is crisscrossed with dikes of coarsely crystalline pegmatite dikes or fine-grained aplite. These are formed when fresh magma flows into cracks that form as the granite cools and contracts.

The thin, acid soils at the summit favor red spruce (*Picea rubens*), balsam fir (*Abies balsamea*), and lowbush blueberry (*Vaccinium myrtilloides*).

You have to wander around the open rock areas of the summit to take in all the views. They extend as far as the Presidential and Franconia ranges in New Hampshire, but the real charmers are the scenes of Camel's Hump and other Green Mountain summits framed by local hills and ponds.

A steep dirt road ends at a picnic pavilion within just 0.1 mile of the summit, which is reached by a short trail with old stone steps built by CCC crews in the 1930s. There is also a more leisurely ascent via a 1.5-mile trail from New Discovery State Park.

Directions: On US 302 about 2 miles west of Groton, turn on VT 232, heading north. Turn right about 7.3 miles from the junction to reach the picnic pavilion. Turn right about 8 miles from the junction to reach New Discovery State Park.

Trail: 0.1 mile one-way from picnic area, 1.5 miles one-way from New Discovery State Park.

Elevation: 1,746 to 1,958 feet.

Degree of difficulty: Easy to moderate.

Surface and blaze: Rocky footpath, stone steps, and ledge. Blue blazes.

BIG DEER AND LITTLE DEER MOUNTAINS

[Fig. 44] Big Deer and Little Deer mountains embrace the southern end of Osmore Pond and can be approached from either New Discovery State Park (see page xx) to the north or Stillwater State Park (see page xx) to the south. The mostly wooded summit of Big Deer has nice views of Peacham Pond and Peacham Bog, while Little Deer looks down the length of Groton Pond.

Trail: From New Discovery State Park and Stillwater State Park one-way and loop hikes of 1.5 to 5 miles.

Elevation: Around 1,000 to 1,992 feet.

Degree of difficulty: Easy to moderate.

Surface and blaze: Old road and rocky footpath. Blue paint blazes or orange diamonds.

SPRUCE MOUNTAIN

[Fig. 44] Spruce Mountain is on the western border of Groton State Forest and is approached from the town of Plainfield in the upper Winooski River valley. An abandoned fire tower in a clearing at the summit puts your head above the spruce and fir for some of the broadest views in the region, including the state forest lands and White Mountains to the east and river-bottom farm lands and Green Mountains to the west.

Directions: From center of Plainfield, about 0.5 mile east of the junction of US 2 and VT 214, turn south on Brook Road. About 4 miles from the turnoff, turn left on

East Hill Road, and after another 0.7 mile turn right on Spruce Mountain Road. Turn left at the next junction and park below the gate, about 0.7 mile up. The trail starts at the gate.

Trail: 2.2 miles one-way.
Elevation: 1,700 to 3,037 feet.
Degree of difficulty: Moderate.
Surface and blaze: Old road and rocky footpath. Unblazed.

MONTPELIER AND WELLS RIVER RAIL TRAIL

[Fig. 44(3)] The nineteenth-century Montpelier and Wells River Railroad that traded tourists for timber was closed in 1956, barely 80 years after its opening. It is now the backbone of a great backwoods mountain bike loop that circles the hills on the eastern side of Groton State Forest, passing through deep woods and along the shore of Marshfield Pond. The return leg involves more strenuous riding on jeep roads, but the old railroad grade is easy riding. In Plainfield and outside of the state forest, the trail passes near Lord's Hill, an undeveloped state natural area with a stand of old-growth northern hardwood–hemlock forest. The trail is also used by hikers, skiers, and snowmobilers.

Directions: The southern end of the rail trail is at Ricker Pond State Park (*see* page 260), with additional access points near Stillwater Campground (*see* page 261), Kettle Pond (*see* page 263), and Marshfield Pond. The return leg of the full loop follows an old jeep road over Hardwood Mountain, shown on the state forest trail map.

Trail: 23.5-mile loop, 8 miles one-way to Marshfield Pond, or shorter one-way sections.
Elevation: 1,000 to 1,800 feet.
Degree of difficulty: Easy to strenuous, depending on route.
Surface and blaze: Old railroad bed and jeep road, unblazed.

LEVI POND WILDLIFE MANAGEMENT AREA

[Fig. 44(11)] Just outside Groton State Forest, Levi Pond is a standout among the numerous small ponds in the region because of an ecological curiosity. The largest and healthiest colony of great laurel (*Rhododendron maximum*) in the state grows along the eastern shore, forming a broad band between shrub communities along the waterfront and the forest farther inland. This is at or near the northernmost extent of the natural range of the species, and it is otherwise rare enough in Vermont that it is listed as a state threatened species.

The pond is not more than 20 feet deep, with floating aquatic plants such as yellow water lily (*Nuphar variegatum*), pondweeds (*Potamogeton* spp.), and bladderworts (*Utricularia* spp.) along its shallow margins. Some parts of the shoreline support bog mats, with leatherleaf (*Chamaedaphne calyculata*), sheep laurel (*Kalmia*

Craftsbury Area

Located near the Canadian border, Craftsbury Outdoor Center can always be counted on to have snow.
During the summer, mountain biking, camps and educational programs are offered.

DANIELS POND

1 LITTLE HOSMER POND

Mud Island Road

Shadow Lake Road

• Craftsbury Common

Wylie Hill Road

Rocking Rock Road

Shadow Lake Rd

• Craftsbury

(14)

Gebbie Road

LONG POND

East Craftsbury Road

2

LAKE ELLIGO

3

Baker Hill Road

CASPIAN LAKE

• Greensboro

The Bend Road

(16)

1 Craftsbury Outdoor Center
2 Barr Hill Natural Area
3 Highland Lodge

⌂ Ref: DeLorme Vermont
N State Atlas & Gazetteer

angustifolia), huckleberry (*Gaylussacia dumosa*), and some northern pitcher plants (*Sarracenia purpurea*).

To avoid disturbance, there are no trails through the great laurel colony, so it is best visited by canoe.

Directions: From Groton, go west on VT 302 about 1.3 miles and turn right on Goodfellow Road. At about 1.5 miles from VT 302, where another road comes in from the right, turn left on the road to the pond.

Activities: Canoeing, wildlife-watching.

Facilities: None.

Dates: The entrance road is not plowed in winter.

Fees: None.

Closest town: Groton, 4 miles.

For more information: Vermont Department of Fish and Wildlife, 324 North Main Street, Barre, VT 05641. Phone (802) 479-3241.

Craftsbury

▨ CRAFTSBURY OUTDOOR CENTER

[Fig. 45(1)] Vermont cross-country skiers have a secret, and it's Craftsbury Outdoor Center. With its location not far from the Canadian Border, Craftsbury can always be counted on to have snow, and lots of it.

The center is located on the fringe of historic Craftsbury Common, one of the most picturesque villages in northern Vermont. More than 100 kilometers of ski trails offer skiers access to every delight Vermont has to offer, from classic rolling hills and dairy farms to the wild thickets along the Black River.

The center is open year-round. Summer offerings include a mountain bike center and week-long adult camps on everything from rowing to running to Elderhostel educational programs.

Directions: From Hardwick, at the junction of VT 15 and VT 14, go north on VT 14 approximately 7 miles to a right-hand turn on Cemetery Road to Craftsbury. Turn left at the T-junction onto Wylie Hill Road, and drive through Craftsbury to Craftsbury Common. Pass through the village on the east side of the village common and follow signs to the Outdoor Center, approximately 1.5 miles from the common.

Activities: Hiking, snowshoeing, cross-county skiing, mountain biking, canoeing, bird-watching.

Facilities: 100 kilometers of ski trails, 10 kilometers of snowshoeing trails, 200 miles of dirt roads and trails for mountain biking, lodging, family-style meals, ski shop, and rental shop.

Dates: Open year-round.

Fees: There is a charge to use the trails and facilities.

Closest town: Craftsbury Common, 1.5 miles.

For more information: Craftsbury Outdoor Center, PO Box 31, Craftsbury Common, VT 05827. Phone (800) 729-7751.

HIGHLAND LODGE

[Fig. 45(3)] This family lodge has been operating since 1954 on the shores of Caspian Lake. With its wide porches, lovely lake views, fine dining, and network of excellent cross-country ski trails, Highland Lodge is a place where Vermonters go to get away when they don't want to leave Vermont. The resort's trails connect with those of the Craftsbury Outdoor Center, which means a skier could spend a week here exploring and still have places to visit.

During the summer, guests can fish or swim in the sandy-bottomed Caspian Lake, or hike to nearby Barr Hill Natural Area, a 256-acre preserve owned by The Nature Conservancy.

Directions: From Hardwick and the junction of VT 15 and VT 14, look for Maple Street and follow it out of the village, where it becomes Center Road, and north toward Hardwick Center about 2 miles. From Hardwick Center continue on Center Road north for another 4 miles to Greensboro. From Greensboro village, bear left on the East Craftsbury Road and keep left for 2 miles to the lodge at the end of the lake.

Activities: Hiking, cross-country skiing, sledding, tennis, fishing, canoeing.

Facilities: Lodge, cottages, 50 kilometers of ski trails, hiking trails, tennis courts.

Dates: Open year-round.

Fees: There is a charge for lodging and to use the facilities.

Closest town: Greensboro, 2 miles.

For more information: Highland Lodge, Caspian Lake, Greensboro, VT 05841. Phone (802) 533-2647.

BARR HILL NATURAL AREA

[Fig. 45(2)] Scenic vistas, old sugar maples (*Acer saccharum*) and red spruce (*Picea rubra*), apple trees (*Malus sylvestris*) left from the days when the land was a homestead, and boulders left behind by the glacier all combine to make the Barr Hill Natural Area a fascinating place to visit.

The Nature Conservancy maintains two self-guided nature trails that pass the parcel's most interesting features. Near the summit of Barr Hill, the gritty bottom of the continental ice sheet gouged a narrow trough in the 400-million-year-old phyllites that make up the stone outcrop here. This glacial trough is one of the best examples of its kind to be found in northern Vermont.

The balsam fir (*Abies balsamea*), and red and white spruces (*Picea rubra* and *P. glauca*) are good habitat year-round for boreal chickadees (*Parus hudsonicus*), and, during the breeding season, for Cape May warblers (*Dendroica tigrina*). Both have been observed nesting in the preserve, which is near the southern limit of their breeding ranges.

Moose (*Alces alces*), bear (*Ursus americanus*), white-tailed deer (*Odocoileus virginianus*), and Eastern coyote (*Canis latrans*) all use the area, as do smaller mammals such as red squirrels (*Tamiasciurus hudsonicus*), woodchucks (*Marmota monax*), and snowshoe hare (*Lepus americanus*). Biologists have also found pygmy shrews (*Microsorex hoyi*); at roughly 3 inches long including tail and weighing in at 0.1 ounce, this is the smallest mammal in New England and one of the world's smallest mammals.

Directions: From the center of Greensboro, go north to the Town Hall and turn right. Turn left at the next fork, and follow the road to the gate at the George Hill Farm. At the farm, open the gate to allow your vehicle to pass, then close the gate behind your car. Look for parking and the trailhead beyond the gate.

Activities: Hiking, picnicking, cross-country skiing, bird-watching.

Facilities: Nature trails, stone fireplaces near Barr Hill summit.

Dates: Open year-round.

Fees: None.

Closest town: Greensboro, 2.5 miles.

For more information: Vermont Chapter of The Nature Conservancy, 27 State Street, Montpelier, VT 05602. Phone (802) 229-4425.

Fairbanks Museum and Planetarium

[Fig. 46(6)] A century ago, Victorians liked to keep what they called a cabinet of curiosities, loaded with interesting natural history and cultural objects. Saint Johnsbury resident Franklin Fairbanks, founder of the company that invented the platform scale, had a curio cabinet larger than most. In fact, he built the stately Fairbanks Museum in 1891 to keep his vast collection.

These days, the museum has more than 160,000 objects that range from pictures made out of insect bodies (the only such known in the world), to Japanese silks and netsuke. Rocks and minerals, bird eggs and nests, stuffed birds, including the largest collection of mounted hummingbirds in North America, dinosaurs, and Egyptian mummified animals are just part of the collection. One part of the museum is devoted to nineteenth-century life in northern Vermont and includes farm implements and tools, household implements, toys, dolls, and memorabilia collected by local residents. The museum also houses a collection of Fairbanks scales and other products made by Fairbanks's company, including Civil War stirrups and stoves.

Even if you don't visit the museum itself, the building is worth a look: Built of red sandstone and limestone, its Romanesque towers, arches, and carved bas relief have earned the building a place on the National Register of Historic Places.

Directions: From I-91 take Exit 20 and go north on US 5 approximately 1.5 miles to Main Street. Go north on Main Street roughly 2 miles to the Fairbanks Museum and Planetarium on the right side of the street.

Facilities: Three floors of museum exhibits, planetarium, gift shop.

Dates: Open year-round.

Fees: There is a charge for visiting the museum.

Closest town: Saint Johnsbury.

For more information: Fairbanks Museum and Planetarium, Main Street, Saint Johnsbury, VT 05819. Phone (802) 748-2372.

Burke Mountain

▓ DARLING STATE PARK

[Fig. 46(4)] The campground that was once the heart of this 2,000-acre state park was traded to Burke Mountain Ski Resort in the 1970s. In exchange the state was given land on the south end of Lake Willoughby, one of Vermont's more picturesque lakes. The ski resort leases most of the rest of Darling State Park for its ski trails, but the land remains public property. That means the summit road, hiking trails, and remaining lean-tos in the park are available for public use. The proximity of I-91, along with the road to the summit, makes this a popular place during the fall foliage season. A drive to the top gives a magnificent view of hundreds of square miles of blazing reds and yellows of maples and birches contrasted with the rich dark greens of the evergreens in the boreal forests.

The park is also part of a larger regional effort by a coalition of area businesses and residents to build a network of trails for hiking, mountain biking, and cross-country skiing, called the Kingdom Trails. The network as it exists now includes the hiking trails in Darling State Park, a link into Victory State Forest, and trail networks near the ski resort base area and in East Burke .

Directions: From I-91, take Exit 23 and go north on US 5 through Lyndonville. About 1.5 miles from the interstate, turn north on VT 114 and go about 6.5 miles to Burke Mountain Road on the right.

Activities: Hiking, mountain biking, skiing and other resort activities, primitive camping.

Facilities: Lean-tos, fire tower, paved road to summit, hiking trails, ski resort, facilities.

Dates: Open year-round.

Fees: There is a charge to use resort facilities.

Closest town: East Burke, 1.5 miles.

For more information: Vermont Department of Forests, Parks, and Recreation,

324 North Main Street, Barre, VT 05461-4109. Phone (802) 476-0170. Kingdom Trails Association, Inc., Box 204, East Burke, VT 05832. Phone (802) 626-9924.

CCC ROAD/WEST PEAK TRAIL

[Fig. 46(3)] This combination of trails brings hikers to the summit of Burke Mountain, which, with its summit fire tower, commands fabulous 360-degree views. The northern Presidential Range in the White Mountains of New Hampshire lies southeast, but probably the most stunning view is northwest, where the glacially oversteepened cliffs of Mounts Pisgah and Hor frame Lake Willoughby. The trail passes several lean-tos that make for good picnic stops or camping. It's possible to follow the CCC Road into Victory State Forest, past the turnoff for the West Peak Trail. The CCC Road is also open to mountain biking, and extends to a 1.3-mile-long woods road, which then links to a 3.5-mile-long public road leading to the Victory-Granby Road.

Directions: From I-91 take Exit 23 and go north on US 5 through Lyndonville. About 1.5 miles from the interstate turn north on VT 114 and go about 6.5 miles to Burke Mountain Road on the right. Drive to the unused toll house and park. The CCC Road, now a hiking trail, begins from the toll road 0.6 mile up on the right.

Trail: CCC Road to West Peak Trail, 1.7 miles one-way; West Peak Trail to summit, 1.3 miles one-way. CCC Road to Victory State Forest, about 3.5 miles one-way.

Elevation: 1,900 feet to 3,267 feet.

Degree of difficulty: Moderate.

Surface and blaze: Grassy abandoned road grading into rocky footpath. Blue blazes.

BURKE MOUNTAIN RESORT

[Fig. 46(2)] Burke Mountain calls itself Vermont's hidden jewel. Most of the state's big ski areas are to the south and along the main spine of the Green Mountains, leaving Burke somewhat separate from the pack, which is the way the mountain's fans like it. The slopes are uncrowded and the views are spectacular. The resort was purchased in the mid-1990s by a British investment group, which in recent years has expanded snow-making and added a new snowboard park.

Directions: From I-91 take Exit 23 and go north on US 5 through Lyndonville. About 1.5 miles from the interstate, turn north on VT 114 and go about 6.5 miles to Burke Mountain Road on the right.

Activities: Alpine and cross-country skiing, snowshoeing, ice skating, mountain-biking, tennis.

Facilities: 43 alpine ski trails, 4 lifts, snow-making, snowboard park, 80 kilometers of cross-country trails, summit road (summer), ice-skating rink, townhouses, condominiums.

Dates: Open year-round.

Fees: There is a charge to use the facilities.

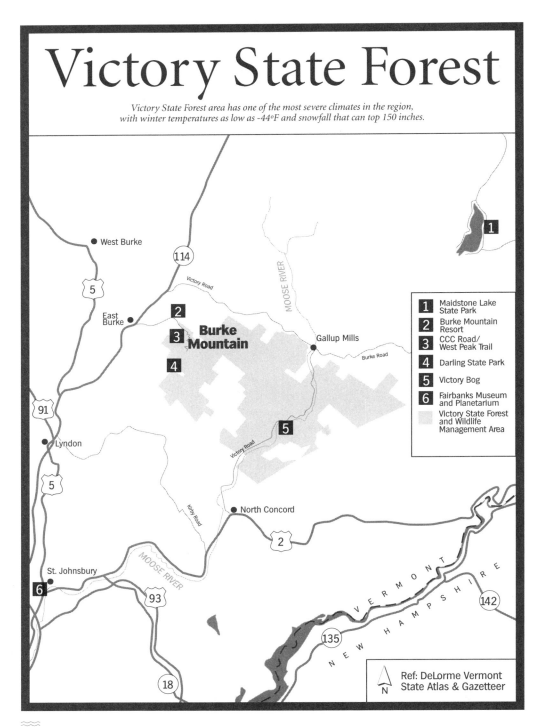

Victory State Forest

Victory State Forest area has one of the most severe climates in the region, with winter temperatures as low as -44°F and snowfall that can top 150 inches.

West Burke

114

5

Victory Road

MOOSE RIVER

East Burke

2

3 **Burke Mountain**

Gallup Mills

Burke Road

4

91

5 Victory Road

Lyndon

5

Kirby Road

North Concord

2

MOOSE RIVER

St. Johnsbury

6

93

18

135

142

VERMONT

NEW HAMPSHIRE

1	Maidstone Lake State Park
2	Burke Mountain Resort
3	CCC Road/ West Peak Trail
4	Darling State Park
5	Victory Bog
6	Fairbanks Museum and Planetarium
	Victory State Forest and Wildlife Management Area

N

Ref: DeLorme Vermont State Atlas & Gazetteer

Closest town: East Burke, 1.5 miles.

For more information: Burke Mountain, Northern Star Ski Corporation, PO Box 247, Mountain Road, East Burke, VT 05832. Phone (802) 626-3305.

Victory State Forest and Wildlife Management Area

[Fig. 46] Stunted spruce trees, bogs, and meandering rivers give visitors to the Victory State Forest and Wildlife Management Area—collectively known as Victory Basin—the feeling that they've been transported several hundred miles north to the Canadian subarctic. The sheer size of the public parcel helps, too: The state forest covers nearly 16,000 acres in four towns, and the wildlife management area another 5,000 acres.

The basin's subarctic feel has a basis in reality: The area has the one of the most severe climates in the region, with winter temperatures as low as -44 degrees Fahrenheit, and snowfall that can top 150 inches. The mean annual temperature here is only 37 degrees Fahrenheit—the same as Quebec City, 100 miles to the north.

The bowl shape of the basin helps explain part of its climatic severity. The area is underlain by granite from the New Hampshire plutonic series, rocks that were formed about 400 million years ago and cooled slowly beneath the Earth's surface. Erosion eventually exposed the pluton, and weathering carved a bowl-shaped depression out of the coarse-grained granite at the basin's center. More resistant, fine-grained granite forms surrounding hills that ring the basin at an elevation of roughly 2,000 feet. The bottom of the basin is at only 1,000 feet, and cold air tends to pool here.

It may be that water has pooled here, too, in the past. Much of the area shows signs of the passage of the glacier 15,000 years ago and more. There are eskers, moraines, and kame terraces. Some researchers think Victory Basin might have been an enormous lake just after the glaciers passed, based on a layer of impermeable clay that lies at the base of Victory Bog. The boreal nature of the area attracts birds and animals common in the north: otter (*Lutra canadensis*), mink (*Mustela vison*), fisher (*Martes pennanti*), and, possibly, marten (*Martes americana*) and lynx (*Lynx canadensis*) may all be found here.

Scattered throughout the basin are stands of black spruce (*Picea mariana*), but the more dominant spruce is red spruce (*Picea rubra*), growing in association with balsam fir (*Abies balsamea*). Red maple (*Acer rubrum*), yellow birch (*Betula alleghanensis*), and the occasional American beech (*Fagus grandifolia*) grow on drier knolls. Beaver (*Castor canadensis*) ponds abound, as do beaver meadows, the wet leftovers from abandoned beaver ponds. In Victory Bog proper, sphagnum peat dominates; close to streams, alders (*Alnus incana*) make for good spring browse for moose (*Alces alces*).

The forests have been commercially logged since the early 1800s. A sawmill was built in nearby Granby in 1810, and another in Victory in 1830. Loggers used the Moose River to carry logs to sawmills on the Passumpsic or Connecticut rivers; historians estimate that 14 sawmills once operated in the area. Logging boomed when the Victory Branch Railroad was built beginning in 1882.

A 12-mile offshoot of the Saint Johnsbury and Lake Champlain Railroad, the branch traveled north from North Concord roughly parallel to the Moose River. With the branch line came people, and a mill and settlement were built on Bog Pond. By 1885, the settlement was the largest in the town of Victory, with 20 houses, a store, and a school. The mill burned in 1900 and the village was then abandoned, but hikers who want to walk the railroad line from Damon's Crossing north can look for ruins of the mill dam and foundations from the mill and homes.

The area is a hunter's paradise. While hiking and primitive camping are permitted, there are no developed facilities and only one main hiking path, the old abandoned railroad bed that travels some nice country but has no real destination. Another trail, the CCC Road, comes into the northern part of the area from Darling State Park. Visitors who want to explore Victory Basin should come prepared with a compass, topographic map, and plenty of blaze orange. Shooting season for deer typically begins in mid-November, but hunting for other animals or birds, or with other weapons, bridges a much longer period in the fall and spring.

Directions: From North Concord on US 2, go north on Victory Road approximately 3 miles to the town of Victory. Continue north on this road, now called River Road or Town Highway 1 through the wildlife management area. There are five parking areas along the road, known from south to north as Mitchell's Knoll, Damon's Crossing, Charles Damon Parking Area, an unnamed area, and Lee's Hill.

Activities: Bird-watching, hiking, hunting, canoeing, bushwhacking, snowshoeing.

Facilities: None.

Dates: Open year-round, but check with Vermont Fish and Wildlife Department about hunting seasons.

Fees: None.

Closest town: Victory.

For more information: Vermont Fish and Wildlife Department, 184 Portland Street, Saint Johnsbury, VT 05819. Phone (802) 751-0100.

▓ VICTORY BOG

[Fig. 46(5)] One of only a few raised bogs in Vermont, Victory Bog has a thick, slightly domed mat of sphagnum (*Sphagnum* spp.) at its center and relatively low plant diversity. As bogs in Vermont go, Victory Bog is considered extremely fragile, and land managers have worked hard to keep the bog inaccessible. Their job is made easier by the prodigious blackfly (family *Simuliidae*), mosquito (family *Culicidae*), and deerfly (family *Tabanidae*) populations that plague hikers here in the summer: The open water makes for ideal breeding grounds, and the thick vegetation excludes any possibility of relief from wind. Those determined to visit Victory Bog usually bring head nets.

One way to reach the bog is to bushwhack south from the pull-out at the Charles Damon Parking Area. A line of stunted black spruce (*Picea mariana*) rings the bog's true edge, while farther away from the bog center, the spruce grow larger (though research has shown that they are the same age). These two spruce forests have little in common other than spruce. Away from the bog center and near a small stream that bounds one edge of the area, the spruce forests are more typical of wet areas where nutrients are more plentiful than in a true bog. Balsam fir (*Abies balsamea*), red maple (*Acer rubrum*), mountain ash (*Sorbus americana*), checkerberry (*Gaultheria procumbens*), and bunchberry (*Cornus canadensis*) can all be found here, along with several species of sphagnum moss.

But closer to the bog, where the spruce shrink in size, plants more typical of wetlands with poor nutrient status appear: rhodora (*Rhododendron canadense*), leatherleaf (*Chamaedaphne calculata*), wren's egg cranberry (*Vaccinium oxycoccus*), and Labrador tea (*Ledum groenlandicum*). Closest to the bog, true bog plants appear: bog rosemary (*Andromeda glaucophylla*), cottongrass (*Eriophorum spissum*), and northern pitcher plants (*Sarracenia purpurea*).

Many of the boreal birds and animals common in Victory Basin are found here. But the bog proper may be home to two more unusual mammals as well: One biologist believes two rare lemming species, southern bog lemming (*Synaptomys cooperii*) and northern bog lemming (*Synaptomys borealis*), use hummocks in the bog for breeding.

Directions: From North Concord on US 2, go north on Victory Road approximately 3 miles to the town of Victory. Continue north on this road, now called River Road or Town Highway 1 through the wildlife management area, and continue to the second of five pull-outs on the road at Damon's Crossing. Park here and bushwhack roughly 0.5 mile southeast to find the bog.

Activities: Bird-watching, botanizing.

Facilities: None.

Dates: Open year-round.

Fees: None.

Closest town: Victory.

For more information: Vermont Fish and Wildlife Department, 184 Portland Street, Saint Johnsbury, VT 05819. Phone (802) 751-0100.

MOOSE RIVER

[Fig. 46] Much of the Moose River is challenging whitewater paddling, but the short stretch of river traversing the Victory Wildlife Management Area is generally

Moose

When Europeans first settled Vermont in the 1700s, the state was mostly forested, and moose were widespread. Historical accounts include regular mentions of moose; one Abenaki was said to have killed 27 moose near Crystal Lake in Barton during the winter of 1783–1784.

As forests fell to the axe, moose habitat disappeared and so did the moose. By 1896, when all but 25 percent of the state was agricultural land, the Vermont legislature prohibited moose hunting—a token effort at best, because the animals had been all but extirpated.

The gradual shift in land use during the next century eventually allowed the moose to re-establish itself in Vermont. Recovery was slow.

By 1960, state officials estimated there were only 25 moose in Vermont. But by 1980, numbers had climbed sufficiently that Vermonters began asking the state to institute a hunting season, both as a way to limit the number of moose-car collisions and for the hunt itself. But it wasn't until 1993 that the state officially opened a limited hunting season when biologists determined there were about 1,100 moose in the state, mostly in the Northeast Kingdom. Since then, numbers have grown to about 2,500 animals, and the state continues to offer a limited moose season in mid-October.

passable at medium- to high-water conditions and is a pleasant half-day paddle. Its chocolate-brown waters, stained by tannins and organic acids, give the river a mysterious feel and obscure the bottom where the river runs deep.

Though it may be necessary to get out and drag your canoe over beaver dams or low spots, given the area's thick vegetation and lack of trails, paddling the river may be one of the best ways to enjoy Victory Basin.

The alder swamps, open areas in the river's floodplain, and the river itself are abundant in plant species. Swamp candles (*Lysimachia terrestris*), St. Johnswort (*Hypericum* spp.), and reed-meadow grass (*Glyceria grandis*) fringe the river's edge. This rich floodplain is ideal for woodcock (*Scolopax minor*), and numerous boreal birds inhabit the surroundings, including Canada jay (*Perisoreus canadensis*), yellow-bellied and olive-sided flycatchers (*Empidonax alnorum*, *E. flaviventris*, and *Contopus borealis*), golden-crowned and ruby-crowned kinglets (*Regulus calendula* and *R. satrapa*), boreal chickadees (*Parus hudsonicus*), and, if you're lucky, rusty blackbirds (*Euphagus carolinus*). Anglers may wish to bring a rod; brook trout (*Salvelinus fontinalis*), brown trout (*Salmo trutta*), and rainbow trout (*Oncorhynchus mykiss*) can all be found here.

Directions: From North Concord on US 2, go north on Victory Road approximately 3 miles to the town of Victory. Continue north on this road, now called River Road or Town Highway 1 through the wildlife management area. Mitchell's Landing is the first parking area on the left, or north side of the road, where a snowmobile bridge crosses the Moose River. This is the take-out. Continue north approximately 4 miles to the put-in at Lee's Hill. The river is across the road from the parking area at an unmarked put-in.

Activities: Canoeing, fishing, bird-watching.

Facilities: Parking pull-outs.

Dates: Open year-round, but check with Vermont Fish and Wildlife Department for hunting season dates.

Fees: None.

Closest town: Victory.

For more information: Vermont Fish and Wildlife Department, 184 Portland Street, Saint Johnsbury, VT 05819. Phone (802) 751-0100.

Maidstone Lake State Park

[Fig. 46(1)] Maidstone State Park and its pretty lake are probably the most remote state lands in all of Vermont. A 5-mile-long drive on a dirt road brings you to the southern end of this large, deep lake. Even though camps dot the shoreline, the thick spruce-fir forests, the calls of nesting loons, and the occasional glimpses of moose give the park a marvelous secluded feel. The special nature of the area was recognized early on in Vermont's development of its state lands. The Civilian Conservation Corps used the area, designated as a park in 1938, as a camp and subsequently built fireplaces and tent sites for camping, as well as the picnic shelter.

Glaciers are thought to have carved the deep basin that cradles the lake, which is 120 feet deep in places. The clear cold water supports a good trout fishery, with some lake trout (*Salvelinus namaycush*) topping 25 pounds. Brook trout (*Salvelinus fontinalis*), rainbow trout (*Oncorhyncus myskiss*), and yellow perch (*Perca flavescens*) also abound.

MOOSE
(Alces alces)
The largest member of the deer family, the moose grows up to 10 feet tall and to more than 1,000 pounds in weight. Its habitat is the northern forest, often near freshwater where it feeds on aquatic plants.

What draws most people, however, are the nesting loons (*Gavia immer*). Maidstone's remote nature and good fishery make the lake ideal for the birds, which are considered an endangered species in Vermont. In each of the 20 years Vermont has been monitoring loon populations, the birds have been found here, and the lake remains one of the state's most productive in terms of nesting success. Maidstone is second only

Willoughby State Forest

In 1984, Willoughby's Mt. Pisgah became the first location in Vermont where peregrine falcons reoccupied a nest site on their own.

Orleans

8 **9**

Lake Willoughby

10

Westmore

16

5

Bald Mountain

91

Long Pond Road

MAY POND

Wheeler Mountain

LAKE WILLOUGHBY

Barton **7**

P

4

6

Haystack Mountain

CRYSTAL LAKE

WHEELER POND

P

1

91

2

5

VAIL POND

3

11

P

BEAN POND

MARL POND

P

P

DOLLOFF PONDS

5A

Ref: State of Vermont Department of Forests, Parks & Recreation

N

1 Mount Pisgah	**7** Crystal Lake State Park
2 Herbert Hawkes Trail	**8** Willoughby Falls WMA
3 Mount Hor	**9** South Bay WMA
4 North Trail	**10** Town Beach
5 South Trail	**11** Cheney House
6 Long Pond-Mount Pisgah Loop Trail	Willoughby State Forest
	Trail

1 MILE

5

To West Burke

to Green River Reservoir in the number of surviving chicks, with 23 fledged over two decades.

The forests here are dominated by red spruce (*Picea rubens*) and balsam fir (*Abies balsamea*). This northern coniferous forest attracts birds less common elsewhere in Vermont, including evening and pine grosbeaks (*Coccothraustes vespertinus* and *Pinicola enucleator*) and red and white-winged crossbills (*Loxia curvirostra* and *L. leucoptera*).

Because Maidstone is surrounded by undeveloped paper company land, many of Vermont's larger mammals pass through or den here. It's not uncommon to find tracks or scat from moose (*Alces alces*), black bear (*Ursus americanus*), porcupine (*Erethizon dorsatum*), red fox (*Vulpes fulva*), and, occasionally, bobcat (*Lynx rufus*).

Several short hiking trails travel the southern end of the lake. The ranger station has trail maps.

Directions: From Guildhall, go north on VT 102 approximately 11 miles, through Maidstone and to Maidstone Hill Road on the left. Take Maidstone Hill Road 5 miles to the park entrance.

Activities: Hiking, fishing, canoeing, camping, picnicking, bird-watching.

Facilities: 45 campsites, 37 lean-tos, restrooms, hiking trails, swimming beach, picnic shelter.

Dates: Open mid-May to mid-Oct.

Fees: There is a charge for camping and day use.

Closest town: Bloomfield, 10 miles

For more information: Maidstone State Park, RFD 1, Box 455, Guildhall, VT 05905. Phone (802) 676-3930 (summer). Vermont Department of Forests, Parks, and Recreation, 324 North Main Street, Barre, VT 05461-4109. Phone (802) 476-0170 (winter).

Willoughby State Forest

[Fig. 47] Uncle Joe Hyde, a longtime Westmore resident who had more than enough time to spin a yarn in his 94 years, remembered a time when "Mount Pisgah was just a good size anthill and Willoughby Lake was just a puddle." Other visitors to the lake have chosen to describe the scene in considerably more dramatic and grandiose terms, to the point where, by sheer weight of verbiage, it ranks as one of Vermont's finest landscapes. Indeed, a first glimpse of Lake Willoughby can be a bit of a shock: It looks like a 5-mile arm of a Norwegian fjord transplanted to the gentle hill country of eastern Vermont. The steep cliffs of Mount Pisgah on the east side and Mount Hor on the west frame the cold, 300-foot-deep waters of the lake, which occasionally give up lake trout (*Salvelinus namaycush*) or landlocked salmon (*Salmo salar*) that tip the scales at over 20 pounds.

BOREAL CHICKADEE
(Parus hudsonicus)
This brown-capped bird sings its "chick-a-dee" in a buzzy voice.

The Willoughby pluton, a 10-mile-wide body of resistant granite, forms a mountain range in miniature, complete with a scattering of mountain ponds and steep cascading brooks. Ice Age glaciers filed a deep notch through the granite, dividing the range, and left a moraine dam at the southern end to form the basin of the northward-draining lake.

Unlike the smaller lakes in the region, the shores of Lake Willoughby are too steep to nurture extensive wetlands, and a stiff southerly wind blowing across the full fetch of the lake can whip up a fair chop, so this is a place to think twice before putting a canoe in the water. But catch it on a fair day and paddle close in under the white cedars (*Thuja occidentalis*) and mossy boulders along the wild southwestern shore, and it doesn't take much imagination to make it a morning in Alaska.

The state forest wraps around the southern end of the lake, and there is a state boat ramp on the eastern shore, about 1.2 miles south of the junction of VT 16 and 5A. A small town beach at the northern end, immediately west of the same junction, provides swimming and canoe access. The Youth Conservation Corps swimming beach at Cheney House, at the south end of the lake, also provides canoe access.

While there are no campgrounds in the state forest, primitive camping is allowed, and there are private campgrounds at the south end and off VT 5A about 0.5 mile north of the lake. The state-run Cheney House, at the southern end of the lake, provides hostel-style accommodation for groups of up to 25 from September 1 through May 31. There is also hotel accommodation on VT 5A along the east shore of the lake.

Directions: The junction of VT 5A and VT 16 is at the north end of Lake Willoughby. VT 5A south of this junction runs along the eastern shore, entering the state forest about 3 miles south of the junction.

Activities: Canoeing, kayaking, fishing, hiking, ice climbing, primitive camping, developed camping nearby.

Facilities: Boat ramp, swimming beach.

Dates: Open year-round.

Fees: None for access to the lake or state forest lands.

Closest town: Westmore.

For more information: Vermont Department of Forests, Parks, and Recreation, 324 North Main Street, Barre, VT 05461-4109. Phone (802) 476-0170.

MOUNT PISGAH

[Fig. 47(1)] Mount Pisgah's west face presents a stark band of 500-foot-high cliffs to Lake Willoughby. The cliffs are carved out of the limy schist and phyllite that surround the Willoughby pluton. The granite pluton was formed as a bubble of magma that cooled gradually deep underground. The magma also worked its way into cracks in the surrounding rock, forming numerous light-colored veins or dikes that stand out clearly on the face of Mount Pisgah, which is near the contact between the two rock types.

The cliffs are kept wet by water seeping over and through the rock, enough so as to discourage rock climbing but to make for acres of steep ice climbing in the winter. The seeps, enriched by water flowing through the limy bedrock, also feed a hanging garden of rare plants, including bird's-eye primrose (*Primula mistassinica*), purple and yellow mountain saxifrages (*Saxifraga oppositifolia* and *S. aizoides*), and several rare fern species such as wall-rue (*Asplenium ruta-muraria*) and smooth woodsia (*Woodsia glabella*). The broad, mostly stabilized talus slopes beneath the cliffs support rich forest communities with still more rare plants, including yellow lady's slipper (*Cypripedium calceolus*).

In 1984, Mount Pisgah became the first location in Vermont where peregrine falcons (*Falco peregrinus*) reoccupied a nest site on their own, without prior release of captive-bred birds. A breeding pair now returns annually, and 24 young have fledged here in the last 14 years. The adults can be seen doing their spectacular courtship flights in the spring months, and young are fledged by midsummer. This is also a good place to watch for hawks during migration, especially accipiters and large buteos, which ride the updrafts generated by westerly winds flowing up and over the cliff face.

Three trailheads give access to the dramatic views from the top of the cliffs.

SOUTH TRAIL

[Fig. 47(5)] The most popular and direct way up Mount Pisgah begins by bridging a wet meadow near a beaver pond, then keeps a steady, moderate grade over the 1,500-foot climb to the wooded summit. Pulpit Rock, about halfway to the summit in both distance and elevation, is the first of several dramatic viewpoints along the cliff brow, and it is a good short hike destination. The best viewpoints are a short distance past the summit on the North Trail.

Directions: From the junction of VT 16 and VT 5A in Westmore, drive south on VT 5A about 5.8 miles to a trailhead parking area on the right.

Trail: 1 mile one-way to Pulpit Rock, 1.7 miles one-way to the summit, and about 2 miles one-way to the viewpoints north of the summit.

Elevation: Trailhead, 1,280 feet; Pulpit Rock, about 1,800 feet; summit, 2,751 feet.

Degree of difficulty: Moderate.

Surface and blaze: Rocky footpath. Blue blazes.

NORTH TRAIL

[Fig. 47(4)] The North Trail ascends gradually through the forests on the steep slopes north of the cliff band, meeting the south trail at the summit. You can close a 6.9-mile loop by walking the 3-mile stretch of VT 5A between the North and South trailheads. The road follows the lakeshore, providing plenty of scenery in its own right.

Directions: From the junction of VT 16 and VT 5A in Westmore, drive south on VT 5A about 3 miles to the trailhead on the left. There is limited roadside parking.

Trail: 2.2 miles one-way.

Elevation: 1,180 to 2,751 feet.

Degree of difficulty: Moderate.

Surface and blaze: Old road and rocky footpath. Blue blazes.

LONG POND–MOUNT PISGAH TRAIL

[Fig. 47(6)] This trail approaches Mount Pisgah from Long Pond, where trails also leave for Haystack and Bald mountains. It passes through a saddle between Pisgah and Hedghog Mountain, and joins the North Trail about 0.5 mile north of the summit.

Directions: From the junction of VT 16 and VT 5A in Westmore, go south on VT 5A about 1.5 miles, turn left on Long Pond Road. About 1.8 miles from VT 5A, turn right onto a logging road and park at a gate.

Trail: 2 miles one-way to the North Trail; 2.7 miles one-way to the summit of Mount Pisgah.

Elevation: 1,840 to 2,440 feet.

Degree of difficulty: Moderate.

Surface and blaze: Old road and rocky footpath. White blazes.

BALD MOUNTAIN

[Fig. 47] The hike over Bald Mountain provides a nice extension to the Pisgah hike for those willing to make a car drop and with enough miles in their legs: The total distance is about 10 miles. It is the highest summit in the Willoughby area, and the summit fire tower is a nice day hike destination with views stretching from the northern Green Mountains and several summits in Quebec to New Hampshire's distant Presidential Range.

Directions: From the junction of VT 16 and VT 5A in Westmore, go south on VT 5A about 1.5 miles, turn left on Long Pond Road. Park at the Long Pond Access Area and walk up the road to the trailhead on the left. To reach the northern end of the trail, go south on VT 5A about 1 mile and turn left on Goodwin Road. Near the top of the hill, bear right at a fork onto Coles Road, and go 1.7 miles and park near the entrance to an old road on the right.

Trail: 2.1 miles one-way to the summit from Long Pond; 2.8 miles one-way from Coles Road.

Elevation: 1,600 to 3,315 feet.

Degree of difficulty: Moderate.

Surface and blaze: Old road and rocky footpath. Yellow blazes.

HAYSTACK MOUNTAIN

[Fig. 47] The wooded summit of Haystack Mountain has lookouts to the south, east, and west, and it can be reached by hiking a 3.3-mile loop, including a 1.2-mile section of Long Pond Road.

Directions: From the junction of VT 16 and VT 5A in Westmore, go south on VT 5A about 1.5 miles, turn left on Long Pond Road. The trailhead is on the left, about 0.6 mile past the Long Pond Access Area.

Trail: 3.3-mile loop.

Elevation: 1,800 to 2,712 feet.

Degree of difficulty: Moderate.

Surface and blaze: Old road and rocky footpath, orange or yellow blazes.

MOUNT HOR

[Fig. 47(3)] Without Mount Hor on the west to complement Pisgah on the east, the Lake Willoughby landscape would be decidedly lopsided, and might not have attracted nearly as much praise as it has over the years. But, fortunately, Hor is there, and it provides fine views of its eastern counterpart and of the lake in between. The cliffs are geologically and floristically similar to those on Mount Pisgah, with many of the same rare plant species.

HERBERT HAWKES TRAIL

[Fig. 47(2)] The cliffs overlooking the lake are the main objective of this trail, but a side trail leads over the summit to a viewpoint overlooking Burke Mountain and several small ponds in the western part of the state forest. A rough, 5-mile side trail leads west over Moose Mountain to Wheeler Pond.

Directions: From the junction of VT 16 and VT 5A in Westmore, drive south on VT 5A about 5.8 miles and turn left on the unpaved CCC Road. Park on the right about 1.8 miles from VT 5A.

Trail: 1.4 miles one-way.

Elevation: 1,900 to 2,656 feet.

Degree of difficulty: Easy to moderate.

Surface and blaze: Old road and rocky footpath. Blue blazes.

WHEELER MOUNTAIN

[Fig. 47] Unlike Mounts Pisgah and Hor, Wheeler Mountain is set back from the shore of Lake Willoughby, with expansive views that take in the lake and its surrounding summits and sweep the Green Mountains from Jay Peak to Mount Mansfield. A trail passes over the mountain summit and descends slightly to a cliff overlooking hill pastures and the lake.

Directions: From the junction of VT 5 and VT 16 in Barton, go south on VT 5 about 5 miles and turn left on Wheeler Mountain Road. There is trailhead parking on the left, 1.9 miles from VT 5.

Trail: 1.3 miles one-way. A steeper, slightly shorter alternate route to one section of the trail is blazed in red.

Elevation: 1,700 to 2,371 feet.

Degree of difficulty: Moderate.

Surface and blaze: Rocky footpath and ledge. White blazes; alternate route blazed in red.

MAY POND

[Fig. 47] Hidden away in the hills between Crystal Lake and Lake Willoughby, May Pond makes up for its small size by providing the wildness that the bigger lakes lack. The shores are lined with bands of marsh and thickets of berry-bearing shrubs—great habitat for wetland and forest edge species. A pair of common loons (*Gavia immer*) nests in the south cove, so it is best to give them plenty of room during the breeding season. A big beaver lodge dominates the southern end of the pond, and otter (*Lutra canadensis*) are sighted regularly, often feeding on the pond's abundant crayfish. The lake is deep and cold enough to support brook trout (*Salvelinus fontinalis*).

Directions: From the junction of VT 5 and VT 16 in Barton, take VT 16 north about 1.6 miles and turn right on Pond Road. Bear right at a fork and at 2.1 miles from VT 16, turn left into the state fishing access.

Activities: Canoeing, fishing, wildlife-watching.

Facilities: State boat ramp.

Dates: Open year-round.

Fees: None.

Closest town: Barton, 3 miles.

For more information: The Vermont Nature Conservancy, 27 State Street, Montpelier VT 05602. Phone (802) 229-4425.

CRYSTAL LAKE STATE PARK

[Fig. 47(7)] Crystal Lake State Park is open for day use only, so campers will have to find other places to pitch their tents. The lake has almost a mile of sandy shoreline and plenty of deep cold water for rainbow and brown trout (*Oncorhynchus mykiss* and *Salmo trutta*), while chain pickerel (*Esox niger*), and smallmouth bass (*Micropterus dolomieui*) lurk along the shoreline.

Directions: From the junction of US 5 and VT 16 in Barton, go east on VT 16 about 0.6 mile and turn right on Pageant Park Road. The state park entrance is about 0.2 mile down on the right.

Activities: Swimming, picnicking, boating, fishing.

Facilities: Extensive beach, picnic area, boat rentals. There is a boat ramp on US 5 near the south end of the lake.

Dates: Open late May to Sept.

Fees: There is a fee for day use.

Closest town: Barton, 0.8 mile.

For more information: Crystal Lake State Park, Barton, VT 05822. Phone (802) 525-6205 (summer). Vermont Department of Forests, Parks, and Recreation, 324 North Main Street, Barre, VT 05461-4109. Phone (802) 476-0170 (winter).

WILLOUGHBY FALLS WILDLIFE MANAGEMENT AREA

[Fig. 47(8)] Eleven months out of the year, Willoughby Falls is not all that wild a place. Just north of the village of Orleans and barely out of sight of the houses on Maple Street, the Willoughby River slides over a broad, sculpted ledge, falling all of about 4 feet—not much of a waterfall.

But in April, as the river swells with highland snowmelt until it stretches nearly 100 feet across the ledge from bank to bank, wildness swims upriver to Willoughby Falls. Steelhead, the migratory form of rainbow trout (*Oncorhynchus mykiss*), charged up with vernal hormones and fattened by several years of good living on the international cuisine of Lake Memphremagog, run up the river to spawn in the gravel beds of shallow headwater streams. In a spectacle that is rare in the East's tamed rivers, they leap tirelessly through the cold, cascading water of the falls, 2-foot streaks of silver against white foam.

Rainbow trout are not native to eastern waters, and here they have likely replaced landlocked Atlantic salmon (*Salmo salar*), which are now reoccupying another Memphremagog tributary, the Clyde River, following the removal of a much-disputed hydroelectric dam in 1996.

The falls can be viewed from the Brownington Road bridge, but by walking along the stream bank you can sometimes get within a few feet of the leaping fish.

While it is not one of Vermont's more dramatic falls, it can make a nice summer picnic stop.

Directions: From the junction of US 5 and VT 58 in Orleans, proceed east on VT 58 through the center of town. Bear left on Brownington Road and park at the Vermont Fish and Wildlife lot near the bridge.

Activities: Wildlife-watching, picnicking.

Facilities: None.

Dates: The trout usually run in the last two weeks of Apr. or the first week of May.

Fees: None.

Closest town: Orleans.

For more information: Vermont Department of Fish and Wildlife, 184 Portland Street, Saint Johnsbury, VT 05819. Phone (802) 751-0100.

SOUTH BAY WILDLIFE MANAGEMENT AREA

[Fig. 47(9)] Lake Memphremagog straddles the Vermont-Quebec border, and with the town of Newport near its south end, plenty of summer camps along its shores, lots of big boat traffic, and the whitecaps kicked up by stiff breezes out of just

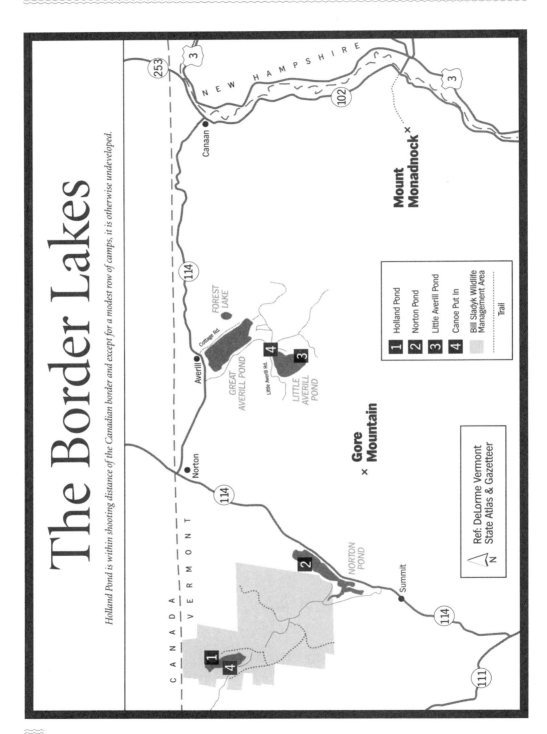

The Border Lakes

Holland Pond is within shooting distance of the Canadian border and except for a modest row of camps, it is otherwise undeveloped.

NEW HAMPSHIRE

Canaan

Mount
Monadnock ×

Gore
Mountain ×

FOREST
LAKE

Cottage Rd.

Averill

GREAT
AVERILL POND

Little Averill Rd.

LITTLE
AVERILL
POND

Norton

NORTON
POND

Summit

CANADA

VERMONT

1 Holland Pond
2 Norton Pond
3 Little Averill Pond
4 Canoe Put In
Bill Sladyk Wildlife
Management Area
.... Trail

Ref: DeLorme Vermont
State Atlas & Gazetteer
N

about any quarter, it is not all that friendly a place for canoes or other small boats. But south of Newport, where a bridge on US 5 crosses a narrows, the lake opens out again into 2-mile-long South Bay. The Barton River empties into the south end of the bay, amid a 2.5-mile-long stretch of wetlands–floating gardens of water lilies (*Nuphar variegatum*) and pickerelweed (*Pontederia cordata*), vast stands of bulrushes (*Scirpus* spp.), cattails (*Typha latifolia*) and burreed (*Sparganium* spp.), and stands of silver maple (*Acer saccharinum*) along the river levees.

The open waters of the bay are often within earshot of the roads and train tracks of Newport, but the several miles of the Barton River channel and the backwater sloughs of the marshes are a world apart. This is prime habitat for numerous wildlife species, from snapping turtles (*Chelydra serpentina*) and American bittern (*Botaurus lentiginosus*) to beaver (*Castor canadensis*), mink (*Mustela vison*), and otter (*Lutra canadensis*). The refuge is an important migratory stopover for a variety of duck species, and one of a handful of black tern (*Chlidonias niger*) nesting sites in the state.

Directions: From the junction of VT 191 and US 5/VT 105 in Newport, take US 5/VT 105 south across the South Bay Bridge, and take the first left after the bridge onto Coventry Street. There is a boat access about 0.5 mile down on the left. There is also an unmarked access on a marsh channel at the south end of the bay: from the junction of VT 191 and US 5/VT 105 in Newport, take US 5/VT 105 south 0.2 mile and turn left on Glen Road. About 2.5 miles down Glen Road, look for a dirt road on the right that leads to the water.

Activities: Canoeing, fishing, wildlife-watching.

Facilities: Boat access ramp.

Dates: Open year-round.

Fees: None.

Closest town: Newport.

For more information: Vermont Department of Fish and Wildlife, 184 Portland Street, Saint Johnsbury, VT 05819. Phone (802) 751-0100.

The Border Lakes

[Fig. 48] The northern tier of Vermont towns along the Canadian border east of Lake Memphremagog is, in some ways, the wildest stretch of the state. It is a rolling hinterland of forest and swamp, pocked with lakes, that is the stronghold of boreal plant and bird species like white spruce (*Picea glauca*) and spruce grouse (*Dendragapus canadensis*), and served as the beachhead for the return of moose (*Alces alces*) and loons (*Gavia immer*) to the state—perhaps a harbinger of other species to come. It is also wild in the sense that it is not, and never has been, heavily settled. Much of the land has passed through the hands of big paper or logging companies and has seen intensive management throughout at least the first half of this century, resulting

The Clyde River Dam

In May 1994, the Clyde River, fueled by heavy rains, breached the Newport Number 11 Dam, the last of a series of hydropower dams in its course, just 0.25 mile up from the mouth of the river on Lake Memphremagog. It was a small dam, and the floodwaters did no significant damage. The breach was far larger in significance. It was the first time in nearly 40 years that the waters of the Clyde had flowed freely down a 2,000-foot stretch of riverbed that was still remembered for its superb run of landlocked salmon (*Salmo salar*). The dam had shunted water around the riverbed in a man-made bypass to feed hydropower generators downstream, leaving the spawning beds dry for most of the year, and salmon-less for all of those 40 years.

The breach was a symbolic turning point in a controversy that was raging over the fate of the dam, which was up for review and relicensing by the Federal Energy Regulatory Commission (FERC). While the out-of-state utility that owned the dam stood firm on its "right" to continue running the dam as it pleased, the Northeast Kingdom Branch of Trout Unlimited had spearheaded a campaign to have the dam removed.

By the time the dam broke, the Vermont Water Resources Board, along with other state and federal agencies, had come around to support removal of the dam. The battle wasn't over, but in 1996 FERC ordered removal of the dam, one of the first such decisions in the nation. The company then withdrew its objections and voluntarily removed the dam.

The salmon have returned to the Clyde.

in a mosaic of mostly young hardwood and coniferous forests. Their fate still hangs in the balance as the lands come up for sale and social and political forces in the region seek new ownership and tax structures that will help keep this, and other lands in the great swath of the northern forest from New York to Maine, a healthy, working forest.

HOLLAND POND AND BILL SLADYK WILDLIFE MANAGEMENT AREA

[Fig. 48(1)] Holland Pond is within shooting distance of the Canadian border, and far enough away from anywhere else to winnow out all but the most ardent outdoor enthusiasts. Many of these, in the right season, are hunters and fisherman, out to harvest the zoological bounty of the 10,000-acre Bill Sladyk Wildlife Management Area, which runs from the area around Holland Pond eastward nearly to Norton Pond. But this is also promising country for those who bag their prey with binoculars. It offers visitors a good chance of seeing boreal bird species such as gray jays (*Perisoreus canadensis*), boreal chickadees (*Parus hudsonicus*), and black-backed woodpeckers (*Picoides arcticus*).

Holland Pond has a modest row of camps along the western shore but is otherwise undeveloped. Like other northern ponds, it is an important breeding and feeding area for common loons (*Gavia immer*). Some sections of the lake may be closed during the breeding season. Wetlands border the shallow inlets on the southern and northeastern shores, and from the northeastern bay a 200-yard carry will take adventurous canoeists to tiny but pristine Turtle Pond. A semicircle of smaller ponds north of Holland Pond are accessible by trail.

Bill Sladyk is also accessible by road from the Norton Pond area (*see* below). Old logging roads fan out from a parking area at road's end, some heading northeastwards towards Holland Pond, others wandering up into the northwestern corner of the refuge. There are no grandiose views here, just acres of woodlands—a good place to practice map and compass skills or try out a handheld GPS receiver.

Directions: From the junction of VT 114 and VT 111 north of Island Pond, go north on VT 111 to the village of Morgan Center and turn right on Valley Road. Continue north 4.7 miles through the village of Holland, where you turn right onto a dirt road. Bear right 3 miles out of the village, then bear left at 5 miles and continue to the Holland Pond boat access.

Activities: Canoeing, hunting, fishing, wildlife-watching, hiking.

Facilities: Boat ramp.

Dates: Open year round.

Fees: None.

Closest town: Morgan, about 10 miles.

For more information: Vermont Department of Fish and Wildlife, 184 Portland Street, Saint Johnsbury, VT 05819. Phone (802) 751-0100.

NORTON POND

[Fig. 48(2)] The southern bays and sloughs of Norton Pond are a quiet water maze that is well out of sight of the few scattered camps, the road, and the railroad line on the west side of the pond. A pair of loons (*Gavia immer*) nests regularly on a small island in the pond, and nonbreeding loons frequently stop by to feed, often to be chased away by the breeding pair. Mammalian residents include beaver (*Castor canadensis*), mink (*Mustela vison*), and otter (*Lutra canadensis*).

A road around the southern end of the pond, which crosses private forest lands, serves as the south entrance to Bill Sladyk Wildlife Management Area.

Directions: From the junction of VT 105 and VT 114 in Island Pond, go 9 miles north on VT 114 and turn left on a dirt road, which goes about 0.25 mile to a state boat ramp. For Bill Sladyk Wildlife Management Area, turn left on Hurricane Brook Road, about 7.5 miles north of Island Pond, and follow it about 4 miles to a parking area.

WOOD DUCK
(Aix sponsa)

Activities: Canoeing, fishing, hunting, wildlife-watching, hiking.

Facilities: Boat ramp.

Dates: Open year-round.

Fees: None.

Closest town: Island Pond, 9 miles.

For more information: Vermont Department of Fish and Wildlife, 184 Portland Street, Saint Johnsbury, VT 05819. Phone (802) 751-0100.

LITTLE AVERILL POND

[Fig. 48(3)] The 13-mile stretch of VT 114 between Norton and Canaan is never less than 1 mile from the Quebec border, and it's far enough away from anyplace else in Vermont that a first-time visitor might not expect to see a whole lot of civilization. But just over the border, the wrinkled hills of the Northeast Kingdom give way to the broad plain south of the Saint Lawrence Seaway, a land of prosperous Quebecois farms. Like their southern neighbors, these people like to hunt, fish, or otherwise while away summer afternoons at rustic summer camps. But to do so, many of them head south—to the Northeast Kingdom. So the border highway is not as lonely as you might expect, especially if tu parles Francais.

Like many a lake farther south, the shores of Great Averill Pond sport plenty of summer camps and noisy summer fun and frolic. But just 1 mile or so south, Little Averill Pond, like many of its northern brethren, is quiet enough for breeding loons (*Gavia immer*), which have been breeding here at least since 1977—as good a litmus test of wildness as any.

On the northwestern shore of the pond there is a 200-yard-long example of the many-miles-long coastal barrier beach and salt marsh systems that develop along ocean shores. A small creek provides a supply of sand and gravel, which is reworked by waves whipped up by winds blowing across the pond. The waves angling into the shore winnow the sediment, leaving the big chunks near the river mouth while picking up the sand and sweeping it northwards along the shore, eventually piling it up to form a low sand berm that divides the marshy shallows from the rest of the lake. The berm has a sparse shrub community with scattered gray birch (*Betula populifolia*), while the wetlands support a variety of sedges (*Carex* spp. and *Scirpus* spp.) and horsetails (*Equisetum* spp.). The shallow creek can be negotiated, by twists and turns, through a small wetland delta. Much of the beach and wetland area is Nature Conservancy land and may be closed in early summer to protect breeding loons.

The steep cliffs and talus of Brousseau Mountain, just north of the pond, provide a dramatic backdrop for the northern shore, and other forested slopes rise from the southern shores.

Directions: From Norton, on VT 114 about 16 miles north of Island Pond, take VT 114 west 3.4 miles and turn right on a dirt road. Bear right at 3 miles from VT

114, then turn left into a gravel boat ramp about 0.2 mile farther.

Activities: Canoeing, fishing, wildlife-watching.

Facilities: Boat ramp.

Dates: Access road is not plowed in winter.

Fees: None.

Closest town: Averill, about 4 miles.

For more information: Vermont Department of Fish and Wildlife, 184 Portland Street, Saint Johnsbury, VT 05819. Phone (802) 751-0100.

MOUNT MONADNOCK

[Fig. 48] Mount Monadnock is a lonely, windswept, spruce-and-fir-covered peak that has the distinction of being the northeastern-most summit in the state. It is a symmetrical evergreen dome rising some 2,000 feet above the winding upper reaches of the Connecticut River, just 10 miles or so south of where the river spills out of the hills of northernmost New Hampshire to become Vermont's eastern border. (The river, however, is New Hampshire's, for the border runs down the western bank).

Like Ascutney, in a similar position 35 miles to the south, Monadnock has some loyalties to the eastern side of the river. It is a small, granitic pluton, the core of an extinct volcano, one of a string of volcanoes that erupted, mainly across New Hampshire and southwestern Maine, following the tectonic birth of the Atlantic Ocean some 250 million years ago. Monadnock is only 140 feet lower than Ascutney, but at 171 million years, it is fully 50 million years older than its southern cousin.

Without the somewhat rickety summit fire tower, Monadnock wouldn't offer much in the way of views, but the mountain's isolation means that once you get your head above the trees, you can scan the northern White and Green mountains and look north across the hills and plains of southern Quebec.

Directions: From the junction of US 3 and NH 26 in Colebrook, NH, take NH 26 east over the Connecticut River and park on VT 102 just south of its junction with NH 26. The trail to the summit fire tower begins as a dirt road on the west side of VT 102 about 100 feet south of the bridge.

Trail: 2.5 miles one-way.

Elevation: About 1,000 to 3,140 feet.

WHITE-THROATED SPARROW
(Zonotrichia albicollis)

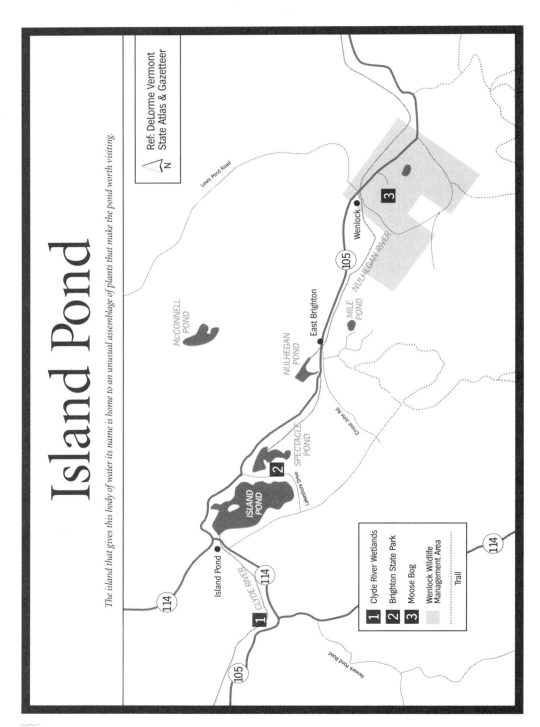

Island Pond

The island that gives this body of water its name is home to an unusual assemblage of plants that make the pond worth visiting.

Ref: DeLorme Vermont
State Atlas & Gazetteer

N

Lewis Pond Road

Wenlock

105

NULHEGAN RIVER

3

McCONNELL
POND

MILE
POND

East Brighton

NULHEGAN
POND

Ernest John Rd.

SPECTACLE
POND

2

Lakeshore Drive

ISLAND
POND

Island Pond

CLYDE RIVER

114

114

1

105

114

Newark Pond Road

1 Clyde River Wetlands
2 Brighton State Park
3 Moose Bog
Wenlock Wildlife
Management Area
·········· Trail

Degree of difficulty: Moderate.
Surface and blaze: Rocky footpath. Unblazed.

Island Pond

▨ BRIGHTON STATE PARK

[Fig. 49(2)] Tiny Spectacle Pond, the location of Brighton State Park, gives visitors a hint of the forces that shaped much of this remote area. Glaciers scoured hillsides, dumped sediments in rivers and lakes, and here, left a chunk of ice that was covered by sediments during glacial retreat. Eventually, the ice melted and left a depression, which filled with water and became Spectacle Pond. Geologists call ponds formed in this way kettle ponds.

The pond is shallow, less than 10 feet deep, and has no true inlet or outlet.

Much of the vegetation around the pond is what botanists call boreal—northern trees and plants. The area is fragrant with the scent of balsam fir (*Abies balsamea*); elsewhere, look for red spruce (*Picea rubens*), and on the eastern shore, a red pine (*Pinus resinosa*) forest. Underfoot, look for goldthread (*Coptis trifolia*), twinflower (*Linnaea borealis*), and bunchberry (*Cornus canadensis*), all typical boreal forest floor plants.

The healthy conifers make for a lively (and noisy) red squirrel (*Tamiasciurus hudsonicus*) population, but they aren't the only creatures that will wake campers from their slumber. Loons (*Gavia immer*) come to fish the pond from nearby nests on Norton and Little Averill ponds.

Directions: From Island Pond center at the junction of VT 105 and VT 114, go east on VT 105 approximately 2 miles to the state park turnoff on Lakeshore Drive on the right. Go south, or right, on Lakeshore Drive 0.8 mile to the park entrance.

Activities: Canoeing, fishing, hiking, swimming, camping.

Facilities: 63 tent sites, 21 lean-tos, restrooms, swimming beach, nature museum, boat rentals, playground, nature trail.

Dates: Open mid-May to Oct.

Fees: There is a charge for camping and day use.

Closest town: Island Pond, 2 miles.

For more information: Brighton State Park, Island Pond, VT 05846. Phone (802) 723-4360 (summer). Vermont Department of Forests, Parks, and Recreation, 324 North Main Street, Barre, VT 05461-4109. Phone (802) 476-0170 (winter).

▨ ISLAND POND

[Fig. 49] Looking for all the world like a great fried egg sunny side up, Island Pond and its little round island sit on the western side of Brighton State Park, with a small state-owned swimming area (which is actually part of the state park), a parking lot, and a boat ramp at the pond's southern end. Island Pond is moderately developed, but the island that gives the water body its name is home to an unusual assemblage of plants that make the pond worth a visit.

The island pokes above the lake level by about 60 vertical feet, and the forests here are dominated by red pine (*Pinus resinosa*), with a scattering of white pine (*Pinus strobus*), red maple (*Acer rubrum*), and white birch (*Betula papyrfera*). The forest is believed to date from after a fire in the late nineteenth century, making this island stand one of the older naturally occurring stands of red pine in the state.

Cold north winds trim the vegetation low on the northern tip of the island, which allows for the growth of a tiny round-leaved heath plant, mountain cranberry (*Vaccinium vitis-idaea*). Mountain cranberry is more typically found in high mountain or arctic areas. There's tons of it above treeline on the flanks of Mount Washington in New Hampshire, for example, and the Laplanders in northern Scandinavia pick berries of the exact same species to make into a sauce they serve with reindeer meat. But in Vermont, mountain cranberry is found in only two other spots.

Directions: From Island Pond center at the junction of VT 105 and VT 114, go east on VT 105 approximately 2 miles to the state park turnoff on Lakeshore Drive, on the right. Go south, or right, on Lakeshore Drive.

Activities: Canoeing, fishing, bird-watching.

Facilities: Boat ramp, swimming beach.

Dates: Open year-round, with swimming beach open mid-May to Oct.

Fees: There is a charge for the swimming beach and parking.

Closest town: Island Pond, 2 miles.

For more information: Brighton State Park, Island Pond, VT 05846. Phone (802) 723-4360 (summer). Vermont Department of Forests, Parks, and Recreation, 324 North Main Street, Barre, VT 05461-4109. Phone (802) 476-0170 (winter).

CLYDE RIVER WETLANDS

[Fig. 49(1)] In its upper reaches, the Clyde River travels in lazy arcs across the landscape, passing through several fine examples of one of Vermont's more unusual habitats—northern white cedar (*Thuja occidentalis*) swamp. Other flood-tolerant habitats are part of this complex wetland, including red maple (*Acer rubrum*) and black ash (*Fraxinus nigra*) swamps.

From a canoe access just west of Island Pond, the river wanders 12.5 miles to Pensioner Pond, where there is a canoe access on the northwestern side of the pond. For those who don't wish to paddle the entire 12.5-mile leg, two fine cedar swamps are visible in the first 2 miles of river paddling. The cedar swamp nearest the canoe put-in on VT 105 is relatively nutrient-rich and includes alder-leaved buckthorn (*Rhamnus alnifolia*) and marsh cinquefoil (*Potentilla palustris*). The second cedar swamp west of Webster Brook is relatively nutrient-poor and shares some species with bogs, such as black spruce (*Picea mariana*) and Labrador tea (*Ledum groenlandicum*).

The jumble of habitats—slow-moving river, wooded swamps, open marshes—makes this a good area to look for black-backed woodpeckers (*Picoides arcticus*), olive-sided flycatchers (*Contopus borealis*), winter wrens (*Troglodytes troglodytes*), ruby-crowned and golden-crowned kinglets (*Regulus calendula* and *R. satrapa*), and boreal chickadees (*Parus hudsonicus*).

Directions: From the center of Island Pond, where VT 114 splits off from VT 105, go south on VT 114/105 approximately 1.6 miles to where VT 105 heads west. Go west on VT 105 and look for a canoe put-in on the north, or right-hand side of the road not far past the road junction. The Pensioner Pond fishing access is on the west side of VT 105 about 10 miles from Island Pond or about 0.8 mile south of the junction of VT 105 and VT 5A in Charleston.

Activities: Canoeing, bird-watching, botanizing, fishing.

Facilities: Canoe access off VT 105 and on Pensioner Pond.

Dates: Open year-round.

Fees: None.

Closest town: Island Pond, 1.5 miles.

For more information: Vermont Nongame and Natural Heritage Program, Fish and Wildlife Department, 103 South Main Street, Waterbury, VT 05671. Phone (802) 241-3716.

WENLOCK WILDLIFE MANAGEMENT AREA

[Fig. 49] This 1,900-acre parcel, purchased by the state with money from hunting and fishing fees, is managed by Vermont's Fish and Wildlife Department primarily for the benefit of the population that paid for the land: hunters and anglers. As such, the forests are left mostly in a primitive state, and trail development is kept to a minimum. Much of this area is former paper company land, so it's possible to follow old logging roads for some distance, but you'll want to wear blaze orange during hunting season. Carry a topographic map and compass if you plan to venture far from the road.

The Wenlock is distinct from the state's nearly 85 other wildlife management areas because of its population of spruce grouse (*Dendragapus canadensis*), a species known to breed only here in Vermont and protected by the state's endangered species law. The spruce grouse has given wildlife managers a major headache because it is difficult to tell from ruffed grouse at the distances a hunter would typically see a bird.

The Wenlock Wildlife Management Area also contains one of the state's largest and most important white-tailed deer (*Odocoileus virginianus*) wintering areas, called a deer yard. Typically, deer take shelter under conifers because the winter snowpack is shallower than in a deciduous forest, and deer will browse on twigs, needles, and buds.

Because of its thick forest cover and relative inaccessibility, bears (*Ursus americana*) are attracted to the wildlife management area to feed on blueberries (*Vaccinium* spp.), raspberries (*Rubus* spp.), and beech nuts from American beech (*Fagus grandifolia*).

Directions: From the center of Island Pond at the junction of VT 105 and VT 114, go east on VT 105 approximately 7 miles, and look for road signs announcing boundaries of the wildlife management area.

Activities: Hiking, bushwhacking, hunting, fishing, canoeing.

Facilities: None.

Dates: Open year-round, though caution should be exercised in the fall during hunting season.

Fees: None.

Closest town: Island Pond, 2, miles.

For more information: Vermont Fish and Wildlife Department, Saint Johnsbury Regional Office, 184 Portland Street, Saint Johnsbury, VT 05319. Phone (802) 751-0100.

▓ MOOSE BOG

[Fig. 49(3)] The still waters in the center of Moose Bog are a nearly perfect mirror for the low, wraparound hills of the Nulhegan Basin. Just a 15-minute walk from VT 105 in the Wenlock Wildlife Management Area, this peaceful, beautiful bog may be Vermont's most accessible. Its accessibility doesn't take away from the variety and species diversity here: birders especially will delight in the boreal species that nest in the shrubs and swamp thickets surrounding the 15-acre open bog area.

The bog is ringed by a black spruce (*Picea mariana*) and tamarack (*Larix laricina*) swamp, a combination that makes for a striking combination in the fall, when the bright yellow of the tamarack is a startling contrast to the deep blue green of the spruce.

Closer to the bog's wet center is the shrub zone, where a thicket of plants makes wearing long pants a good idea even on a warm day. Leatherleaf (*Chamaedaphne calyculata*), Labrador tea (*Ledum groenlandicum*), and bog laurel (*Kalmia polifolia*) are interspersed with tawny cottongrass (*Eriophorum virginicum*), northern pitcher plants (*Sarracenia purpurea*), and wren's egg cranberry (*Vaccinium oxycoccus*). Botanists have documented uncommon plants species here, as well. Sedge experts should look for bog sedge (*Carex exilis*); also reported are bog aster (*Aster nemoralis*) and, floating in the bog waters, hidden-fruited bladderwort (*Utricularia geminscapa*).

The thickets of trees and shrubs draw boreal birds during nesting season. Spruce grouse (*Dendragapus canadensis*), which are protected by Vermont's endangered species law, are known to nest here. Other uncommon birds include gray jays (*Perisoreus canadensis*), black-backed woodpeckers (*Picoides arcticus*), ring-necked ducks (*Aythya collaris*), rusty blackbirds (*Euphagus carolinus*), white-winged cross-bills (*Loxia leucoptera*), Lincoln's sparrows (*Melospiza lincolnii*), and boreal chickadees (*Parus hudsonicus*).

Directions: From the center of Island Pond at the junction of VT 105 and VT 114, go east on VT 105 approximately 8.7 miles to a small turnout on the south side of road.

Activities: Bird-watching, botanizing.

Facilities: None.

Dates: Open year-round.

Fees: None.

Closest town: Island Pond, 8 miles.

For more information: Vermont Fish and Wildlife Department, Saint Johnsbury Regional Office, 184 Portland Street, Saint Johnsbury, VT 05319. Phone (802) 751-0100.

NULHEGAN POND

[Fig. 49] More than 10,000 years ago, the Nulhegan River roared with meltwater from glacier ice in the Island Pond area, but the river was so steep it carried its load of gravel all the way to the Connecticut River, or so geologists reckon. The Nulhegan still roars with water, though at a much smaller scale and only in places. The Nulhegan is a place of contrasts. The river tumbles through gorges that challenge the limits of what a whitewater kayaker can run, while other sections of the river wind through alder swamps. A small section of the river near its headwaters in Island Pond runs lazily along on granite bedrock, creating a series of swamps and a small impoundment, Nulhegan Pond.

In spite of its name, Nulhegan Pond is probably best described as a lowland bog and fen. It's small and shallow with a peat bottom, ringed by wetland shrubs and with one area a grassy fen. The pond's distinction lies mainly with its bird and insect population; northern harrier (*Circus cyaneus*) have been reported nesting here and can often be seen wheeling in the air above the area. The pond also has one of the most diverse populations of dragonflies and damselflies in the state, as well as two rare plants, small yellow-eyed grass (*Xyris montana*) and bog aster (*Aster nemoralis*). Canoeists are more likely to see a moose (*Alces alces*) here than probably any other area in the state. And anglers take bullhead (*Ictalurus nebulosus*) and chain pickerel (*Esox niger*) from the pond's shallow waters.

Directions: From the center of Island Pond at the junction of VT 105 and VT 114, go east on VT 105 approximately 8.7 miles. From Island Pond, go east on VT 105 approximately 3.2 miles to the John Boyland Airport. Look for the Nulhegan River on the north side of VT 105 just east of the airport. It flows into Nulhegan Pond just north of the VT 105.

Activities: Canoeing, fishing, bird-watching.

Facilities: None.

Dates: Open year-round.

Fees: None.

Closest town: Island Pond, 3 miles.

For more information: Vermont Fish and Wildlife Department, Saint Johnsbury Regional Office, 184 Portland Street, Saint Johnsbury, VT 05319. Phone (802) 751-0100.

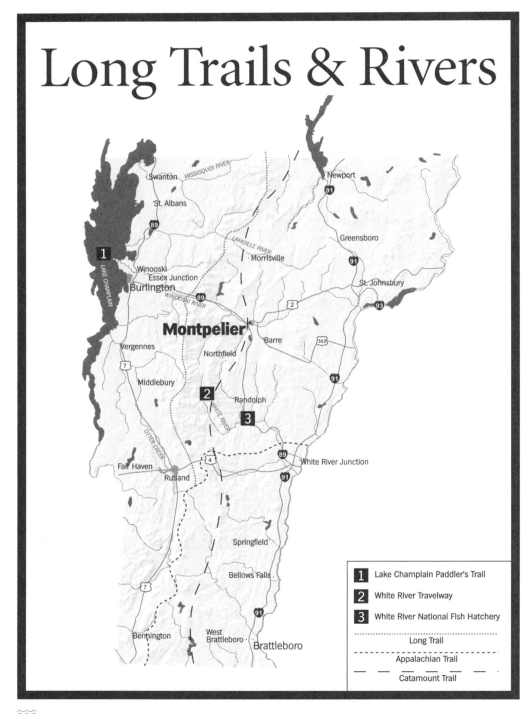

Long Trails & Rivers

Swanton

MISSISSQUOI RIVER

Newport

91

St. Albans

89

Greensboro

LAMOILLE RIVER

91

Morrisville

1

Winooski

Essex Junction

Burlington

LAKE CHAMPLAIN

St. Johnsbury

89

WINOOSKI RIVER

2

93

Montpelier

Barre

302

Vergennes

Northfield

7

91

Middlebury

2

WHITE RIVER

Randolph

3

OTTER CREEK

Fair Haven

4

89

White River Junction

Rutland

91

Springfield

Bellows Falls

7

91

Bennington

West
Brattleboro

Brattleboro

1	Lake Champlain Paddler's Trail
2	White River Travelway
3	White River National Fish Hatchery
·········	Long Trail
- - - - -	Appalachian Trail
— — —	Catamount Trail

Long Trails and Rivers

F or most people, it usually happens after about three nights out, away from cars, TVs, and Web sites. Contentious talk of politics, goings-on at the office, or even environmental issues fades away. It is replaced by fundamental questions like "What's for supper?", "Did you hear that owl last night?", "What's for breakfast?", "What kind of mushroom is that?", "Can you eat it?", "What's for lunch?"

You know you're back to the basics when food becomes a dominant topic of conversation—and thought. Vermont's Long Trail and the other long-distance passages described in the following pages provide opportunities to get back to basics; by boot, snowshoe, or ski, over and through the mountains; by canoe along the rivers that rush out of the mountains and wind through farmlands and wetlands; or by kayak along the length of Lake Champlain.

[*Above:* A kayaker below the Palisades, Lake Champlain]

The Long Trail

[Fig. 50] The nation's oldest long-distance hiking trail, Vermont's Long Trail spans 270 miles from the Massachusetts border to Quebec. Looped along the spine of the Green Mountains, the trail travels Vermont's wildest places, but frequent road crossings make it possible to break the hike up into manageable pieces. Many people hike the entire trail in segments, taking years to complete the journey. For those who want to hike the trail in one stretch, the trip typically takes three weeks to a month to finish.

The Long Trail is the brainchild of James P. Taylor, assistant headmaster at the Vermont Academy in Saxtons River. Taylor was a hiker, and he thought the boys at the school should be able to enjoy Vermont's mountains. But in the early 1900s, relatively few mountains had trails to the summit, and, as the story goes, Taylor spent a wet night on the side of Stratton Mountain and got to thinking: Why couldn't there be a trail linking the line of mountains that ran the length of Vermont?

In March 1910, Taylor gathered 23 like-minded men in Burlington with a common goal: to build a trail that would run the length of the Green Mountains. They called themselves the Green Mountain Club, and with $100 in assets, began a two-decade odyssey to do what had never before been done in North America. It was an incredible feat both at the time and in retrospect. The trail was cut with hand tools, not power saws. Trail crews, all volunteer, had to cut corridors through the thick second-growth spruce and fir that cap Vermont's taller mountain peaks and bridge mountain streams where no bridges had ever been built. They called it the Long Trail, because at the time it was the longest trail in the country.

Now, the Long Trail is a part of the fabric of Vermont, so prized by residents that the Vermont Legislature has appropriated $250,000 or more each year to help with a multiyear effort to buy a protective corridor along it. More than 40,000 people climb Mount Mansfield on the Long Trail each year, and hundreds set out to hike it end-to-end.

While the route is popular year-round, the trail is most heavily used in the summer and early fall. The southern 100 miles of the Long Trail are shared by the Appalachian Trail, and hikers on this section may meet through-hikers, or people who typically take six months to hike the 2,150 miles of the Appalachian Trail, which goes from Georgia to Maine. By the time through-hikers reach southern Vermont, they are still nearly 600 miles from the Appalachian Trail's terminus on Mount Katahdin in northern Maine.

A majority of mountains crossed by the Long Trail are included in this book, as all but a fraction of the trail's mileage is on state or federal land. Roughly 130 miles of side trails lead off the trail like nerves off a spinal cord, making it possible to break a Long Trail hike into smaller sections.

The Green Mountain Club, founder and protector of the Long Trail, continues to maintain the 270-mile-long path and its side trails. Like its sister trail, the Appalachian Trail, the Long Trail is blazed with 2-by-6-inch rectangular white blazes. Side trails are typically blazed in blue.

For more information: Guidebooks, maps, and other publications related to hiking the Long Trail are available from the Green Mountain Club, 4711 Waterbury-Stowe Road, Waterbury Center, VT 05677. Phone (802) 244-7037.

Appalachian Trail

[Fig. 50] There's poetic justice in the fact that the Long Trail and Appalachian Trail are one and the same through most of Vermont: Benton MacKaye, a forester, planner, and founder of the Appalachian Trail, often said he got his inspiration for the trail while on the summit of Stratton Mountain. Stratton, of course, is where Long Trail founder James Taylor stood in 1909, frustrated that he couldn't get to the summit without bushwhacking. Taylor's frustration led to the construction of the Long Trail beginning the following year.

MacKaye's story is a little different: He told of climbing to the top of a tree on Stratton's summit to get a better view of the mountains.

"I felt as if atop the world, with a sort of 'planetary feeling.'" he later wrote. "Would a footpath someday reach far southern peaks from where I was then perched?"

In 1921, MacKaye wrote an influential article calling for the construction of the Appalachian Trail. Sixteen years later, on August 14, 1937, workers cut the final swath of the 2,150-mile-long trail in Maine.

In Vermont, the southern 100 miles of the Long/Appalachian Trail travel the rugged ridge of the Green Mountains. But when the Long and Appalachian trails split at US 4 in Sherburne, the remaining 46 miles of Appalachian Trail in Vermont veer east over a series of rolling ridges. As the trail approaches the Connecticut River, which is the New Hampshire border, it travels through abandoned farmland. Everywhere, stone walls and cellar holes under second-growth hardwood forests speak of the past land use.

As it splits away from the Long Trail, the Appalachian Trail also leaves the billion-year-old rocks that characterize the southernmost extension of the Green Mountains, and travels into a highly convoluted mix of younger rock, which averages around 400 million years old.

Unlike the bare ridges and rock outcrops common on the Long Trail, however, there are few outcrops along this section of the Appalachian Trail. Instead, the trail is mantled in a thick blanket of till, left from the passage of the glaciers and the source of all the stone that's piled in the well-preserved stone walls that mark the way.

For more information: Guidebooks, maps, and other publications related to hiking the Appalachian Trail can be obtained at area outfitters or by contacting the Appalachian Trail Conference, PO Box 807, Harpers Ferry, WV 25425. Phone (304) 535-6331 or the Appalachian Trail Conference, New England Regional Office, PO Box 312, Lyme, NH. Phone (603) 795-4935.

Catamount Trail

[Fig. 50] Backcountry skiing is not for everyone. There is little room for rest in the winter cold, when 10 minutes of cooling off can call for an hour of hard work to get warm again. For many people, a snowy landscape is sterile, unconscious even of the stirrings of life that will begin again in spring. And when the thermometer dips below zero, just getting dressed and out to the car can seem like a valiant struggle.

But to those who learn the ways of winter, there are days that seem like dreams, when the air is so diamond-clear that sight and sound seem magnified. With the gentle greens of summer gone, the winter landscape is a constantly changing etching in gray and white, with rock and bough sometimes pillowed with tufts of snow, sometimes graced with sparkling feathers and flakes of hoarfrost, sometimes encased in clear coffins of ice.

And though the trees are dormant, the summer flowers reduced to dry, rattling stems above the snow, and many birds have fled south, the hardy winter resident mammals and birds must keep foraging. Fresh snow is a palimpsest of wildlife that can record in detail the hurried, tree-to-tree dash of a deer mouse, the cat-and-mouse contest of fox and hare, or the nocturnal strike of an owl. Backcountry skiers know the sudden shock of a grouse bursting out from under ski tips, with no trace of its journey to its subnivean hideaway left on the surface. Spend enough time on snow and you may meet a day when a cow moose stares you off the trail rather than give way herself.

For founder Steve Bushey, the Catamount Trail is a 280-mile dream come true. As a geography student at UVM and backcountry skier, Bushey, along with Paul Jarris and Ben Rose, schemed to ski the length of Vermont from Massachusetts to Quebec, on a route parallel to the Long Trail, much of which is too steep or narrow for cross-country skiing. Bushey built a thesis on the idea, and the threesome completed the first end-to-end ski tour in 1984. A year later, the Catamount Trail Association was founded to develop and maintain the trail.

The trail, 92 percent open in 1998, links groomed trails in 15 cross-country ski centers with long backcountry stretches, sometimes sharing a right-of-way with snowmobiles, sometimes using hiking trails or old woods roads. It runs by many of the mountains, lakes, and streams covered in this book, from the busy slopes of major ski areas to the remote interiors of wilderness areas and state forests. The trail can be broken down into a series of 26 half- or full-day tours ranging in length from

3 to 23 miles. Many of the cross-country ski centers are run by inns, providing the possibility of inn-to-inn touring on some sections. But there are also long stretches where you'll need to be totally self-sufficient, especially if you haven't posted a car at the far end of the trail.

While sections of the Catamount Trail are amenable to beginners, the more difficult sections require strong intermediate skills, with perhaps more emphasis on survival than technique, and there are a few thrilling runs for telemark skiers. As with other backcountry ski tours, sections that are relatively easy in good conditions can become very difficult when the snow is icy, crusty, or heavy and wet.

For more information: Catamount Trail Association, PO Box 1235, Burlington, VT 05402. Phone (802) 864-5794.

White River

With its headwaters in the Breadloaf Wilderness, the White River offers anglers a chance to cast a line for Vermont's only native stream-dwelling trout, the brook trout (*Salvelinus fontinalis*). Cold, steep mountain streams such as the headwaters of the White are the best places to find wild trout in Vermont and some people consider these upper reaches of the White a fly-fisherman's dream. In the quick tumble of water that characterizes the smallest tributaries of the White, the brookies are wild but small: A brook trout more than 8 inches long is considered a prize.

The White's attraction goes beyond its trout. It is a tributary of the Connecticut River, and fisheries biologists are working to re-establish a native strain of Atlantic salmon (*Salmo salar*) in the entire river drainage. Downstream at the White River National Fish Hatchery [Fig. 50(3)] in Bethel, millions of salmon fry are produced each year for stocking Connecticut River tributaries. The hatchery has a visitor center with information on the salmon life cycle and the restoration program, and visitors can view salmon in raceways, including some large adult brood fish.

On the 25-mile stretch of river between Hancock and Stockbridge, the Green Mountain National Forest maintains a series of roadside, wheelchair-accessible river accesses, collectively called the White River Travelway. Most have interpretive signs on the natural and social history of the river. The accesses, typically on sandy point bars, are also good habitat for ostrich fern (*Matteuccia struthiopteris*) and spotted sandpipers (*Actitis macularia*). River otter (*Lutra canadensis*) are common, and wood turtles (*Clemmys insculpta*) seek out these sandy streamsides to lay eggs.

Near the Peavine river access, bats have adopted an abandoned talc mine for winter hibernation. In the twilight of late autumn evenings, they can be seen flying over the river by the hundreds. The state-endangered Eastern small-footed bat (*Myotis leibii*) is among the species known to hibernate in the mine.

The White River is canoeable at high water from Granville to Bethel, and passable in all but dry summers below Bethel. The difficulty ranges mainly from quickwater to Class II, but a series of ledge drops below Sharon are a favorite Class II–III practice and play spot for area boaters. Some of the tributary branches of the White are also passable at medium to high water.

WHITE RIVER TRAVELWAY

[Fig. 50(2)] **Directions:** From the junction of VT 125 and VT 100 in Rochester, go north on VT 100 about 2 miles. The Green Mountain National Forest Rochester District Ranger Station, on the right (east) side of VT 100 has information on the White River Travelway. Signed travelway sites are located along VT 100 between Hancock and Stockbridge (location of the Peavine site), with two more on VT 73 near Rochester.

Activities: Fishing, bird-watching, picnicking, canoeing.

Facilities: Picnic tables, interpretive sites, wheelchair-accessible streamside sites.

Dates: Open year-round.

Fees: There is a fee for a Vermont fishing license.

Closest town: Rochester.

For more information: Green Mountain National Forest, Rochester Ranger District, RR2 Box 35, Rochester, VT 05767. Phone (802) 767-4261.

WHITE RIVER NATIONAL FISH HATCHERY

[Fig. 50(3)] **Directions:** Take Exit 3 off of I-89 and go west on VT 107 to Bethel. Continue on VT 107 approximately 2 miles to the hatchery on the right.

Activities: Fish-watching.

Facilities: Hatchery with visitor center.

Dates: Open year-round.

Fees: None.

Closest town: Bethel.

For more information: White River National Fish Hatchery, RR2 Box 140, Bethel, VT 05032. Phone (802) 234-5400.

Otter Creek

Otter Creek collects water from both the Green and Taconic mountains, carries it northward through the limestone lowlands of the Valley of Vermont, and empties into Lake Champlain near its wasp-waisted Narrows. Along the way it passes through Rutland, the state's second largest city; Proctor, for 150 years the center of Vermont's marble industry; and the miniature city of Vergennes, once the shipbuilding capitol of Lake Champlain.

With about 100 canoeable miles, mostly flatwater and quickwater, Otter Creek is

Vermont's longest river, and most of it remains passable at low to medium flows. The dam-free stretch from Proctor to Middlebury provides 36 uninterrupted miles of floating, even at low water, complete with bucolic farms, a half dozen covered bridges, and extensive wetlands around Brandon and the Cornwall Swamp Wildlife Management Area.

Winooski River

The water of Vermont's highest pond, tiny Lake of the Clouds on Mount Mansfield, finds its way to Lake Champlain, the state's lowest and greatest lake, by way of the Winooski River. The waters of streams flowing eastward off the slopes of Camel's Hump and the Monroe Skyline do likewise. But most of the Winooski's water comes from the piedmont hills east of the Green Mountains, and flows westward across the range through a deep valley between Mount Mansfield and Camel's Hump, the state's first and fourth highest peaks.

In its rush to get through the mountains, the river once raged through gorges of Green Mountain Schist and over a bouldery bed in Middlesex and Bolton, now the sites of two of the six dams that punctuate the river for power and profit. Take-outs, carry trails, and put-ins are provided at these dams for canoeists running the full length of the river.

Above and below the water gap the river flows over gravel riffles and around deep looping bends through broad farmland floodplains, picking up and depositing sediment in the restless rhythm of a meandering river. Before its final winding run to Lake Champlain through Burlington's intervale, it flows through another series of gorges cut into the marbles and quartzites of the Champlain Valley, which also serve as dam sites.

For the angler, the Winooski River serves up smallmouth bass (*Micropterus dolmieui*), rainbow and brown trout (*Oncorhynchus mykiss* and *Salmo trutta*), walleye (*Stizostedion vitreum*), and, in the lower reaches, landlocked salmon (*Salmo salar*) and steelhead, the migratory form of rainbow trout. The river alternates long, gravelly, unproductive shallows with fast water and deep holes, with especially fine trout fishing in the stretch between Montpelier and Bolton. From the Bolton Falls Dam to Lake Champlain the river is open to fishing year-round, but only for warm-water species during the late fall and winter months; it is one of only five year-round rivers in the state.

About 80 of the river's 90 miles are canoeable, beginning below the Green Mountain Power dam at Molly's Pond in Marshfield. The uppermost reach from Marshfield to Montpelier can be run only at high water, and offers intermittent stretches of Class II–III water, with an 8.5-mile stretch from Marshfield to Plainfield that ranges from quickwater to Class II. Below Montpelier the river is generally passable at any

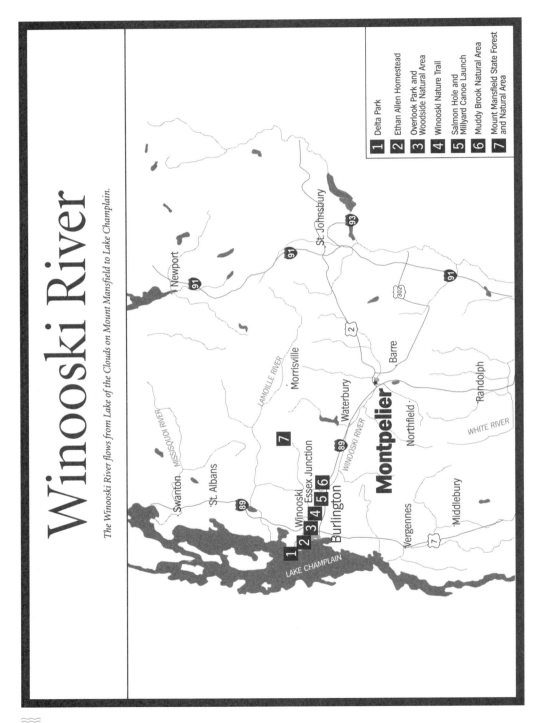

Winooski River

The Winooski River flows from Lake of the Clouds on Mount Mansfield to Lake Champlain.

1 Delta Park
2 Ethan Allen Homestead
3 Overlook Park and Woodside Natural Area
4 Winooski Nature Trail
5 Salmon Hole and Millyard Canoe Launch
6 Muddy Brook Natural Area
7 Mount Mansfield State Forest and Natural Area

water level, with a few Class II rapids and some fairly long carries around the dams.

For naturalists, the real rewards are in the rich riparian forests, and their residents, that border the river for long stretches. The best of these are protected in a series of riverside parks, managed by the Winooski Valley Park District, that are rich in natural and human history and make worthwhile stopovers for both canoeists and terrestrial travelers. The park district publishes a free pamphlet on trails in its parks and a canoe guidebook to the Winooski River that is available at area bookstores.

MUDDY BROOK NATURAL AREA

[Fig. 51(6)] Canoeists wanting to run as much of the river as possible will find themselves making a long carry around Essex Dam. Muddy Brook Natural Area provides an easy alternate put-in just 0.5 mile below Essex Dam, with access to a short Class I stretch and the slow float on down to the next dam at Lime Kiln Gorge. The natural area also has picnic tables and two short loop trails running through old field and second-growth forest along the riverbank.

Directions: From Tafts Corner (the junction of US 2 and VT 2A in Williston, just off I-89 Exit 12), take VT 2A north about 1.6 miles and turn left onto River Cove Road. The park is on the right about 0.8 mile west of VT 2A, just after the bridge over Muddy Brook.

Activities: Hiking, canoeing, fishing.

Facilities: Picnic area, canoe access, trails.

Dates: Open year-round.

Fees: None.

Closest town: Williston, 2.5 miles.

For more information: Winooski Valley Park District, Ethan Allen Homestead, Burlington, VT 05401. Phone (802) 863-5744.

OVERLOOK PARK AND WOODSIDE NATURAL AREA

[Fig. 51(3)] VT 15 between Winooski and Essex can be a trying stretch of road—four busy lanes that serve Saint Michael's College, the National Guard reservation, a hospital, and a host of small businesses, each with its own parking lot. Drivers intent on safe passage may never notice the small pullout just east of the hospital where a couple of picnic tables and a short trail overlook a quiet pocket of riparian forest and wetland tucked in under the steep slopes below the highway and railroad tracks. A gated road gives canoe and hiker access to the river, where a 1-mile trail circles the cattail marshes and beaver ponds.

A mile below the put-in the river passes under a high bridge and makes a sharp S-bend through Lime Kiln Gorge. Predictably, the gorge is the site of a hydropower dam, but the short paddle down to the safety barrier above the dam is magical. The flannel-gray limestone walls of the gorge rise straight up out of the water to heights of up to 75 feet, and the surrounding bustle of Winooski and Burlington can seem centuries away. In the 1900s this gorge and the Winooski Gorge immediately down-stream of the dam were renowned for an assortment of rare plant species, but most are now gone, driven out by development and perhaps overcollecting by unscrupu-lous collectors. Sharp eyes may be able to spot clumps of smooth cliff brake (*Pellaea glabella*), an uncommon fern, growing in cracks in the steep walls.

Directions: From Exit 15 off I-89, take VT 15 east about 1.5 miles and, opposite the Dalton Drive entrance to Fort Ethan Allen, turn right onto a dirt road. The parking and picnic areas are to the left, and the road continues to a gate 0.2 mile above the river and canoe access.

Activities: Picnicking, canoeing, hiking, fishing.

Facilities: Picnic area, canoe access, trails.

Dates: Open year-round.

Fees: None.

Closest town: Essex.

For more information: Winooski Valley Park District, Ethan Allen Homestead, Burlington, VT 05401. Phone (802) 863-5744.

WINOOSKI NATURE TRAIL

[Fig. 51(4)] Above the bridge between Winooski and Burlington, block-long brick mills converted to shopping centers and condominiums crowd the river on both sides, while the river itself runs over stairstep ledges at the entrance to Winooski Falls. Amidst all this brick, pavement, and rock, there seems precious little space for trees, herons, or beaver. But upstream of the Old Mill shopping complex the parking lots give way to scruffy old fields under siege by black locust (*Robinia pseudoacacia*), boxelder (*Acer negundo*), and green ash (*Fraxinus pennsylvanica*). These trees are the vanguard of the levee forest of green ash and silver maple (*Acer saccharinum*) that fills in an often-flooded 0.5-mile stretch of riverbank farther upstream and below the noisy I-89 bridge.

Close to the river Eastern cottonwoods (*Populus deltoides*) and black willows (*Salix nigra*) soak up the sun and fresh nutrients delivered by the river to grow wood faster than any other trees in the region. The 4-foot-diameter grandmother willows leaning out over the river may in fact be teenagers in tree terms—likely less than 100 years old.

Behind the levee is an extensive cattail marsh teeming with frogs, mammals, and birds, all stones in an ecological pyramid built on the burst of summertime growth that is limited more by the length of the growing season than the availability of water or nutrients. In spite of the proximity to the city, it would be no great surprise to find mink (*Mustela vison*) here, along with beaver (*Castor canadensis*), muskrat (*Ondatra zibethicus*), meadow vole (*Microtus pennsylvanicus*), and star-nosed mole (*Condylura cristata*).

A nature trail descends a steep bank from VT 15 down to the floodplain, then wends its way along the wetland boundary out to the riverbank, where you can explore up- or downstream.

Directions: From the junction of US 2/7 and VT 15 in the center of Winooski, take VT 15 east (East Allen Street) about 0.5 mile and turn into a small dirt parking area on the right.

Activities: Hiking, fishing.

Facilities: Trails.

Dates: Open year-round.

Fees: None.

Closest town: Winooski.

For more information: Winooski Valley Park District, Ethan Allen Homestead, Burlington, VT 05401. Phone (802) 863-5744.

SALMON HOLE AND MILLYARD CANOE LAUNCH

[Fig. 51(5)] Approximately 550 million years ago, give or take 10 million years, a trilobite crawled like an insect bulldozer over tide-rippled sands in a shallow tropical estuary, leaving a 2-inch-wide, curved track. That track and the ripples it cuts across, along with tracks of other trilobites, the burrows of worms, and even mud cracks and the impressions of rain drops, can all be seen clearly on the broad, gently sloping shelves of red Monkton Formation Quartzite that step down to the river at Salmon Hole. Once buried under thousands of feet of younger rock, and even more thousands of feet of thrust fault slices, the trilobite track has been exposed by hundreds of millions of years of erosion, ending with the scouring of Pleistocene ice and the raging glacial rivers that cut the gorge just above Salmon Hole and below Winooski Falls.

The gray and buff-colored walls of the gorge, just upstream of the quartzite ledges, are made of dolomite of the Winooski Formation. At the head of the gorge, the river plunges and foams away from the recently revitalized Winooski One hydro-electric dam, the last of Green Mountain Power's dams on the river. The spray from the falls is a critical habitat element for early thimbleweed (*Anemone multifida*), a state-endangered species now found only in this location. Because of their preference for spray-drenched limy gorge walls, other Vermont populations of the species have succumbed to hydropower development.

Native Americans once fished Lake Champlain's landlocked salmon as they worked their way over the falls to spawn. Although they have suffered from overfishing and dams that block spawning runs, the salmon still return up the Winooski every spring. They are trapped below the dam, trucked upstream, and released to continue the spawning run to higher reaches of the river and its tributaries. Salmon Hole is also remembered as an important spawning area for lake sturgeon (*Acipenser fulvescens*), another endangered species. The ledges at Salmon Hole are still a favorite local fishing spot, but the area is closed to fishing during the spawning season.

Lake Sturgeon

Although the lake sturgeon (*Acipenser fulvescens*) was known and valued by Native Americans, it was later scorned as a bottom-feeder that fouled nets set for more valuable fish and was fed to pigs or even dried and stacked up like cordwood to fuel riverboats. By the mid-1800s sturgeon came to be valued for smoked filets, caviar, skins for leather, and a curious byproduct—gelatin extracted from the swim bladder that was used to clarify beer and wine, among other uses. As with other long-lived fish species subject to sudden, intensive harvest, catches of sturgeon in northeastern lakes declined by 80 percent to 90 percent, often in less than a decade. Now the lake sturgeon is listed as threatened or endangered over much of its range, including Vermont.

The lake sturgeon is easily the largest fish in Lake Champlain, formerly reaching lengths approaching 8 feet and weights of over 200 pounds. The fish can live more than 150 years, and do not breed until they are at least 20 years old. They are primitive fish with a cartilaginous skeleton and a sleek body lined with distinctive rows of bony plates. The Cyrano de Bergerac-esque snout is whiskered with sensory barbels, and the mouth tucked under it works like a vacuum cleaner. Lake sturgeons scour lake and river bottoms for mussels, crayfish, and insect larvae: If it moves slowly enough and fits in their mouth, they'll eat it. In early spring they swim upriver to spawn in fast-moving water, often near the base of impassable falls.

Lake sturgeon are endangered in Vermont, so it is illegal to fish for them or harm them in any way.

Just across the river, behind the Millyard Condominiums in Winooski, there is a parking area and canoe launch that is a perfect put-in for the 8-mile float down the home stretch of the river into Lake Champlain.

Directions: From the junction of US 2/7 and VT 15 in the center of Winooski, take US 2/7 south across the Winooski River Bridge then bear left on Riverside Avenue. The Salmon Hole Park parking area is about 100 yards up on the right. For the Millyard canoe access, turn right off US 2/7 onto Canal Street, then left again into the parking area for the Millyard condominiums. Drive around the west end of the building and down to a gravel parking area above the river.

Activities: Hiking, fishing, canoeing.

Facilities: Trails, canoe launch.

Dates: Open year-round.

Fees: None.

Closest town: Burlington.

For more information: Winooski Valley Park District, Ethan Allen Homestead, Burlington, VT 05401. Phone (802) 863-5744.

ETHAN ALLEN HOMESTEAD

[Fig. 51(2)] Vermont founding father Ethan Allen built his own farm on a rise near the edge of the complex of swamp forests and marshes along the Winooski River known as the Intervale. The rise was high enough to keep the farm buildings above the floodwaters, but gave ready access to the fertile bottomlands that Allen cleared and planted. The homestead now serves as the headquarters of the Winooski Valley Park District. The old farmhouse has exhibits that illustrate the history of the farm and its founder, and guided walking tours are available for a small fee. A hiking and mountain biking trail system consisting of several loops allows exploration of the marshes, swamps, and fields, and includes a marsh boardwalk with interpretive signs that illustrate marsh ecology.

The park's longest trail, the Peninsula Loop, follows the river around a narrow neck of land on the inside of a sharp bend. The walk along the riverbank illustrates the dynamics of a meandering river. Near the farmhouse, the trail passes along a steeply cut bank on the outside of a bend, where the water flows fastest and has energy to cut away at the soft sediment of the floodplain, often undercutting the bank so that sections of bank slump downwards to be carried away. On the opposite shore, the river is building a complementary point bar by depositing sediment on the inside of the bend, where the water moves relatively slowly. By this process of cutting and filling, the meander becomes more exaggerated until it folds back on itself and may eventually be cut off to form an oxbow pond. The narrow neck of land connecting the farthest reach of the peninsula and the homestead will likely be breached in this way. The swamp forests of green ash (*Fraxinus pensylvanica*) and silver maple (*Acer saccharinum*) that have become established on some sections of the riverbank can help to slow, but not stop, the erosion.

Cyclists can reach the homestead by Burlington's bike path system, which includes a paved link that runs between VT 127 and the Intervale wetlands. Fat tire riders can ride on some of the homestead's trails and pick up a 2-mile mountain bike trail through riverbank forests and fields to Riverside Avenue in Burlington. Canoe access to the river is available by way of a 0.2-mile carry from the homestead parking area.

Directions: Ethan Allen Homestead is off Burlington's Northern Connector, VT 127, which emerges from the maze of streets in Burlington's old north end. From I-89 Exit 14 take VT 2 (Main Street) west toward downtown Burlington. Partway down the hill, turn right on North Willard Street, then left after about 0.6 mile onto North Street. Follow North Street through several lights and take a right onto North Champlain Street, then left at the T intersection with Manhattan Drive. Move into the right lane and bear right onto VT 127. Take the first exit for North Beach, but bear right off the exit ramp onto the paved road leading to the homestead.

Activities: Hiking, bicycling, canoeing, fishing.

Facilities: Visitor and educational centers, picnic shelter, hiking and biking trails, canoe access.

Dates: Trails are open year-round, visitor center closed in winter months.
Fees: No entry fee; there is a fee for a guided tour of the homestead.
Closest town: Burlington.
For more information: Winooski Valley Park District, Ethan Allen Homestead, Burlington, VT 05401. Phone (802) 863-5744.

▒ DELTA PARK

[Fig. 51(1)] The Winooski River enters Lake Champlain near the broadest part of the lake, where waves and currents whipped up by the prevailing southerly winds, as well as those from west to north quarters, can rework the sediment that the river delivers to its delta front. Over the last century, the southerly longshore drift has built a sandbar that curls northward from the mouth of the river, enclosing a productive patch of sedge and cattail marsh. The sandbar is accessible by a trail that follows the bed of a railroad that once spanned the Winooski River at its mouth. An observation platform along the rail trail provides a view across the marshes, which can be explored by walking along the sand bar.

Although the river is constantly delivering sediment and building the delta out into the lake, the balance between deposition by the river and wave erosion is constantly shifting in response to changes in sediment supply and distribution. Along one stretch of the bar the beach is littered with fallen, bleached cottonwoods (*Populus deltoides*) that were undercut by waves as they pushed the sand back into the wetland edge.

The far stretch of the bar is a fine place to take off your shoes and feel the sand between your toes as you wander among the willows (*Salix* spp.) that are rapidly colonizing the narrow stretch of new land. The broad lake has the grand backdrop of the Adirondacks on one side, while on the other side there is the more intimate landscape of the marsh, a favored haunt of great blue and green herons (*Ardea herodias* and *Butorides virescens*), as well as more cryptic marsh birds such as American bittern (*Botaurus lentiginosus*), common snipe (*Gallinago gallinago*), Virginia rail (*Rallus limicola*), and marsh wren (*Cistothorus palustris*).

Canoeists can put in at the Vermont Fish and Wildlife boat ramp that is just a short walk from the park and paddle along the riverbank wetlands, around the end of the sandbar, and into the bay behind the bar. On windy days, the lake can be rough—maybe too rough for canoes. Once inside the bay, you can land on a driftwood-littered beach and make a short but rough carry back to the Delta Park parking area. The path is bordered by fences that protect a small population of beach pea (*Lathyrus japonicus*), a relict of the Champlain Sea that is abundant along the Atlantic coast but threatened in Vermont.

Upstream of the boat ramp is a 30- to 40-foot-high bluff of exposed sands that were part of a marine delta built by the Winooski on the shore of the Champlain Sea. Alert naturalists will notice scattered pitch pines (*Pinus rigida*) in the housing development on the drive in. The coarse, dry sands of the marine delta favored the development of pitch pine–oak forests that are renewed by periodic fires. These were once abundant in Burlington and Colchester but have fallen to development—the sand is flat, easy to dig, and allows for much better septic systems than the lake bottom clays found in other areas near the lake.

In 1998, a local group began operating a free experimental ferry for pedestrians and cyclists across the mouth of the Winooski River, tying the dirt railroad bed bike trail in Colchester to the paved Burlington Bike Path, which also follows the old railroad bed. While the future of the ferry is uncertain, it makes it possible to visit Delta Park via the Burlington Bike Path; check with the Winooski Valley Park District for an update.

Directions: From Exit 16 off I-89, take US 2/7 north about 3.5 miles and turn left on VT 127. Follow VT 127 west along the shore of Mallets Bay, but where it turns left (south) continue straight ahead on Holy Cross Road. At a stop sign, go straight ahead onto Airport Road, then take the second left onto Windermere Way. The boat ramp is by a big dirt parking area on the left, and the parking area for Delta Park is 0.1 mile farther, also on the left.

Activities: Hiking, picnicking, canoeing, fishing.

Facilities: Picnic tables, trails, observation platform, canoe access.

Dates: Open year-round.

Fees: None.

Closest town: Colchester.

For more information: Winooski Valley Park District, Ethan Allen Homestead, Burlington, VT 05401. Phone (802) 863-5744.

Lamoille River

As it travels from its headwaters north of Greensboro west to its destination in Lake Champlain, the Lamoille River winds through scenic river valleys where dairy farmers grow corn and hay. The river is big and deep enough in its lower reaches that it offers something most Vermont rivers don't: enough water so that it's possible to paddle even in the summer.

The name "Lamoille" is a corruption of the French words for the gull, *la mouette*. Legend has it that the river's discoverer, Samuel de Champlain, or a later map-maker, failed to cross the Ts in LaMouette, leaving later generations with Lamoille, a meaningless but euphonious name.

The uppermost 8 miles, from Greensboro to Hardwick, can be run only at high water with a mix of Class I–III rapids. The 60 miles of river between Hardwick and Milton (punctuated by 4 dams) can generally be run at any water level and range mostly from winding flatwater to Class I with a couple of important exceptions. Just above Johnson there are two dangerous Class IV to V drops that are best portaged by mere mortals. Ithiel Falls, a scenic drop halfway between Johnson and Jeffersonville, is considered Class II in summer but may be more difficult in high water. Finally, there is a continuous 4.5-mile stretch of Class I–III water between Fairfax and Arrowhead Mountain Lake in Milton.

The final 13 miles from Arrowhead Mountain Lake west to Lake Champlain offer intermittent reaches of easy Class II whitewater. There are several areas where canoeists will have to portage around dams, but for the most part the water is quick and passes through lovely scenery.

Bird watchers will most enjoy the lowest reaches of the Lamoille, just before the river enters Lake Champlain. The last few miles of river meander through a huge wetland established on the river's old delta. The higher ground is colonized by an extensive silver maple (*Acer saccharinum*) swamp. Oxbow lakes, the abandoned elbows of the river, are dotted here and there and are especially rich with wading birds and ducks.

Great blue herons (*Ardea herodias*) frequent the delta, standing still as statues in the weeds to fish. Osprey (*Pandion haliaetus*), considered an endangered species in Vermont, nest on several platforms at the river's mouth and in nearby Sandbar State Park.

It's also possible to see the secretive black-crowned night heron (*Nycticorax nycticorax*), wood duck (*Aix sponsa*), common goldeneye (*Bucephala clangula*), and belted kingfisher (*Ceryle alcyon*). Pileated woodpeckers (*Dryocopus pileatus*) are common in the wetlands and can occasionally be seen flying across the river. The area is also the only known nesting locality in Vermont for Cerulean warblers (*Dendroica cerulea*).

Along with its bird diversity, the Lamoille delta's extensive wetland habitat makes it ideal for water-loving mammals such as beaver (*Castor canadensis*), muskrat (*Ondatra zibethicus*), and river otter (*Lutra canadensis*). It is an especially good spot to see muskrat houses, dome-shaped structures about 1 foot high and typically built of cattail (*Typha latifolia*) leaves.

The Lamoille is considered one of the better fisheries in the state for brook trout (*Salvelinus fontinalis*) in its upper reaches and rainbow trout (*Oncorhynchus myskiss*) in its middle reaches. Closer to Lake Champlain, where the current is slow and the water deeper, the fishing is good for large- and smallmouth bass (*Micropterus salmoides* and *M. dolomieui*). The lower stretches of the river are closed during spawning season but upper reaches are open to fishing for warm-water species year-round.

For more information: No one group manages the Lamoille River. The Vermont Fish and Wildlife Department can answer questions about state fishing and canoeing accesses on the Lamoille. Vermont Department of Fish and Wildlife, 111 West Street, Essex Junction, VT 05452. Phone (802) 878-1564.

Missisquoi River

The Missisquoi is an international river. It rises on the east side of the Northern Green Mountains and makes a 10-mile, leisurely northwest passage through Quebec farmlands before returning to Vermont for its final westward run to Lake Champlain. Its 68 canoeable miles, between North Troy and Lake Champlain, are interrupted by five dams and a couple of ledges that are best left for experts. Most of the river is passable in summer, with a nice mix of flatwater and mostly Class I–II rapids, and some short Class III pitches near Richford. Boaters making the Canadian passage should report at Canadian customs on VT 5A before putting in at North Troy and land at the bridge in East Richford to check in with U.S. Customs. The final reach from Swanton to Lake Champlain passes through the Missisquoi National Wildlife Refuge, perhaps Vermont's largest and most diverse wetland complex (see page 39).

Above North Troy, the upper reaches of the Missisquoi are good brown trout (*Salmo trutta*) waters, with some sizeable brook trout (*Salvelinus fontinalis*) lurking in the headwater streams. As it comes out of the mountains, the river slows down, warms up, and picks up agricultural runoff from valley farms. It begins to favor warm-water species in the pools and backwaters.

For more information: Vermont Department of Fish and Wildlife, 184 Portland Street, Saint Johnsbury, VT 05819. Phone (802) 751-0100. Vermont Department of Fish and Wildlife, 111 West Street, Essex Junction, VT 05452. Phone (802) 878-1564.

Lake Champlain Paddlers' Trail

Called by some the "sixth Great Lake," 120-mile-long Lake Champlain is ideal for kayakers who want to explore. Public campsites on both the New York and Vermont sides of the lake make it possible for the enterprising kayaker to link together a multiday trip.

It's not just the proximity of campsites, but the scenery that makes Lake Champlain so perfect for kayaking. Much of its shoreline is undeveloped, especially on the New York side, where from the water the unspoiled hills of the Adirondacks seem to go on forever.

There's some fascinating natural history that is best seen from the water, too.

Though they are difficult to find, the low rock cliffs on the western side of Isle La Motte are home to the oldest known coral reefs in the world. Three-foot-diameter, 500-million-year-old mushroom-shaped organisms, called stromatoporoids, are visible as lighter inclusions in the gray limestone. The reefs are a relict of the time when the Adirondacks were the east coast of North America, with the tropical Iapetus Ocean lapping the foothills.

Farther south on the Vermont side of the lake is another geologic landmark that tells of the enormous forces that built the Green Mountains. Beginning about 440 million years ago, as the Iapetus Ocean closed and the North American and African plates collided, the huge compressive forces caused a thick slice of rock to break free and be forced up and over rocks much younger in age. This thrust fault is easily seen from the water at Lone Rock Point, on Burlington's northern shore, where early Cambrian-age Dunham Dolomite sits on top of rocks that are 100 million years younger, the black shales of the Iberville Formation.

The spectacular geology is matched by the varied bird and animal life. Peregrine falcons (*Falco peregrinis*) wheel and glide from the 100-foot-high cliffs at the Palisades, on the New York side. Spiny softshell turtles (*Apalone spinifera*), like weird floating dinner plates with long snouts, bask on logs in the Sandbar Wildlife Management Area at the mouth of the Lamoille River. Common terns (*Sterna hirundo*), which are uncommon in Vermont in spite of their name, nest by the hundreds on tiny Poppasquash Island, a bird refuge owned by the Green Mountain Audubon Society.

Anglers also flock to the lake to troll for the warm-water and cold-water species that abound. Each year the Vermont Fish and Wildlife Department stocks the lake with hundreds of thousands of fish, chiefly lake trout (*Salvelinus namaycush*), brown trout (*Salmo trutta*), and landlocked salmon (*Salmo salar*). In the shallow wetlands near major river mouths, look for northern pike (*Esox lucius*), chain pickerel (*Esox niger*), and small- and largemouth bass (*Micropterus dolomieui* and *M. salmoides*).

The Lake Champlain Committee, an advocacy group, joined with state agencies and the National Park Service to create the Lake Champlain Paddlers' Trail. The first sites opened in 1996, and now 18 locations are part of the trail, with more than 50 campsites. The Lake Champlain Committee has written a guide to the paddlers' trail, which can be obtained by purchasing a membership with the group.

For more information: Lake Champlain Committee, 14 South Williams Street, Burlington, VT 05401. Phone (802) 658-1414.

Appendices

A. Books and References

25 Bicycle Tours in Vermont by John Freidin, Backcountry Publications, Woodstock, Vermont 1996.

50 Hikes in Vermont by Bob Lindemann and Mary Deaett, Backcountry Publications, Woodstock, VT 1997.

200 Years of Soot and Sweat: The History and Archaeology of Vermont's Iron, Charcoal, and Lime Industries by Victor R. Rolando, Vermont Archaeological Society, Burlington, VT 1992.

AMC River Guide: New Hampshire, Vermont edited by Roioli Schweiker, Appalachian Mountain Club, Boston, MA 1983.

Amphibians and Reptiles of New England: Habitat and Natural History by Richard M. DeGraaf and Deborah D. Rudis, University of Massachusetts Press, Amherst, MA 1983.

Appalachian Mountain Club Quiet Water Canoe Guide: New Hampshire, Vermont by Alex Wilson, Appalachian Mountain Club, Boston, MA 1992.

Bogs of the Northeast by Charles W. Johnson, University Press of New England, Hanover, NH 1985.

Catamount Trail Guidebook edited by Rosemary V. Shea, Catamount Trail Association, Burlington, VT 1995.

Classic Northeastern Whitewater Guide by Bruce Lessels, Appalachian Mountain Club, Boston, MA 1998.

Day Hiker's Guide to Vermont, The Green Mountain Club, Waterbury Center, VT 1992.

Field Guide to the New England Alpine Summits by Nancy G. Slack and Allison W. Bell, Appalachian Mountain Club, Boston, MA 1995.

Fishing Vermont's Streams and Lakes by Peter F. Cammann, Backcountry Publications, Woodstock, VT 1992.

Green Mountain Adventure, Vermont's Long Trail by Jane Curtis, Will Curtis, and Frank Lieberman, Green Mountain Club, Montpelier, VT 1985.

A Guide to Bird Finding in Vermont by Walter G. Ellison, Vermont Institute of Natural Science, Woodstock, VT 1983.

Hiker's Guide to the Mountains of Vermont by Jared Gange, Huntington Graphics, Huntington, VT 1996.

Into the Mountains: Stories of New England's Most Celebrated Peaks by Maggie Stier and Ron McAdow, Appalachian Mountain Club, Boston, MA 1995.

Long Trail Guide, The Green Mountain Club, Waterbury Center, VT 1996.

Manual of Vascular Plants of Northeastern United States and Adjacent Canada by Henry A. Gleason and Arthur Cronquist, New York Botanical Garden, Bronx, NY 1991.

Mount Ascutney Guide edited by Sharon Harkay, Ascutney Trails Association, Windsor, VT 1992.

Mountain Bike! Vermont by Kate Carter, Menasha Ridge Press, Birmingham, Alabama 1998.

The Nature of Vermont by Charles W. Johnson, University Press of New England, Hanover, NH 1998.

Roadside Geology of Vermont and New Hampshire by Bradford B. van Diver, Mountain Press, Missoula, MT 1987.

The Surficial Geology and Pleistocene History of Vermont by David P. Stewart and Paul MacClintock, Vermont Geological Survey, Department of Water Resources, State of Vermont, Montpelier, VT 1969.

Vermont Atlas and Gazetteer, DeLorme, Freeport, ME 1996.

Vermont Wildlife Viewing Guide by Cindy Kilgore Brown, Falcon Press Publishing, Helena, MT 1994.

Wild Mammals of New England by Alfred J. Godin, Johns Hopkins University Press, Baltimore, Maryland 1977.

B. Conservation Organizations

The following are some of the larger nonprofit organizations dedicated to the preservation and/or enjoyment of the rich natural heritage of Vermont's mountains.

Appalachian Trail Conference, National Office, PO Box 807, Harpers Ferry, WV 25425. Phone (304) 535-6331. This national group is the parent organization of the chiefly volunteer-staffed trail clubs that maintain the 2,150-mile Appalachian Trail. The group publishes guidebooks and maps, and has been delegated by Congress to maintain and protect the trail and its corridor.

Appalachian Trail Conference, New England Regional Office, PO Box 312, Lyme, NH 03768. Phone (603) 795-4935. Coordinates regional trail-related activities for the Appalachian Trail.

Catamount Trail Association, PO Box 1235, Burlington, VT O5402. Phone (802) 864-5794. Promotes and maintains the Catamount Trail, Vermont's end-to-end cross-country ski trail.

Champlain Kayak Club, c/o Schumacher, 4461 Shelburne Road, Shelburne, VT 05482. Phone (802) 651-8758. Founded in 1992 to promote kayaking on Lake Champlain, the all-volunteer organization sponsors slide shows, Wednesday evening paddles, skills workshops, and trips to more far-flung destinations outside of the state.

Conservation Law Foundation, 21 East State Street, Montpelier, VT 05602. Phone (802) 223-5992. Promotes environmental advocacy on issues such as energy efficiency and land and water policy.

Green Mountain Audubon Nature Center, 255 Sherman Hollow Road, Huntington, VT 05462. Phone (802) 434-3068. Owns and maintains 300-acre sanctuary with hiking trails, working sugarbush, summer nature camps, Halloween haunted forest, and workshops.

Green Mountain Club, 4711 Waterbury-Stowe Road, Waterbury Center, VT 05677. Phone (802) 244-7037. Protects and maintains the 270-mile Long Trail and its side trails. Offers trail advice, publishes guidebooks and maps, conducts outdoors and natural history workshops, and coordinates trail work.

Lake Champlain Committee, 14 South Williams Street, Burlington, VT 05401. Phone (802) 658-1414. A citizens group, with members in Vermont and New York, devoted to promoting a clean and accessible Lake Champlain. Manages the Lake Champlain Paddlers' Trail.

National Wildlife Federation, Northeast Natural Resource Center, 58 State Street, Montpelier, VT 05602. Phone (802) 229-0650. Sponsors comprehensive environmental education programs and advocates for sound environmental policies in Vermont, New England, and across the U.S.

The Nature Conservancy, Vermont Field Office, 27 State Street, Montpelier, VT 05602. Phone (802) 229-4425. Purchases and manages areas of ecological significance, offers educational workshops and field trips, and aids other private and state agencies with land purchases.

Northern Forest Alliance, 43 State Street, Montpelier, VT 05602. Phone (802) 223-5256. A consortium of environmental groups from Maine, New Hampshire, New York, and Vermont that focuses on the protection of the 26-million-acre swath of forests along the northern tier of the four states.

River Watch Network, 153 State Street, Montpelier, VT 05602. Phone (802) 223-3840. Coordinates volunteers in schools or citizen advocates to monitor river health and promote river protection nationwide.

Shelburne Farms, 102 Harbor Road, Shelburne, VT 05482. Phone (802) 985-8686. At this 1,400-acre working farm, there is an environmental education center that sponsors workshops and educational programs and tours and walking trails on the lakeside property.

Vermont Audubon, 65 Millet Street, Richmond, VT 05477. Phone (802) 434-4300. The state branch of the National Audubon Society; sponsors workshops, field trips, and promotes environmental activism. Focuses on protecting birds and other wildlife and their habitat.

Vermont Institute of Natural Science, Church Hill Road, Woodstock, VT 05091. Phone (802) 457-2779. An environmental education group that also hosts a Raptor Center where injured birds are rehabilitated and returned, if possible, to the wild. Publishes books, sponsors research and school programs.

Vermont Land Trust, 8 Bailey Avenue, Montpelier, VT 05602. Phone (802) 223-5234. Protects Vermont's agricultural and forest-related heritage through conservation easements or land purchase.

Vermont Natural Resources Council, 9 Bailey Avenue, Montpelier, VT 05602. Phone (802) 223-2328. Environmental advocacy group that focuses on wise resource use and land protection through research, legislative lobbying, and educational programs.

Vermont Public Interest Research Group, 43 State Street, Montpelier, VT 05602. Phone (802) 223-5221. Works on consumer protection and environmental health issues in Vermont through education, grass-roots organizing, and legislative lobbying.

Winooski Valley Park District, Ethan Allen Homestead, Burlington, VT 05401. Phone (802) 863-5744. Acquires and manages riverside parks in seven member towns along the lower Winooski River in Chittenden County.

C. Special Events, Fairs, and Festivals

JANUARY

Ski Fest Celebrations—Woodstock Ski Touring Center in Woodstock hosts guided tours or orienteering as part of a nationwide effort to attract people to cross-country skiing. Early January. Phone (802) 457-6674.

White-Out Days Winter Carnival—Burke Mountain Resort in West Burke holds fun races for kids, entertainment, torchlight parade. Mid-January. Phone (802) 626-3305.

Annual Harriman Ice Fishing Derby—Harriman Reservoir derby, entry fee. Mid-January. Jacksonville. Phone (802) 368-2773.

Vermont Farm Show—Animal judging, equipment, food contests. Barre City Auditorium Complex. Late January. Phone (802) 828-2433, (802) 828-2431.

Stowe Winter Carnival—Music, ski races, ice sculptures, dogsled races all week long in various locations. Stowe. Late January. Phone (802) 253-7321.

FEBRUARY

Burlington Annual Winter Festival—Family activities, crafts, dogsled rides, snowshoe demo and race, snow sculpture at various downtown locations. Three-day event. Burlington. Early February. Phone (802) 864-0123.

Newport Winter Carnival—Skating, dancing, fireworks, contests, and more at various times and locations. Newport. Phone (888) 884-8001.

Brattleboro Annual Harris Hill Ski Jumping Competition—Features U.S. Ski Team jumpers and European jumpers. Brattleboro. Mid-February. Phone (802) 254-4565.

Brattleboro Annual Winter Carnival—Activities for the whole family. Various locations. Brattleboro. Late February. Phone (802) 258-2511.

Middlebury College Winter Carnival—Rikert Touring Center and Middlebury College Snow Bowl. Ripton. Late February. Phone (802) 388-4356.

MARCH

Annual American Snowboard Tour North American Championships—Mount Snow Resort. West Dover. Phone (800) 245-SNOW.

Sugar on Snow Party—Family activities and tours. Green Mountain Audubon Nature Center, Huntington. Mid-March to end of syrup season. Phone (802) 434-3068.

Cavendish Sugar-On-Snow Supper and Craft Sale—Baptist Church. Cavendish. Mid-March. Phone (802) 226-7602.

APRIL

Waitsfield Annual Sugarbush Triathlon—Watch or participate in Vermont's largest team sporting event; canoe or kayak, run, bike, and cross-country ski. Sugarbush ski area. Early April. Waitsfield. Phone (802) 496-7907.

St. Albans Annual Vermont Maple Festival—Parade, exhibits, products, pancake breakfasts, arts and crafts, antique show, and more. St. Albans. Late April. Phone (802) 524-2444, (802) 849-6038.

MAY

Annual Plowing Match—Dozens of teamsters competing with draft horses and oxen. Billings Farm and Museum, Woodstock. Early May. Phone (802) 457-2355.

Annual Vermont Square and Round Dance Convention—Features square, round, clogging, and line dancing. Spaulding High School, Barre. Early May. Phone (802) 563-2777, (802) 748-8538.

Manchester Festival Weekend—Features flytiers, canoe makers, artists, and casting instructors. American Museum of Fly Fishing, Manchester. Early May. Phone (802) 362-3300.

Shelburne Museum Lilac Festival—Family activities and entertainment; collection of more than 400 lilac bushes. Shelburne Museum, Shelburne. Late May. Phone (802) 985-3346.

Vermont Canoe and Traditional Small Craft Day—Displays; activities, workshops; old and new canoes, kayaks, boats on display; used equipment swap. Camp Aloha Hive, Fairlee. Late May. Phone (802) 333-3405.

JUNE

Annual Discover Jazz Festival—Weeklong festival, more than 50 locations. Burlington. Mid-June. Phone (802) 863-7992.

Annual Kids' Maritime Festival—Lake Champlain Maritime Museum, Ferrisburgh. Mid-June. Phone (802) 475-2022.

Ethan Allen Days—Weekend of historic battle re-enactments and encampments, craftsmen, and food. Held on Route 7A, 4 miles north of Arlington, Sunderland. Late June. Phone (802) 375-2800, (802) 362-4213.

Lake Champlain International Fishing Derby—Lake Champlain. Based in Burlington. Late June. Based in Burlington. Phone (802) 862-7777.

The Green Mountain Chew Chew—Family-oriented festival featuring more than 40 area restaurants and Vermont Food Producers. There is also music and events. Waterfront Park, Burlington. Late June. Phone (802) 864-6674.

Ben & Jerry's One World One Heart Festival—Live music from nationally and internationally renowned artists, family activities, crafts, food, free Ben & Jerry's ice cream. Sugarbush Resort, Warren. Late June. Phone (802) 800-BJ-FESTS.

JULY

Hermann's Royal Lipizzan Stallions—Traditional equestrian ballet with world famous flying white Lipizzan Stallions. Route 2, North Hero. Early July–late August. Phone (802) 372-5683.

Rokeby Museum Wool Festival—Shearing, border collie, and spinning demonstrations; house tours. Rokeby Museum, Ferrisburgh. Mid-July. Phone (802) 877-3406.

Lake Champlain Small Boat Show—On-water boat trials, rowing and paddling races, demonstrations, kids' activities, music, food. Lake Champlain Maritime Museum, Ferrisburgh. Mid-July. Phone (802) 475-2022.

Living History Program—Revolutionary War encampment and demonstrations of period military tactics. Hubbardton Battlefield, Hubbardton. Mid-July. Phone (802) 464-5569.

Annual Vermont Quilt Festival—Exhibits, displays, and vendors. Over 60 classes and lectures with teachers/quilters from throughout the U.S. Norwich University, Northfield. Mid-July. Phone (802) 485-7092.

Vermont Forestry Expo and Lumberjack Roundup—Lumberjack and jill events, equipment, games, crafts, Vermont products. Barton Fairgrounds, Barton. Late July. Phone (802) 533-9212.

Annual Soldiers on the Mount—Full authentic British and American encampments, cooking, crafts, artillery and musket demonstrations. Mount Independence State Historic Site, Orwell. Late July. Phone (802) 464-5569.

AUGUST

Champlain Valley Folk Festival—Concerts, dancing, workshops, storytelling, informal jam sessions, family activities. UVM Redstone Campus, Burlington. Late July–early August. Phone (800) 769-9176.

Annual Dowsing School and Convention—Weeklong dowsers convention and school. Lyndon State College, Lyndon. Early August. Phone (802) 684-3417.

Morgan Horse Farm Open House—Demonstrations of versatility and training of Morgans; stallions, mares, and foals shown. UVM Morgan Horse Farm, Weybridge. Mid-August. Phone (802) 388-2011.

Annual Orleans County Fair—Orleans County fairgrounds, Barton. Mid-August. Phone (802) 525-6210.

Mount Snow-Chevy Truck NORBA National Championship Series Mountain Bike Finals—Amateurs and top international riders compete. Mount Snow Resort, West Dover. Late August. Phone (800) 245-SNOW.

Deerfield Valley Farmers Day—Country fair. Middle/High School and fairgrounds, Wilmington. Late August. Phone (802) 464-5277.

Annual Scottish Festival—Vermont Championship Sheepdog Trials, demonstrations, exhibits; pipe bands, Scottish dancing, music, food, games. Polo field, Quechee. Late August. Phone (802) 295-5351, (802) 496-2213.

SEPTEMBER

Champlain Valley Fair—Vermont's largest fair. Champlain Valley Exposition grounds, Essex Junction. Late August–early September. Phone (802) 878-5545.

Vermont State Fair—Horse shows, music, arts and crafts, derbies, carnival, and more. Fairgrounds, Rutland. Early September. Phone (802) 775-5200.

Tunbridge World's Fair—Traditional country fair. Fairgrounds, Tunbridge. Late September. Phone (802) 889-3704.

Annual Northeastern Open Atlatl Championship—Contests for accuracy, distance, and weapon style with demonstrations of Native American skills and craft. Chimney Point State Historic Site, Addison. Mid-September. Phone (802) 759-2412.

National Traditional Old Time Fiddlers and Step Dancers Contest—Barre Municipal Auditorium, Barre City. Late September. Phone (802) 728-5188.

OCTOBER

Bethel Annual Forward Festival—Entertainment, street festival, crafts, activities. Main Street, Bethel. Early October. Phone (802) 234-9070.

Stowe Foliage Art and Fine Craft Fair—175 professional juried artists, demonstrations, food, entertainment. Topnotch Field, Stowe. Mid-October. Phone (802) 253-7321.

Weston Annual Craft Show—Playhouse, On the Green, Weston. Mid-October. Phone (802) 824-3476.

Shelburne Museum Apple Days—Celebration of apple traditions, demonstrations, apple-related activities. Shelburne Museum, Shelburne. Early October–mid-October. Phone (802) 985-3346.

NOVEMBER

Stowe Rescue Squad Annual Barn Dance and Raffle—Annual dance to raise money for Stowe Rescue Squad. Percy's Garage, Stowe. Early November. Phone (802) 253-9060.

Walden Hunters' Supper—Gathering for hunters and families to celebrate the hunting season. Church, Walden. Mid-November. Phone (802) 563-2472.

DECEMBER

Annual Messiah Sing—Community sing along. Center Congregational Church, Brattleboro. Early December. Phone (802) 257-1961.

Wassail Celebration—Parade, caroling, Yule log burning, dancing, and more. Woodstock. Phone (802) 457-3555.

Vermont's Largest and Greatest Potluck Supper—Community-wide celebration and pot luck. Begins at Hildene with music and tours, to Equinox Hotel, with dancing at First Congregational Church, Manchester. Early December. Phone (877) DECEMBR.

Fairbanks Museum Holiday Open House—Museum decked out in holiday finery. Music, refreshments, planetarium shows. Fairbanks Museum and Planetarium, Saint Johnsbury. Mid-December. Phone (802) 748-2372.

Hildene Annual Candlelight Tours—Sleigh rides to main house; decorations, candlelight, Aeolian organ music. Hildene, Manchester. Late December. Phone (802) 362-1788.

D. Outfitters, Guides, and Suppliers

The following outfitters and guides are listed alphabetically.

Alpine Shop, 1184 Williston Road, South Burlington, VT 05403. Phone (802) 863-4362. Hiking, paddling, and ski equipment; rentals.

Adventure Guides of Vermont and Vermont Outdoor Guide Association, PO Box 3, North Ferrisburgh, VT 05473. Phone (800) 425-8747 or (802) 425-6211. Statewide guide association offering links between clients and guide companies. Represents more than 60 activities, from rock climbing to whitewater kayaking.

Adventure Outfitters, 97 Main Street, Brattleboro, VT 05301. Phone (802) 254-4133. Hiking, camping, rock climbing, backcountry skiing, canoeing, and kayaking equipment.

Canoe Imports, 370 Dorset Street, South Burlington, VT 05403. Phone (802) 651-8760. Equipment, rentals, maps, workshops; local contact for Champlain Kayak Club.

Climb High, 2438 Shelburne Road, Shelburne, VT 05482. Phone (802) 985-5055. Technical equipment outfitter for rock and ice climbing, backcountry skiing, snowshoeing, hiking, and camping.

Clearwater Sports, Route 100, Waitsfield, VT 05673. Phone (802) 496-2708. Guided canoe trips, moonlight paddles, canoe and kayak rentals and equipment, whitewater instruction, shuttles.

Country Walkers, PO Box 180, Waterbury, VT 05676. Phone (800) 464-9255. Walking tours, inn-to-inn hiking.

East Burke Sports, PO Box 189, East Burke, VT 05832. Phone (802) 626-3215. Cycling, skiing, and hiking equipment, local trail advice, maps for Kingdom Trail network.

Eastern Mountain Sports, 100 Dorset Street, South Burlington, VT 05403. Phone (802) 864-0473. Hiking, camping, rock climbing, kayaking, snowshoeing, and cross-country ski equipment, clinics.

The Mountain Goat, PO Box 2182, Manchester, VT 05255. Phone (802) 362-5159. Sales and rental of outdoor equipment and clothing; ice climbing, rock climbing, mountaineering, and backcountry skiing clinics and private instruction.

Mountain Travelers, 147 Route 4, East Rutland, VT 05701. Phone (802) 775-0814. Hiking, camping, canoeing, kayaking, snowshoeing, and backcountry skiing equipment; guidebooks.

North Wind Hiking and Walking Tours, PO Box 46, Waitsfield, VT 05673. Phone (800) 496-5771. Hiking and walking tours, inn-to-inn hiking, nature tours.

Northern Vermont Llama Company, 766 Lapland Road, Waterville, VT 05492. Phone (802) 644-2257. Full-day or half-day llama treks from the village of Smugglers Notch.

Onion River Sports, 20 Langdon Street, Montpelier, VT 05602. Phone (802) 229-

9409. Hiking and ski equipment.

Orvis Company, Historic Route 7A, Manchester, VT 05254. Phone (802) 362-3750. Fly-fishing and hunting clothing and equipment; guide service; fly-fishing and shooting instruction.

Paddleways Kayak Touring, 89 Caroline Street, Burlington, VT 05401. Phone (802) 660-8606. Instruction and guided tours on Lake Champlain and in the region.

The Ski Rack / Downhill Edge, 81 Main Street, Burlington, VT 05401. Phone (802) 658-3133. Downhill and cross-country ski equipment, cycling and boating equipment and repairs.

Umiak Outdoor Outfitters, 849 South Main Street, Stowe, VT 05672. Phone (802) 253-2317. Hiking and paddling gear, canoe rentals, area lake and river shuttles.

Vermont Bicycle Tours, PO Box 711, Bristol, VT 05443. Phone (800) 245-3868. Guided bicycle tours.

Vermont Horse Council, PO Box 105, 400 Country Road, Montpelier, VT 05601. Phone (800) 722-1419. Riding clubs and information.

E. Glossary

Acidic—Characterized by an excess of hydrogen ions; typically detrimental to soil fertility or lake inhabitants.

Bog—Peat-dominated wetland, generally acidic, poor in nutrients.

Boreal—Descriptive of a northern coniferous forest and its inhabitants.

Coniferous—Cone-bearing trees; evergreens or softwoods.

Deciduous—Trees that lose their leaves in winter; hardwoods.

Delta—Fan-shaped deposit of river-borne sediments that forms at the mouth of a river as it enters a lake or ocean.

Eutrophic—Nutrient-rich; in lakes, usually characterized by heavy algae growth.

Fen—Peatland that is relatively rich in nutrients brought by a water source, either a river or a spring.

Gneiss—Banded metamorphic rock.

Iapetus—Ocean separating ancient North America from other continents.

Kame terrace—Sediments deposited by running water that fill the space between a glacier and an adjacent hillside.

Kettle pond—Pond formed where blocks of glacial ice are left behind by retreating glacier and buried in sediments before the block melts. When the ice block melts, it leaves a depression that fills with water and forms a pond.

Klippe—Remnant of the upper plate of a thrust fault, isolated by erosion.

Krummholz—German for twisted wood; used to describe stunted trees that grow in alpine areas.

Marsh—Wetland dominated by grasslike herbaceous vegetation such as sedges and cattails.

Metamorphic—Rocks formed from other rocks under intense pressure and temperature, typically due to mountain building.

Monadnock—A hill or mountain of resistant rock that stands above the surrounding low-lying area.

Oligotrophic—Nutrient poor.

Outcrop—Exposed bedrock.

Orogeny—Mountain-building event.

Pangaea—Super-continent formed from Laurasia and Gondwanaland about 350 million years ago.

Pluton—A body of molten rock that solidifies deep in the Earth.

Quartzite—Metamorphic rock formed from sedimentary rocks, typically sandstones in which the main element is quartz.

Roche moutonée—Literally "sheep rock," a form left when a glacier advances over a rock and shapes it asymmetrically, with a smooth slope on the upstream side of the glacier and a steep face on the downstream face. The smooth slope is abraded by the glacier, and the steep face results when ice shatters and plucks rock away from the cliff.

Striae—Parallel scratches or grooves in a rock outcrop, cut by the sandpaper-like passage of a grit-filled glacier.

Schist—Layered metamorphic rock formed from shales and characterized by parallel layers of platy minerals, such as mica.

Scree—Accumulation of stones, typically fist-sized and smaller, at the foot or base of a cliff, resulting from stones that weather from the cliff face and tumble down.

Sedimentary—Rocks formed when sediments—sand, mud, plant material, sea shells—are deposited in a place and accumulate over millions of years.

Shale—Rock formed by weak metamorphosis of muds and clays. Typically very fine-grained, dark gray. Breaks into thin layers.

Swamp—Wetlands colonized by perennial trees or shrubs.

Succession—A change in vegetation over time, with new tree and plant species replacing older ones, the pattern of which is determined by seed source, soil type, moisture availability, and amount of light.

Talus— Accumulation of stones, typically larger than a fist, at the foot or base of a cliff, resulting from stones that weather from the cliff face and tumble down.

Till—Silt, sand, gravel, and boulders frozen into or on top of a glacier that are left as an unsorted mixture on the earth after the ice melts.

Understory—Shrubs and nonwoody plants that live underneath trees in a forest.

Index